מסורה

ArtScroll Series®

Rabbi Nosson Scherman / Rabbi Meir Zlotowitz

General Editors

WASSERMAN EDITION

Published by
Mesorah Publications, ltd

REB MOSHE

The Life and Ideals of HaGaon Rabbi Moshe Feinstein

BY RABBI SHIMON FINKELMAN

WITH RABBI NOSSON SCHERMAN
FOREWORD BY RABBI MEIR ZLOTOWITZ

EXPANDED 25TH YAHRZEIT EDITION

FIRST EDITION
First Impression … December 1986

REVISED AND EXPANDED EDITION
Five Impression … February 2011 — September 2020
Sixth Impression … February 2021

Published and Distributed by
MESORAH PUBLICATIONS, Ltd.
313 Regina Avenue / Rahway, N.J. 07065

Distributed in Europe by
LEHMANNS
Unit E, Viking Business Park
Rolling Mill Road
Jarrow, Tyne & Wear NE32 3DP
England

Distributed in Australia & New Zealand by
GOLDS WORLD OF JUDAICA
3-13 William Street
Balaclava, Melbourne 3183
Victoria Australia

Distributed in Israel by
SIFRIATI / A. GITLER — BOOKS
POB 2351
Bnei Brak 51122

Distributed in South Africa by
KOLLEL BOOKSHOP
Northfield Centre, 17 Northfield Avenue
Glenhazel 2192, Johannesburg, South Africa

ARTSCROLL® SERIES
WASSERMAN EDITION
REB MOSHE
© *Copyright 2011, by* MESORAH PUBLICATIONS, Ltd.
313 Regina Avenue / Rahway, N.J. 07065 / (718) 921-9000 / www.artscroll.com

---

ITEM CODE: EREMH
ISBN 10: 1-4226-1084-5 / ISBN 13: 978-1-4226-1084-8

Typography by CompuScribe at ArtScroll Studios, Ltd.

Printed in the United States of America
Bound by Sefercraft, Quality Bookbinders, Ltd., Rahway N.J.

WASSERMAN EDITION

*J*t is our pleasure and honor to dedicate this biography of one of the greatest Torah authorities and saintly personalities American Jewry has ever known.

HaGaon Rabbi Moshe Feinstein זצוק״ל,

Rosh HaYeshivah of Mesivtha Tifereth Jerusalem

and the Yeshiva of Staten Island

For nearly half a century, the most difficult questions of Jewish law came to him. The entire world recognized his towering stature. But he was equally attentive to the needs of the humblest Jew. Very, very few can aspire to his heights of scholarship, but we can all learn from his kindness, sensitivity, humility, and dedication to the needs of the individual and the nation. It is our privilege to help keep his memory and lessons alive through this biography.

Klal Yisrael is indeed fortunate that the Rosh Yeshivah's legacy is carried on by his great successors, the *geonim* **Rabbi David Feinstein שליט״א** and **Rabbi Reuven Feinstein שליט״א**. Thanks to such families, the Torah's promise that the Torah will not be forgotten is being fulfilled.

Stanley and Ellen Wasserman
and our children and grandchildren:

Alan and Svetlana Wasserman
Sasha, Jesse, Talya, Jacob, Bella, and Aiden

Neil and Yael Wasserman
Yeshayahu, Shiri, Yonatan, Ruth, and Aviva

Mark and Anne Wasserman
Joseph, Bailey, Erin, Rebeccah, and Jordyn

Stuart and Rivka Berger
David, Gabrielle, and Jack

בס"ד תתברכו

Patrons

A group of distinguished friends of the Yeshiva
who have endowed the 25th yahrzeit campaign.

JOSEPH & CHARLES ALPERT	MR. & MRS. JACK LEVINE
ANONYMOUS PATRON	THE PARNES FAMILY
MR. & MRS. BENJAMIN ARYEH	MR. & MRS. SHIMON PELMAN
MR. & MRS. MICHAEL ARYEH	MR. MOSHE PODOLSKI
MR. & MRS. MOSHE BEINHORN	DR. AND DR. MARK RAMER
MR. & MRS. EZRA BEYMAN	MR. & MRS. NORMAN SCHMUTTER
MR. & MRS. MARTIN COHEN	MR. & MRS. RUBIN SCHRON
MR. & MRS. EZRA ERANI	MR. & MRS. SHELDON SEIDMAN
RABBI & MRS. AHRON FOGEL	MR. CHAIM SINGER
MR. & MRS. JACK FORGASH	MR. & MRS. A. JOSEPH STERN
MR. & MRS. MICHEL FRANKEL	MR. & MRS. STANLEY WASSERMAN
YAD AVRAHAM INSTITUTE	MR. & MRS. JERRY WILLIAMS
MR. & MRS. RALPH HERZKA	MR. & MRS. MOSHE WILLIAMS
RABBI & MRS. HOWARD ZUCKERMAN	MR. & MRS. HARVEY WRUBEL
MR. & MRS. MARVIN JACOB	MR. & MRS. MEL ZACHTER
MR. & MRS. JIMMY KHEZRIE	RABBI & MRS. MEIR ZLOTOWITZ

MR. & MRS. MENDY ZWICK

The ideals and heritage of the Rosh HaYeshiva,

HaGaon Rabbi Moshe Feinstein זצ"ל

continue to be alive and vibrant through his *sefarim*
and the living examples of his sons

Hagaon Harav David Feinstein, Shlita
and
Hagaon Harav Reuven Feinstein, Shlita

The Jaffa Family Foundation

לז"נ

האשה החשובה
אשת חיל
אם משפחתנו

חוה בתלא יהודית בת ר' יוסף ע"ה
Judith Williams ע"ה
נפטרה כ"ו תשרי תשס"ח

שמשה דמות לצניעות ומסירות למשפחתה
זכתה לדורות ישרים ההולכים בדרך ה'
פיה פתחה באמת ודרכיה נאות ואצילות
ידיה היו מלאות בחסד ובצדקה
בטח בה לב בעלה ותשחק ליום אחרון

תנצב"ה

נר זכרון

לע"נ ידיד נאמן של מרן ראש הישיבה שליט"א

וידיד מסור לישיבה הקדושה

חכם רפאל ע"ה

בן חכם רבי חייא זצ"ל

ומלכה בת ר' אליהו זצ"ל

בן בנו של הדיין המצויין המפורסם

לשם ותהילה חה"ש מאור הגולה

הרב הדיין חכם רפאל אריה ס"ט זצוק"ל מקשאן-פרס.

נלב"ע במוצאי שבת קודש ד' שבט התשנ"ז

תנצב"ה

עד אשר יקיצו וירננו שוכני עפר

יהיה זכרו ברוך

הונצח ע"י

אשתו ובניו ובנותיו

למשפחת אריה

This Dedication is
in memory of

Mr. Irwin Saks ע״ה

A generous donation was given
To
Mesivtha Tifereth Jerusalem
In his memory

By
The Irwin Saks Irrevocable Trust
Miami Beach, Florida

לעילוי נשמת

יצחק בן אברהם ע״ה

תנצבה

*I*pay tribute and express profound gratitude
to the **Roshei HaYeshivah** שליט״א
and their **Rebbetzins** שתחי׳
for the more than 30 years
that they have made me feel like part
of their families. With warm hearts
and open hands they remove barriers
and pay me the high honor of making
me feel at home in their
בתי מקדש מעט

לרפו״ש להרב אברהם יעקב הלוי
בן רבקה דבורה שיחי׳ עמו״ש

לזכר נשמת משה ב״ר שמואל אברהם הלוי ע״ה
ורעיתו רבקה דבורה בת שלום ז״ל

ולזכר נשמת יצחק ב״ר יששכר דוב ע״ה
ורעיתו גאלדה בת זאב ז״ל

תנצב״ה

מאת
יששכר שמואל הלוי גינזבערג

It is our privilege to join in dedicating this biography
of the preeminent *posek hador*

HaGaon Rabbi Moshe Feinstein זצ"ל

His eight volumes of *Igros Moshe* and his many volumes of
Dibros Moshe demonstrate that he would have been revered as a
gaon even in earlier centuries. This volume shows that he was as
great a person as he was a Torah giant.

May his successors and his yeshivos flourish in the service of
Klal Yisrael.

עד ביאת הגואל בב"א

Rabbi Dr. and Mrs. Neil Maron

Dedicated to the memory of
our dear friends and mentors

Rabbi Max and Mrs. Chana Schiff, ע"ה

תנצב"ה

Who brought so much Torah and beauty
to our lives

Kerry & Josh Gotlib

MESIVTHA TIFERETH JERUSALEM

לעילוי נשמות

הרב יצחק בן הרב מרדכי ז״ל

ד׳ טבת תשנ״ט

רחל בת איסר ע״ה

כ״ה מנחם אב תשנ״ז

Rabbi and Mrs. Yitzchok and Ruth Gottlieb

Riverdale, New York

A stellar couple whose lives exemplified the ideals of Torah and Chesed, whose wise counsel and sincere concern greatly enriched their family and friends and enhanced every cause they supported. May their good deeds, always performed with heartfelt love and kindness, continue to inspire their family and all of those whose lives they touched.

MESIVTHA TIFERETH JERUSALEM

לעילוי נשמת

יעקב בן ר׳ ישראל מרדכי ע״ה

נפטר כ׳ שבט תשס״א

ת.נ.צ.ב.ה

Ruth Salamon

Moshe & Esther Beinhorn

Motty & Estee Salamon

MESIVTHA TIFERETH JERUSALEM

We are pleased to join in this
special yahrzeit publication on the life of

HaGaon Harav Moshe Feinstein, זצוק"ל

dedicated
in memory of

Judge Paul P.E. Bookson, ע"ה

Mrs. Tova Bookson
Bryna and Michael Klein
Rochel and Moshe Schlusselberg
Shoshana and Saul Stromer

לזכר נשמת

לאנא בת ר' מאיר ז"ל

ע"י משפחתה

TABLE OF CONTENTS

Every Jewish Child / Inspiring Love of Torah / With His Own Children / Seemingly Regular / The Visitors / Everyone's Father

DOCUMENT AND PHOTO CREDITS

Agudath Israel of America	Rabbi Aryeh Don Greher	Meir Melnicke
Michael Aryeh	Rabbi Mordechai Gottlieb	Rabbi Ephraim Lenchitz
Rabbi Efraim Barenbaum	Hamodia	Family of R' M. Mendel Pollak
Rabbi Avrohom Biderman	Rabbi Avrohom Y. Heschel	Mr. and Mrs. Neil Powers
Rivkah Blau	Rabbi Indich	C.S. Rosenthal
Rabbi Yehoshua Blum	Rabbi Heshy Jacob	Rabbi Dovid Schwartz
Shulamis Bluming	Nosson Josephy	Menachem Stern
Rabbi Pesach Broyde	Dr. David Katz	Frank Storch
Shloime Dachs	Jeffrey Kaufman	Rabbi Hillel Tendler
Jerry Esterson	Rabbi Aharon Kovitz	Trainer Studios
Rabbi Hertz Frankel	Rabbi Aharon Machlis	Rabbi Yitzchok Twersky
Mimi Fried	Rabbi Moshe Maline	Shaul E. Wasserteil
Jay Greenfield	David & Mermelstein families	Kalman Zeines Studios
Rabbi Shmuel Greenberg	Mordechai Mehlman	Rabbi Menachem Zwick

Many of the photos in this volume are from the archives of Moshe D. Yarmish and Tsemach Glenn

Dear readers: If you recognize unidentified people who are pictured in this book, please notify us at comments@artscroll.com

Twenty-fifth
Yahrzeit Edition

A T THE FIRST YAHRZEIT GATHERING IN MESIVTHA TIFERETH Jerusalem in memory of the *gaon* Harav Moshe Feinstein זצ״ל, his illustrious son, HaRav David Feinstein, שליט״א, said that his father was still alive in a very real sense. For when people were confronted with issues of Halachah, they invariably wanted to know, "What did the Rosh Yeshivah hold?"

Twenty-four years later, this is still true. Wherever and whenever Halachah is discussed, one wants to know Reb Moshe's ruling. There can be no greater testimony to his greatness in Torah. And there can be no greater testimony to Reb Moshe's sterling personality than to be in the presence of his children who, like their father, are paragons of *chesed* and *anavah* (modesty).

This past November, I attended the annual dinner of Mesivtha Tifereth Jerusalem and Yeshivah of Staten Island. I was moved by the palpable, mutual feeling of love between the roshei hayeshivah and the alumni, and by the feeling of love and awe for Reb Moshe, that permeated the entire evening. Again, it was a testimony not only to his status as *gadol hador,* but also to the greatness of his character and as someone whose relationship to his talmidim was like that of a father to a son. In fact, one of the talmidim who was interviewed for this book, who learned under Reb Moshe in the 1950s, wept as he reminisced. "He was like a father to me," he said.

A few weeks after the original *Reb Moshe* was published before his first *yahrzeit,* one of the *gedolim* of our time phoned me and said, "I finished the book and I think I am a better person because of it." While I appreciated the phone call, the caller's sentiments were more a commentary to the book's subject than to the writer's abilities. How can one read about Reb Moshe and not be inspired?

Now, with the approach of Reb Moshe's 25th *yahrzeit,* those who lived in his era have an opportunity to renew their connection to him, to reawaken the memories of greatness that made Reb Moshe the revered and beloved leader that he was. And those of the next generation have an opportunity to learn of the life and ideals of someone who, by the testimony of his peers, ranked with the *gedolim* of an earlier era.

This book is, essentially, a new book. While it contains almost all of the original material, a significant amount of the text is new, as are scores of photos and documents. The goal of this new edition is to give a more complete picture of Reb Moshe's greatness, both in Torah and *middos.* To this end, many new interviews were conducted with family, talmidim, and others, whose relationship with him may have been as early as the 1940s or as late as the 1980s. Additionally, during the past quarter-century many articles on Reb Moshe have appeared, in both Hebrew and English, in which many authentic anecdotes and observations of family and close talmidim were recorded.

I am deeply grateful that in preparing this project I was privileged to interview Reb Moshe's illustrious sons, Harav David Feinstein, Rosh Yeshivah of Mesivtha Tifereth Jerusalem, and Harav Reuven Feinstein, Rosh Yeshivah of Yeshivah of Staten Island, and their rebbetzins. May I offer a *bircas hedyot* that the Roshei Yeshivah continue to guide and inspire their talmidim and *Klal Yisrael* for many years to come, and that they and their rebbetzins see much *nachas* from their families and talmidim.

I thank all those who gave of their time to be interviewed and share their recollections of Reb Moshe. Their names appear in the anecdote(s) in which they were personally involved. I must make mention of a few distinguished individuals who went to special lengths to assist me with this project:

Rabbi Yisroel H. Eidelman, Executive Vice President of Mesivtha Tifereth Jerusalem and a longtime friend of our family, has been a tremendous help from the project's inception to its completion.

Rabbi Dovid Weinberger, Rav of Congregation Shaarei Tefillah in Lawrence and son-in-law of Reb Moshe's close talmid, Rabbi Nissan Alpert זצ"ל, provided anecdotes, tapes of hespeidim, and important contact information.

Rabbi Simcha Bunim Cohen, Rav of Khal Ateres Yeshaya in Lakewood, gave of his time for an extensive interview, for which he prepared with notes, and provided me with written insights and divrei Torah that he heard from Reb Moshe.

Rabbi Michel Shurkin, a Rosh Yeshivah at Yeshivah Toras Moshe in Jerusalem and a close talmid of Reb Moshe, kindly sent me the second volume of his Meged Givos Olam and allowed me to quote freely from both volumes.

Twenty-five years ago, I interviewed Rabbi Elimelech Bluth, who stood faithfully at Reb Moshe's side for 16 years, learning from him and attending to him. Today, Rabbi Bluth is the distinguished Rav of Congregation Ahavath Achim in Kensington, where our family has davened for over forty years. We are privileged to consider Rabbi Bluth a member of our family, and we know that he feels the same way. I thank him for his input for this new book and for all that he has done for our family over the years. May he and his rebbetzin merit good health, long life, and much nachas from their family and kehillah.

My thanks to Rabbi Chaim Dovid Zwiebel, Executive Vice-President of Agudath Israel of America; Rabbi Nisson Wolpin, editor of The Jewish Observer for most of its existence; Rabbi Efraim Barenbaum, son of the Mashgiach of Tifereth Jerusalem, Harav Michel Barenbaum, זצ"ל; and Rabbi Eliezer Hamburger for their contributions; and to Rebbetzin Zelda Alpert, wife of Rabbi Nissan Alpert זצ"ל, for sharing her recollections with me.

No words can express my gratitude to Rabbi Meir Zlotowitz and Rabbi Nosson Scherman for granting me the zechus to write the original biography of Reb Moshe, and now this expanded edition. It was Rabbi Zlotowitz, a close talmid of Reb Moshe and a devoted friend of the Feinstein family and Mesivtha Tifereth Jerusalem, who was the driving force behind the original biography and who conceived of this new edition. I can attest that, for him, this book was truly a labor of love. He carefully read the entire manuscript, made important editorial changes, compiled the index, and added poignant personal anecdotes. His concern for clarity, both in style and message, and his intense desire that the book be a true *kavod* to the Rosh Yeshivah's memory, have enhanced the final product immeasurably. I take this opportunity to thank Rabbi Zlotowitz for the kindness he has shown me over the years. May he be granted many more years in good health, to continue to accomplish for *kvod haTorah* and *kvod Shamayim*.

Rabbi Nosson Scherman edited and wrote portions of the original book. I cannot adequately thank Rabbi Scherman for all that he has done for me since my youth. I would like to take this opportunity to grant him a *zechus* — by relating something from which all of us can learn.

Twenty-five years ago, when I was approached to write the biography of Reb Moshe, I was somewhat of a novice in the writing field. I had never written a book for adults; I was both excited and apprehensive at the prospect of writing such a book. About a week after I had begun work on the project, I phoned Rabbi Scherman and reported whom I had already interviewed and whom I was planning to interview soon. A couple of days later, I received a letter from Rabbi Scherman. He was writing to "congratulate" me on what I had already accomplished, and to express his confidence that the book would be a success.

I recall how good I felt upon receiving that letter. It definitely boosted my confidence. I doubt that Rabbi Scherman recalls this incident, but to me it is a great lesson of how a small act of *chesed* can be very meaningful.

May Rabbi Scherman enjoy many years of good health so that he may continue to accomplish for *kvod haTorah* and *kvod Shamayim*.

My thanks to my dear friend, Rabbi Avrohom Biderman, who did his best to assist me even while being in overdrive with his own book. Mendy Herzberg coordinated the production of this book with enormous patience, pleasantness, and efficiency; it's a pleasure to work with him and I truly appreciate his efforts.

The aesthetic beauty of this book is a credit to the graphics brilliance of Rabbi Shea Brander, whose talents enhance countless *sifrei kodesh* and books. My thanks to him and to Reb Eli Kroen for the beautiful cover.

I thank Mrs. Judi Dick for reviewing the manuscript; Mrs. Estie Dicker and Mrs. Toby Goldzweig for typing portions of the book, and Mrs. Reizy Ganz for her expert paginating. My thanks also to Danny Kay for his work on the photographs, and to the entire staff at ArtScroll/Mesorah.

As a former talmid of Yeshivah of Staten Island, Moshe D. Yarmish has a special feeling for Reb Moshe, which is reflected in his vast archive of photos. This book has been greatly enhanced by the photos that he provided; I thank him for his gracious assistance.

I am also very appreciative to Tsemach Glenn, who provided photos from his archives and also made a special effort to obtain photos for this book from those close to Reb Moshe.

Our sincerest thanks to the many who responded to the advertisements in Jewish periodicals to submit photos and documents for this book. Those whose material was used are listed in the credits box elsewhere in this volume. Our apologies to the many whose submissions could not be included. Your efforts *l'hagdil Torah ul'haadirah* are surely noted in Heaven.

I am grateful to my brother, Rabbi Dovid Finkelman, to Rabbi Mendel Manne and Rabbi Eliyahu W. Ferrell, and to my son, Yisroel Menachem, נ"י, for directing me to sources I otherwise would not have found.

My thanks to my *chaveirim* Rabbi Yosef C. Golding and Rabbi Mordechai Gottlieb; to authors Rabbi Binyomin Pruzansky and Rabbi Nachman Seltzer; and to Rabbi Moshe Benoliel and Rabbi Avrohom Eidelman for their help with this project.

I am fortunate to teach Torah at Yeshivah Darchei Torah, one of America's premier Torah institutions. I thank our Rosh HaYeshivah, Rabbi Yaakov Bender, for all that he has done for me and my family; our yeshivah's very special President, Mr. Ronald Lowinger, for all that he has done for the yeshivah and for me personally; the *menahalim* of the Junior High School division, Rabbi Dovid Frischman and Rabbi Dovid Presser; our *menahel emeritus,* Rabbi Raphael Skaist; and all the wonderful rebbeim with whom I am privileged to work on a daily basis.

I take this opportunity to express my *hakaras hatov* to Rabbi Shlomo Avigdor Altusky, Rosh Yeshivah of Darchei Torah's Beis Medrash Heichal Dovid. Having grown up in the Lower East Side, Rabbi Altusky had a number of encounters with Reb Moshe and took time from his busy schedule to share them with me.

I am fortunate to spend my summers at "Ruach Country," otherwise known as Camp Agudah. My thanks to our wonderful Director, Meir Frischman; our great Head Counselor, Rabbi Simcha Kaufman; and the rest of the Camp Agudah family. I must make mention of Agudath Israel of America's late Executive Secretary, Rabbi Boruch Borchardt, ז"ל, who meant so much to everyone at camp and is sorely missed.

Whatever I have merited to accomplish can be attributed to the *ahavas haTorah* of my father, עמו"ש, and the *tefillos* of my mother, ע"ה. May this effort at *harbatzas haTorah* be a *zechus* for a *refuah sheleimah* for my father,

ר׳ שמואל אביגדור בן חי׳ גיטל בתוך שאר חולי ישראל; and a source of merit for the *neshamah* of my mother, מרת פריידא זעלדא רחל בת ר׳ משה ע״ה.

My wife's parents, Mr. and Mrs. Philip Shapiro שיחיו, are consistently teaching by example. Their sincerity, commitment to Torah, and happiness with their lot are an inspiration. May we merit to be inspired by them for many years to come.

I could not accomplish anything were it not for my wife Tova, תחי׳ שלי; שלה. May Hashem reward her with the fulfillment of all her heart's desires.

I thank the *Ribono shel Olam* for allowing me to undertake and complete this project. May the lessons of Reb Moshe's life inspire us to greater service of Hashem, and to a strengthening of our feeling and concern for each other. In this merit, may we soon witness the end of this *galus* through the coming of Mashiach, speedily and in our time.

Shimon Finkelman

Adar Rishon 5771

"In the Rosh Yeshivah's Presence — as His Talmidim Saw Him"

by Rabbi Meir Zlotowitz

פגע בו רבי עקיבא מן קיסרי ללוד. היה מכה בבשרו עד שדמו שותת לארץ [והיה צועק ובוכה ואומר "אללי לי עליך רבי, אללי לי עליך רבי ומורי, שהנחת כל הדור יתום!" (אבות דרבי נתן כה:ג)]. פתח עליו בשורה ואמר "אבי אבי רכב ישראל ופרשיו! הרבה מעות יש לי, ואין לי שולחני להרצותן!" (סנהדרין סח).

Rabbi Akiva encountered [the bier of his rebbi, Rabbi Eliezer ben Hyrcanus] being brought from Caesaria to Lod. He began striking his flesh until his blood flowed to the earth. [He was crying out, weeping and saying, "Woe is to me, my rebbi, over you! Woe is me, over you, my rebbi, my master, for you have left the entire generation orphaned!" (Avos d'Rabbi Nassan 25:3).]

In the row of mourners, he introduced his eulogy with this verse, " 'My father, my father, chariot of Israel and its rider!' (II Kings 2:12). I have many coins, but I have no money-changer to evaluate them!" (Sanhedrin 68a; see Tos. there and Yevamos 13b; Yoreh Deah 180:6).

◆§ Orphaned

RABBI AKIVA EXPRESSED HIS GRIEF WITH THE VERSE THAT THE prophet Elisha exclaimed when his teacher and guide Eliyahu was taken from this world. *Maharsha (Sanhedrin 68a)* explains that Eliyahu was likened to the chariot and riders that lead the way in battle, overcoming defenses and conquering new lands and peoples for the service of their sovereign. So, too, Eliyahu waged the battles of Torah, refining and reinforcing old concepts, resolving insurmountable difficulties, and opening new vistas of knowledge.

Rabbi Akiva compared himself to the possessor of a hoard of coins; some ordinary and some precious, some negotiable and some invalid. How could he know the value of each unless he could find a trustworthy, experienced, knowledgeable money-changer to teach and guide him? Rabbi Akiva was a repository of Torah but he needed his teacher, Rabbi Eliezer, to polish his brilliance, direct his knowledge, resolve his questions. Now Rabbi Eliezer was gone and the world was orphaned. Rabbi Akiva was overcome with grief, as his tears and blood flowed to the ground.

This was the reaction of Rabbi Akiva, who lived in a world still peopled by giants of Torah. The Sanhedrin was in Yavneh and the *tannaim* of the Mishnah were the acknowledged leaders of the nation. If in such a generation a sage of Rabbi Akiva's stature could feel bereft and adrift, what words have we to describe our world without Maran HaGaon HaRav Moshe Feinstein, the *gadol hador* and father of his nation? Rabbi Akiva had coins; what have we? Rabbi Akiva at least had the words to shriek in grief; we are mute.

Our sense of orphanhood is compounded by the quantum loss within less than a year of three of our era's most revered and venerable sages: Maran HaGaon HaRav Yaakov Yisrael Kanievsky, the Steipler Gaon; Maran HaGaon HaRav Yaakov Kamenetsky; and finally, the Rosh Yeshivah, Reb Moshe, זכר צדיקים וקדושים לברכה. We have often heard that the passing of a great man signifies the end of an era, but for American Jewry, surely, the twin losses of Reb Moshe and Reb Yaakov — especially coming within two weeks of one another — marked a sunset. In his *hesped* on the Chofetz Chaim, Reb Elchonon Wasserman asked how one can know when an era is over. He explained that when a great leader dies and there is no one left to compare with him, no one who can be a bridge to *his* level of greatness, then an era has ended and the world moves down a rung. With the death of the Chofetz Chaim, he said, a period was closed. There was none to succeed him. In our time, we have faith that the sun will rise again — but meanwhile Reb Moshe is gone and an era is over.

If a third of a million Jews in America and Israel came to bid the Rosh Yeshivah farewell, then it was because his people recognized him as their *gadol hador* and father.

Everyone perceived the Rosh Yeshivah in his own way, according to his own experience and needs, but one thing is indisputable: there is not an observant family in the world that has not been touched by the Rosh Yeshivah in some way, by his person or by his halachic decisions.

Many have noted that his funeral was the largest in Eretz Yisrael since the time of Rabban Yochanan ben Zakkai. It was not coincidental. Rabban Yochanan ben Zakkai and Reb Moshe led their people after unprecedented destructions; both elevated the stature of Torah and the authority of Halachah in generations when the faint-hearted feared for the future of *Klal Yisrael.* Heroically and farsightedly they prepared the way for others. Rabban Yochanan ben Zakkai laid the groundwork for Rabban Gamliel. Reb Moshe and his illustrious fellow *gedolei Yisrael* laid the groundwork for — we know not yet the history of the next generation, but one thing is clear: these *gedolim* had faith that Torah will never be forgotten from the Jewish People, and by their self-sacrifice and greatness, they assured that it would not be.

☙ Totality of Greatness

THE ROSH YESHIVAH LEFT US MANY LEGACIES, AND AN ENTIRE BOOK COULD BE written about each one. He was a giant in Torah, Halachah and *Aggadah,* a giant in fear of Hashem, a giant in prayer, a giant of inspiration to his countless talmidim, a giant in modesty, a giant in kindness, a giant in understanding people and situations with a perception born of the profundity of Torah. No one knew the *complete* Reb Moshe. Certainly the *moreh hora'ah* [halachic authority] who came to him with a complex question of *agunah* knew a different Reb Moshe than the woman who regularly asked him to translate a letter in Russian from her sister. The people who came to him for blessings and miracles knew a different Reb Moshe than those who marveled at his phenomenal intensity in prayer.

In the responsive reading of the Song at the Sea, *Chazal* tell us that Moshe called out אָשִׁירָה לַה׳ כִּי גָאֹה גָּאָה, *I will sing to Hashem for He is exceedingly great,* and the Jewish people responded, סוּס וְרֹכְבוֹ רָמָה בַיָּם, *He has hurled the horse and its rider into the sea.* Moshe saw the total greatness of Hashem, but the rest of the people could not perceive that. They could see only that Hashem had toyed with mighty Egypt and exerted His mastery over horse and rider.

So it was with the Rosh Yeshivah. Great men saw him in all his grandeur; the rest of us saw him according to our own needs and experiences. That, too, was part of his greatness. He could relate to each of us according to our individual needs. And the miracle of the man was that in every one of his roles, he was great beyond measure.

I write as a talmid who felt a personal closeness to him as to no one else. My picture of the Rosh Yeshivah is in many ways personal but it is also the reflection of the way countless others saw him. One of the most distinguished of today's middle-aged rabbis is an exceptional *talmid chacham* with the mind of a genius who has written a major halachic work. When he was working on his own *sefer,* he found it difficult to make time to respond to complex halachic inquiries and to attend *simchos* and institutional affairs. He was so totally engrossed in his own subject that he could not immerse himself in foreign subjects. "I am not Reb Moshe," he once told me. "I'm thankful that the *Ribono shel Olam* lets me devote all my time to my *sefer;* I don't have the capacity to be available for so many things and to do each one as if that is the only thing on my mind." To him, the Rosh Yeshivah's greatness was demonstrated by his incredible ability to retain total command of every area of activity — to respond with equal facility to every manner of halachic question, to teach, to write, to comfort troubled Jews, to lead organizations, to attend weddings and *brisos* — and to do each without seeming distracted or preoccupied with something more important.

As HaGaon Reb David, the Rosh Yeshivah's older son and successor as Rosh Yeshivah of Mesivtha Tifereth Jerusalem and as *posek,* puts it, "My father had more than a photographic memory. He had a total grasp of the entire spectrum of Torah. Whatever subject one brought to him, he could instantly and without distraction focus upon it every source and nuance from his lifetime of immersion in Torah."

◆§ Immersion in Torah

TOTAL IMMERSION IN TORAH — THAT WAS THE ROSH YESHIVAH'S ESSENCE. The public is familiar with the legends that he finished *Shas* more than two hundred times and Shulchan Aruch more than six or eight hundred times. Those who knew him best insist that these are exaggerations; what truly matters is that learning was his life and that if it could be said of anyone that he was a living Torah, it was the Rosh Yeshivah. When he was saying the twice-weekly *blatt shiur* for us, he lived in the Gemara. When there was a humorous passage, he smiled and laughed with obvious pleasure. When there was a tragic story or a discussion of Jewish sorrow, pain and grief would be etched on his face and tears would come to his eyes.

To him a mitzvah was a joyous privilege and never an effort. As part of his role as Rosh Yeshivah, he would invite groups of talmidim to be present at a *chalitzah* so that we could learn how such rare mitzvos are to be performed. With a basin of water beside him, he would go down on his hands and knees and examine the bare foot of the man, to make sure it was free of any extraneous matter that might disqualify the performance of the mitzvah, and he would wash the foot himself, if necessary. A lack of dignity? Not at all! What could be more dignified than the performance of a mitzvah?

His extreme simplicity was misunderstood by some as naiveté, but he had a full grasp of every facet of a situation. The most intractable disputes came to him and he had to sift the truth and apply the Halachah in disputes at which both sides were presented by forceful, learned, influential people. Once, during a recess of a heated *din Torah*, he remarked to me as he passed my seat, "They think they are fooling me."

Disputes between institutions invariably came to him. Often they were cases where both sides were right, but one was a bit more right. He had to decide the Halachah in cases that were clear cut only to him. The Rosh Yeshivah had his ways of deciding who was sincere and identifying the underlying, truly crucial issues. For example, during the course of a celebrated, long-running dispute, he wanted to force one gentleman to forgo long-winded rhetoric and articulate the real issues as he saw them. The Rosh Yeshivah asked him, "Simply speaking, if it were up to you, what would you want the result to be, realistically?"

⋙ A Talmid's-Eye View

HIS TALMIDIM CAN BEST DESCRIBE THE ROSH YESHIVAH FROM THE VANTAGE point in his beis midrash. The Rosh Yeshivah was utterly devoted to his institutions, on the Lower East Side and in Staten Island, and he was always available to anyone and everyone, especially his talmidim. He always seemed to be writing and learning. After *Shacharis,* he would review Mishnayos while removing his *tallis* and *tefillin.* In the earlier years, he would eat breakfast in the dining room, but when walking the steps became difficult for him, he began eating at his desk in the beis midrash. Breakfast was always the same: a roll, a soft-boiled egg, and a glass of coffee. As soon as he finished eating and *bentching* he would begin writing in his hard-cover composition notebooks with usually only a gemara open before him. Then he would go into his office to prepare for his *shiur.*

We hesitated to disturb him because we knew that every second was so precious to him, and we knew how he avoided *bitul Torah.* But we knew that if we *ever* had to speak to him, he was warm and gracious. Our consciences told us to beware of interrupting, but nothing he *ever* did or said ratified that reluctance. When we went over to him, we would stand and wait until he noticed us. It never took more than a few seconds, and then he would put down his pen and give us his complete attention. He was very happy if we had a *kushya* on the Gemara or a probing comment on his *shiur.* Rarely did we have to complete a *kushya* before he knew what we meant. He was always way ahead of us, but he never interrupted. We wanted to finish making our point and he wanted to hear us develop it, even though he knew what we planned to say. He would answer, and if we didn't understand him, he would repeat and explain his answer until we did. If we came to him with a personal problem or request, he gave us the same uninterrupted attention, and all the thought and sympathy our dilemma required.

When we were finished and ready to leave, he always gave a *berachah* or encouragement. We never left him without a good word. And we knew he was concerned with our problem. He expected us to report back to him, and if we didn't, he would seek us out and ask. There was an exception: If the query was of a very personal nature, he would not inquire because we might have felt embarrassed. He would never pry, and he scrupulously returned private letters or papers, lest they fall into the wrong hands.

We approached him with reverence, and that feeling of awe was still upon us as we left him. We knew we were standing before the *gadol hador* and we felt that his throat was our conduit from Mount Sinai. Whether or not he used a *pasuk* or quote from the Sages to buttress what he was telling us, we knew that his *every* word and thought were growing from the lush soil of *kol haTorah kulah.* Even if his judgments had been coming merely from a man of experience, concern and enormous wisdom, he would have been a treasure to us, but he was much more. Whether one studied Scriptures, Talmud, Midrash, or Mussar, the descriptions of the ideal human being could have been written about him. To be near him was to be in the courtyard of a *Beis HaMikdash* and to hear his word was like hearing a holy voice emanating from between the Cherubim. Even his genius at humility could not obscure that.

As he walked through the beis midrash and noticed a group of talmidim learning well, disputing one another vociferously over the *p'shat* of some commentary, he would pause and look on with obvious pleasure. Sometimes he would diffidently look over a shoulder to see what the to-do was about, but he would not come close to us because he knew that would make us self-conscious and interfere with our learning. Yet we knew he was there, and the thought that the Rosh Yeshivah was pleased with our efforts made us extend ourselves further in the fray of Torah.

He understood talmidim well and pushed them gently to come closer to realizing their potential. When we were studying for *semichah* [ordination], he would test us whenever we said we were ready. We could ask to be tested on one *siman* or on an entire section. He let us know that the main thing in learning was to know something thoroughly; then we would be able to find sources and apply them to questions as they arose. "Cramming" was not the way, because things that are learned hastily and under pressure are soon forgotten. A rav has to know how to decide Halachah; if he remembers everything clearly, so much the better. But memorization is not a substitute for thorough knowledge.

New talmidim were always flabbergasted by the way he looked up a page in the gemara. He did not look at the page number at the *top* of the page. He would turn up the bottom of the page and look at the few words at the bottom corner. That was enough for him to know what page he was on. Total recall.

◈§ Part of the *Klal*

HE FELT A TREMENDOUS RESPONSIBILITY FOR *KLAL YISRAEL;* THAT IS WHY HE always managed to find time for so many causes and individuals. People usually manage to do what they *must* do, and to him attending the needs of Jewry was something that must be done. He was fully cognizant of his personal role in the Jewish destiny, and he sometimes groaned that he was personally liable for Jewish tragedy, because if he were more worthy, the nation would have merited Divine help. In a sense, he felt he was like the *Kohen Gadol,* who was held responsible for those who were exiled to a city of refuge [עִיר מִקְלָט] for manslaughter. Since the most complex halachic questions came to him, he was subject to a constant flow of tragic news. He once remarked sadly to this writer, "Situations that the *Rishonim* dealt with as abstract, hypothetical questions come to me as realities."

The Rosh Yeshivah complained about few things, but those he did complain about were most expressive of the kind of person he was. It bothered him that his talmidim and others did not inform him of happy occasions. "People come to me with their problems and woes, why don't they come to me with their joys?" Those who would call him hysterically for his blessings and prayers in cases of illness or business crisis usually did not tell him when the patient recovered or the business remained solvent. In fairness, many of us did not do so because we knew how he treasured every second of Torah and we didn't want to intrude on him. We failed to realize that it was not an intrusion. We were all his children — does a father resent the interruption when he is told that his child has weathered a crisis?

It bothered him that he was seldom asked halachic questions about the distribution of tzedakah or about the education of children. He once remarked that almost the only people who consult him about giving tzedakah are kollel scholars who, in many cases, are not required to give. Don't people realize that the Shulchan Aruch speaks about tzedakah and chinuch just as it does about kashrus and interest?

He could not understand why many more people did not attend the melaveh malkahs and dinners of his institutions. The Mesivtha Tifereth Jerusalem and later Yeshivah of Staten Island, where his son HaGaon Reb Reuven is Rosh Yeshivah, were very precious to him. He took personal financial responsibility for the institutions because his allegiance to talmidim, to the Jewish community of the Lower East Side, and to the transmission of Torah to future generations was so intense. His salary was modest beyond belief; he took only what he needed to maintain his very simple standard of living. It pained and mystified him, therefore, that many people ignored his appearances on behalf of the yeshivos.

◄§ Where Are They?

OCCASIONALLY, IN HIS LATER YEARS, HE WOULD VOICE THIS COMPLAINT PUBlicly when he spoke at a melaveh malkah. Where are the people, he wondered, who call early in the morning and late at night with *she'eilos* and requests? When we devote time to fund-raising, we are torn from learning and from responding to the questions that come to us from everywhere. Why does the Jewish public force its roshei yeshivah to steal time from Torah and talmidim to raise money? Shouldn't people who value Torah go out of their way to give the roshei hayeshivah the financial support to which they and their institutions are entitled without the need for a melaveh malkah?

He had a remarkable ability to detach himself from his role. It was hardly possible for a human being to be more modest and personally self-effacing, but he was very much aware of what he was. The Rosh Yeshivah accepted the homage that was due to his Torah, his responsibilities, his position — but he never considered that the individual Jew named Reb Moshe Feinstein was entitled to any honors. That is why he did not shrink from deciding complicated and consequential questions of Halachah that no one else in the world would touch, or why he was ready to oppose the consensus of *poskim* if he was sure he was right. Despite his enormous respect for the *Chasam Sofer* or the *Mishnah Berurah,* he would rule differently from them if his research so dictated. In someone else, this could have seemed arrogant, but there was no one in the world who could associate haughtiness with the Rosh Yeshivah. He had no ego; he had only the Torah of which Hashem had made him a caretaker. It was his duty to interpret the Torah, convey it to talmidim, and apply it to situations. That he did, and if his Torah conflicted with the opinion of others, so be it. As he constantly reiterated, any qualified rabbanim had a right to differ with him, provided they were positive in their own minds that they had mastered all the relevant Talmudic and halachic sources.

◈§ Breadth of Halachah

IT IS ALMOST IMPOSSIBLE TO CONVEY A FULL PICTURE OF THE AMAZING BREADTH of his expertise. However, we can glean an inkling of his Torah greatness from a very brief sampling of the halachic inquiries that came to him:

— Are heart and other organ transplants permitted?

— What is the halachic definition of "time of death"?

— What is the halachic status of marriages and divorces performed and witnessed by people who do not accept the Divine origin of the Torah?

— When a woman is in labor, may her husband ride with her to a hospital on Shabbos?

— A response to Governor Hugh Carey of New York who asked the Rosh Yeshivah to explain the halachic status of the civil death penalty.

— The permissibility of plastic surgery for purely cosmetic purposes.

— Responses to several long series of medical inquiries regarding such matters as "pulling the plug," deciding priorities on who is more entitled to receive scarce medical treatment, prolongation of life which would involve great suffering but no hope of cure, abortion, and so on.

— The use of frozen meat that was not washed within seventy-two hours after slaughter.

— Severing Siamese twins if only one will survive.

— Bringing a seeing-eye dog into a synagogue.

— The halachic status of a deaf-mute from birth, who had been trained to function to a significant degree.

— If a business in Israel is owned by a Diaspora Jew, may it open for business on the second day of Yom Tov?

— Under what circumstances may an *eruv* be constructed in a metropolitan area?

— How can a child make restitution to parents after a long period of minor pilfering from them?

— What is the status of the laws of interest with regard to corporations?

When we consider that the seven volumes of *Igros Moshe* respond to thousands of such queries and that the Rosh Yeshivah decided countless *agunah* questions, we must stand in open-mouthed amazement at how a single human being could know so much, write so much, be available to so many people and institutions, grace so many *simchos* and tzedakah affairs, and accomplish so much in just one lifetime, even though it was nine decades long!

The Rosh Yeshivah was more than merely the sum of many parts; he was the embodiment *par excellence* of many perfect wholes.

✔§ The Greatest Miracle

IT IS TOLD THAT REB LEIB, THE CHOFETZ CHAIM'S ELDEST SON, ONCE VISITED A town where he was surrounded by people who asked to hear of his father's miracles. "My father's greatest miracle," Reb Leib said, "was that he fulfilled, to the letter, the word of Hashem." Similarly, those who were very close to Reb Moshe insist that the greatest lessons we must learn from him are not tales of miracles, but the far greater miracle of his personal behavior.

Though this book cannot offer more than a bare glimpse of the Rosh Yeshivah's Torah greatness, it can give us some idea of the man and his character traits. This is a very important, very worthwhile undertaking, because there is much for us to learn from him. He was our Rosh Yeshivah and model in virtually *every* area of sublime human activity. There is much to emulate; even if we but make the attempt, we will have benefited ourselves and our surroundings.

Because he is no longer among us, it is even more important that we preserve his legacy. It is not enough to mourn, we must preserve. And to paraphrase the Sages, we must ask ourselves, "When will my deeds approach the deeds of the Rosh Yeshivah?"

The Talmud relates that Rabbi Eliezer wept upon observing the incomparable beauty of his teacher Rabbi Yochanan. He explained, להאי שופרא דבלי בעקרא קא בכינא; אמר ליה, על דא ודאי קא בכית. ובכו תרוייהו, "Because of this beauty that will shrivel in the earth do I weep." [Rabbi Yochanan] said to him, "For this it is surely proper that you weep," and then they both wept *(Berachos* 5a).

The *Avnei Nezer* cited the above passage in his eulogy of the *Nefesh Chayah.* He commented that Rabbi Yochanan was a very old man, probably over a hundred years of age, when that meeting took place. How physically beautiful could he have been, and why did Rabbi Eliezer cry? The *Avnei Nezer* explains that Rabbi Yochanan's beauty was spiritual. In his long lifetime he had unceasingly scaled the ladder of Torah, piety, kindness, and service to his people. This spiritual glow radiated from him — and this beauty was his alone. He was not born with it and no one presented it to him as a gift. It was the product of a lifetime of striving and self-perfection. Rabbi Yochanan and Rabbi Eliezer both knew that he would not live forever, and that children with the potential to succeed him would and had been born. But would they ever become great enough to duplicate his glory? Who would replace the spiritual radiance of Rabbi Yochanan when his time would come? At that thought, they both wept, as well they might.

The Rosh Yeshivah is gone. His beauty is gone. His wisdom is gone. Who will replace him? Well may we weep. At the same time, we are reassured by our faith and our history. *Klal Yisrael* survives and new *Gedolei Yisrael* have always arisen. The Rosh Yeshivah's heroic work for Torah will not be in vain. In his *hesped* after the *shivah,* Reb David Feinstein noted, "Just as my father was accessible during his lifetime, his final resting place is accessible to everyone. He was laid to rest at the side of the road, where every Jew can come to pour out his heart and beseech him to pray for us now, just as he did in life."

He is still accessible. He still prays for us. May he implore our Maker to help his children. We mourn him and we miss him. May we learn from him and be worthy of his lifetime of dedication to *Klal Yisrael.*

תנצב"ה

CHAPTER ONE

Origins of Greatness

RABBI YISRAEL MEIR HAKOHEN, BETTER KNOWN AS THE CHOFETZ Chaim, was wont to say that the Heavenly map of this world differs greatly from our own. In Heaven, major cities are not determined by population, level of industry, or seat of government. Rather, a place is deemed worthy of note if its inhabitants are especially G-d-fearing, steeped in the study of Torah, and meticulous in their observance of its mitzvos.

Moshe Rabbeinu's Namesake

The village of Uzda was one such place. Tiny in size, it would most likely go unnoticed by someone scanning a map of 19th-century White Russia, but this small suburb of Minsk dwarfed a host of famous landmarks as a wellspring of holiness and purity. It was there that Rabbi David Feinstein, an outstanding *talmid chacham, posek,* and *tzaddik,* served as Rav; and it was there that on the 7th of Adar, 5655 (1895), a son was born to Reb David and his wife, Rebbetzin Faya Gittel. Having been born on the birthday of Moshe Rabbeinu, the child was named Moshe.

It would seem as if a spark of *ruach hakodesh* had inspired Reb David and his rebbetzin to give their child this name. For, like his namesake

Moshe Rabbeinu, their son would one day sit from early morning until evening, studying and teaching Torah and answering *Klal Yisrael's* questions. And, like Moshe Rabbeinu, their son would be so devoted to his people that he would always be ready to sacrifice himself for their benefit.

REB DAVID FEINSTEIN, WHO DESCENDED FROM A LINEAGE STUDDED WITH brilliant *talmidei chachamim*, was a direct descendant of the Vilna Gaon's

Distinguished Lineage brother, author of *Sefer Maalos HaTorah.* He had been named after his paternal grandfather, who earned a livelihood as a common laborer, but was an exceedingly devout and G-d-fearing Jew, as can be seen from the following incident:

When Reb Moshe's great-grandfather was hired by a gentile employer, he stipulated that he be granted time off from work each day to recite

the daily *tefillos.* While the gentile agreed to this condition, he seethed inwardly that precious time would be "wasted" because "the Jew had to say his prayers." His anger increased manifold when he saw that Reb David's *Shemoneh Esrei* was recited carefully and with intense concentration — and took far more time than was necessary, as far as the employer was concerned.

This the gentile would not stand for. He decided to send a message to his worker, one which he was sure the Jew would not forget for a long time.

One day, as Reb David stood with his eyes closed, praying the *Shemoneh Esrei*, his employer moved stealthily behind him, a shotgun poised in his hands. As Reb David bowed at one point, a shot rang out and a bullet

Rebbetzin Faya Gittel Feinstein

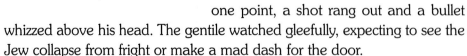
whizzed above his head. The gentile watched gleefully, expecting to see the Jew collapse from fright or make a mad dash for the door.

He was greatly disappointed. Reb David continued to pray as if nothing at all had occurred. The employer told Reb David later that he had been angry enough to kill him if he had run or even turned around when the shot was fired. But when he saw how intensely Reb David was concentrating on his prayer, he realized that Reb David was truly a G-d-fearing man. Never again did the gentile complain about the length of "his" Jew's *Shemoneh Esrei*.

Reb Moshe's great-grandfather Reb David passed away at a relatively young age. His son, Reb Yechiel Michel, was a scholarly layman and a chassid of the Admor of Koidenov. In America, Reb Moshe was especially warm to the descendants of the Rebbe out of a feeling of *hakaras hatov*.[1]

REB MOSHE DESCRIBED THE GREATNESS OF HIS FATHER AND MOTHER IN THE introduction to *Dibros Moshe* to *Bava Kama*, the first of many *sefarim*

A Righteous Couple

which he was to write during his incredible lifetime. Reb Moshe writes of his father:

> He was a great gaon, a tzaddik, chassid and anav … there was hardly a likeness to him, in middos and in the performance of every deed for Heaven's sake alone, as well as his love of Torah and those who study it, and in his love for every Jew. He learned more than two sedarim (orders) of Gemara with me and my holy brothers, of blessed memory,[2] and a large portion of Choshen Mishpat[3] …

Elsewhere Reb Moshe wrote, "I lived near his town, and as long as he lived I consulted him in all complicated halachic questions; his responses were as if from Sinai itself."

The late Ponevezher Rosh Yeshivah, Rabbi Elazar Menachem Shach, recalled:

---

1. From *Sar HaTorah — The Life of Rabbi Yechiel Mechel Feinstein* (of Bnei Brak).
2. Reb Moshe's siblings were: Rebbetzin Shaindel, who married Rabbi Shaul Yaffen, *Hy"d*, a Rav in Rassein and other cities; Rebbetzin Chana, wife of Rabbi Isaac Small, who emigrated to America and was a Rav in Chicago; a girl, Shoshanah, and a boy, Yitzchak, who passed away as children; Reb Avraham Yitzchak, named after his deceased brother (with a name added as is the *minhag haGra* as a *segulah* for long life) — he was the father of the late *gaon* Rabbi Yechiel Michel Feinstein of Bnei Brak; Reb Yaakov, *Hy"d*; Reb Yissochor Ber, *Hy"d*; Shlomo, who passed away suddenly at age 17 while studying at Yeshivas Mir; and Reb Mordechai, Rav and Rosh Yeshivah in Shklov, *Hy"d*.
3. The section of Shulchan Aruch that deals with money matters.

Whoever knew Reb Moshe's father, Reb David "Starobiner," and was familiar with his righteousness, his saintliness, and his extraordinarily fine character, which are beyond description, and whoever had the privilege of beholding his countenance — which was comparable to seeing an angel of G-d — can easily understand the source of Reb Moshe's greatness in his family heritage, from which he drew.[4]

Another person recalled, "*Ahavas Yisrael* simply gushed forth from Reb David."

From age 13 to 17, Reb David studied at the famed Yeshivas Volozhin, where he rose to great heights in Torah learning and character development. His *hasmadah* was such that as Rav of Starobin, aside from his daily walks from his home to the town beis midrash, he rarely ventured outside.[5] Once, when he walked through the streets on his way to deliver a *hesped*, Jewish children pointed with their fingers in amazement and exclaimed, "Look — the Rav is walking in the street!"[6]

❧ ❧ ❧

Reb Moshe's mother, Rebbetzin Faya Gittel, was of royal Torah lineage.

Her father, Rabbi Yitzchak Yechiel Davidowitz, was the scion of a rabbinic family that went back for many generations, and included Rabbi Yom Tov Lipmann Heller (author of *Tosafos Yom Tov*), and Rabbi Yechiel Halprin (author of *Seder HaDoros*), while her mother's family traced itself back to the famed *Shelah HaKadosh* and the *Maharshal*.

The famed *gaon* Reb Eliyahu "Pruzhaner" was married to a daughter of Reb Yitzchak Yechiel.[7] When a younger daughter reached marriageable age, R' Yitzchak Yechiel asked his son-in-law to find a suitable mate for her. R' Elya's inquiries left him convinced that there could be no one more suitable for the young *tzadekes* than a budding *gaon* and *tzaddik*, Reb David Feinstein.[8]

Reb Moshe writes of his mother:

---

4. From *The Rosh Yeshivah Remembers* compiled by Rabbi Asher Bergman (ArtScroll/Mesorah Pulications).
5. The same is said of the *posek hador* Rabbi Yosef Sholom Elyashiv of Jerusalem.
6. Related to Rabbi Yitzchok Silberstein by Rabbi Yechiel Michel Feinstein (from *Sar HaTorah*).
7. Pruzhan was the town in which Reb Elya grew up. His last name was Feinstein but he was not a blood relative of Reb Moshe — Reb Elya was a Levi; Reb Moshe was a Yisrael.
8. *Sar HaTorah*.

She had no peer in fear of Hashem and love of Torah. All she aspired for was that we become great in Torah; she expended every effort in seeing that we not waste any time at all from our learning.

During the first World War, many Russian women earned money by selling home-baked bread to the various armies passing through their cities. In Starobin, Rebbetzin Faya Gittel earned a reputation among the soldiers for her integrity and was their first choice when they needed to buy bread.[9]

Rabbi Elya Pruzhaner

All his life, Reb Moshe was awestruck when speaking of his mother's sublime righteousness. He humbly attributed his accomplishments in Torah to the merits of his parents, and said that his mother taught him the value of time.

There was an elderly woman on New York's Lower East Side who remembered the Feinstein family from Russia. The men and boys were always learning, she said, all of them; Torah was their life.

UZDA AND ITS ENVIRONS ABOUNDED WITH WONDROUS STORIES ABOUT REB David. One such tale centered around his means of livelihood — the sale

Miracle of the Yeast

of yeast by his Rebbetzin. The income from this business could not have been much, but together with the small salary Reb David received as Rav, it was enough to provide his large family with their basic needs.

Then, a gentile opened a store in Uzda which sold baking supplies, including yeast. His sales were enough to encroach on the Rav's business, to the point that he, his Rebbetzin and their children were literally going hungry. Reb David, however, steadfastly refused to seek help in getting the gentile to curtail his yeast sales; instead, he placed his full trust in Hashem.

One day, the gentile's wagon, laden with yeast, chanced down a path that brought it past Reb David's house. As it came directly in front of the house, the horse pulling the wagon came to an abrupt halt, for no expli-

---

9. *Sar HaTorah.*

cable reason. The driver's repeated whippings and commands were to no avail; the horse simply would not budge.

Well aware of what effect his business had had on the Rav's livelihood, the gentile understood the horse's strange behavior as a Divine warning that he had done wrong. He jumped off his wagon, knocked on Reb David's door, and begged forgiveness for having caused anguish to him and his family — and he promised not to sell another speck of yeast.

The gentile then returned to his wagon — and the horse started down the road without a moment's delay.

> In 1901, when Reb Moshe was 6 years old, a pogrom forced Reb David, his family, and the other Jews of Uzda to run for their lives. When the Rav and his family returned six weeks later, they found that a *talmid chacham* who had come to the town in the interim had declared himself Rav and was occupying the Rav's seat in the main beis midrash. Reb David absolutely refused to involve himself in anything that smacked of *machlokes*. While the townspeople continued to recognize him as their Rav and he still maintained the Rav's yeast business, from then on Reb David and his sons *davened* in the town's chassidic shul. Thus, at a very young age, Reb Moshe learned to flee from strife and to get along with those whose background and customs differed from his own.[10]

MOSHE'S BIRTH BROUGHT HIS PARENTS SPECIAL JOY, FOR HIS mother had suffered a number of miscarriages before receiving a blessing

In His Father's Footsteps

for a child from Reb Yisrael, the Karlin-Stoliner Rebbe. The joy of this noble couple surely increased manifold as it became apparent that their son possessed many rare qualities.

It was evident from his early youth that Moshe Feinstein was destined for greatness. He had been blessed with a brilliant mind, possessed sterling character traits and had an appreciation for the value of Torah study that belied his young age.

> When he was about 6 years old, Moshe and a friend became involved in a "serious" discussion. "When I grow up," the other boy said, "I would like to become a tailor, like my father."
>
> "It is good for a child to go in the ways of his father," young Moshe replied. "When I grow up I hope to become a rav."

---

10. From the biographical preface to *Igros Moshe* Vol. VIII, prepared for publication by Rabbi Shabsi Avraham HaKohen Rapaport and the Feinstein family.

He was a talented chess player in a country where chess was a popular pastime among Talmudic scholars. Yet, at age 8, he gave up playing the game. In later years he explained why. "I told myself that if one is already using his mind, it should better be used for the study of Torah."[11]

An elderly contemporary remembered him as a child. He was popular and used to play with the other boys, but after five or ten minutes of play, he would excuse himself and go back to his *sefer.*

Rabbi Yitzchak Chaim Krasnitsky was dean of Yeshivah L'Metzuyanim in Israel, and knew Reb Moshe from his boyhood days in Russia. When asked to relate interesting episodes from those days involving young Moshe Feinstein, he replied, "There is nothing to relate. All his time was spent learning."

An elderly Jew in the Bronx told a talmid of Reb Moshe, "I remember him as a little boy in Uzda. He was always learning. We all knew he would be a great *talmid chacham,* but we never dreamed that our friend would become the *gadol hador!*"

Before sending Moshe to a *melamed,* Reb David taught him all of *Tanach.* Reb Moshe was amazingly fluent in *Tanach* and its commentaries, and throughout his life, he began his day by learning two chapters of *Tanach.*

When he was still very young, Moshe was brought to a *melamed* who was teaching Gemara to boys a few years older than he. On Moshe's very first day in the class, the rebbi pointed to the word אִיתְּמַר in the gemara and asked for someone to read the word. Moshe raised his hand and, since the gemara had no punctuation, misread the word as אִיתָמָר (the son of Aharon HaKohen). The *melamed* reprimanded the other boys when they laughed at Moshe's mistake.

Reb Moshe would later say that he learned two lessons for life from that incident: In learning, one should never assume that his initial approach is the correct one. Rather, he should approach a topic from every angle and entertain the possibility that the correct explanation is one that he never before considered.

The second lesson was one of *middos.* Reb Moshe never forgot how he felt when his classmates laughed at his mistake. He resolved never to laugh at people or ridicule them in any way, no matter how foolishly they spoke or acted.[12]

❦ ❦ ❦

11. He once told his grandson, Rabbi Aryeh Don Greher, another reason why he gave up chess: it bothered him that he always won. He did not like any game in which there is a winner and a loser, because he always felt bad for the loser.
12. Preface to *Igros Moshe,* Vol. VIII.

Before reaching his 10th birthday, Moshe already knew the tractates *Bava Kama, Bava Metzia* and *Bava Basra,* a total of 410 *blatt* in three of the Talmud's most difficult tractates. On a Yom Kippur eve before his bar mitzvah, Moshe remained awake all night studying *Masechta Yoma* with his father. By the time morning services began, the two had completed the entire tractate.

Reb Moshe related how his father not only studied with him, but also carefully supervised his education. Reb David personally paid for a private Gemara rebbi for his son and three other boys, to foster their maximum growth. Indeed, the group completed the entire *Masechta Gittin* with all of *Tosafos* that year. Here in the United States, Reb Moshe told that story to the president of a yeshivah who had argued that he could not afford the expense of a second rebbi for an oversized class.

Reb David knew that the youngster had unlimited potential and, as Reb Moshe wrote in the introduction to the first volume of his responsa *Igros Moshe*:

> … My father said to me that he hoped and was virtually positive that many would inquire of me regarding Halachah, which is the word of Hashem, both orally and in writing, and that I would answer correctly, with G-d's help.

That comment illustrated a unique characteristic of Reb Moshe, a trait that represented another of his similarities to Moshe Rabbeinu. On the one hand, his modesty was incredible. He was uncomfortable with honor, never felt that he had learned or accomplished enough, and gave respect and honor even to children and unlearned people. On the other hand, like Moshe, he knew that he had a responsibility to lead, to rule on the most complex questions of Halachah, and even to disagree with other great rabbis if he was sure he was right. He had the very unusual ability to differentiate between himself as an individual Jew and the Torah that he knew. As a person, no one could be more humble; but he felt he had no right to be humble where Hashem's Torah was concerned.

EVEN AT THAT EARLY AGE, MOSHE WAS COMMITTING HIS ORIGINAL TORAH thoughts to writing. It is told that when a thought would come to mind and there was no paper on hand, he would record the *chid-*
Unlimited Potential *dush* on any available substitute, even a stone. Throughout his long life, during which time he wrote many thousands of pages of *chiddushei Torah* and *teshuvos*, Reb Moshe would fill each page from top to bottom before beginning the next page. He explained to

his talmidim that in Russia, paper was often scarce and prohibitively expensive. He had no choice but to fill *every* inch of the paper with his writing. This was a habit that remained with him his entire life.[13]

When Moshe was about 11 years old, he once entered a room where his father was meeting with a number of prominent rabbanim, including Reb David's renowned brother-in-law, Reb Elya Pruzhaner. As soon as they noticed Moshe's presence, the rabbanim all rose in respect for the young Torah genius. He turned red from embarrassment, and his father was terribly upset. Reb David asked his son to go bring refreshments for his guests. However, with the door closed, Moshe was able to hear his father's next words.

"What are you doing to me?" Reb David demanded of the others. "You are destroying my child! You will turn him into a *baal gaavah* … "

WHEN MOSHE WAS 12 YEARS OLD, HIS FAMILY LEFT UZDA FOR STAROBIN, A CITY teeming with Torah scholars. It was said that there were one hundred

The Fruits of Diligence

Starobin working men knowledgeable enough to serve as rabbanim. This was a play on the Russian words *sta* (one hundred) and *rabbin* (rabbis), but it was an accurate description of the level of Starobin's Jews. It was this golden community that chose Reb David Feinstein as its new Rav.

Young Moshe Feinstein became a fixture in the town's main beis midrash. Reb Leib Meislik, a *tzaddik* whose incredible life story is recorded in *Voices in the Silence*,[14] related:

> Once during my basic training in the Czar's army, our regiment camped near the town of Starobin. I had a friend who was also a former yeshivah student, and we used *every* leave we were given to good advantage: We would go to the town shul and learn a *blatt Gemara* together.
>
> In the corner of Starobin's shul, near the *aron kodesh,* we always found a charming boy of about 13 sitting and learning. His eyes shone with a penetrating light as he sat over his gemara, never wasting a moment. His older sister even brought him his lunch to eat there in the shul, to save him the few minutes it would take to go home and come back. He would eat upstairs in the women's balcony and then go right back to his studies.

---

13. From *Sar HaTorah.*
14. By Rabbi Shlomo Zalman Sonnenfeld, published by Feldheim.

Rabbi Isser Zalman Meltzer

He was known in the town as *"Moishe'le dem Rav's zun"* ("Moishe'le the Rav's son"). His father, who would learn with us, was Rav David Feinstein, Rav of Starobin. The older sister was later known as Rebbetzin Chana Small of Chicago. And the boy was the future Rav Moshe Feinstein, whose Torah lit up the world.

❦ ❦ ❦

Shortly before Moshe became a bar mitzvah, his father deemed him ready to leave home and study under one of the foremost Torah giants of that time. Off to Slutzk he went, to the Yeshivah Eitz Chaim, headed by the famed Rabbi Isser Zalman Meltzer. It was through his closeness to the Rosh Yeshivah that, in later years, Moshe became friendly with Reb Isser Zalman's son-in-law, Rabbi Aharon Kotler, with whom he worked hand in hand in guiding Torah Jewry in the United States and elsewhere after 1940.

In Slutzk, Moshe quickly earned a reputation for himself for his amazing brilliance and incredible diligence. The "Starobiner *Iluy*," as he was known, would remain in the beis midrash far into the night, sleeping barely five hours. By the time he turned 13, Moshe was fluent in two complete orders of *Shas*. Forty years later, Reb Isser Zalman would relate with admiration some questions and *chiddushim* of the 13-year-old Moshe Feinstein.

Reb Moshe related an incident that occurred a few years after he left Slutzk. A renowned contemporary told him that he had occasion to sit together with Reb Isser Zalman and Rabbi Yeruchom Leib Perlmutter, known as "the Minsker *Gadol*." Reb Isser Zalman related a *chiddush* of Reb Moshe and said it was *"l'amitah shel Torah* (absolute Torah truth)." The *talmid chacham* continued, "Reb Isser Zalman and the Minsker *Gadol* held like you, but I refuted the *chiddush*." Reb Moshe smiled and replied, "If my rebbi and the Minsker *Gadol* held like me, that is good enough for me."

AFTER MOSHE HAD ALREADY LEFT SLUTZK, ANOTHER FUTURE TORAH LEADER arrived there. Rabbi Elazar Menachem Mann Shach became a prize talmid

Rav Shach of Reb Isser Zalman and later married his niece. When Reb David Feinstein would travel to Slutzk to preside over *dinei Torah* alongside Reb Isser Zalman, Reb Moshe would accompany

Rabbi Elazar Menachem Shach

him and visit his rebbi. It was during these visits that Reb Moshe and Rav Shach would "speak in learning," developing a deep friendship that transcended time and continents.

At Reb Moshe's funeral in Jerusalem, Rav Shach cried:

> I have known him since his younger days in Slutzk. His *hasmadah* knew no bounds. Day and night he did not cease from studying Torah — this is no exaggeration.

On another occasion, Rav Shach commented that he recalled Reb Moshe reviewing all of *Masechta Shabbos* in a single Shabbos.

As Rav of Luban, Reb Moshe corresponded with Rav Shach regarding difficult *sugyos* in *Seder Nashim* and *Seder Nezikin*. In their correspondences decades later, Reb Moshe addressed Rav Shach as "*yedid nafshi* (the friend of my soul) from our youth."

Rav Shach's family is in possession of a letter of apology from Reb Moshe. In his *Igros Moshe*, Reb Moshe published each letter in its original form. The *sefer* contains letters to Rav Shach written when the two were young men. Reb Moshe apologized because in those early letters, the salutations with which he addressed his lifelong friend were not befitting someone who now was a *gadol hador*.[15]

---

15. From *Maran HaRav Shach* (English — *Path to Greatness*) by Rabbi Asher Bergman, published by Feldheim.

ASIDE FROM BEING HEADED BY A ROSH YESHIVAH, MOST YESHIVOS OF HIGHER
learning are guided by a Mashgiach, who is responsible for the spiritual

Rav Pesach Pruskin growth of the talmidim in areas outside of actual Torah study. Yeshivah Eitz Chaim's Mashgiach was Rabbi Pesach Pruskin, who himself had been a student of Reb Isser Zalman when he studied as a young man in Slutzk. Following his marriage, Reb Pesach became a night watchman in an orchard, which afforded him time to study on his own and to meditate while he sat among the trees. He became well versed in areas of Torah *hashkafah* (outlook), completing the Rambam's classic, *Moreh Nevuchim*. Meanwhile rumors abounded that Reb Pesach was one of the thirty-six hidden *tzaddikim* in whose merit the world exists. During this period, he met Reb Isser Zalman, who invited him to return to Slutzk as Mashgiach. After some delay Reb Pesach accepted the offer, and proceeded to inspire the yeshivah's talmidim with his impassioned *mussar* talks and his own angelic ways.

While Reb Pesach was respected as a *tzaddik* and an expounder of *mussar*, he was deemed only average as a Talmudic scholar. Although he applied himself diligently, he was considered of ordinary intelligence.

When a heated discussion on a topic in *Bava Kama* took place one day, Reb Pesach offered his opinion. Those taking part in the discussion were not impressed in the least by Reb Pesach's comment; they fell silent and a mocking smirk appeared on the lips of one or two of the participants. Reb Pesach noted the reaction and he retreated to his corner, deeply humiliated. He began to weep until he fell asleep. He dreamed that he was commanded to continue his Torah study and was promised *siyata diShmaya* (Heavenly assistance) in achieving greater success in his learning.

Reb Pesach began to study with new confidence, and in a short time, a noticeable change had taken place. He spent a summer in the company of Rabbi Chaim Soloveitchik of Brisk, and, with his newfound depth and clarity, assimilated Reb Chaim's analytical approach to learning to an extent that amazed everyone. As time went on, he amassed a vast amount of knowledge and, combining this with diligence and his newly acquired sharpness of mind, Reb Pesach went on to become one of the foremost *geonim* of his day.

Rabbi Nosson Tzvi Finkel ("*der Alter*" of Slabodka) advised Reb Pesach to leave Slutzk and start his own yeshivah in Shklov, where he would serve as rosh yeshivah. Seeking to assure the success of the new yeshivah, Reb Isser Zalman had lots drawn to select a group of outstanding talmidim who would accompany Reb Pesach and become the nucleus of his new beis midrash. Among those selected was the Starobiner *Iluy*, Moshe Feinstein, then all of 15 years old.

Rabbi Pesach Pruskin

> Years later, when Reb Moshe was an acclaimed giant of his generation, a 15-year-old naively asked him, "Does the Rosh Yeshivah study only those tractates in *Talmud Yerushalmi* to which there is no *Bavli*, or does he study the others as well?"
>
> "By the time I was your age," replied Reb Moshe with a warm and friendly smile, "I had already written *chiddushim* on the entire *Yerushalmi* tractates of *Bava Kama, Bava Metzia* and *Bava Basra.*" It was his gentle way of encouraging young students to feel that they could accomplish much more in learning. He felt that people were usually held back not so much by lack of ability as by lack of confidence in themselves and a deficiency of ambition to attain major goals.

At the dedication ceremonies for the new yeshivah in Shklov, attended by many prominent rabbanim, Moshe offered a halachic discourse that amazed the entire gathering. Sixty years later, he included this *shiur* — with only minor changes — in a volume of his *Dibros Moshe.*

IN 1911, UPON THE ADVICE OF RABBI CHAIM SOLOVEITCHIK, REB PESACH accepted the invitation of the Jews of Amtsislav that he serve as their Rav.

His Rebbi's Pride The community accepted Reb Pesach's condition that his yeshivah be relocated in their city. Thus, when Reb Pesach departed Shklov he was joined by his talmidim, including Moshe, who studied under Reb Pesach until he was 19, and always considered Reb Pesach his primary rebbi.

By age 17 Moshe had already mastered all of *Shas* with *Tosafos,* and in another two years he had completed all four sections of *Tur* and *Shulchan Aruch.* It was then that, at his father's urging, he began to write halachic responsa. One of these *teshuvos,* dealing with the complex laws of *shechitah,* was later printed in his classic *Igros Moshe,* a multi-volume collection of *teshuvos* [responsa] spanning a breathtaking array of halachic topics.

Around this time, Reb Pesach remarked with pride about Moshe, "I have a student who has surpassed me in learning as well as in Halachah."

In 5729 (1969), many of Reb Pesach's lectures were published by his grandson under the title *Shiurei Rabbi Pesach MiKobrin*.[16] The work contains a *haskamah* (approbation) from Reb Moshe, in which he writes:

> *I was extremely joyful to hear that the writings of my rebbi, the great gaon ... (are being published) ... Many great giants and geniuses in Torah became great by serving him and learning his holy ways in the method of Torah study. I recall the great pleasure I experienced when hearing his shiurim and chiddushim in the years I merited to serve him ...*

In the 1960s, a talmid of Reb Moshe became engaged. When the wedding date was set, he asked Reb Moshe to serve as his *mesader kiddushin*. Reb Moshe replied that he could do so only if the *chuppah* would be late, because he first had to attend the wedding of a grandchild of Rav Pesach Pruskin. The talmid felt bad; he did not want to delay his *chuppah*, since many of his relatives lived out of the New York area and wanted to leave the wedding at an early hour. Reb Moshe also felt bad, but said that he could not change his plans regarding the first wedding. The talmid said, "May I ask: Does the Rosh Yeshivah know either the *chassan* or *kallah* at the other wedding?" Reb Moshe replied that he did not. "But I am the Rosh Yeshivah's *talmid*!" the talmid argued.

Reb Moshe responded, "And I am Rav Pruskin's *talmid*. I learned by him."[17]

Reb Moshe sent a wedding gift to one of Reb Pesach's grandchildren, with the following note: "This gift which I send you is nothing in light of the deep appreciation I feel towards my rebbi ... "

Reb Moshe had an older sister, Shaindel. She was married to a great *gaon*, Rabbi Shaul Yaffen, who served for a time as Rav of Rassein. When Moshe was 18, his brother-in-law had to flee the city because of a libelous accusation. Before departing, he designated Moshe to serve as interim Rav, a position he held for six months. He then returned to Reb Pesach's yeshivah.[18]

---

16. Kobrin, Reb Pesach's birthplace, was where he spent the last 17 years of his life, serving as both rav and rosh yeshivah.
17. In the end, the two *chuppos* were scheduled to everyone's satisfaction.
18. Preface to *Igros Moshe*, Vol. VIII.

REB MOSHE HAD A CLOSE RELATIONSHIP WITH HIS UNCLE, THE *GAON* RABBI
Yaakov Kantrowitz, author of *Tzelusa D'Shmait'sa.*[19] Reb Yaakov was

Rav Yaakov Kantrowitz born and raised in Uzda, and it was the town's Rav, Rabbi David Feinstein, who arranged the match between him and Reb David's wife's sister. When Reb David left Uzda to become Rav of Starobin, Reb Yaakov succeeded him as Rav. Ten years later, when Reb Yaakov left Uzda to become Rav of Shatzk, Reb Moshe succeeded him.[20]

In his youth, Reb Moshe initiated an exchange of letters with Reb Yaakov on a topic in *Masechta Kiddushin.* Reb Yaakov's initial response opened with:

> With great delight, I perused your thoughts that are so precious to me, the chiddushim presented with wisdom and understanding, the fruits of your study — may every mother give birth to one like you!

Thus began a correspondence that lasted years. As a young rav, Reb Moshe wrote *teshuvos* in Halachah to his famed uncle. These letters were so precious to Reb Yaakov that he brought them with him when he emigrated to America in 1928, and they were subsequently published in *Igros Moshe.*[21]

Their correspondence led to one between Reb Yaakov and Reb Moshe's brother, the *gaon* Reb Mordechai, *Hy"d.* Reb Mordechai's initial letter begins:

> In truth, it is a while that I have desired to enter into a correspondence with his honor, the gaon. Now, when I am a guest at the home of my brother, the gaon [Reb Moshe], shlita, I read his honor's letter and derived much pleasure from it. Therefore, I have decided to be so bold as to trouble his honor to peruse my simple words of Torah and to respond to me.

During his years in the United States, Reb Yaakov served as *Av Beis Din* in Trenton, New Jersey. In 1933, at the request of Rabbi Shraga Feivel Mendlowitz, he became Rosh Yeshivah of Mesivta Torah Vodaath. He would spend half the week at the yeshivah and the other half in Trenton.

---

19. The material in this section was gleaned from an appreciation of Reb Yaakov by his grandson, Rabbi Shlomo Lipschitz, published in the *Yeshurun* Torah journal (#21).
20. See the following sub-chapter.
21. See, for example, *Orach Chaim*, Vol. I, #13-19.

Rabbi Yaakov Kantrowitz

However, one year later he was injured in a fall and was forced to resign his position as Rosh Yeshivah.[22] He passed away on Hoshana Rabbah 5706 (1945).

After Reb Yaakov's passing, Reb Moshe prepared his *Chiddushei HaGaon R' Yaakov* for publication.[23] In his preface to that work, Reb Moshe wrote:

My uncle, the great gaon, Moreinu HaRav Yaakov Kantrowitz, zt"l, was a true Torah personality from his youth until his very last day, in all his ways and deeds. He did not leave the four amos of halachah, for he was exceptionally diligent in his studies all his days and virtually never ceased from studying words of Torah. All his learning was with great depth and he was amazingly fluent in all of Shas and its commentaries, and all sections of Tur and Shulchan Aruch with their commentaries. When one discussed any Talmudic topic with him, it was as if he had been studying it that day [for such was his clarity]. He propounded great insights in Torah and was a genuine master of psak halachah. [I know this because] I knew him for many years and exchanged letters with him in deep Talmudic discussions and practical Halachah.

---

22. At the behest of Rabbi Chaim Ozer Grodzensky of Vilna, Rabbi Shlomo Heiman was chosen to succeed him.

23. Rabbi Yaakov Moshe Shurkin, a Rosh Yeshivah at Mesivta Rabbi Chaim Berlin, was a son-in-law of Reb Yaakov. In *Meged Givos Olam*, his son, Rabbi Michel Shurkin, relates the following:

At Reb Yaakov's funeral, his son-in-law Reb Yaakov Moshe approached a Mr. Milner, who was a member of the Trenton *kehillah* and had deep respect for Torah and its students. "Do you want to live a long life on this world?" he asked. "Then listen to my advice. As they are lowering my father-in-law's pure body into the ground, say the following: 'Rebbi: I accept upon myself to publish your holy writings, and in this merit, I would like to live long on this earth.' "

Mr. Milner did as instructed; that very day, he gave the family $5,000 to cover publishing costs. The manuscripts were then given to Reb Moshe, who prepared them for publication.

In 5745 (1985), upon Reb Moshe's directive, Reb Yaakov's remains were re-interred in Eretz Yisrael. A few days later, Mr. Milner passed away at a very old age and was buried alongside Reb Yaakov.

He served as Rav in four distinguished European communities, and in his later years in America. His greatness in Torah was matched by his exceptional humility — total self-negation, as was known to all his scholarly friends, both in his youth and his later years. His piety and good, beloved middos were likewise exceptional; he dealt with every individual with unusual feeling and love. He was an embodiment of "'And you shall love Hashem, your G-d' — that the Name of Hashem should become beloved through you ... "[24]

AT THE OUTBREAK OF WORLD WAR I IN 1914, MOSHE LEFT AMTSISLAV AND rejoined his father in Starobin, where they studied together and where he

The Chofetz Chaim's Blessing

began teaching local youths. His *shiurim* gained broad acclaim and he was quickly hailed as a young giant of Torah and *psak*.

During the second year of the war, with the Czar's army being mauled on the western front, a conscription order was issued for all young men of Moshe's age. Aside from the dangers of fighting in a war, serving in the Russian Army meant forced transgression of certain mitzvos, and of course little time for Torah study. To Moshe and his parents, these considerations were sufficient reason to seek a deferment from service through any means available. He traveled many miles to see an attorney who was said to have connections with government officials. However, the attorney proved to be of little help and Moshe began his journey home empty-handed.

On the way back to Starobin, Moshe stopped off in Smilovitz where the Chofetz Chaim and his yeshivah had been forced to relocate because of the war. Moshe headed for the yeshivah's beis midrash to seek the blessing of the Chofetz Chaim, whom he had never met.

When Moshe entered the beis midrash, he found the Chofetz Chaim with his most famous disciple, Rabbi Elchonon Wasserman. As Reb Moshe retold the story to his students half a century later, "I went to see the Chofetz Chaim and he was sitting with Reb Elchonon. We spoke in learning and when he saw that I knew *(ven ehr hot gezehn az ich ken)*, he gave me his blessing."[25]

---

24. *Yoma* 86a.

25. It was typical of Reb Moshe's modesty that all his life he never said much about his visit to the Chofetz Chaim. Even to his family, he would say only that he had spoken to the Chofetz Chaim very briefly, and only to ask for his blessing. On Purim afternoons, his students used to visit his New York home to celebrate the festival with him. At those times he would be unusually jovial and outgoing, and on a few occasions he related the conversation with the Chofetz Chaim.

The Chofetz Chaim

Rabbi Elchonon Wasserman

The Chofetz Chaim had heard much about the "Starobiner *Iluy*" and was concerned when Moshe explained the gravity of his situation. The Chofetz Chaim and Reb Elchonon both rose and escorted their young visitor from the beis midrash. The Chofetz Chaim then turned to Moshe and said:

> *Chazal* tell us, *Whoever accepts upon himself the yoke of Torah — the yoke of government and of worldly responsibilities are removed from him.*[26] It would seem that, rather than "removed from him," a more proper phrase would have been "are not placed upon him."
>
> There is, however, a fundamental message in this carefully worded statement of *Chazal*. One whose deeds are purely for the sake of Hashem will merit that even decrees that have already been proclaimed upon him will be removed.

With these words, the Chofetz Chaim bade Moshe farewell. Not long afterward, the government proclaimed that, in view of the successful mobilization of the Russian Army, all call-ups of rabbis were suspended until further notice. In that proclamation, Reb David saw a legal way to protect his son from the draft. Uzda, Moshe's birthplace, was seeking a new rav at the time, so — at Reb David's suggestion — they accepted Moshe as their Rav. His trials were not over, however, because he was ruled too young and able-bodied for a deferment. Nevertheless, he even-

---

26. *Avos* 3:6.

tually succeeded in gaining an exemption. Despite the superficially natural means through which he gained his freedom, he attributed his success to the Chofetz Chaim's blessing.

More than half a century later, someone mentioned a halachic issue to Reb Moshe which had been debated by 19th-century *poskim*. Reb Moshe replied that in this matter, he followed the opinion of Rabbi Dovid Friedman of Karlin, and quoted the latter's *teshuvah* on the subject. Then, he remarked parenthetically, "I came across this *teshuvah* during the First World War when I had to travel somewhere because of a draft notice I received. While I was waiting to see someone, I entered a beis midrash and found a *sefer* of R' Dovid's *teshuvos*."

The fact that Reb Moshe, at that unsettling hour, had the ability to study the *teshuvah* and retain it so that he could quote it over fifty years later illustrates the degree to which he had already accepted upon himself the "yoke of Torah."

WHEN REB MOSHE WAS INVITED TO SERVE AS RAV IN UZDA, THE INHABITANTS WERE filled with pride over the glowing reports concerning their former Rav's son.

The Young Rav Twenty years old and as yet unmarried, Reb Moshe assumed his first rabbinic position. Soon after Reb Moshe's arrival, his former *melamed* publicly served him, like a servant before his master. Reb Moshe was visibly upset that his rebbi had accorded him such honor. However, the *melamed* had a different view, saying that his heart was filled with joy when he saw how great his talmid had become.

Years before, Reb Moshe's father had declared his confidence that his son would become a respected *posek*. In Uzda it became clear that Reb David's words were indeed prophetic.

> In his very first year as Rav, a delicate halachic query was brought to him, involving a man and woman who had been wed in a marriage ceremony whose validity was questionable. After carefully reviewing the case, Reb Moshe issued a thirteen-page *teshuvah* in which he concluded that the ceremony was invalid, thus permitting the woman to remarry without obtaining a *get*. Forty-four years later, this *teshuvah* too was published in *Igros Moshe*.[27]

Reb Moshe's halachic rulings were also sought by many people outside of Uzda, for already then his *psak* was known to be clear, concise, and based on a knowledge of Torah that was breathtaking in range and dazzling in depth.

---

27. *Even HaEzer*, Vol. I, # 82.

In his first years in Uzda, Reb Moshe wrote an intricate *teshuvah* (also found in *Igros Moshe*) on the complicated laws of *ribis* (interest). Many years later, Rabbi Tuvia Goldstein, Rosh Yeshivah at Yeshivah Emek Halachah, expressed amazement to Reb Moshe that he could have had such a broad scope of knowledge at so young an age. In one of only two occasions when Reb Tuvia saw him display a touch of pride, Reb Moshe responded by commenting that he had sent the *teshuvah* for review to Reb Isser Zalman Meltzer, and his former rosh yeshivah had lavishly praised the piece as *emes l'amitah,* the quintessential truth.

Reb Moshe had a brother, Reb Yaakov, *Hy"d,* who was married to a relative of the famed Rav of Brisk, Rabbi Chaim Soloveitchik. During Reb Moshe's years in Uzda, he received a letter from Reb Chaim, saying that he had heard much about him and inviting him to come study with him. Reb Moshe would have readily accepted the invitation but for the responsibility he felt toward the Jews of Uzda.[28]

IN UZDA, AS WHEREVER HE WENT, REB MOSHE WAS LOVED AND ADMIRED NOT only for his greatness in Torah, but for his angelic character traits and his love for every Jew.

Appetite for Goodness

The Jewish community in Uzda provided him with all his basic needs, some of which were slightly unusual for a rav, since Reb Moshe remained unmarried during his years there. One of the local women was assigned the task of cooking his meals, a task she performed gladly.

One day, Reb Moshe's sister Chana arrived in Uzda to visit her brother. "I see you are being treated very well," she commented upon seeing him. "You've put on a little bit of weight."

"I *am* being treated well," Reb Moshe replied. "The woman who cooks for me prepares a heaping plate of food for each meal. I always finish all that is served, not wanting her to think I find her food lacking. However, she sees my clean plate as a sign of hunger and she promptly serves me seconds — which I also partake of, for her sake. And so, yes — I have put on weight."

Later that day, Chana joined him for a meal at the woman's house. She took one bite — and found that it tasted so awful that she was tempted to spit it out. With a heaping plate of food staring at her and not wishing to insult her hostess, she saw no way out of her dilemma but to clear the food off the plate when the woman was not looking.

---

28. Preface to *Igros Moshe*, Vol. VIII.

Rabbi Dovid
Povarsky

Rabbi Yeruchom
Levovitz

Rabbi Nechemiah
Yerushalemski

Rabbi Chaim
Kavalkin

In later years, Rebbetzin Small would relate this story to her grandchildren, expressing her admiration for her brother who, day after day, for
three years, ate this woman's cooking, two portions at a time! Difficult as
it may have been to eat the badly prepared food, Reb Moshe, who would
one day be remembered as "a *gaon* in *middos*," found it far more difficult
to hurt the woman's feelings.

IN THE YEAR 1920, REB MOSHE ACCEPTED AN INVITATION TO SERVE AS RAV IN
Luban, a town twenty miles from Slutzk. Torah and fear of Hashem were

Luban found in abundance in Luban. A group of working men formed
a *Chevrah Shas,* in which the members divided the entire Talmud
among themselves for study, with a *siyum* being held each year on
Chanukah. Most parents in the town sent their sons to study in the great
yeshivos of Eastern Europe, where many of them developed into outstanding Torah personalities. Luban was the birthplace of Rabbi Yerucham
Levovitz, legendary Mashgiach of the Mirrer Yeshivah in Europe; and Rabbi
Dovid Povarsky, late Rosh Yeshivah at the Ponevezh Yeshivah in Bnei Brak.

In discussing the concept of מַאן מַלְכֵי? רַבָּנָן (Who are [the true] kings?
the Sages),[29] Reb Moshe said that *Chazal* meant this in a literal sense. To
illustrate this, he recounted the manner in which the Jews of Luban treated
him when he became their Rav:

> An elderly man would come to the shul at 4:00 a.m. in order to heat
> the oven so that the Rav would be warm when he learned at that
> early hour. When Reb Moshe protested, "But I am a young man!" the

---

29. See *Gittin* 62a.

Jew responded, "If the Rav will not permit me to do this, I will have no choice but to take him to a *din Torah*."

The Ponevezh Rosh Yeshivah, Rabbi Dovid Povarsky, who was about Reb Moshe's age, related that his own father would stand before Reb Moshe like a servant before his master.

The townspeople assigned a *"gabbai"* to accompany Reb Moshe whenever he walked in the street, for they felt it improper for the Rav to walk alone.

That Reb Moshe was chosen for such a distinguished position at so young an age says much for his stature in the Torah world at that time. Reb Moshe did not disappoint the people of Luban. There his brilliant light would shine forth ever stronger. There he would emerge as a courageous leader of his people.

CHAPTER TWO

A Rabbi Under Communism

THE RAVAGES OF WORLD WAR I LED TO WORSENING CONDITIONS and resulted in revolution in Russia. Relatively minor at its outset, the revolution quickly took on a different dimension when govern-

Revolution and Violence
ment troops, ostensibly loyal to the Czar, banded with his enemies to force the government's collapse. A new government was formed, but this was not enough to satisfy the Bolsheviks (Communists), who sought full control of the state and total elimination of their opposition.

In October of 1917 the Bolsheviks took power, supported by their Red Army, and the country was then plunged into a four-year civil war as the counter-revolutionary White Army battled the Reds for control of the land.

As the scene of battle moved through the Russian terrain, soldiers on both sides of the conflict would often vent their fury on the Jewish communities that stood in their path. While the Red Army was, at least officially, opposed to such behavior, this was not so of its opposition. The fact that many Jews were in the forefront of the Revolution and most other Jews embraced it — due to its official stand against anti-Semitism — was enough to reinforce the age-old anti-Semitism of the Czar's supporters.

Many battalions in the White Army were composed of Cossack forces, who popularized the battle cry, "Strike at the Jews and save Russia!" Countless Jews in the Ukraine, where the Cossacks were primarily to be found, lost their possessions, their homes, and often their very lives at the hands of these beastly hordes.

White Russia, the province in which Minsk, Starobin, and Luban were located, remained relatively quiet until mid-1920.

TOWARD THE END OF 1920, HOWEVER, WHITE RUSSIA WAS INVADED BY BANDS of bloodthirsty Cossacks. Starobin became the scene of a terrible pogrom.

Reb David's Courage The Cossacks pillaged Jewish homes, mercilessly slaughtering many of their inhabitants. Afterwards, they seized Reb David Feinstein and led him away to the outskirts of the town, while demanding an exorbitant ransom from the remaining Jews in exchange for the safe return of their beloved Rav.

Well aware of the poverty prevalent in his town and the untrustworthiness of the Cossacks, and probably afraid that payment of the ransom would encourage the Cossacks to repeat this practice in other Jewish towns, Reb David was prepared to die rather than allow the townspeople to submit to his captors' demands. He somehow sent word to the townspeople that as Rav he strictly forbade them to pay the ransom.

> Reb David's grandson, Rabbi Yechiel Michel Feinstein, recalled that horrifying time vividly. Fearful for his grandfather's fate, he sat in a room together with his uncle, Reb Moshe, who began reciting *Tehillim* from memory. Reb Moshe said each word slowly and distinctly so that his young nephew could repeat after him.

Soon after, for no explicable reason, the Cossacks decided to release Reb David. However, before letting him go, they insisted that he repeat a certain declaration that they recited to him in Polish, a language with which he was unfamiliar.

"I will not say something that I do not understand," Reb David responded. The Cossacks again threatened him with death, but he remained unshaken. Finally, Reb David was released unharmed and returned to his grateful community and family.[1]

---

1. Reb David passed away on 27 Tishrei 5688 (1927) at age 71. Though he was paralyzed for the last six months of his life, he insisted on sleeping in the *succah* on yom tov. After yom tov, his condition worsened and he lost his power of speech. As he felt his end drawing near, he indicated that he wanted to take leave of the community whom he had

IN LUBAN ON LAG BAOMER OF 1921, REB MOSHE SEEMED TO HAVE SENSED AN ominous atmosphere. He packed his most precious belongings — his

The Pogrom

Torah manuscripts — and fled the town. Minutes later, Luban was struck by a pogrom, and a bomb was detonated in the Rav's house. The assumption was that Reb Moshe had perished in the explosion. Reb Moshe continued in his flight from the area until several days later when he simply collapsed.

A Russian peasant found the package of writings and brought them to Reb Isser Zalman Meltzer, who recognized them as belonging to Reb Moshe. He saw it as grounds to fear the worst, for Reb Moshe would never be separated willingly from his writings. Yet, when an inquiry came to him from Reb David Feinstein, asking if he had heard anything about Reb Moshe, Reb Isser Zalman replied, "I am confident that he is alive."

Sure enough, in a matter of days, a fatigued Reb Moshe Feinstein found his way to Slutzk, where he stayed with Reb Isser Zalman for an extended period of time.[2]

> When the Cossack threat passed, Reb Moshe and the others who had survived the pogrom returned to the ruins that had once been their homes. Infused with the Rav's spirit, faith and love, the survivors fought to overcome their personal tragedies and rebuild life anew. With the help of the surrounding communities, life in Luban slowly returned to normal. To commemorate the Lag BaOmer pogrom, Reb Moshe never took advantage of the break in the *Sefirah* mourning period that Lag BaOmer offers. His mourning bridged the entire period without interruption.

After that brief separation from his precious writings, Reb Moshe bought a handsome leather carrying-case for the sole purpose of taking his manuscripts with him whenever he traveled.

A year later on 10 Teves, on his way to visit his father and show him a manuscript of his *chiddushim* on *Yerushalmi*, the briefcase was stolen at a train station, probably because it was of such high quality. As a result, the

---

served with such devotion. Men, women, and children filed past his bed and he nodded to each one in a sign of blessing and farewell (preface to *Igros Moshe* Vol. VIII).

2. Almost half a century later, the *seudas bar mitzvah* for a great-grandson of Reb Isser Zalman was held in Lakewood in the midst of a snowstorm. Reb Moshe asked his son, Reb Reuven, to drive him there despite the weather conditions. "I must go for the *kavod* of the *alter Rebbetzin*," a reference to Rav Aharon Kotler's wife, who was Reb Isser Zalman's daughter. (Reb Aharon had already passed away.) "I lived in her parents' home for six months."

fast of the Tenth of Teves always had an extra dimension of gravity in the Feinstein household.[3]

IN THE FOLLOWING YEAR, REB MOSHE MARRIED SIMA (PRONOUNCED SHIMA), the daughter of Rabbi Yaakov Moshe HaKohen Kastonowitz, Luban's

Marriage *shochet* and *mohel* and head of the Jewish community. When the *shidduch* was suggested, Reb Yaakov Moshe told his daughter, "The Rav may be small in stature, but the day will come when he will surpass all his peers."

In the preface to the first published volume of *Dibros Moshe*, Reb Moshe wrote:

> *To the eternal remembrance of my holy father-in-law, who was a great tzaddik. All his life, he was involved in tzedakah and good deeds. He was a talmid chacham and spent much of his time learning, and he assisted me in all communal matters so that I would not have to lose time from my learning.*

A family portrait. Reb Moshe and his Rebbetzin (at right) with his in-laws, Reb Yaakov Moshe (at left) and Rivka Kastonowitz. The child in the center is the oldest Feinstein child, Faya (Shisgal).

---

3. In the preface to the first published volume of *Dibros Moshe* (*Bava Kamma*, vol I), Reb Moshe writes: "Many correct *chiddushim* that I propounded were forgotten when the writings of my youth were lost on Asarah B'Teves 5682."

Reb Moshe attempted to restore the lost *chiddushim*. He contacted those to whom he had written *teshuvos* and talmidim who had transcribed his *shiurim*. He also rewrote what he recalled from memory. However, all his efforts resulted in only partial success (preface to *Igros Moshe* Vol. VIII).

Reb Sholom learned in Slutzk at the same time as Reb Moshe. (They were around the same age.) He received semichah from Reb Isser Zalman Meltzer and later from Reb Moshe, and was certified as a shochet by his older brother, Reb Yaakov Moshe. Reb Sholom emigrated to America in the 1920s where he continued to practice shechitah.

With his father-in-law's younger brother, Rabbi Sholom HaKohen Katz (Kastonowitz)

Once, a boy in Reb Yaakov Moshe's town strayed from the path of Torah and became an outcast in the community. Later, this boy was stricken with tuberculosis. The only known treatment at that time was a regimen of medicines that were prohibitively beyond the means of this boy's family. In similar situations, the entire community had donated to the cause and the necessary funds were provided. However, in this boy's case, many people — who were already impoverished — did not want to contribute.

Reb Yaakov Moshe vehemently disagreed. He said that a Jew is a Jew; regardless of his level of religious observance, there was an obligation to save the boy's life.

Single-handedly, Reb Yaakov Moshe managed to raise the necessary sum and the boy received the medicines.

Years later, when Reb Moshe was Rav of Luban, the Communists planned to seize all gold rubles and American dollars from private citizens. A number of Luban's Jews were arrested and thrown into a crowded prison pending their interrogation and compliance with the authorities.

Reb Moshe himself was summoned for questioning. When he stated his name, the Jewish commissar in charge of the investigation exclaimed, "Wait, I recognize that name! This man's father-in-law is one of the greatest men in all of Russia. When my brother — who like myself is not religious — was deathly ill, the Rabbi's father-in-law provided him with the medicines that saved his life. Let the Rabbi go, and grant him whatever he wants!"

Reb Moshe asked that those arrested be freed, and his request was granted.[4]

REBBETZIN SIMA FEINSTEIN, WHO WOULD BE REB MOSHE'S FAITHFUL PARTNER in life for the next 64 years, bore him five children: two daughters, Faya

A Home Permeated With Torah and Sifra; and three sons, Pesach Chaim (who died of whooping cough as an infant[5]), David and Reuven. All were born in Luban

except Reuven, who was born in the United States.

---

4. Related by Rav Elazar Menachem Shach. See *The Rosh Yeshivah Remembers*.

5. The heading to a *chiddush* in *Dibros Moshe* reads, "… said at the *seudas bris milah* of my first son, Pesach Chaim, who was taken from us, due to our many sins, on 5 Elul, 5686 (1926), and who will be returned to us at the time of *techias hameisim*."

In *Igros Moshe* (*Yoreh De'ah* I, #198), Reb Moshe writes: "During my days of mourning for my dear son, Pesach Chaim, *a"h* … from which I arose ten days ago, may Hashem comfort me among the other mourners of Zion and Jerusalem, I saw something perplexing in the *Shach* … regarding a mourner changing his place [in shul] on Shabbos … "

Reb Yaakov Moshe appreciated the great merit of having Reb Moshe as his son-in-law. Recognizing Reb Moshe's legendary diligence in Torah study, he did his utmost to ensure that nothing would disturb it. Reb Yaakov Moshe was once present when his daughter was faced with the common dilemma of trying to wash the floor while the children required supervision. Seeing the possibility that Reb Moshe would be forced to close his gemara and tend to the children, Reb Yaakov Moshe quickly said to his daughter, "His job is to learn; I will wash your floor and *you* tend to the children." Years later, Rebbetzin Feinstein would recall this incident as having impressed upon her the value of her husband's learning.

> Reb Moshe's total concentration on Torah was legendary in Luban already in those years. One of his admirers was an elderly *talmid chacham* who could well appreciate the Torah greatness of the young Rav. In those days, the only time Reb Moshe took a nap during the day was on Shabbos. The elderly scholar would jokingly tell Rebbetzin Feinstein, "Don't let the Rav sleep! You are not allowed to let him sleep! Too much Torah is lost when he is not awake."

In general, the Rebbetzin took upon herself the burden of all material matters in the home, making certain that all was in order without interrupting Reb Moshe's holy work. She bore this responsibility with happiness and dignity, realizing full well that her husband's mission in life was greatly dependent on her. It can certainly be said that without the Rebbetzin's dedication, Reb Moshe might not have become the Torah giant that he was.

The Ponevezh Rosh Yeshivah, Rabbi Dovid Povarsky, recalled that the Feinstein household shone with exemplary *middos*. The respect this earned them among the town's inhabitants, including non-religious Jews as well as gentiles, would figure prominently in their surviving the many years of Communist oppression that lay ahead.

Communist Domination

BY THE END OF 1921, THE COMMUNISTS HAD CONQUERED ALL OPPOSITION AND were in full control of what became known as the Union of Soviet Socialist Republics (USSR). While the Communists were opposed to all forms of religion and especially Judaism, they were too preoccupied in the formative years of their regime to make a concerted effort to subvert religious practices.

There was, however, one section of the Communist Party that, from its inception, expended great energy in attempts to destroy Jewish religious life. This was the *Yevsektsia,* the notorious "Jewish Section." It was composed of Jews who had shorn all traces of their Jewishness in the hope that this would gain them acceptance among the Communists.

The *Yevsektsia* advocated the death of the Jewish religion. They opened a network of kindergartens, schools, and youth clubs where there was no mention of Jewish history or faith and where "G-d" was treated as a superstition of backward people, ר"ל. Instead, Communist ideology and culture was taught with enthusiasm and fervor.

The *Yevsektsia's* open war against the religion of its ancestors began with ridicule of Jewish laws and customs. On the eve of Pesach they would send the local rav a loaf of bread; they would choose the night of Yom Kippur to hold their mass meetings at which non-kosher food was served; and they would demonstrate in front of *chadarim* (religious elementary schools) bearing placards with slogans such as: "Down with the *chadarim* and yeshivos!" "Down with the black rabbis!" and "Let freedom live!" As time went on, *chadarim* in Russia were forced to close and teaching Torah to the young became a crime against the State.

In his addresses delivered in the main shul of Luban, Reb Moshe would allude to the new regime's edicts against his people. In an address delivered on the Shabbos before Pesach, 5682 (1922), he said:

> We are redeemed, in a sense, even while we are in exile, for our own spirit can never be exiled. No one can claim mastery over our spirit; the decrees against us can only affect our bodies …
>
> … This is cause for great rejoicing. We must, therefore, celebrate the Yom Tov of Pesach with much beauty and splendor …[As we say in the *Haggadah,*] "Had Hashem not taken our ancestors out of Egypt, we would still be [spiritually] enslaved to Pharoh in Egypt" — meaning, we would be enslaved either to Pharoh, or some other nation, or to our physical passions. But now [that we we were redeemed and are a nation of Torah], we are not slaves, for our spirit cannot be subjugated by anyone or anything. We have no master but Hashem.[6]

In Luban, the Jewish community was spared the wrath of the Party and the *Yevsektsia* until 1930, when the ruthless anti-Semite Joseph Stalin crushed the last remnants of opposition to his power, thus allowing him to turn his full attention to the Jews.

---

6. *Darash Moshe* (Hebrew), *Drush #7.*

At one point, when the NKVD (Russian secret police) were seeking to arrest a certain Jew on trumped-up charges, Reb Moshe hid the man in his house for six months. Then, with the authorities closing in on their target, Reb Moshe told the man, "I am not concerned for my own safety; I would be prepared to hide you longer. But I have no right to endanger my wife and children." Reb Moshe presented the man with a plan as to how he could flee the country. The plan succeeded; some time later, Reb Moshe received a letter from the man thanking him in the most superlative terms.

In relating this episode to Rabbi Michel Shurkin, Reb Moshe said, "I never understood why I was deserving of such praise. I simply did what any Jew would have done."[7]

IN FACT, REB MOSHE CONSIDERED THE FIVE YEARS FROM 1925 TO 1930 AS THE most productive of his life. It was during this period that he wrote a famous

Most Productive Years

teshuvah that challenged a ruling by Rabbi Yechezkel Abramsky, then Rav of Slutzk. The responsa were brought to the attention of Rabbi Chaim Ozer Grodzensky, in Vilna, who sided with Reb Moshe. He commented: "I have heard of the two brothers (Reb Moshe and his brother Reb Mordechai) deep in the Russian heartland, who learn Torah as it was studied a century ago!"

Rabbi Chaim Ozer Grodzensky

When, in 1936, Reb Moshe passed through Vilna on his way to America, he visited Reb Chaim Ozer, who was then the recognized leader of world Jewry and its foremost *posek*. During the course of their conversation, Reb Chaim Ozer mentioned that he had read Reb Moshe's above-mentioned teshuvah. "I have also written on this subject," he told his much younger visitor, "and my conclusion concurs with yours. However, your line of reasoning is superior to mine."

---

7. *Sefer Meged Givos Olam.*

Throughout the 1920s, Reb Moshe responded in writing to halachic questions, sending *teshuvos* to Jews in Slutzk, Starobin, Amtsislav and elsewhere. Many of these *teshuvos* were subsequently published in *Igros Moshe,* where we find among his correspondents his father, Reb David; Rav Yechezkel Abramsky; and Reb Moshe's friend from his visits to Slutzk, Rav Elazar Menachem Shach.

REB MOSHE MAINTAINED A LIFELONG FRIENDSHIP WITH RAV YECHEZKEL Abramsky, corresponding with him when the latter served as *Av Beis Din*

Rav Abramsky
in London and later when he emigrated to Eretz Yisrael where he was recognized as one of the generation's great Torah leaders.

Reb Moshe delivered a lengthy and moving *hesped* when Rav Abramsky passed away in 5736 (1976). He said that during his years in Russia, Rav Abramsky was a symbol to *bnei Torah* of incredible Torah knowledge and relentless *hasmadah* (diligence). Every striving *ben Torah* sought to emulate him.[8]

In 1947, Reb Moshe published his first volume of *Dibros Moshe.* He sent a copy to Rav Abramsky, then residing in London, along with a letter:

Rabbi Yechezkel Abramsky

> *To his honor, my friend, the great, renowned gaon, splendor of Israel, pillar of Torah, HaRav R' Yechezkel Abramsky, shlita, formerly Av Beis Din of Slutzk and presently leader of the rabbanim of London,*
>
> *Peace and all that is good unto the gaon, his wife and precious children, forever …*
>
> *It is my honor to send to the gaon the sefer which I have just now published, and which I named "Dibros Moshe." It is on Masechta Bava Kamma until Perek HaChovel.*
>
> *Recalling our friendship yet in Russia, it is my hope that the honored gaon will accept the sefer with happiness and that it will find favor in his eyes. It would make me very happy if the honorable gaon would examine the sefer and write to me his esteemed opinion of it.*

8. Ibid.

*At a meeting in Jerusalem during the 1964 Knessiah Gedolah; center, right to left:
Reb Eliezer Silver (pointing), Reb Moshe, Reb Yechezkel Abramsky,
Reb Zalman Sorotzkin*

> *As the cost of publishing is high, I was unable to publish on the entire masechta at the present time. I have left the remainder for some future time, when Hashem Yisborach will help me to accomplish it.*
>
> *May the honorable gaon and his family be blessed with a chag kasher v'sameiach, and merit the Final Redemption, together with the entire Jewish nation.*
>
> *His friend, who loves him with all his heart and soul, Moshe Feinstein*[9]

On Purim one year in New York, with his talmidim gathered around him, Reb Moshe related a timeless thought he had heard from Rav Abramsky:

> *Megillas Esther* relates that after Mordechai's refusal to bow to Haman, "It seemed contemptible to him [Haman] to lay hands on Mordechai alone, for they had made known to him the people of Mordechai. So Haman sought to destroy all the Jews … "[10]
>
> Why did Haman want to eradicate Mordechai's people only after he had learned their identity? Why did he did not want to destroy them as soon as Mordechai refused to bow? Rav Abramsky explained:
>
> Initially, Haman thought that he could force Mordechai into submission. Once that happened, Mordechai's nation, whoever

---

9. From *Melech B'Yafyo* (Hebrew) on the life of Rav Abramsky.
10. *Esther* 3:6.

they were, would follow their leader and also submit themselves to Haman's orders and whims. But upon learning that Mordechai was a Jew, Haman realized that this would never work. The Jewish people look up to their leaders only as long as those leaders embody the teachings of Torah. The moment they cease to follow the Torah, the people lose all respect for them. If Mordechai could be coerced to follow Haman's lead, the Jews would cease to respect him.[11]

The courage shown by both Reb Moshe and Rav Abramsky during the dark Stalin era exemplified Torah leadership in times of persecution, a lesson that Mordechai had taught so well. Rav Abramsky was banished to Siberia for the "crime" of teaching Torah to Jewish children, and Reb Moshe, as we will see, led his community in Luban despite persecution and threats by the Communist regime.

IN THE EARLY 1930S, THE JEWS OF LUBAN WERE SUBJECTED TO THE RELIGIOUS oppression that was already a way of life for communities in other parts of

The War Against the Rabbis Russia. The *chadarim* and main synagogue were closed down. A heavy tax was levied on the importation of religious articles. With many Jews suffering economically as punishment for their adherence to Torah, it became necessary for Luban and four neighboring towns to share in the purchase of a single *lulav.* Everyone fulfilled the mitzvah of *arbaah minim* by the minimal requirement of lifting the species, save for the five rabbanim who performed the *naanuim* ritual. After Succos, the *lulav* was carefully preserved and made to last for *another two years.*[12]

The Communists levied special taxes against rabbis to force their resignations. Most rabbis gave in to the Soviets and resigned their positions. Those who did not paid the consequences, which were severe. The Lubavitcher Rebbe, Rabbi Yosef Yitzchok Schneersohn, had already been imprisoned and expelled from the country in 1927. Rav Abramsky was sentenced to hard labor in Siberia in 1930, and served for two years before foreign intervention gained his freedom. Other rabbis were arrested and mistreated; many were never heard from again.

---

11. From the *hakdamah* to *Darash Moshe* (Hebrew).
12. The carefully wrapped *lulav* hung on a nail in Reb Moshe's apartment, high above the reach of children.

  The Soviets permitted the importation of *esrogim* like any other edible fruit. *Hadassim* and *aravos* were homegrown, making it possible to procure fresh ones each year. *Lulavim,* however, are not food and were not grown in Russia. The prohibitive import tax left the Jews with no choice but to smuggle in a *lulav* once in 3 years.

While Reb Moshe fell victim to Soviet oppression in the 1930s, he remained at his post as Rav in Luban until his departure for America in 1936. Whenever a rabbi resigned his position, the Communist press would feature the news with blaring headlines about how another rabbi had seen the true light. Reb Moshe considered this to be a public *chillul Hashem* and felt that it was forbidden for him to relinquish his position, even at the risk of death. In later years, Reb Moshe remarked that, ironically, the rabbanim who remained at their posts, though suffering for their recalcitrance, generally escaped deportation or prolonged imprisonment, while virtually all of those who acceded to the government's demands were exiled to Siberia.

> Without a doubt, Reb Moshe's quiet, respectful manner and his avoidance of public confrontation with the Communists kept him in relatively good standing with the regime and its supporters. Though there was no doubt where the Rav stood on religious issues, the government could tolerate a man who did not, at least publicly, attempt to show the fallacy of their brutal policies.
>
> In private, though, Reb Moshe defied the Communists as much as anyone, if not more. When his father-in-law was forced by the government to cease practicing *shechitah,* Reb Moshe mastered the skill and became the town *shochet.* He continued to study Gemara with the men of the town, while inspiring and encouraging his people to remain strong in their faith and observance of every mitzvah, despite the persecutions.

Many years later, while discussing a particular page in *Masechta Kreisus,* Reb Moshe remarked wistfully, "This was the last *daf* I studied with the men of Luban."

PERHAPS THE SINGLE MOST IMPORTANT FACTOR IN REB MOSHE'S BEING allowed to remain Rav was the reverence he inspired from both Jew and

The Mikveh

gentile alike. While the religious Jews of Luban were in awe of his overall greatness, all were impressed by his wisdom and earnestness. Many *Yevsektsia* members were children of religious families and they could not bring themselves to make life difficult for the man whose mere mention evoked awe in their parents' home; in fact, some Jewish Communists tried secretly to protect him.

One particular incident illustrates both Reb Moshe's courage and effectiveness during those years. There was no possibility of maintaining a mikveh openly, but Reb Moshe found a way, nevertheless. With a combination of ingenuity, personality, daring and — most important — faith, he succeeded

Shul in Luban where Reb Moshe learned

in having a mikveh built — with the aid of the Communists themselves.

A municipal bathhouse and swimming pool were being built in Luban. Reb Moshe prevailed upon the non-Jewish contractor to build the pool in such a way that it would be a kosher mikveh. With the construction taken care of, a problem of a different sort had to be solved. Men and women were expected to use the pool at the same time, something no religious Jew in Luban would dream of doing. Unless this situation could be changed, the pool would be useless as a mikveh.

Reb Moshe approached a high-ranking official whose respect he had earned and put the dilemma to him this way: The religious community wanted very much to enjoy the new sanitary facilities generously provided by the government, but would not bathe in mixed company. It was important, then, in the interest of public hygiene that the bathhouse have a few separate men's and women's nights. The official agreed and the Jews had themselves a mikveh, the only one for miles around.

A responsum in *Igros Moshe* begins:

> *In our city Luban, after it became possible, through Hashem's kindness, to construct a mikveh (during the years of evil decrees) in a bathhouse run by the government, which was unaware that it was, in fact, a kosher mikveh* ...[13]

13. *Igros Moshe, Orach Chaim* I, #126.

The persecutions increased as time went on. The Feinstein family was forced out of its house by an exorbitant clergy tax, and Reb Moshe was harassed with the intention of forcing him to resign as rabbi. He answered that he was ready to turn over his meager earnings to the state — an offer the Communists graciously accepted — but he could not relinquish his position.

Reb Moshe's family moved into a room adjoining the Schneiders' Shul [Tailors' Synagogue], the only synagogue in Luban still in Jewish hands. There, Reb Moshe, his Rebbetzin and their young children were forced to live along with Reb Moshe's in-laws and two other relatives. Even then, Reb Moshe's diligence in study did not slacken. He continued to write voluminously and the Jews of Luban continued to revere him. Hashem was their G-d, Reb Moshe was their king, and they clung to him tenaciously.

IN THE PREFACE TO THE FIRST PUBLISHED VOLUME OF *DIBROS MOSHE,* Reb Moshe writes:

Tenacity Under Fire
I must make take this opportunity to praise and bless Hashem Yisborach for all His kindness that He has done for me to this day. He took me from the place of shmad (forced transgression of mitzvos) ten years ago. And even when I was there in my suffering and persecution, He helped me so that I did not lose much time from my learning …

Reb Moshe would later say that it was during this period, with so many others sharing the same room, that he learned to study amid all sorts of distractions. When notebooks were often unavailable, he wrote his *chiddushim* on anything he could find. The Feinstein family still has old used ledger sheets on which he wrote between the columns of numbers.

What is incredible is how, throughout such frightening times, with the sword of interrogation and imprisonment constantly over him, Reb Moshe was able to put *every* fear and distraction out of his mind and grow uninterruptedly in Torah. One can only conclude that Hashem was rewarding his utter devotion to Torah with Divine assistance, for such greatness under these circumstances seems nothing less than supernatural.

RABBI NOTA GREENBLATT, A RENOWNED RAV AND *POSEK* IN MEMPHIS, Tennessee, is among Reb Moshe's closest talmidim. In his *Sefer K'reiach*

The Essence of Holiness
Sadeh, he discusses the Torah's command *You shall be holy, for I, Hashem, your G-d, am holy.*[14] Hashem is holy beyond human comprehension; at the same time, His holiness does not prevent Him from involving Himself with the needs

---

14. *Vayikra* 19:2.

of every creature, especially the poor and downtrodden whom others tend to shun.

Moshe Rabbeinu achieved this type of dual existence. Rambam writes that Moshe reached a level akin to *malachim*, yet his own brother and sister did not perceive that he was above and beyond their level of prophecy. For Moshe, with all his spiritual greatness, was able to involve himself with the needs of his people and deal with the mundane problems that others faced.

Rabbi Greenblatt comments:

> Fortunate are we who merited to be in the close proximity of *gedolim*. The way of the author of *Dibros Moshe, zt"l,* who excelled in this quality, was something wondrous. For many years, he lived with his family in Russia, in a cauldron of hatred and persecution. He resided in a cramped apartment, and there he studied Torah with amazing *hasmadah*. And precisely under these conditions, he authored the great treatises upon which most of his *chiddushei Torah* — both on *Shas* and in Halachah — are based.
>
> This quality, of being able to separate himself from his surroundings and totally immerse himself in Torah, served him well even after he was rescued (from the Soviet Union) and was totally involved on these shores in the study and dissemination of Torah. I recall that during the days of wrath, when the frightening reports regarding the Jews of Europe reached us and it became virtually humanly impossible to focus one's mind on learning and deep analyses, he, *zt"l,* continued with his regular *shiurim* and the writing of his *chiddushei Torah* as if what was transpiring was not relevant to him, *chas v'shalom*— save for the river of tears that flowed from his eyes during *tefillah* and the reciting of *Tehillim*.
>
> His *chiddushim,* which encompass most topics in *Shas,* and his halachic responsa to the countless petitioners who came to him bear witness to the strength of his ability to always divorce himself from his surroundings and focus his entire being and depth of thought on words of Torah.
>
> And yet, did this quality prevent him from sharing the burden of his fellow Jews? He was, in fact, the leading patron of the yeshivos and *chesed* organizations, and he was a ready listener for every broken, dispirited soul.[15]

---

15. Rabbi Greenblatt writes: "I merited to pray in the old Jewish cemetery of Altona

ONCE, REB MOSHE WAS TAKEN FROM HIS ROOM IN THE MIDDLE OF THE NIGHT
for interrogation by the secret police. A prime purpose of such interroga-

**Interrogation
and Harassment**
tion was to trap the befuddled person into making
a statement that could be used as proof that he
was an "enemy of the State." Responding with
wisdom and forethought, Reb Moshe did not fall into such a trap. He
acquitted himself so well that the inquisitor apologized, saying that he had
only wanted to gain insight into Judaism. In addition, thirty Jewish political prisoners were released in Luban.

Rebbetzin Feinstein vividly recalled those fearful times. "When the
government evicted us from our home it seemed as if the next step was
Siberia, but Hashem provided us with great miracles … "

When Reb Moshe was unable to pay the tax levied upon all rabbanim,
the government said that he would have to pay the tax by digging ditches.
Rebbetzin Feinstein would not permit "the Rav," as she often referred to
him in public, to be humiliated in this way. She approached local officials
and said, "If you are doing this because you really need the work done,
then you should allow me to do it instead. I am stronger than my husband
and can do a better job of digging ditches." Permission was granted; the
Rebbetzin took shovel in hand and went to work.

In later years, she tried to minimize her self-sacrifice. "Of course I did
the digging," she said, "I was better at it!"

(Germany) at the graves of the "cedars of Lebanon, giants of Torah," who served the
קהלת אה"ו (communities of Altona, Hamburg, and Wansbeck) during their golden era,
and to examine the engravings on their tombstones, each one an original work unto itself.
I found that on the tombstone of the *Baal HaTumim*, zt"l (Rabbi Yonasan Eibeschutz) was
the appellation "*Rabbeinu HaKadosh*" — which even in the days of the Mishnah was
reserved for only one individual (Rabbi Yehudah HaNasi).

"I thought long and hard about this appellation, and then some time later I came
across an entry in the *pinkas* (ledger) of these communities which was written during
the "days of wrath" when the terrible *machlokes* (involving R' Yonasan and R' Yaakov
Emden) raged all around him. [The ledger stated] that throughout that period, the *gaon*
R' Yonasan, zt"l, delivered *shiurim* to his talmidim in his great yeshivah as if nothing was
transpiring.

"Perhaps this is the meaning of 'Rabbeinu HaKadosh.' In the midst of the conflagra-
tion that attacked his very being, for he was accused of heresy, *chas v'shalom*, he sat and
learned Torah as if nothing was happening — as if there was no *machlokes*, no conflagra-
tion. This is the essence of *kedushah*. Such a person can be called 'Kadosh' — 'Rabbeinu
HaKadosh.'"

REB MOSHE'S REBBETZIN AND THEIR CHILDREN SUFFERED THEIR SHARE OF PERsonal abuse at the hands of the Communists. The Feinstein girls, Faya and

Tormenting the Family

Sifra, were among the honor students of the local government school, which they were required to attend, but they were hardly welcomed with open arms.

When a gathering was to be held at the government school for a group of outstanding students — Faya among them — and their parents, the Rebbetzin was very reluctant to go. She had already experienced an unpleasant exchange with a school official in her own home and, as she put it, "If they treated me this way in my own home, what sort of treatment could I hope for in their school?" In the end, however, she decided to attend the gathering, for Faya's sake.

As soon as the gathering commenced, an official announced that those who did not follow Communist Party ideology — such as the Rav's wife — were not welcome. The Rebbetzin was roundly booed and forced to leave the auditorium, as her humiliated daughter looked on.

Such anecdotes vividly illustrate both the torment and the courage of those who refused to relinquish their rabbinic positions. It is easier to endure poverty and harassment than to see one's wife and children tormented and humiliated. The Communists understood this quite well; it was part of their psychological warfare against the rabbis who would not surrender.

IN 1936, REB MOSHE AND HIS FAMILY WERE EVICTED FROM THEIR CRAMPED dwelling which, along with the adjoining Schneiders' Shul, was being

The Situation Worsens

taken over by the government. Ignoring the risk involved in taking the Rav's family into his home, the old Jewish shoemaker of Luban invited Reb Moshe to come live with him. Of this brave Jew, the Rebbetzin said, "He, like the local wagon-driver, was fluent in all of *Shas*. During the time that we lived in the shul, I would see the two of them studying throughout the night."

The accommodations which the poor shoemaker could offer Reb Moshe's family were not very much. He took planks from a barn, and used them to erect makeshift walls near the kitchen stove. It was in this "room" that Reb Moshe's family lived, along with the mice that came to warm themselves near the fire.

A distinguished rav once asked Reb Moshe why he remained at his post for so long and why he had let so many years pass before finally attempting to leave Russia. Reb Moshe answered simply that he was the only practicing Rav remaining in his area and he saw it as an obligation to stay and guide the Jews of Luban and its neighboring towns. He sought to emigrate only after it became clear to him that there was no longer any alternative.

> In 1939 in New York, the renowned *posek* Rabbi Moshe Bick was present at a conversation between Reb Moshe and Rabbi Elchonon Wasserman, who was visiting America to raise funds for his yeshivah. Reb Moshe remarked that there were people who were upset with him for "deserting" his brethren in Russia. Reb Elchonon responded that the Chofetz Chaim said that a country where it is forbidden to speak Hashem's Name is tantamount to a bathroom. "No one," Reb Elchonon concluded, "can be expected to spend his whole life in such a place."

In a postcard sent to his rebbi, Reb Isser Zalman Meltzer,[16] Reb Moshe wrote that his efforts to leave Russia first began in 1929. However, leaving Russia was far from simple. At one point, the government announced that for one day only, exit visas would be granted to anyone who would register. On that frigid winter morning, Reb Moshe arose at 5:00 a.m. to stand on line with hundreds of others. At 11:00 p.m., with only two people ahead of him, registration was closed. Two days later it became known that whoever had registered had been sent to Siberia.[17]

REB MOSHE SENT WORD TO FRIENDS AND RELATIVES IN ERETZ YISRAEL AND America, requesting their help in gaining admittance to their respective

The Road to Freedom

countries. Time after time, Reb Moshe's applications for an exit visa were rejected — with one exception. A cousin of Reb Moshe, reputed to be a millionaire, had fled across the Russian border to freedom. The authorities guaranteed Reb Moshe's family a visa if he would help them locate this man. Of course, Reb Moshe refused.

Once, Reb Moshe donned peasant's clothing and slipped into Moscow, in the hope of somehow procuring a visa there. A kind gentile family provided him with a place to sleep while he subsisted on a diet of potatoes and water. Whatever time was not needed for his mission he spent study-

---

16. The text of that note to Reb Isser Zalman appears later in this chapter.
17. Related by Reb Moshe to Rabbi Yaakov Moshe Shurkin, as recorded in *Sefer Meged Givos Olam.*

ing in a local beis midrash, where he blended in with the other Jews and would not be noticed by government agents.

One night while studying in the beis midrash, Reb Moshe became so engrossed that he failed to note the passage of time. When he finally looked up at the clock, the hour was well past midnight. Realizing that he would very likely wake someone in the household were he to return to his lodgings, Reb Moshe decided to spend the night in the beis midrash.

The next morning, he was greeted with incredible news. The previous night the secret police had raided homes in the district in search of those who had gained illegal entry into the city. By not returning to his lodgings, Reb Moshe had escaped discovery and certain arrest.

A BROTHER AND SISTER OF REBBETZIN FEINSTEIN AND A SISTER OF REB Moshe were able to get out of Russia and came to the United States. They

American Intervention

were to become Hashem's agents in saving Reb Moshe and his family from the Communist purgatory and the Nazi Holocaust. Rabbi Nechemiah Kastonowitz, who shortened his name to Katz, became a rabbi in Toledo, Ohio, where he served for forty-eight years until his retirement. His sister Rebbetzin Zlata Levovitz lived in New York. Reb Moshe's sister Rebbetzin Chana Small lived in Chicago.

Upon learning that Reb Moshe was trying in vain to leave Russia, they attempted to secure congressional assistance in gaining his family's freedom. Senator William Edgar Borah (a Republican from Idaho) was one of the powers of the United States Senate. Until Roosevelt's Democratic landslide, Borah had been chairman of the Senate Foreign Relations Committee, and was still the ranking Republican of that committee. Although Borah was an arch-conservative and isolationist, he had been one of the first to champion the cause of United States recognition of the Communist regime. As a result, he enjoyed a personal friendship with Soviet Ambassador Yanovsky. Rabbi Katz and Rebbetzin Levovitz were convinced, therefore, that if Senator Borah would be willing to use his influence with Yanovsky, an exit visa could be pried out of the Soviets.

But how could they reach Borah? Their initial attempts failed. They went to visit two congressmen from New York to ask them to intercede with Borah, but New York's liberal New Dealers wanted nothing to do with him. Instead, they provided personal letters to Yanovsky on Reb Moshe's behalf. Undaunted, Rabbi Katz then took his case to his own congress-

Rabbi Isaac Small   Rabbi Nechemiah Katz

man, who arranged an appointment with Senator Buckley of Rabbi Katz's state of Ohio, in addition to providing his own letter to Yanovsky. Buckley, too, gave Rabbi Katz a personal letter for the Russian ambassador and, having a good relationship with Borah, he contacted the Senator, who agreed to provide his own letter as well.

When Rabbi Katz came to Borah's office, the senator was away, and one of his assistants, an elderly, sympathetic gentleman, received him very graciously. The man had instructions to give Rabbi Katz a letter on Borah's personal stationery — but his typewriter was broken. Seeing Rabbi Katz's disappointment, he placed a call to the Russian Embassy and requested, in the name of Sen. Borah, that the rabbi be given an audience with the ambassador. After some persuasion, the request was granted. As an elated Rabbi Katz was about to leave the office, the gentleman tried again to repair the typewriter and succeeded. He typed the letter and Rabbi Katz, accompanied by Rebbetzin Levovitz, who spoke an eloquent Russian, were soon heading toward the Russian embassy, carrying with them letters from two senators and three congressmen.

Meanwhile, Reb Moshe's brother-in-law, Rabbi Isaac Small, worked through his own congressman, Adolph Sabath of Chicago, one of the most senior members of the House, who also exerted efforts on Reb Moshe's behalf. Yanovsky was not in the least sympathetic to the plight of a rabbi in Luban. Rabbi Katz and his sister pleaded that they were not anti-Soviet; they merely wanted to be united with their family.

Reb Moshe's passport and exit visa, 1936

Finally, in deference to Borah's "personal request," the ambassador said that he would forward all five letters to Moscow. In Moscow, too, the strong congressional sentiment, given added weight by the venerated name of William Edgar Borah, turned the tide. Finally, the Feinsteins were granted an exit visa.

DAYS BEFORE HIS DEPARTURE, REB MOSHE WROTE AN EIGHTEEN-YEAR CALEN-
dar for the Jews of Luban, since publishing a Jewish calendar was prohib-

Farewell ited by the Communists. The calendar was used until 14
Kislev 5702 (1941), when the accursed Germans liquidated
the community.[18]

Reb Moshe had expected to encounter difficulties in taking along his
hundreds of pages of manuscripts, so he devised a method for transport-
ing many of them safely out of Russia. Every day he would mail several
pages of his writings to each of some thirty relatives in America in the
guise of correspondence, mailing them from different villages to ward off
suspicion. He did not put a return address on the envelopes or enclose a
signed personal note, lest the authorities concoct some accusation against
him. He had hoped that the relatives would understand that the writings
were his and why he mailed them. His hopes were vindicated, for almost
all of the "mail" eventually was returned to him in the States.

Before he departed Luban, Reb Moshe was given a *ksav preidah* (certificate of parting) by the community leaders that could be shown to other
communities who might consider him for a position:

> *We, the leaders and treasurers of the community of the city of Luban
> in the province of Minsk, certify and bear witness that the Rav, the
> great gaon, our master, Rav Moshe, son of the gaon Rav David
> Feinstein, served as Rav of our city for more than fifteen years, from
> 9 Nissan 5681 (1921) until 5 Elul 5696 (1936), the day on which he
> took leave of us and left our country.*
>
> *All the members of our community hold this honored gaon in
> very high esteem; we will never forget him. On behalf of the entire
> community, we thank him for all his good efforts on our behalf, and
> for leading our community in the path of Torah and fear of G-d, and
> for disseminating Torah through his daily shiurim in Mishnah and
> Gemara and his precious derashos on the yamim tovim.*
>
> *He fulfilled all the obligations of a rav towards his community with
> all his heart and soul, with truth and faithfulness.*
>
> *To all of the above, we affix our signatures on the day he took
> leave of us, Sunday, 5 Elul 5696, here in Luban.*

On 5 Elul, the Feinstein family — Reb Moshe, his Rebbetzin, and their
three young children — and the Jews of Luban bid one another their sad

---

18. Preface to *Igros Moshe* Vol. VIII.

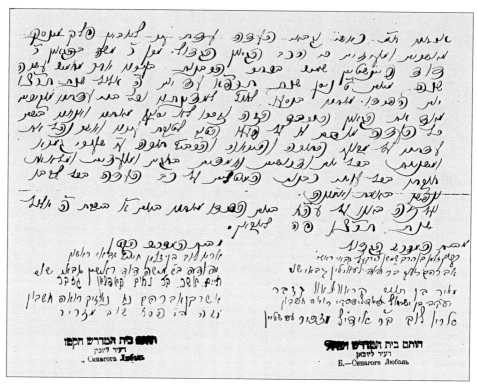

The ksav preidah given by the Luban community to Reb Moshe

farewells. Many of his dear ones remained behind in and around Luban: his in-laws, who were later murdered by the Nazis; his brother, Rabbi Mordechai Feinstein, the Rabbi of Shklov, who was taken from his holiday table on Shavuos and deported to Siberia where he died; and many others.

Even though the Feinsteins had all the documents they needed to leave Russia legally and safely, they still feared that the Communist authorities in Luban might prevent their departure. To help avoid this possibility, they left town under cover of darkness, in a horse and wagon that would take them to the nearest railroad station. The townspeople, too, did not want to endanger their beloved Rav and his family by a public farewell. They slipped out of the town at night and parted from Reb Moshe on the road.

THE FAMILY WENT TO MOSCOW TO PICK UP ITS EXIT VISA, AND THEN TO RIGA, Latvia. At the border between the USSR and Latvia, the Russian border

Journey to Freedom

authorities confiscated a package of Reb Moshe's writings, claiming it was anti-Soviet propaganda. Other manuscripts were left behind in Luban. They were destroyed by the Nazis.

On the train to Riga, Reb Moshe found himself wondering how he would impact upon the Jews of America, whose language he did not speak and who, for the most part, were not steeped in Torah as were the Jews of Luban and other Eastern European communities. As he pondered this thought, he fell asleep and as he awoke, the verse וְשָׁמְעוּ אֲמָרַי כִּי נָעֵמוּ, *They heard my words so pleasant,*[19] came to mind. *Chazal* teach that when a verse from *Tanach* comes to mind as one awakens, it is a portent of future tidings.[20] This infused Reb Moshe with confidence that he would, indeed, influence the masses in his new land.

Upon arriving in Riga, he was asked to deliver a *derashah* before a large crowd and his words were warmly received. He took this as yet another good omen for the future.[21]

BUT THERE WAS STILL A FORMIDABLE HURDLE TO OVERCOME. THOSE WERE THE years when it was impossibly difficult for Jews to come to the United

More Obstacles

States. America was not keen on accepting immigrants who had no way of self-support. Thus, when the Feinsteins arrived in Riga, they still had not been granted a visa to enter the U.S.

In Riga, Reb Moshe was invited to become Rav of Dvinsk, as successor to the famed Rogatchover Gaon, who had recently passed away. At the same time, he received a telegram from a relative in America suggesting that he remain in Latvia where his fame would almost certainly ensure him a position worthy of his stature. Such positions were difficult, if not impossible, to find in America. However, Reb Moshe did not want to remain in Eastern Europe. His primary reason was his concern for the *chinuch* of his children. He feared that the forces which had destroyed Torah life in Russia might do the same in Latvia with the passage in time, a fear that would be realized. Reb Moshe said that he was prepared to clean streets in America as long as his children could be raised and educated as Torah Jews.[22]

A postcard sent three days after Reb Moshe left Luban provides some fascinating information. On 8 Elul, his brother-in-law Rabbi Shaul Yaffen sent a postcard from Riga to Rabbi Isser Zalman Meltzer in Jerusalem

---

19. *Tehillim* 141:6.
20. *Berachos* 55b.
21. Preface to *Darash Moshe*.
22. Preface to *Igros Moshe* Vol. VIII.

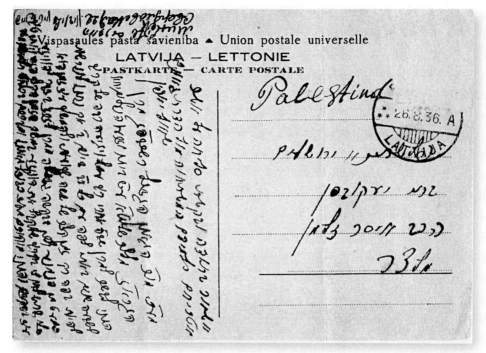

The postcard sent by Reb Shaul Yaffen to Reb Isser Zalman.
Reb Moshe's signature is on top left corner.

regarding his own attempt to leave Eastern Europe.[23] In the remaining space on that postcard, Reb Moshe wrote to his revered rebbi, requesting that he procure for his family a visa to enter Eretz Yisrael:

> To his honor, my master and teacher, the great gaon, leader of the entire diaspora, our master, the gaon Rav Isser Zalman Metzer, shlita, and his exalted family, יחיו:
>
> I wish to inform our master that thank G-d, after much effort and great toil of close to seven years, I have arrived here with my wife and children on Monday. However, we have been granted permission to remain here for but six weeks; to remain longer than that is virtually impossible. Therefore, I beseech our master to expedite the matter of obtaining a visa on my behalf, so that I will receive the visa before this time span elapses — the earlier the better.
>
> One who holds him in great esteem, as his befitting his genius, and who blesses him with all that is good,
>
> His student, Moshe Feinstein from Luban.

---

23. Rav Yaffen never left Eastern Europe and was killed in the Holocaust along with his rebbetzin, who was Reb Moshe's sister.

(left) Reb Moshe and his Rebbetzin with their son David and (behind them) daughters Faya and Sifra; (center) Reb Moshe's brother-in-law Rabbi Shaul Yaffen with his son David; (behind him) his wife Shainda, nee Feinstein, and daughter; (right) Reb Moshe's brother Rabbi Yaakov Feinstein and his family, in Riga 1937

Apparently, the visas to America arrived before any response was received from Eretz Yisrael. Providence had arranged for the future *gadol hador* to settle in the land whose Torah community would mature and flourish under his leadership.

THE VISA TO AMERICA WAS FINALLY GRANTED, IN LARGE MEASURE THANKS TO A plan devised by Rabbi Nechemiah Katz and approved by his congrega-

Congregation Bnei Yaakov

tion. Rabbi Katz called a meeting of his shul's board of directors and proposed the following suggestion: Should Reb Moshe be granted entry into the U.S., Rabbi Katz would resign his position and it would be given to Reb Moshe. This proposal was accepted. In fact, after arriving in America, Reb Moshe served as Rav of Bnei Yaakov for a few weeks. He then resigned the position and it was returned to his brother-in-law.

Rabbi Katz informed the secretary of the Agudas HaRabbanim, Rabbi Yehudah Leib Seltzer, of his shul's decision and Rabbi Seltzer then contacted Senator Robert Wagner of New York. A letter from the American consul in Riga to Senator Wagner dated November 2, 1936, begins:

THE FOREIGN SERVICE
OF THE
UNITED STATES OF AMERICA

DEPARTMENT OF STATE

AMERICAN CONSULATE

Riga, Latvia, November 2, 1936.

The Honorable Robert F. Wagner,
     United States Senate,
          Washington, D. C.

Sir:

I have the honor to acknowledge the receipt of
your letter dated October 6, 1936, in which you request to be advised with regard to the status of the
application for an immigration visa of Rabbi Moses
Feinstein, now a resident of Riga, who desires to
proceed to the United States to join the Congregation
B'nai Jacob of Toledo, Ohio.

In answer to your letter I take pleasure in informing you that Rabbi Feinstein's visa case is having
careful consideration and that this Consulate is dis-
posed to consider favorably his application as soon as
he submits the documents required of an alien who desires
to proceed to the United States for the purpose of continuing his vocation of a rabbi. Rabbi Feinstein stated
that he hoped to be able to present the required documents, among them a document showing that he has been
a rabbi for two years immediately preceding the time
of his application for a visa, within the very near
future as he had requested that they be sent to him.

Very respectfully yours,

William L. Peck,
American Consul.

Letter from the American consul in Riga to Senator Wagner

*I have the honor to acknowledge the receipt of your letter dated
October 6, 1936, in which you request to be advised with regard to
the status of the application for an immigration visa of Rabbi Moses
Feinstein, now a resident of Riga, who desires to proceed to the
United States to join the Congregation Bnei Jacob of Toledo, Ohio …*

However, even this move did not produce immediate results. Again
Rabbi Katz thought of a plan. He appealed to the secretary of the Ohio

Democratic Party, a gentile who was known as a warm, sympathetic person. The secretary enlisted the aid of the state's lieutenant governor, who beamed as he listened to Rabbi Katz's story. The American consul in Riga, Latvia, was an old friend of his! He got word to the consul, who agreed to process the papers for the family. So it was that — as Rabbi Katz put it — they had the indescribable privilege of saving the future *gadol hador!*

Reb Moshe arrived in the United States in Shevat 5697 (1937). When the boat carrying the Feinstein family docked at New York Harbor, it was met by a number of prominent rabbanim who had come to welcome the 41-year-old *gaon* from Luban. While the vast majority of America's Orthodox Jews had never even heard of Rabbi Moshe Feinstein, many *talmidei chachamim* had. The Iron Curtain had not blocked news of Reb Moshe's greatness in Torah.

An issue of the Torah periodical *HaPardes,* published soon after the Feinsteins landed on these shores, heralded Reb Moshe's arrival:

> *… This gaon, renowned in Europe as a great personage, is a giant in Torah, amazingly fluent in all of Talmud Bavli, Yerushalmi, Rishonim and Acharonim, and (is known for) the many original Torah thoughts with which he responds to questions.*
>
> *… It is hoped that he will find a rabbinic position in this country through which the glory of his Torah will be heard.*

Little did anyone dream to what degree the "glory of his Torah" would shine forth for the next fifty years.

CHAPTER THREE

Rebbi of Talmidim

SOON AFTER REB MOSHE ARRIVED IN AMERICA, HE WAS INVITED to deliver a number of *shiurim* in the New York area. Following one such *shiur,* the Torah periodical *HaPardes* wrote, "All the

Bleak Prospects

city's roshei yeshivah and rabbanim were delighted by his extraordinary *shiur,* wondrous *chiddushim,* reasoning and depth."

While all were impressed by Reb Moshe's genius, in no way did this assure him of a position connected with Torah. America in those days had few yeshivos and none of those that existed had anywhere near the large enrollment so many yeshivos boast of today. As such, the chances of Reb Moshe being offered a post as a rosh yeshivah were slim indeed. One yeshivah did offer him a respectable position soon after his arrival, but Reb Moshe rejected it, fearing that a certain member of the yeshivah's administration would resent the appointment as an infringement on his own position. Opportunities to serve as a rav were also difficult to find.

Reb Moshe experienced more than one discouraging encounter as he tried to find a position. "What will you *do* in America?" people wondered. Such questions did not unsettle Reb Moshe. "I will do what Reb Sholom the *melamed* did back home," came his even reply.

Reb Sholom the *melamed* was a teacher of Torah to the Jewish children of Luban — until the Bolsheviks took control. After that, he was forced to spend his days cleaning the town's streets.[1] Reb Moshe meant to say that, come what may, he would not let his spirit be broken. He was eternally thankful to have escaped the oppressive Communist rule. Certainly he would try his utmost to obtain a position that would afford him the opportunity to spread the word of Hashem, but he was prepared to accept whatever lay ahead — even something along the lines of the occupation poor Reb Sholom the *melamed* was forced to undertake.

A relative offered to establish Reb Moshe as a *mashgiach* (kashrus supervisor) in a large slaughterhouse, a post that would have allowed him to support his family in reasonable comfort. Reb Moshe, however, refused the offer, for he was not yet ready to give up on becoming a rosh yeshivah or rav. Annoyed and surprised, the relative argued, "America does not *need* roshei yeshivah; you will never make a living your way!" However, Reb Moshe was adamant. He had lived in peril in Luban for the Torah's sake, and he was not yet ready to surrender the chance to instill America's Jews with its message, unless he had no choice.

RABBI YEHUDAH LEVENBERG WAS ONE OF THE PIONEER TORAH BUILDERS IN America. He had established a yeshivah in New Haven, Connecticut, but

Rosh Yeshivah had relocated his institution to Cleveland, Ohio. Reb Moshe accepted Rabbi Levenberg's invitation to become a rosh yeshivah in his institution. A few months later, Rabbi Levenberg died and the yeshivah disbanded. Almost immediately came the call to serve as rosh yeshivah of Mesivtha Tifereth Jerusalem on New York's Lower East Side. It was this position that Reb Moshe held with such distinction for the rest of his life, nearly forty-nine years.

One of his original talmidim in Tifereth Jerusalem recalls how Reb Moshe was introduced to them. The yeshivah's principal was Rabbi Yosef Adler, a distinguished and popular local rav. Rabbi Adler told the students, "Whenever we needed a rosh yeshivah, I brought a great *talmid chacham* from Europe. Sometimes, I went to Europe myself to recruit people. *Baruch Hashem,* you boys learn well and, before long, I have to bring you a new rebbi who knows even more Torah. I am not a young man anymore, so

---

1. Reb Sholom merited having a son who became one of the greatest roshei yeshivah of his time, the late Rabbi Dovid Povarsky of Ponevezh.

Rabbi Yosef Adler

I decided to bring you someone who knows so much that no matter how much you learn, he will always know more than enough for you."

A story is told that relates what it was that ensured Reb Moshe's appointment. Reb Moshe's father, Rabbi David Feinstein, once stopped at an inn overnight while on a journey. The innkeeper recognized the Rav of Starobin and accorded him the service due someone of his stature. The innkeeper brought his only urn into Reb Dovid's room should the Rav desire a cup of tea during the night.

A short while later, a *chasan* and *kallah* arrived at the inn. When they asked the innkeeper for use of his urn, he told them that the urn was in the Starobiner Rav's room and he would ask the Rav if they could borrow it for a short while.

When the request was put forth to Reb David, he replied, "What is the question? In fact, I think it would be best to keep the urn in the room of the *chassan* and *kallah* the entire night; they deserve to be treated royally."

The *chassan* and *kallah* were none other than Rabbi and Mrs. Yosef Adler. When Reb Moshe was being considered for the position in Tifereth Jerusalem, Mrs. Adler reminded her husband of this incident and suggested that the son of the Starobiner Rav most likely had the superlative *middos* of his father and would be a very positive influence upon the yeshivah's talmidim.

Divine Providence had arranged that Reb Moshe should fulfill his desire to dedicate his life to the study and teaching of Torah. However, his initial months as Rosh Yeshivah were far from easy. The Feinsteins' first apartment in New York was located in the East New York section of Brooklyn. Reb Moshe's starting salary was not enough to cover his family's basic needs *and* his train fare. So until they found an apartment on the Lower East Side, Reb Moshe slept on a bench in the beis midrash throughout the week, returning home only for Shabbos.[2]

---

2. Preface to *Igros Moshe,* Vol. VIII.

WHEN REB MOSHE ASSUMED THE LEADERSHIP OF TIFERETH JERUSALEM, THE Lower East Side was a vibrant, teeming center of Jewish life, with syna-

Tifereth Jerusalem

gogues on virtually every block. Down East Broadway from the yeshivah were Ezras Torah, where the great *tzaddik, gaon* and *posek* Rabbi Yosef Eliyahu Henkin directed a world-wide *chesed* apparatus; and the Agudas HaRabbanim, the organization of European-trained rabbis who had the Talmud and *Shulchan Aruch* at their fingertips. Sadly, there was still an appalling shortage of yeshivos. The Jewish establishment looked down on Orthodoxy and had little respect for its rabbis or institutions, and younger generations of Jews were slipping away from Torah and mitzvah observance. There were a few strong Zeirei Agudath Israel branches here and there, but the Agudath Israel of America had not yet been founded in its present form. Thus, Jewish life on the Lower East Side was strong, but its future was not promising.

Reb Moshe and his yeshivah quickly became a center of Torah life on the East Side. At its peak, Tifereth Jerusalem enrolled over 500 talmidim, but it was more than a yeshivah, just as Reb Moshe was more than a rosh yeshivah. Tifereth Jerusalem included a shul where Reb Moshe not only delivered *shiurim* to his talmidim, but the traditional *Shabbos HaGadol* and *Shabbos Shuvah drashos* to large audiences of *lomdim* (scholars) — usually on Talmudic themes related to *Kodashim* (sacrificial order).

His primary role, however, was as a *posek*, a decider of halachic questions, and before long, word spread that a *posek* of the first rank was there — and available. Distinguished rabbis converged on him with knotty problems and so did local housewives with their strange-looking chicken parts —

because he belonged equally to them all. Two middle-aged *talmidei chachamim* whose fathers were butchers on the East Side remember being sent frequently to Reb Moshe with *she'eilos*. As children they knew him as the nice, friendly man who never made them feel unimportant — as some others understandably did. As they grew older, they realized with a shock that their "friend" was one of Jewry's greatest people.

Mesivtha Tifereth Jerusalem

Reb Moshe with the yeshivah's semichah candidates, early 1940's

Seated (left to right): Rabbis Abraham Brown, Pesach Levovitz, Saul Lasher, Mr. Lazarus, the Rosh Hayeshivah ל״צז, Rabbis Meir Lazar, Bernard Greenfield, Norman Zdanowitz

Standing (left to right): Rabbis Morris Haft, Bernard Gottlieb, Joseph Maza, Mandelbaum, Joseph Schiff, Max Oldak, Gabe Maza, Shmuel Grossman, Jacob Rapaport

It is not surprising that one woman used to call him every Friday afternoon to inquire about the time to light candles; he would answer and pleasantly wish her *a gutten Shabbos* — as he would have done in Uzda or Luban. Did it make any difference whether he was a 20-year-old beginner in a tiny *shtetl* or the teacher of *Klal Yisrael?* His responsibility was to answer the queries of all Jews who needed him.

REB MOSHE DELIVERED THREE KINDS OF SHIURIM: A *BLATT SHIUR,* ON THE text of the Gemara and the basic commentaries of *Rashi* and *Tosafos;* a

The "Blatt Shiur" *pilpul shiur,* in which he would discuss a breathtakingly broad and deep range of material and concepts, and relate them to the text being studied; and a Halachah *shiur,* in which he taught the text and basic commentaries of the *Shulchan Aruch.*

The *blatt shiur* was generally delivered on Mondays and Wednesdays, for one and a half to two hours. As Reb Moshe once told Rabbi Avraham Kalmanowitz (legendary *hatzalah* figure and founder and Rosh Yeshivah of the Mirrer Yeshivah in Brooklyn), "When my talmidim come to the *blatt,* they already know the *Gemara, Rashi* and *Tosafos.* I have to show them *how* to learn it properly."

In other words, the *blatt shiur* was intended to train his students to analyze and understand the basic textual material. What is the significance of a seemingly superfluous word or phrase? What has the Gemara added by citing a particular question and answer? What is the key to a Talmudic dispute? Why do *Rashi* and *Tosafos* differ? What forced *Rashi* to interpret the text a certain way despite the objection raised by *Tosafos?* The goal of this *shiur* was to deal with the text as it is stated, not with abstract theories. If the text was properly understood, the underlying principles and concepts would follow of their own accord and the major commentaries would have a framework in which to be understood properly.

As is true of all master teachers, the greater the scholar the more he puts into even his most elementary elucidation of a Scriptural verse or Talmudic passage. Reb Moshe's basic translation of a simple *Rashi* was colored and flavored by his thorough knowledge of the entire Torah.

Until his later years, he would be in the beis midrash from *Shacharis* until after *Minchah,* to be available to the talmidim who had questions about their learning. After *Minchah,* he would leave and devote the rest of the day to study, responsa, individual petitioners, and communal needs. The only exception was the one afternoon a week when he would return to Tifereth Jerusalem to deliver a Halachah *shiur.* This would be along the general lines of the *blatt,* but it would lay down the general principles upon which practical halachic decisions are based.

Reb Moshe enjoyed when his talmidim challenged something he had said in his *shiur,* taking pleasure in debating the matter with them until it was clarified. As a talmid of Reb Moshe, Rabbi Michel Shurkin would regularly

Standing (left to right):
Rabbi Avraham Pam,
Rabbi Reuven Feinstein,
Rabbi Yehoshua Blum

interrupt his Friday *shiur* with questions.[3] One day, a distinguished member of the yeshivah's kollel told Rabbi Shurkin that it was disrespectful to interrupt the *shiur* of a *gadol hador*. The next week, Rabbi Shurkin sat quietly throughout the *shiur*. The moment the *shiur* ended, Reb Moshe hurried towards him and asked, "Are you not feeling well today? Why were you quiet today?" It was obvious that Reb Moshe welcomed the interruptions. The following week, Rabbi Shurkin made sure to interject with a number of questions.[4]

ONE OF THE GREAT CHALLENGES THAT EDUCATORS FACE IS TEACHING IN A way that can be understood and appreciated by *every* type of student. In

A Rebbi for Everyone

Reb Moshe's case this should have been especially difficult, because his brilliance lent itself to *shiurim* that were deep and complex. He told his *talmid* Rabbi Yehoshua Blum that this was especially challenging in his early years at

---

3. Rabbi Shurkin adds that most of the time his questions were a result of his failure to fully grasp the depth of Reb Moshe's thoughts.
4. From *Meged Givos Olam*. Reb Moshe included some of Rabbi Shurkin's insights in *Dibros Moshe*.

Tifereth Jerusalem when there was a wide gap between the stronger and weaker talmidim. He solved this dilemma through total dedication to his talmidim's needs. The *shiur* was always geared to the stronger students. However, he would stay late after the *shiur* had been delivered to review it privately with those who had difficulty comprehending it.

Rabbi Blum recalls that in his own days as a talmid, Reb Moshe made sure to uplift and encourage the weaker talmidim. It happened sometimes that a talmid would interrupt the *shiur* with a question that showed a total lack of comprehension. Sometimes, stronger talmidim could not help but smile at what, apparently, made no sense. In the midst of his *shiur*, in which he was totally engrossed and had invested so much toil, Reb Moshe paused to uplift the questioner. "What you probably meant to ask is this," he would begin, and then proceed to ask a *kushya* that was clear and incisive. The talmid who had posed the question could not have felt better.

Sometimes, a talmid would approach Reb Moshe after the *shiur* and ask him to repeat a point that he had not understood. Slowly and patiently, he would review the material step by step. When the *bachur* prepared to return to his seat, Reb Moshe would say, *"Host gut farshtanen?"* ("Do you understand it well?") *"Oib nisht, kum tzurik."* ("If not, come back [to me] again.")

REB MOSHE'S PILPUL *SHIURIM,* WHICH HE WROTE AS HE PREPARED THEM, FORM the bulk of his *Dibros Moshe* on the Talmud. These *shiurim* were exceed-

The Making of the "*Dibros*"

ingly complex. First would come a long list of as many as twenty *kushyos* [difficult questions] regarding the Gemara and then a series of intricately woven frameworks upon which an approach to the entire subject would be fashioned. Only the most accomplished of his talmidim could follow his reasoning. For the rest, the *shiur* provided flashes of insight and a demonstration of the vastness of Torah knowledge.

His preparation of the *pilpul shiur* was exceptionally rigorous. The day of the *shiur*, Reb Moshe would arise at 2 a.m. and review all the major sources. Sometimes he would surround himself with chairs upon which he would put the many *sefarim* to which he referred, while he sat on the floor referring to several of them at once. After *Shacharis* in the yeshivah, he would lock himself in his office and rehearse the *shiur* aloud, perfecting it as he went along.

Though Reb Moshe had hundreds of *shiurim* in writing, he would still construct new *chiddushim* in the early hours of Friday morning to be

Addressing his talmidim at Tifereth Jerusalem

used in that day's *shiur.* Rabbi Tuvia Goldstein once asked him why he strained himself so to prepare new material when he could have certainly managed well with his existing *shiurim.* Reb Moshe replied, "As long as the *Ribono shel Olam* gives strength, one must seek to originate anew." Reb Tuvia then remarked that one evening might not always be sufficient to construct the kind of involved *shiurim* for which Reb Moshe was famous. What did Reb Moshe do when time was running out and the *shiur* was not near completion? Reb Moshe allowed himself a slight smile and said simply, *"Baruch Hashem; baruch Hashem."*

Reb Moshe once felt dizzy minutes before he was to deliver a *shiur* and asked someone to get him a glass of water. After doing so, the person said, "I will take the Rosh Yeshivah home so that he can rest." Reb Moshe replied, "What do you mean? I must say the *shiur!*"[5]

---

5. In relating this story, the person involved said, "Reb Moshe did everything according to the *Shulchan Aruch.* No doubt he was sure that saying the *shiur* would not endanger his health, otherwise he would have gone home. Once he decided that his health was not endangered, he felt obligated to go on with the *shiur."*

First Chag HaSemichah 1944

seated (left to right): Rabbis J. Frankel, Balaban, P. Levovitz; the Rosh HaYeshiva זצ"ל, the Menahel, Rabbi Shmuel Greineman; Rabbis M. Lazar, A. Ziegelman, S. Lasher

standing (left to right): Rabbis J. Maza, M. Haft, N. Zdanowitz, A. Brown, S. Krischer, J. Schiff. Not shown: Rabbis B. Greenfield, S. Gertz

Some years ago, Rabbi Yaakov Feitman was asked to deliver a *shiur* at a certain shul. It was a stormy night when few ventured outdoors. Only a handful of men attended the *shiur,* one of whom was an elderly gentleman. At the *shiur's* conclusion, this man approached Rabbi Feitman and told him not to feel bad. "When Rabbi Moshe Feinstein first arrived in America, he would say a Gemara *shiur* for *baalei batim.* I was a regular attendee, and the usual crowd was about what you had tonight."

The man related that he once said to Reb Moshe, "From the *shiur's* content, and the enthusiasm with which the Rosh Yeshivah delivers it, one would think that there were hundreds of people in attendance. Why does the Rosh Yeshivah invest so much effort for such a small crowd?"

Reb Moshe replied that when he prepares or delivers a *shiur,* he does not think about the size of the crowd. He thinks about *nitzchius,* eternity. The study and teaching of Torah is an other-worldly experience and should not be affected by the fact that very few are in attendance.[6]

---

6. The man added that a number of those *shiurim* are found in *Dibros Moshe.*

Rabbi Nissan Alpert

RABBI NISSAN ALPERT, WHOSE UNTIMELY PASSING CAME ONLY A FEW MONTHS after Reb Moshe's, was one of his closest and greatest disciples. In a

With Fire and Feeling *hesped* for Reb Moshe, Reb Nissan related a personal anecdote that illustrates how Reb Moshe's passion for Torah and unusual sensitivity for others went hand in hand. The story centered around Reb Moshe's *pilpul shiur.*

To help his listeners better appreciate the story, Reb Nissan spoke of Reb Moshe's demeanor during a *shiur.* The attendees included current and former talmidim, kollel *yungeleit* from other yeshivos, and an array of laymen. During one period, both a professor and a *chazan* attended the *shiur* regularly. Whoever wanted to learn was welcome.

Often, Reb Moshe would be interrupted by questions, to which he responded patiently. In Reb Nissan's words, "The weaker the student, the more patience the Rosh Yeshivah showed." However, said Reb Nissan, those talmidim like himself who were especially close to Reb Moshe were able to perceive that beneath the calm demeanor during the *shiur* there burned a fire. It was the fire born from love of Torah, from having devoted hours of relentless toil to refining and perfecting a two-hour *shiur,* ensuring that *every* word conformed to Torah truth. So fine-tuned was each *shiur,* said Reb Nissan, that Reb Moshe would not hesitate to issue a halachic ruling based on a *pilpul shiur.*

Could it be possible for a Torah giant who is fully focused on the very complex *shiur* he is delivering to, at the same time, perceive that a talmid who was present appeared somewhat dispirited?

For Reb Moshe, it was possible.

Once, during the *shiur,* Reb Moshe said a *chiddush* that shed new light on the *sugya.* Reb Nissan recognized the *chiddush* as his own. He had been excited to have thought of it and had told it to the Rosh Yeshivah. But the Rosh Yeshivah did not credit him for it during the *shiur!* "I felt very bad," he recalled.

That day, Reb Nissan walked Reb Moshe home after the *shiur,* as he often did. Reb Moshe turned to his talmid and said, *"Az men geit oif a gleichin veg, treft men zich* (If two walk a straight path, they end up meeting one another)." Reb Moshe was letting Reb Nissan know that he had thought of this *chiddush* before Reb Nissan had told it to him, and that is why he did not credit his talmid during the *shiur.* Later, Reb Nissan realized that the *chiddush* was not really his own; it was based on a *chiddush* that Reb Moshe had said on a different *masechta.* In relating this story, Reb Nissan expressed his amazement that in the midst of the *shiur,* Reb Moshe noticed when his *talmid's* face fell and immediately perceived the reason for it.

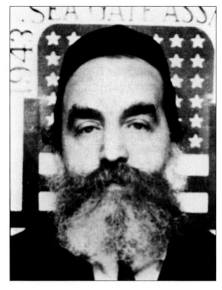

Reb Moshe in 1943

> A poor man who was not associated with the yeshivah would sit in the back of the beis midrash from time to time and disturb others with his loud reading of the *siddur,* which was particularly irritating because he often mispronounced the words. Once, during Reb Moshe's Friday *shiur,* this man walked in and started screaming, "How come the Rosh Yeshivah gives others money and he doesn't give me anything?" Reb Moshe calmed the man down; later, he spoke to some talmidim and asked them to put aside some money so that the next time the man came, a sizable amount would be prepared for him.

NEVER DID REB MOSHE PERMIT HIS RESPONSIBILITIES TO *KLAL YISRAEL* AS A whole to interfere with his guidance of the yeshivah and its students. His

For a Talmid's Sake

many talmidim who became rabbanim and roshei yeshivah would never forget the love, warmth, and respect shown them by their revered rebbi.

Renowned *posek* Rabbi Ephraim Greenblatt, who for decades served as a prominent Rav in Memphis, Tennessee, is among

Reb Moshe's closest disciples. He vividly recalls his first day in Tifereth Jerusalem on an Erev Shabbos, as a 19-year-old who had arrived by boat from Jerusalem only a day earlier. Rabbi Greenblatt entered the beis midrash while Reb Moshe was in his office, preparing his *shiur*. When Reb Moshe entered the beis midrash and noticed the newcomer, he hurried over and greeted him, asked his name, and said that they would talk after the *shiur* had ended. When they spoke again, Reb Moshe told the newcomer to return on Sunday when they would "talk in learning" and he would arrange a study partner for him.

Rabbi Greenblatt wrote:

> The very first time I met him, on an Erev Shabbos in Cheshvan 5711 (1950), his *middos tovos* made an impression upon me for a lifetime. He had the ability to transform a talmid in an instant to someone who wants to learn and develop good character traits.[7]

As soon as Reb Moshe recognized his new talmid's potential in deciding matters of Halachah, he began taking Rabbi Greenblatt aside when questions were brought to him, to demonstrate his method of analyzing a problem and arriving at a *psak*. Rabbi Greenblatt was often asked to be present when Reb Moshe was called to preside over the preparation of a *get* and at times he would accompany his rebbi to comfort a mourner. "Come with me," Reb Moshe would say. "You will meet a great person."

During the summer that followed, Rabbi Greenblatt spent a few days with Reb Moshe in his summer cottage in upstate New York. Reb Moshe would come in at night to check if his talmid's blanket had fallen off while he slept. Rabbi Greenblatt recalls his feelings during those first months.

> At first, I felt that he was going out of his way for me. As time went on, I realized that this was how he treated everyone. He brought every talmid close to him and made us each feel as if we were his *only* talmid.

Another of Reb Moshe's talmidim in those years recalls the time when a student with a very poor reputation was accepted in the yeshivah. The student was touched by Reb Moshe's sincerity and gentleness and became a changed person; today he is a respected member of a thriving Torah community.

---

7. From *She'eilos U'Teshuvos Rivevos Ephraim,* Vol. V, Preface 3.

REB MOSHE WOULD SAY THAT THERE ARE TWO PRIMARY DETERRENTS TO A
Torah student's success: a lack of appreciation for the immeasurable value

**Encouragement
and Direction**

of Torah, and depression over not doing as well as
he had hoped. One who diligently applies himself
to his studies should never become depressed. He
should have confidence in the teaching of our Sages that if one claims, "I
have toiled and not found [success in my studies]," do not believe him.[8]
As long as a student does his very best and keeps trying, Hashem will help
him attain the Torah wisdom that he seeks.

> Reb Moshe once entered his beis midrash and found a talmid sitting
> alone, a sullen expression on his face. Reb Moshe wasted no time
> in approaching him. "עִבְדוּ אֶת ה׳ בְּשִׂמְחָה *(Serve Hashem with joy),*"[9]
> he told the student. He then brought the talmid into his office and
> the two spoke together for some time. A student who observed the
> incident recalled, "I do not know what the Rosh Yeshivah told the
> boy, but I do know one thing — the *bachur* came out of the office a
> changed person."

It did not take Reb Moshe long to size up an individual. An aged *talmid
chacham* passed away in Jerusalem after living in the same neighborhood
for decades, but many of his closest acquaintances did not realize his true
worth. When Reb Moshe was in Israel in 1964 to attend the *Knessiah
Gedolah* (World Conference of Agudath Israel) he had met the man briefly,
and remarked, "This man is a *nistar* (hidden *tzaddik);* he studies Torah
lishmah (for its sake alone)."

He made use of this ability to guide his talmidim along the particular
path best suited for each of them. To one of his students he suggested
taking a position in a community that was then a spiritual desert, but the
talmid could not foresee himself living in such an environment. Reb Moshe
said, "If you settle there it will become a place of Torah." The young man
heeded his rebbi's advice. He lived in that same area for half a century,
and today it is a true center of Torah.

Reb Moshe once accepted this talmid's invitation to visit him and his
community. Afterwards, Reb Moshe told him, "I see that what I said has
come true."

Rabbi Yitzchak Gottlieb was a distinguished Rav in Riverdale, New
York, until his passing in 1998. He became a talmid of Mesivtha Tifereth

---

8. *Megillah* 6b.
9. *Tehillim* 100:2.

Reb Moshe escorting his talmid Rabbi Yitzchak Gottlieb to his chuppah. Rabbi Gottlieb's brother, R' Beirish, also a talmid of Reb Moshe, is at right.

Jerusalem in the early 1940s, and maintained a lifelong relationship with his rebbi, Reb Moshe.

When Rabbi Gottlieb was a young man contemplating a choice of careers, he sought his rebbi's counsel. Reb Moshe told him:

> People do many things in life for which they later have *charatah* (regret). A person may start a business or some other venture and then the day might come when he regrets ever having undertaken it. He may enter a partnership that later turns sour and he will regret the day he agreed to it. That is how life is.
>
> But there is one thing that no one ever regrets. I guarantee you that no one who learns a *blatt* Gemara, a *perek Mishnayos* or a *pasuk Chumash* ever wakes up the next day and tells himself, "I'm sorry I did that." Never.

Rabbi Gottlieb would say that this conversation was a turning point in his life. He developed a true passion for learning and devoted his life to the dissemination of Torah and its ideals.

ANOTHER SOURCE OF THE SPECIAL RELATIONSHIP THAT EXISTED BETWEEN Reb Moshe and his talmidim was the great respect he accorded them.

Respect for Talmidim
Rabbi Nathan Lomner, former Hebrew principal of Tifereth Jerusalem and a talmid of Reb Moshe, recalled, "When I was admitted into the beis midrash, I usually made a point of coming on time. One morning I came somewhat late. The

Rosh Yeshivah, when passing near me, stopped for a moment and said, 'Nu, you came a little late this morning; you probably couldn't come any earlier.' Then he turned and went on his way." Reb Moshe had made his awareness of the occurrence known without making the talmid feel uncomfortable in any way.

When testing a class, Reb Moshe was careful never to say anything that might possibly cause anyone humiliation. Rather than ask pointed questions, he would say, "Let us 'speak in learning,'" and then launch into a discussion of the topic. "*We* asked a question" or "*We* had answered" (rather than "*I*") was Reb Moshe's general way of speaking during an examination. As he spoke, he attempted to draw the students into the discussion. In no way could he be fooled. When a class performed poorly they were told to review and prepare to be tested again.

In the 1950s, a new talmid in Tifereth Jerusalem's beis midrash was informed by Rabbi David Feinstein that he had one week to prepare for a private *farher* (examination) to be given by the Rosh Yeshivah on the Gemara, *Rashi* and *Tosafos* he had recently learned. As he related:

> I was petrified. For the next week, I invested enormous effort in *chazarah* (review), trying my best to clarify every point in the Gemara. Finally, the day of the *farher* arrived.
>
> Nervously, I approached his desk near the *aron kodesh*. The Rosh Yeshivah smiled warmly and asked that I be seated. "How are you?" he asked me. "And how are you adapting to learning in our beis midrash?" I responded and the Rosh Yeshivah then asked about my family, adding that he knew my father well. With his kindness and concern, he was trying his best to put me at ease.
>
> However, he was not successful. Due to my extreme nervousness that morning, I could not recall even much of the basic Gemara. The Rosh Yeshivah asked me to read the Gemara and explain it. I knew that my explanations were wrong, but I could not collect my thoughts and correct my mistakes.
>
> The Rosh Yeshivah did not criticize me or even say that what I had said was incorrect. Instead, every so often, he would stop me and gently say, "What you probably meant to say is ... " and he proceeded to say the correct explanation.
>
> When the *farher* ended, the Rosh Yeshivah said, "*Gantz gut* (Pretty good); *es volt nit geshat tzu iberchazeren di Gemara* (it would not hurt to review the Gemara)."
>
> I never forgot the Rosh Yeshivah's kindness on that day. Later, I

became his talmid and maintained a relationship with him until his passing almost thirty years later.[10]

To a *semichah* candidate whose knowledge of a pertinent subject was not up to par, Reb Moshe said, "You *will* be getting *semichah*. But I want you to review the material and in two weeks we'll 'discuss' it again."

A student from another yeshivah came to Reb Moshe for a *semichah* examination. After a few minutes it became apparent that the young man's knowledge was so sorely deficient that a few weeks of review would not do him much good. What the young man needed was to study the laws with someone knowledgeable. Reb Moshe volunteered to study privately with him. They studied together for some time until the young man was fit to receive *semichah*.

NEVER WOULD REB MOSHE DISMISS A *TALMID'S* QUESTION AS IRRELEVANT OR lacking forethought. To one who thought he had disproven a statement of

Self-Esteem

the *Maharam* — because he had totally misunderstood the statement — Reb Moshe said, "What the *Maharam* seems to be saying is *a little* different from your interpretation." If a boy would ask something totally irrelevant, Reb Moshe would say, "You probably mean to ask as follows," and proceed to raise a sound difficulty which the talmid had not intended to ask — but which was sure to prevent the student from feeling ashamed.

A rebbi once asked Reb Moshe if it was correct to use precious class time to give proper answers to foolish questions that students may sometimes ask. Reb Moshe replied, "The person asking the question never thinks of it as foolish."

> Reb Moshe's own self-respect played no role when he and his talmidim were involved in Torah discussion. Once, during the course of a *shiur,* he made an original point. A talmid interjected to say that he thought he had come across the identical point in a section of *Mishneh LaMelech.* Reb Moshe immediately asked that someone bring him the necessary volume so that he could examine the *Mishneh LaMelech's* comment before continuing his *shiur.*

Aside from attending his *shiurim* and observing his behavior, Reb Moshe's talmidim gained much from his private comments and observations. At times, he would give a talmid practical advice on how to get

---

10. From this author's *Living the Parashah*, Vol. I (ArtScroll/Mesorah Publications).

the most out of his studying. He discouraged a talmid who had difficulty understanding Reb Moshe's quickly spoken Lithuanian Yiddish from listening to a recording of the *shiur* (which he could play again and again) rather than hearing it live. One must *see* the rebbi, Reb Moshe would say, for his words to have their maximum impact.

TO ANOTHER TALMID, HE SAID THAT THE COMMENTARIES OF *MAHARSHA, Maharam, Pnei Yehoshua,* and Rabbi Akiva Eiger were most basic to a

Priorities

proper understanding of Gemara with *Rashi* and *Tosafos.* Reb Moshe would also stress the importance of review. At a *siyum* celebration he expressed the wish that "we merit to study, review, and remember."

He encouraged all his students to adopt an 'early to bed and early to rise' schedule, for he placed great value in studying done during the early-morning hours. Once, Reb Moshe became aware that a few diligent students were studying regularly until 4:00 a.m. in their desire to complete a *masechta* before the term's end. After a few hours' sleep, they would rise, *daven* without a *minyan,* and then resume studying. Reb Moshe called

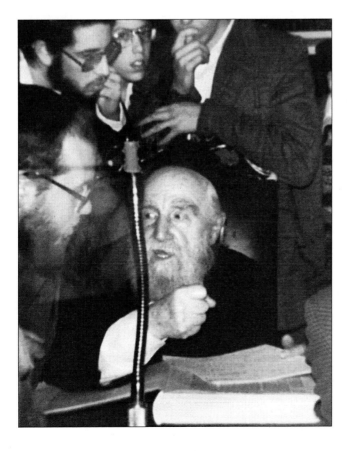

Discussing a shiur at its conclusion with talmidim (l to r): Shlomo Eidelman, Pesach Kuten and Avraham David.

the students aside. "Completing a *masechta* is a wonderful thing," he told them, "but it must not be done at the expense of *davening.*"

As a senior student, Rabbi Shlomo Eidelman felt that the time had come for him to change yeshivos. Since he had become personally close to the Rosh Yeshivah, he felt embarrassed to tell him of his intention, but it would have been wrong not to do so. Trembling, he told Reb Moshe what he wanted to do. Reb Moshe answered, "The Gemara says that one should learn where he feels he will be most successful, so you *should* leave. But I think it is better for you to stay here, so after a few months in your new yeshivah, you should think it over. If you decide to come back, you will be welcome."

Indeed, Rabbi Eidelman *did* return to enjoy the privilege of learning from and serving Reb Moshe for many years.

Reb Moshe stressed to his talmidim the importance of sharing their time to study Torah with those who lack background or ability. In *Dibros Moshe*[11] he points out that Rabbi Preida[12] would review the same lesson with a student *400 times,* though he certainly could have used this time to pursue his own studies. Reb Moshe writes:

> *From this we can prove ... [that just as] one must contribute to others in the areas of tzedakah and gemilas chesed and he may not be exacting even when he needs the money for himself — so it is with regard to the study of Torah. It is forbidden for a talmid chacham to be exacting with his time and to say that he needs it for his own studies, from which he will derive more benefit ... but he must give of his time and teach others, even when it is only the student who stands to gain.*

After suggesting that students of Torah devote one-tenth of their time for the benefit of others, Reb Moshe writes, " ... In this merit, not only will they not lose from their own [success in] Torah, but they will ascend to a more lofty level [than before] ... "[13]

As his son Reb David attests, Reb Moshe was prepared to give even more than ten percent of his time for others. He did not *seek* to give of his

---

11. *Kiddushin* 50:9. See also *Igros Moshe, Even HaEzer* 4:26.
12. See *Eruvin* 54b.
13. Reb Moshe once told a *ben Torah* that learning with a *chavrusa* who is weaker can actually be very beneficial, for it forces the superior student to clarify the subject matter in his mind and explain it well. Also, a weaker student tends to ask many basic questions; this too forces one to gain perfect clarity in the subject matter.

A *ben Torah* once asked the Steipler Gaon if he should agree to learn with a *chavrusa* whose level of learning was not equal to his own. The Steipler replied, "In the *zechus* that you help him with his learning, you will have greater *siyata diShmaya* in your other learning sessions."

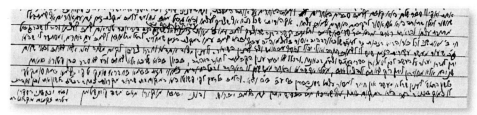

Conclusion of a letter to Rabbi Moshe Friedman in which Reb Moshe writes of the need to give one tenth of one's time to teach Torah to others.

time; nothing was more precious to him than his learning, and if he could have learned uninterrupted, he would have been very happy. However, if someone needed him, he was always ready to help. If the person needed an hour of his time, or even much more, Reb Moshe gave it. No one who needed his help was ever refused.

IN SPEAKING OF BETZALEL, WHO SUPERVISED THE CONSTRUCTION OF THE *Mishkan*, Hashem said, "I have filled him with a G-dly spirit, with wisdom,

Realizing Their Potential

insight, and knowledge, and with every craft."[14] It was, said Reb Moshe, as if Hashem was saying, "I have blessed Betzalel with so much wisdom and natural ability. Why do you think I did this, if not that he should use these inborn gifts to serve Me in the construction of the *Mishkan*?" Every Jew must look into himself, recognize the abilities with which Hashem has blessed him, and then see how best to use them in serving Hashem.

To this end, Reb Moshe did his utmost to ensure that each of his talmidim grow in Torah to the best of his abilities. Whenever a talmid considered leaving Tifereth Jerusalem in pursuit of a livelihood, Reb Moshe would carefully evaluate the *talmid's* personal situation. If he felt that the move should be delayed, he would do his best to keep the talmid in yeshivah for a while longer.

One student found himself in a dilemma. He respected the Rosh Yeshivah's feeling that it was too early for him to leave yeshivah, but could not convince his father of this. The father came to Tifereth Jerusalem to discuss the matter with Reb Moshe personally. Reb Moshe was not swayed by the man's arguments. "It is important for your son to remain in our beis midrash for at least a few more years," he said.

The man was frustrated by Reb Moshe's adamance. He shot back, "Fine, my son will stay in yeshivah — but don't expect to see a penny of tuition from me!"

---

14. *Shemos* 31:3.

Reb Moshe replied calmly, "I already carry the tuition load of many talmidim. I will manage to bear the load of one more."

His words, spoken with utmost sincerity, struck a responsive chord in the man. The talmid remained in yeshivah for a number of years while his father paid tuition and became a staunch supporter of Tifereth Jerusalem.

IN ANOTHER ENCOUNTER, A PARENT'S REACTION TO REB MOSHE'S POSITION WAS shocking. Rather than appreciate the concern shown for his child, the

The Threat

father took the opposite approach.

"Mark my words!" he declared. "I have a younger son and I will not send him to a yeshivah at all!"

This threat upset Reb Moshe tremendously. How could a father threaten to deprive his own child of the Torah's beauty? A very agitated Reb Moshe said to the man, "I will tell you something … no, I had better not say it; once words are uttered they cannot be reclaimed."

Some talmidim who witnessed the episode had never seen Reb Moshe so upset and became fearful for his health. They escorted him to a room in the building and then placed before their rebbi the one thing that was sure to calm him — a gemara. Reb Moshe opened the gemara, immediately became immersed in the subject before him, and remained there studying for two hours.

Meanwhile, the father had remained in the beis midrash, mistakenly thinking that Reb Moshe had been led out to attend to something and would be returning shortly to continue their discussion. When some time had elapsed, he asked a student why the Rosh Yeshivah had not returned.

"Didn't you notice how upset he was?" the student asked incredulously. "Your words hurt the Rosh Yeshivah so, we feared, G-d forbid, that he might suffer a heart attack. We escorted him out to allow him to calm down."

The man had not realized just

how deeply his threat had affected Reb Moshe. He asked the student to direct him to the Rosh Yeshivah so that he could apologize. The student explained that Reb Moshe was now deeply immersed in his studies and it would be wise to leave him alone after the ordeal he had endured.

When Reb Moshe re-entered the beis midrash, the man rushed over to him. "Please forgive me," the father pleaded. "I will certainly send my younger son to the yeshivah. I apologize for having caused the Rosh Yeshivah such anguish. My sincerest ..."

"Apologize?" asked a smiling Reb Moshe. "Whatever for? Nothing happened, nothing happened."

THE SON OF A NOTED MATHEMATICIAN EXCELLED IN HIS TORAH STUDIES; AS he prepared to graduate high school, he wanted to devote at least the next

Simple Arithmetic few years to full-time Torah study. His father, however, wanted him to follow in his footsteps and prepare for a professional career. The *bachur* went to Tifereth Jerusalem to consult with Reb Moshe. "Ask your father to come speak with me," Reb Moshe said.

The father came to Reb Moshe and said, "I am a mathematician and I would like my son to enter the same field. I know that the Rosh Yeshivah feels that he should he pursue his Torah studies, but I have a response to that.

"Our Sages teach that there are three partners in every human being: Hashem, his father and his mother. The Rosh Yeshivah's view represents that of Hashem, but I and his mother respectfully disagree. We are the majority; does not the Torah state,[15] אַחֲרֵי רַבִּים לְהַטֹּת, that the majority opinion prevails?"

Rather than exhibit anger at the man's impudence, Reb Moshe smiled and calmly replied, "Your arithmetic is incorrect. You see, you and your wife are products of the partnership between *their* parents and Hashem. So your shares in your son are not whole ones; Hashem has one third of your share, as well as one third of your wife's. So the computations are as follows: Hashem has His own share in your son, which we will call a three-thirds share; He has one-third of your share; and one-third of your wife's share, a total of five-thirds. You have a two-thirds share in your son and your wife has a two-thirds share, a total of four-thirds. Therefore, Hashem's share is the majority and His will should prevail."

---

15. *Shemos* 23:2.

Leaving Tifereth Jerusalem following Shacharis. Left of Reb Moshe (behind Rabbi Mordechai Schiff, the yeshivah's gabbai. wearing tallis) is Rabbi Mordechai Tendler; Rabbi Moshe Zev Feierstein is at the far left; Rabbi Elimelech Bluth is walking behind Reb Moshe; on right (on sidewalk) is Rabbi Meir Tzvi Ginsberg.

The father was stunned and impressed by Reb Moshe's response. He agreed to allow his son to pursue his full-time Torah studies, and never regretted this decision.[16]

IN *IGROS MOSHE*,[17] REB MOSHE WRITES ABOUT WHAT SHOULD BE THE PRIMARY goal of any Torah teacher:

A Rebbi's Mission *One must realize that teaching Torah to children is unlike teaching any secular subject. [With secular studies,] the teacher must merely explain the material so that the students know it; to the teacher, it is irrelevant whether or not the material penetrates the student's heart and soul to the point that he will practice what he has learned. However, with regard to Torah, the teacher must see to it that the talmidim will absorb what they have learned so that they will perceive in their hearts and souls that this [Torah] is the most important thing in life, and that our true purpose in this world is to fulfill the Torah in all its fine details.*

---

16. From *Along the Maggid's Journey* by Rabbi Paysach Krohn (ArtScroll/Mesorah Publications).
17. *Yoreh De'ah* III, #71.

Moshe Meir Weiss, Reb Moshe and his son, Reb Reuven

Reb Moshe taught not only through his brilliant *shiurim*, but also by example. In the words of Rabbi Yaakov Sable, who as an elementary-school student benefited from Reb Moshe's love and concern, "He was the most beautiful person, and he spoke the most beautiful words to me."

HIS TALMIDIM SOUGHT GUIDANCE ON EVERY IMPORTANT MATTER AND LEARNED from him in other ways. It happened that a talmid of Yeshivah of Staten Island was on the verge of becoming engaged. While his future *kallah* wanted him to study in *kollel* after the wedding, she did not want to live in Staten Island. The *bachur* was troubled by this. Reb Moshe advised him to let the matter rest.

Guiding His Talmidim

A few weeks after the engagement, the *chassan* brought his *kallah* to receive Reb Moshe's *berachah*, accompanied by their parents. When the visit ended and Reb Moshe escorted them to the door, he turned to the *kallah* and her father. "It is my feeling," he said, "that for the *chassan's hatzlachah* (success in his Torah learning) it would be best for them to live in Staten Island and remain in our yeshivah." Hearing these words from the *gadol hador*, everyone agreed that this was the course to follow.

One evening, a married talmid drove Reb Moshe and his own mother home from a *simchah*. When they arrived at the mother's house, the first stop, she could not find her house keys. She accepted her son's suggestion that she spend the night at his house, and he promptly drove her there. When his mother alighted from the car, the son, feeling bad that the hour was late and Reb Moshe was not yet home, remained behind the wheel so that he could drive off as soon as she was in the house. Reb Moshe, however, told him, "You should get out and walk your mother to the door," and he did.

One year, some talmidim of Yeshivah of Staten Island's high school division put forth a serious request. They felt that they could pass at least some of their secular studies courses without attending the scheduled classes. They asked to be excused from these classes so that they could use the free time for Torah study.

When the question was presented to Reb Moshe, he rejected the request. *Bnei Torah,* he said, must know that whatever they do in life, they must do right. If they will "cut corners" in their secular studies, they will do the same when it comes to understanding a *Tosafos.*

When Rabbi Simcha Bunim Cohen was writing *The Radiance of Shabbos,* his first of many works on Halachah, he said to Reb Moshe, "To be perfectly honest, I don't think I'm doing this at all *l'shem Shamayim* (for the sake of Heaven). I think that, from start to finish, I'm doing it for personal prestige."

Reb Moshe's eyes filled with tears. He bent over and kissed Rabbi Cohen. "*Es iz a gutte zach* (It [your motivation] is a good thing)," he said. "If you would say that you're doing it *l'shem Shamayim,* it would be very problematic. You are a young man; do you really expect that at your age, you should be writing a *sefer lishmah?* Do you know why America is not producing enough *gedolim?* Because *bnei Torah* are too preoccupied with the idea of learning *lishmah* [and they become discouraged]. As long as you are not learning to outdo others *(l'kanter),* it is fine. Learn *shelo lishmah,* and with time, you will reach the level of *lishmah.*"[18]

Before his wedding, Rabbi Aryeh Zev Ginzberg asked Reb Moshe what a *chassan* and *kallah* should have in mind as they stand under the *chuppah.* Reb Moshe replied:

> People make a mistake when they seek blessing from Hashem. They think that it is sufficient to ask of Hashem in a general way that everything should be good. However, if this *was* sufficient, the *Anshei Knesses HaGedolah* would not have composed a *Shemoneh Esrei* with so many specific requests.
>
> Each aspect of life requires its own *berachah* and therefore its own *tefillah* that one should merit this *berachah.* When a *chasan* and *kallah* stand under the *chuppah* at this most special moment in their lives, they should beseech the *Ribono shel Olam* for all that is most

---

18. The Gemara states: "A person should always engage in the study of Torah and the performance of mitzvos *shelo lishmah* (not for its own sake), for from *shelo lishmah* one will eventually come to [doing it] *lishmah*" (*Pesachim* 50b).

important in a Jewish home: *shalom bayis*, healthy children whom they can raise to be G-d-fearing Jews, *parnasah* that will allow them to pursue their spiritual goals with peace of mind; and more.

Older talmidim gained lessons for life from watching the manner in which Reb Moshe presided over *dinei Torah*. As *bachurim*, Rabbi Schaye Schonbrun and the late Rabbi Avraham Blumenkrantz studied together only a few feet away from Reb Moshe's desk in the beis midrash. One day, two men came to Reb Moshe to settle a monetary dispute. In the middle of the proceedings, one of the men pointed toward the other and shouted, "He's a liar … a liar!"

Reb Moshe reacted with genuine shock. "How can you say that? He is a Jew who lives by the Torah. How can you accuse such a person of lying?"

To Reb Moshe, it was unthinkable that a G-d-fearing Jew should lie. It was a lesson the two *bachurim* would never forget.[19]

Rabbi Yitzchak Zilberstein of Bnei Brak heard the following from the Rosh Yeshivah of Belz, Rabbi Shmuel Rosengarten:

> I had a talmid who came to me after having learned under Reb Moshe. Before leaving Tifereth Jerusalem for *bein hazmanim* (intercession), he asked Reb Moshe for advice on how to conduct himself while away from yeshivah. This is what the Rosh Yeshivah told him:
>
> "In your shul back home, the rav probably delivers a *Mishnayos shiur* for his congregants between *Minchah* and *Maariv*. An accomplished *ben Torah* like yourself would prefer to spend this time learning a *masechta* of Gemara alone, rather than attend this *shiur* for laymen.
>
> "However, there is something you must understand. If you do not attend the *shiur*, you could be wounding the feelings of the rav in a very serious way, and the participants in the *shiur* might feel insulted as well. Even worse, they might decide that if you feel the *shiur* is not worth listening to, then it is not for them to listen to it either. Instead, they might choose to spend their time between *Minchah* and *Maariv* engaged in idle chatter. This *shiur* might have been their only Torah learning of the day, and you will have been the cause of their doing away with it.
>
> "So make sure that if there is such a *shiur*, you attend."[20]

---

19. Reb Moshe was very astute and could sense when someone was not speaking the truth in a *din Torah*. In this case, he obviously felt that the person was an upright Jew and, as such, would never lie.

20. Rabbi Zilberstein adds that he sometimes visits a certain city where such a *shiur* is held. Always, he is impressed by a certain outstanding *talmid chacham* who sits among

Rabbi Michel Barenbaum

NO DISCUSSION OF REB MOSHE AND HIS TALMIDIM AT TIFERETH JERUSALEM would be complete without mentioning the impact of his beloved col-

Reb Michel league and friend, Rabbi Michel Barenbaum.

Reb Michel was a talmid of the Mirrer Yeshivah and together with his rebbetzin spent the war years with the yeshivah in Shanghai. In 1946, they arrived in New York with no money and few contacts. However, Hashem had already prepared the way for Reb Michel to inspire talmidim for generations to come. Rabbi Shmuel Greineman, who married a sister of the Chazon Ish, was Menahel of Tifereth Jerusalem at that time and he recommended Reb Michel for the position of *Mashgiach Ruchani*.[21] Reb Michel was to serve in that position for more than fifty years.

His first *shmuess* (ethical discourse) was delivered in a classroom. When Reb Moshe learned of this he told Reb Michel, "Next time you will speak in the beis midrash and you will stand at my place!" Reb Michel agreed to the first part of the request but under no circumstances would he stand in

---

the laymen as a participant in the rav's *Mishnayos shiur* (from *Sefer Aleinu L'Shabeiach* to *Parashas Terumah*).

21. Another advocate on Reb Michel's behalf was another member of the Tifereth Jerusalem *hanhalah*, Rabbi Chaim Swiatycki. His father, Rabbi Abba Swiatycki, also married a sister of the Chazon Ish and succeeded his father-in-law, Rabbi Shmaryahu Karelitz, as Rav of Kossowa. On occasions when the elder Rabbi Swiatycki could not deliver his *shiur* to the townspeople, Reb Michel's father would substitute for him.

Left to right: Reb Shmuel Greineman, Reb Yaakov Kamenetsky, Reb Moshe

Rabbi Chaim Swiatycki, menahel and maggid shiur, speaking with Reb Moshe

the Rosh Yeshivah's place. Instead, he had his lectern set up on the side of the beis midrash opposite where Reb Moshe's place was.

Reb Michel would cry when relating the above. "The Rosh Yeshivah was *machayeh* me (brought me to life)." The honor that Reb Moshe accorded him from the day he joined the yeshivah left a profound impression on the yeshivah's talmidim. They realized that, in the eyes of Reb Moshe, their

Reb Michel greeting Reb Moshe at the reception prior to the Tifereth Jerusalem dinner in Reb Moshe's honor

young, new mashgiach was a man of stature. In those early years, Reb Moshe made a point of attending the Mashgiach's addresses [which were intended for the students] and would listen intently to every word.[22]

Reb Michel was not only a *baal mussar;* he was a *gaon baTorah,* and no one recognized this more than Reb Moshe. Reb Michel attended the Rosh Yeshivah's weekly *pilpul shiur* where he often asked pointed questions and would discuss the *shiur* with Reb Moshe following its conclusion. The gen-

---

22. During the Barenbaums' first years in America, they were neighbors with the Feinsteins on Henry Street and the families became very close. When Reb Michel's young son and daughter were given a board game as a gift, they asked their father if they were permitted to use it on Shabbos. "Ring the Rosh Yeshivah's doorbell and ask him," was his reply. The children quickly followed these instructions and presented their question to Reb Moshe, who said that the game could be used on Shabbos.

Reb Moshe was scheduled to speak at the bar mitzvah *seudah* of Reb Michel's son, Efraim, but Rebbetzin Feinstein was concerned that Reb Moshe had not been feeling well that day and she did not want him to speak. However, Reb Moshe's feeling of closeness and *hakaras hatov* would not permit him to not speak at all. He compromised and spoke for a shorter time than he had planned.

Reb Michel's certificate of semichah, presented to him by Reb Moshe

eral practice was that if a talmid wished to pose a *kushya* on Reb Moshe's *shiur,* he would first discuss it with Reb Michel. Only if the Mashgiach said that the *kushya* was a genuine difficulty would talmidim feel free to pose it to the Rosh Yeshivah.[23]

In the 1970s, as Reb Moshe's responsibilities as leader of his generation grew, he found it increasingly difficult to give the yeshivah's *semichah* candidates the required *bechinos* (examinations). He asked Reb Michel to share the burden with him. Reb Michel replied, "How can I test others for *semichah* when I myself am not a *musmach* (ordained rabbi)?"

So it was that Reb Moshe conferred *semichah* upon Reb Michel Barenbaum. The certificate of *semichah* begins:

> *My friend, the rav and gaon who is renowned in his Torah knowledge and fear of Hashem, who for thirty years has stood at my side dissem-*

---

23. There was a natural reluctance on the part of nearly all students to present a question to Reb Moshe unless they were sure it was worthy of his attention — and would reflect well on them.

inating Torah and pure yiras Hashem at Mesivtha Tifereth Jerusalem ... We have discussed many practical matters [of halachah] and have debated in all areas of Torah ...

Reb Michel's *shmuessen* were first published in Hebrew under the title *Sichos Mussar*. In 5756 (1996), in honor of his fifty years as Mashgiach of Tifereth Jerusalem, those *shmuessen* were adapted into English[24] and released at the yeshivah's annual dinner, where a special presentation was made to Reb Michel. In the preface to that volume, Rabbi David Feinstein wrote:

> With such shmuessen, he molded our talmidim into the sort of people worthy to be regarded as students of my father, צ"ל. As a man who is great in both Torah and mussar, the Mashgiach has been able to convey the message of gadlus he not only espouses but embodies.
>
> My father צ"ל described him as "a great man and a gaon in Torah whose chiddushei Torah are worthy of publication"; and he spoke of the yeshivah's talmidim as people who were "influenced by the Mashgiach's words and his mussar and emunah, fear and love of Hashem, the Torah and good character traits." Surely there can be no greater testimony to the Mashgiach's caliber as a talmid chacham and molder of talmidim.

UNTIL THE MID-1950S, REB MOSHE WAS NOT INVOLVED IN THE FINANCIAL ASPECTS of Tifereth Jerusalem. He had been hired to serve as Rosh Yeshivah, to

Financial Responsibility deliver the highest *shiur*, and oversee the *chinuch* of the high school and beis midrash talmidim. The yeshivah's finances were managed by a board of lay-men who made decisions regarding fundraising and salaries.

All this changed when a major fundraising project failed and left the yeshivah deep in debt. For a long time, rebbeim were not paid and there seemed to be no end in sight to the crisis.

Finally, the rebbeim approached Reb Moshe and said that if the current situation continued, they would have no choice but to resign their positions and seek employment elsewhere. To their minds, there was only one way to resolve the crisis: the Rosh Yeshivah should assume full responsibility for the yeshivah's finances.

Reb Moshe knew that the rebbeim were right; as matters stood, the yeshivah was headed toward closure. Well aware of the drain this would be

---

24. That volume, *Reb Michel's Shmuessen,* as well as the original Hebrew work, was published by ArtScroll/Mesorah.

on his time, which was so precious to him, he did what needed to be done.

Without delay, he threw himself into the formidable task of rescuing the yeshivah from financial ruin and establishing a competent financial system that would make it possible for the yeshivah to cover its expenses in the future. Former and present talmidim were recruited to solicit funds. A *bachur* who was a talmid at the time, Shimon Meth, was asked to serve as secretary. He, in turn, approached another talmid, Yitzchak Selengut, on behalf of the Rosh Yeshivah, to request that he assume the position of executive director.[25]

Rabbi Selengut, who remained at that position for three years, recalled:

> It was a very difficult time. The yeshivah was very deep in debt and much of the money was owed to private individuals. In those days, there were few people of means who were *bnei Torah*. Many supported the yeshivah because it was a neighborhood school or because it took in war orphans. And now, these people were owed significant sums of money. We appealed to them to waive these debts in light of the yeshivah's situation and the fact that the Rosh Yeshivah, who had now assumed responsibility for the yeshivah's finances, had been uninvolved until this point. Some did waive the debts, others did not. It took a few years, but, *b'chasdei Hashem*, the yeshivah did pay back all outstanding monies, paid the rebbeim what was owed to them, and once again was on sound financial footing.
>
> During that period, I consulted with the Rosh Yeshivah twice a day. Every day, he would come to my office to discuss matters. Amazingly, though he never diverted his mind from Torah, he was familiar with every detail of the financial operation, and knew exactly how much money would be coming in each and every day. He had assumed responsibility for the yeshivah's future and he took this very seriously.

25. Also especially involved in resolving this crisis were Rabbi Joseph Frankel and Rabbi Saul Lasher, both talmidim of Reb Moshe.

My desk was in an inner office. The outer office had three desks at which sat three secretaries, one of whom was not Jewish. Every day, on his way to my office, the Rosh Yeshivah would stop at each desk to wish each secretary "Good morning."

We took the Rosh Yeshivah to homes of well-to-do individuals to solicit funds. Some of them were not learned, but their fathers or grandfathers were, and this gave them an appreciation for supporting Torah. All this was not easy for the Rosh Yeshivah, but he did it because he determined that this was the *retzon Hashem*.

IN 1966, A BRANCH OF MESIVTHA TIFERETH JERUSALEM WAS FOUNDED IN Staten Island, New York, with Rabbi Reuven Feinstein as its Rosh

Yeshivah of Staten Island

Yeshivah.[26] Today, the Yeshivah of Staten Island is a major Torah institution, where students can escape the tumult of city life and immerse themselves in Torah learning. Until his very last years when illness confined him to his home, Reb

Moshe would deliver a weekly *shiur* in the yeshivah in addition to his visits

Yeshivah of Staten Island main building

---

26. The beautiful Staten Island campus was purchased at a time when Tifereth Jerusalem was experiencing financial difficulties. Someone asked Reb Moshe how he could take responsibility for such a purchase at such a time. Always the man of *bitachon*, he smiled and replied, "Is it a *kuntz* (trick) to buy such property when the yeshivah has money? The *kuntz* is to buy it when the yeshivah does *not* have money!"

With talmidim of Yeshivah of Staten Island. left to right: Shlomo Eidelman, Yaakov Goldstone, Mordechai Sendrovitz and Avraham Ort

there for Shavuos and other occasions. Even when not there in person, Reb Moshe guided the yeshivah from afar, as his son consulted with him in formulating yeshivah policy.

Almost since its inception, the talmidim of Staten Island have enjoyed the summer months on a campus in upstate New York, combining a somewhat less intensive learning schedule with recreation. Until the last summer of his life, Reb Moshe would join the yeshivah for at least one month each summer.

In the camp's early years, on summer Shabbos afternoons, Rebbetzin Feinstein would prepare refreshments for a group of high school boys whom Reb Moshe would join for an *oneg Shabbos* gathering. He would always say a *dvar Torah* and answer any questions the boys might have. In his last years, Reb Moshe's physical condition did not permit the members of Camp Staten Island much more than an opportunity to observe him learning outside his bungalow, going for a short walk, or *davening* in the camp's beis midrash.

On a golf cart at Camp Staten Island

A few years before his passing, the camp's beis midrash was relocated from its original site to a structure only a short distance from Reb Moshe's bungalow, and a path was paved from the bungalow's back door to the beis midrash, so that Reb Moshe could walk to *davening* on level ground. When, in his very last years, even this short walk became too difficult for Reb Moshe, a golf cart would take him to the beis midrash. Reb Moshe would wave to the small children who would sometimes stand along the path as he rode by.

MR. BEINISH KAPLAN RECALLS THE KAVOD AND *SIMCHAS HATORAH* THAT REB

Joy and Honor

Moshe's presence evoked:

When I was younger, I would *daven* on Shabbos morning with my grandfather, Rabbi Avrohom Kaplan, at a local shul where *Mussaf* ended earlier than at Tifereth Jerusalem. Even before my grandfather became Reb Moshe's *mechutan*,[27] we had a Shabbos morning ritual that left a deep impression on me. Before

---

27. Rebbetzin Shelia Feinstein (wife of Reb Reuven) is the daughter of Rabbi Avrohom Kaplan. He was a long-time primary-grade rebbi at Yeshivah Toras Chaim (then in East New York). Among his talmidim were Rabbi David Feinstein, Rabbi Yaakov Perlow (Novominsker Rebbe) and Rabbi Aharon Schechter (Rosh Yeshivah of Mesivta Rabbi Chaim Berlin).

Being oleh to the Torah

going upstairs to my grandparents' home for *Kiddush*, we would wait on the street for Reb Moshe to pass by on his way home from the yeshivah. Many others waited as well.

Reb Moshe never walked home alone. Usually, he was accompanied by an entourage: the Mashgiach, Rav Michel Barenbaum, was to his right, one of the rebbeim to his left, while other rebbeim walked behind them. They were followed by Reb Moshe's sons (who were young men at the time) and talmidim. Reb Moshe smiled and wished everyone *"Gut Shabbos"* as he went by. This weekly demonstration of *kvod haTorah* was something to behold.

Simchas Torah in Tifereth Jerusalem was an unforgettable experience. In the 1950s and early '60s, hundreds of talmidim and neighborhood residents would jam the beis midrash to rejoice with the Torah. I can picture in my mind the *simchah* that Reb Moshe's face radiated as he danced with the *sefer Torah* and the way this energized everyone who was privileged to be there.

After *hakafos,* the *minyan* would accompany the Rosh Yeshivah home, singing as they walked. The Lower East Side was a mixed neighborhood of various ethnic groups, but no one seemed to mind the crowd and the singing in honor of the great rabbi who dwelled in their midst.

CHAPTER FOUR

For the Younger Generation

HE YOUNGER STUDENTS OF TIFERETH JERUSALEM SAVORED
their personal encounters with their revered Rosh Yeshivah.
Rabbi Nathan Lomner recalls his first encounter with the Rosh Yeshivah,

Memorable Encounters
as a youngster of 11. He had come to the United States
with his parents from Germany and was not up to the
level of his class because he did not know Yiddish and
had not yet learned Gemara. Accompanied by Rabbi Shmuel Greineman,
Reb Moshe tested the class, but young Nathan Lomner performed poorly.
Recognizing that the young refugee would be hurt by his failure, Reb
Moshe patiently and sympathetically taught him the Gemara — and then
gave his rebbi a good report about his performance.

> For many years, it was a much-sought-after privilege for a student to
> hold open a *Chumash* for Reb Moshe when he moved close to the
> *bimah* to better hear the Torah reading. Aside from the privilege itself,
> the boy went away with another reward — a gentle pat on the back
> from Reb Moshe.

One day as he left Tifereth Jerusalem accompanied by an entourage of
talmidim and petitioners, Reb Moshe noticed a boy of about ten standing
off to the side crying. Rather than ask someone to find out what was the

matter, he approached the boy himself, patted his cheek affectionately, and asked him what was wrong. The boy was a student in the yeshivah's elementary division; apparently, something had happened in the classroom that made him very upset. Reb Moshe took the child by the hand and accompanied him into the building to resolve the matter.

RABBI LOMNER SERVED FOR A TIME AS THE YESHIVAH'S SIXTH-GRADE REBBI. HE once invited Reb Moshe to test the class on the second chapter of

A Way of Life *Masechta Bava Metzia,* which deals primarily with laws concerning the returning of lost objects. Reb Moshe began by asking the class, "What if someone sees two lost objects, one belonging to his father and the other to his rebbi — which does he return first? Why?" The children answered correctly that the rebbi's object takes priority, for he is the one who, through his teaching of Torah, places his talmidim on the path leading to the World to Come. Reb Moshe then asked a few more questions, all of which were intended to impress upon the talmidim the esteem in which they should hold their rebbi.

His line of questioning then took a very unexpected turn. "How do Hashem's commands affect the way we live?" Reb Moshe asked the boys. One of the students answered that were it not for the commandment that we study Torah, he could be outdoors playing ball. To this Reb Moshe responded, "Children may play ball. But how do Hashem's commandments affect how one plays ball?"

Now the entire class was stumped. After a short pause, Reb Moshe answered the question himself. Jewish boys, he said, should avoid fighting when they play, and they should certainly never lie or use foul language. Even a Jew's recreation must be guided not by what is accepted in the world at that time, but rather by the timeless teachings of the Torah.[1]

One day, one of Rabbi Lomner's students found a dollar in the classroom. Putting into practice a law that the class had learned in the Gemara, Rabbi Lomner had the finder announce that he had found money, so that the loser could prove his ownership by stating the amount and where the money was lost. However, before anyone had a chance to claim the find, one of the boys raised his hand and unwittingly announced that he had seen the finder pick up a dollar in front of the lockers.

---

1. Sometimes, Reb Moshe would leave the yeshivah building when the elementary students were outdoors enjoying their recess. The boys would respectfully stop their games when Reb Moshe passed by. He would tell them, "Don't stop — play! But play like a *Yid* should play."

Listening to the dvar Torah of a bar mitzvah

Almost as soon as this revelation was made, another boy raised his hand and claimed that he had lost a dollar and that it had probably fallen out of his pocket when he had taken out a key to open his locker. To this, the finder retorted that the claimant had probably contrived the whole story after hearing the other boy's announcement.

The case was then brought to Reb Moshe for his ruling. After listening to the finder and claimant state their respective positions, Reb Moshe turned to the finder and said, "It is wrong to accuse your friend of lying. A *yeshivah bachur* would not claim something that was not rightfully his.

"However, you are not obligated to give him the dollar, since the amount of money and the location of the find were made public and as such cannot be used as proof."

Reb Moshe then took a dollar out of his pocket and in his gentle and sincere manner said that he did not need this dollar and was therefore giving it to the boy who said he had lost the money.

When the finder saw this, he immediately exclaimed, "If the Rosh Yeshivah believes him, then I also believe him and I'll give him back the dollar."

"No," Reb Moshe insisted, "you keep your dollar and you take this dollar; both of you should have a dollar."

MESIVTHA TIFERETH JERUSALEM FOLLOWS THE TIME-HONORED TRADITION FOR *has'chalas Gemara* by introducing its young talmidim to the study of

Has'chalas Gemara

Gemara with the second chapter of *Bava Metzia*, which, as mentioned above, deals primarily with the laws of returning lost objects. At some point, there was pressure from parents to follow the practice of some elementary-level yeshivos where Gemara learning begins with *Masechta Berachos*, which deals with laws of *Shema, tefillah,* and blessings. The parents argued that the latter was far more relevant to the children and would capture their interest more.

Reb Moshe called a meeting of the yeshivah's rebbeim and said that the yeshivah's policy in this area was not subject to discussion. He explained the reason for the custom: to impress upon children the importance of being "an *ehrlicher Yid*" (an honest, upright Jew) and that the Torah dictates how a Jew is to behave in the street as much as it teaches how to conduct oneself in shul. Teaching this fundamental of Judaism cannot be postponed until adulthood.

> On the way out of the meeting, Reb Moshe mentioned an additional reason for this custom. In his first year of Gemara study, a child learns only a few *blatt* which he reviews again and again so that he can recite them fluently. And what is he learning again and again in the second chapter of *Bava Metzia*? That we are commanded to return lost objects. In other words, we are not permitted to keep what belongs to someone else. This message will hopefully go a long way in ensuring that the child will grow to be honest in all areas of monetary dealings.

Years later, two ninth-grade students at Yeshivah of Staten Island came to Reb Reuven Feinstein for a *"din Torah."* One had borrowed a cassette recorder from the other and had swung it by its strap, causing it to hit a wall and break. They wanted to know whether the borrower was liable for damages.

At that time, the yeshivah was learning *Bava Metzia* which discusses the laws of *shomrim* (watchmen), including a *sho'el* (borrower). Reb Reuven asked the borrower, "What are the responsibilities of a *sho'el?"* The *bachur* replied correctly that a *sho'el* is liable even for unavoidable accidents *(onsim).* "And certainly he is liable for *pshi'ah* (negligence)," responded Reb Reuven, meaning that there was no question he was liable in this case.

The boys walked away satisfied that their question had been resolved,

Being escorted by talmidim of Yeshivah of Staten Island

but Reb Reuven was troubled that they had come to him with a question whose answer was so plainly obvious. That night he asked his father, "How can it be that they are learning these halachos in yeshivah and they cannot apply it to their own lives?"

Reb Moshe responded, "Ask them what they learned for *has'chalas Gemara*." Reb Reuven followed this directive and discovered that both boys had begun with *Masechta Berachos*. Reb Moshe was not surprised. He said, "In *Berachos*, they learned some things that to their minds are not put into practice. They learned that the ideal time for praying the *Shemoneh Esrei* of *Shacharis* is at sunrise, but how many people actually do this? They learned that there is a deadline each morning for the recitation of *Shema* and *Shemoneh Esrei*, but they may have seen their fathers or older brothers *daven* late and miss these required deadlines. So what have they learned? That there are things in *Yiddishkeit* that are nice to do, but it's all right if you don't do them. So they apply this logic to *Bava Metzia* as well."

ONE TALMID WAS SENT BY HIS FAMILY TO LIVE WITH RELATIVES IN ISRAEL WHEN he was 13 years old. When Reb Moshe attended the *Knessiah Gedolah* in

Simplicity and Concern

1964, the boy stood outside the site of the gathering in Jerusalem waiting to greet him. When they met, Reb Moshe warmly greeted the boy and then stuffed a ten-dollar bill into his hand. "Here," he said, "you'll need this."

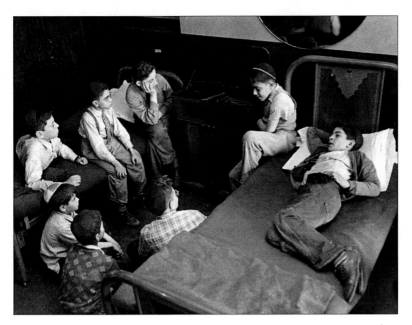

A dormitory room in the early years of the yeshivah

In earlier years, many of Tifereth Jerusalem's students were out-of-towners whose hometown had no yeshivah. The parents of these boys, having been convinced of the importance of providing their son with a Torah education, sent them to attend Tifereth Jerusalem and live in the adjoining dormitory. Naturally, parents were often anxious about such arrangements, and whenever Reb Moshe became aware of this, he did his best to calm these fears.

He could sometimes be found speaking to a mother who sat nervously in the hallway of the yeshivah while her son sat in his new class for the first time. Once, he was seen assuring the mother of a 9-year-old newcomer to the yeshivah that her son would surely overcome his homesick feeling in due time.

> One Friday night, as the congregation filed out of the beis midrash after *Maariv*, Reb Moshe noticed a bewildered-looking out-of-town student. The boy was only too happy to explain his dilemma to the Rosh Yeshivah. It had been arranged for him to eat the Shabbos meal at the home of a neighborhood couple and he was to have met his host in yeshivah after *Maariv*. However, the man was nowhere to be seen and the boy did not know where he lived. Reb Moshe told the student to wait while he looked for the man. Reb Moshe found the man *davening* with a different *minyan*,[2] and then went to get the boy.

2. In those days, a few Friday-night *minyanim* were conducted simultaneously in the yeshivah.

This student later related that it was as a result of this incident, where he saw such extraordinary concern and simplicity from a man so great, that he decided to emulate Reb Moshe in dedicating his life to the spreading of Torah.

He cared for his talmidim like a father. When a *bachur* in the dormitory was ill and had difficulty swallowing the prescribed pills, Reb Moshe would come to his room and crush the pills into small pieces.

One Motza'ei Yom Kippur, minutes after the fast had ended, Reb Moshe entered the beis midrash and found a *bachur* learning. The *bachur* had grabbed a cup of coffee after *Havdalah* and was now preparing for a *bechinah* (exam) that would be administered the next day. Reb Moshe told the *bachur*, "Now is not the time to learn; now one must eat."

IN HIS EULOGY DELIVERED AT THE FUNERAL FOR REB MOSHE IN NEW YORK, Reb Nissan Alpert told of how their close relationship developed. At the conclusion of Reb Moshe's *shiur* on Friday afternoons,

For the Sake of a Talmid

students would usually rush out. Reb Moshe would remain behind to return the *sefarim* to their shelves and climb on benches to shut the lights. As Reb Nissan related, "The *Ribono shel Olam* put an idea into my mind that I should remain with the Rosh Yeshivah and help him shut the lights and return the *sefarim*. When we went home, I would take his briefcase and carry it for him. Through this, I merited a tremendous closeness; I was like a member of the family to the Rosh Yeshivah and the Rebbetzin … "

While Reb Nissan spoke of how he achieved a special closeness with Reb Moshe, their relationship actually began well before that time, when Reb Nissan was 12 years old and the first refugee child to become enrolled at Tifereth Jerusalem during World War II. One day, young Nissan was given an envelope containing a tuition statement which he was to take home to his parents. Unknown to the yeshivah administration, Nissan's father was not well at the time and was unable to work. In no way could he and his wife afford to pay tuition. Nissan noticed that his parents were upset by the bill. Realizing that his parents could not honor the request, he felt ashamed to be seen in yeshivah. The next day he remained at home, rarely venturing out of his room.

A few days went by with no change in the situation. Then, one afternoon, there was a knock on the Alperts' door. It was Rebbetzin Feinstein, accompanied by two other neighborhood women. Nissan was a bright, charming child and had quickly become a popular face in the yeshivah.

His absence had been noticed. The Rebbetzin wondered, was he perhaps not well? The Alperts told her the truth.

The next day again there was a knock on the Alperts' door. This time it was Reb Moshe. He asked to see Nissan. When the boy appeared, Reb Moshe asked him, "Do you want to study Torah?"

"Yes," came the shy reply.

"Then there is nothing to be concerned about. Come with me."

Reb Moshe took Nissan's hand in his own and in this way the Rosh Yeshivah and the young immigrant walked together to yeshivah. Needless to say, Nissan no longer felt ashamed to attend yeshivah and rose to become one of Tifereth Jerusalem's most outstanding products.

IN DARASH MOSHE, REB MOSHE NOTES THAT WHEN THE TORAH COUNTS BNEI Yisrael, the term it uses for counting is שְׂאוּ, whose literal meaning is *lift up*. He explains:

For Every Jewish Child

Sometimes, humility can be counterproductive. A person might tell himself, "I'm a nobody; I can't accomplish much in the way of Torah and mitzvos." To counter this, the Torah "lifts up" every Jew by showing him that when the Jewish people are counted, the simple Jew counts as much as the great tzaddik. This makes one realize that with a proper desire to grow spiritually and a willingness to make the proper effort, every Jew can achieve greatness, each in his own way.[3]

Reb Moshe recognized the potential inherent in *every neshamah* and stood ready to give *every* Jewish boy the opportunity to receive a Torah education.

More than half a century ago, in the town of Tarentum, Pennsylvania, there lived a young Orthodox Jewish family. Mr. and Mrs. Max Palgon were doing their best to raise their three sons to be firmly committed Jews, but it was not easy. After public school hours, the boys would attend Talmud Torah and occasionally would receive a private lesson from the rabbi of the one shul that served fifty Jewish families in Tarentum and two neighboring towns. Thirteen-year-old Arthur could read the *siddur* and knew a bit of *Chumash*. His younger brothers, 11-year-old Louis and 8-year-old Aaron, knew even less.

One day a *meshulach* (fundraiser) from New York came to Tarentum. Mr. and Mrs. Palgon took the opportunity to express their concerns about

---

3. *Darash Moshe* to *Shemos* 30:12.

The Tifereth Jerusalem dining room in the 1930s

their sons' future as faithful Jews. The *meshulach* had a solution: "On Motza'ei Shabbos, you and your sons will accompany me on the train to New York. I will arrange an appointment with a yeshivah."

Sunday morning, Mr. Palgon and his three sons were welcomed by the menahel of a yeshivah. After testing the boys in their studies, he gave their father the bad news: their Torah knowledge was well below par. The yeshivah could not service these boys.

Mr Palgon was devastated. Sadly, he told the boys that they would be heading back to Grand Central Station for the trip home.

However, the kindhearted *meshulach* was not ready to give up. "You came this far; let's try one more yeshivah."

An hour later, without making an appointment, they walked into Mesivtha Tifereth Jerusalem. As they entered the lobby, Reb Moshe was coming down the steps from the second floor. He greeted them and Mr. Palgon explained why they had come.

"Go upstairs to the office and register them," said Reb Moshe.

Mr. Palgon could not believe it. "Register them?" he replied. "But they have not been given a *farher* (examination)!"

"*Zei zenen gekumen lernen* (They came to learn [Torah])," Reb Moshe responded. "First register them, and then we will see which classes to place them in."

The three boys remained in the yeshivah through beis midrash. They raised families of *bnei Torah*; some of their offspring are *marbitzei Torah*. And all because Reb Moshe gave them a chance when others would not.

❦ ❦ ❦

Rabbi Shimon Jakubovic arrived in America as a teenager without his parents in the 1950s. Tifereth Jerusalem welcomed him to the yeshivah with open arms and the subject of tuition was never mentioned. Later, when Rabbi Jakubovic was married and teaching, he and his older brother, who was in the dairy business, found a small way to show Reb Moshe and his family *hakaras hatov*. Each year prior to Pesach, Reb David Feinstein's rebbetzin compiled a dairy order for the Feinstein family for the entire Yom Tov, which Rabbi Jakubovic would personally deliver.

Decades later when the Jakubovics settled in Lakewood, they organized an annual *melaveh malkah* for the benefit of Tifereth Jerusalem. When someone complained that the local *mosdos* should be given priority, Rabbi Jakubovic responded, "Is there an Orthodox Jew anywhere who was not affected by Reb Moshe? Everyone owes his yeshivah *hakaras hatov*." This argument prevailed; the *melaveh malkah* is still held each year and its attendance has grown.

Once, a couple who had children in Tifereth Jerusalem claimed that they could not pay tuition. The yeshivah investigated and determined that they certainly could afford it, but the parents refused to budge. Reb Moshe was asked whether or not the children should be allowed to remain in the yeshivah when the new school year would begin. "Certainly," was his reply. "The fact that the parents are strange people does not mean that the children have to suffer."

IN INSTRUCTING KOHANIM REGARDING THEIR UNIQUE RESPONSIBILITIES, THE Torah[4] uses a seemingly redundant term: first אֱמֹר, *say* [to the Kohanim],

Inspiring Love of Torah

and then וְאָמַרְתָּ, *and you shall say* [to them]. This redundancy, say *Chazal*, is to caution adults with regard to the young, that they too should follow these laws.[5]

Reb Moshe wondered where this is implied in the *pasuk*, for both אֱמֹר and וְאָמַרְתָּ refer to the adult Kohanim, not the children.

Reb Moshe offered a fundamental explanation:

---

4. *Vayikra* 21:1.
5. *Yevamos* 114a cited by *Rashi* ibid.

Conferring his berachah upon a boy soon to become a bar mitzvah

It seems that the Torah is cautioning regarding the chinuch of sons and daughters. It is meaningless to tell children that this is what they must do [regarding mitzvos] unless they see that the mitzvah is something precious to their parents.

If a child hears his father say, "It is a difficult test for us to observe Shabbos and Yom Tov, but we have no choice but to pass the test," this will not teach the children anything positive. The children might say, "Well, we do not have the spiritual resolve of our parents, and we find it hard to prevail over our yetzer hara."

A child must hear from his parents, "Keeping the mitzvos is not a test at all — Torah and mitzvos are our life, they are so very precious!" This is proper chinuch.[6]

The words אָמֹר and וְאָמַרְתָּ are both directed at adults. They must learn the laws of the mitzvos, and they must also learn to love the mitzvos. Then their children will love the mitzvos as well, and will be inspired to observe them in all their fine details.

In a famous speech, Reb Moshe noted the sad historical fact that in America in the early 1900s, children of many Orthodox Jewish immigrants left the path of Torah. Reb Moshe declared that a primary cause of this tragedy was the parents' attitude. Yes, the test of keeping Shabbos was

---

6. *Darash Moshe.*

a difficult one. Most businesses were closed Sunday but open on Saturday, and if a worker stayed home on Shabbos, he quite often received a "pink slip" on Sunday, which meant that he now had to look for a new job.

While some succumbed to this test and came to work on Shabbos, many did not. However, of those who refused to compromise their *shemiras Shabbos,* there were two distinct groups. Some would come home and say to their children, *"Oy, s'iz shver tzu zein a Yid* (Oh, it is hard to be Jewish), but what can we do? We are Jews, and Jews don't work on Shabbos." Children of such parents grew up with the

Delivering an address at a bar mitzvah celebration

feeling that Judaism is a burden; many of them, upon reaching adulthood, decided that they would rather not bear such a burden.

Then there were Jews who had a very different attitude. They would tell their children, "It is not easy to be fired every Sunday for keeping Shabbos and having to search for a new job. But do you know what? It is worth it! How fortunate we are to have the Torah and to keep the mitzvos. No money in the world can make me work on Shabbos. And Hashem will help so that we will have what we need."

Children of such parents grew up with a love and appreciation of mitzvos, and felt in their hearts that nothing would ever sway them from living a Torah life.

A well-known Orthodox leader recalls that he was a young teenager the first time he saw Reb Moshe. The Rosh Yeshivah was the guest speaker at a *siyum* in a small out-of-town shul. His *hadran* was beyond the listener's comprehension, but one part of the address made an indelible impression:

> People destroyed their children by always repeating *Es iz shver tzu zein a Yid* (It is hard to be a Jew). No — it is *not* hard to be a Jew. It is beautiful and joyous to be a Jew.

Testing talmidim at the Karlin-Stolin cheder in Jerusalem during his visit to Eretz Yisrael in 1964

Reb Moshe's face glowed with pride and happiness when he said those simple words, and the then-young listener recalls that he too became suffused with pride in his Jewishness.

Reb Moshe did his best to instill in his talmidim a true love for mitzvos, especially Torah study. Once, when addressing the high school of Tifereth Jerusalem, he said:

> "Moshe commanded the Torah unto us, an inheritance for the congregation of Yaakov."[7] What is the significance of the Torah being our inheritance?
>
> Imagine a bride purchasing a new set of candlesticks before her wedding. Certainly she will be happy, but this will not compare to the joy of a bride who inherited her beloved grandmother's candlesticks. Those are priceless to her; she would not trade them for any pair in the world.
>
> The Torah that we study is the very same one that Moshe transmitted to our people at Sinai. It is our inheritance!

A 13-year-old boy remarked that he could see Reb Moshe's deep love for Torah from the way he embraced and kissed a *sefer Torah* whenever it was carried in shul.

---

7. *Devarim* 33: 4.

Rabbi David Feinstein imbuing Tifereth Jerusalem's young talmidim with love of Torah

A former talmid recalled, "When I first attended the Rosh Yeshivah's *shiur,* I was too young to grasp it, but it was worth coming just to see the look on his face — his *ahavas haTorah,* his love in relating a Torah thought. When someone would interrupt with a question, the Rosh Yeshivah would explain himself again and again (if necessary). When the *bachur* would finally understand, the Rosh Yeshivah would smile — and sometimes even laugh — from joy!"

Rabbi Chaim Krinsky, who for many years was co-Rosh Kollel of Tifereth Jerusalem's Kollel L'Hora'ah, witnessed an incident more than half a century ago in which Reb Moshe's *ahavas haTorah* was plainly evident:

> One day, Reb Moshe entered the beis midrash carrying a new note-book to record his *chiddushim.* He had written in the notebook for around half an hour when he was called to the office to accept a phone call.[8] When Reb Moshe returned to his seat, he turned pale. He said, "Had I lost ten thousand dollars, it would not have been so great a loss." His new notebook had vanished.
>
> The talmidim immediately launched a search for the notebook. Someone noted that the notebook had disappeared during the elementary school's lunch hour. Children would sometimes wander into the beis midrash during this time. Perhaps a boy had noticed the shiny new notebook and taken it.

---

8. Later, a phone was installed in the beis midrash near Reb Moshe's seat.

The classrooms upstairs were searched, and the notebook was found. It contained around a page and a half of *chiddushim*. Reb Moshe's joy upon receiving it was indescribable.

WHEN HIS YOUNGER SON, REB REUVEN, WAS A YOUNG BOY, REB MOSHE WOULD spread out his child's clothing on the radiators in the early hours of cold

With His Own Children

winter mornings. Then he would dress his son under the covers before sending him off to yeshivah. Reb Reuven sees more than a father's concern in this act. "My father did not want me to dread getting out of a warm bed to study Torah. He wanted me to feel that Torah study was something to look forward to, not something that was a burden."[9]

Reb Reuven recalled another incident from his early youth.

> For a number of years, we had an icebox for perishable foods. Later, we had an old-fashioned refrigerator that ran on gas. One day, I came into the kitchen and found my father lying on the floor on his stomach, with paper spread beneath him so that he would not dirty his clothes. He was examining something underneath the refrigerator. My father motioned for me to come lie down next to him. He then explained to me that he was examining how the refrigerator worked in order to determine whether or not it could be opened on Shabbos. Being so young, I did not understand much. but I never forgot how my father made me feel like a partner in his investigation, until "we" decided that the device could be opened on Shabbos.
>
> With time, I came to understand that with all that he did, my father's goal was to instill within me *ahavas haTorah*, and that no aspect of mitzvah observance should ever detract from this love.

---

9. At a *kiddush* in Yeshivah Sh'or Yoshuv in the winter of 5747 (1986), Rabbi Shlomo Freifeld said:

"This week was a very rich week in a way. They came out with a new book about Reb Moshe Feinstein, *zt"l*. There's a story in there about how, on colder winter mornings, Reb Moshe would go and prepare his son's clothing for the next day by placing them next to the hot radiator, so that they would be nice and warm the next morning. He would then dress him in his bed.

"Very nice, right?"

"We have to understand the machinery behind that story — who did it? It was Reb Moshe, the '*Sar HaTorah, mamash,*' the complete master over the entire Torah. His whole life was a discipline in Torah and *avodah*. For him to have the consciousness to put those clothes on the radiator each night … he was concerned about the small things" (from *Reb Shlomo: The Life and Legacy of Rabbi Shlomo Freifeld* by Rabbi Yisroel Besser, published by Judaica Press).

With his son Reb Reuven

One summer, we vacationed near a cattle farm. My father learned with me each morning for a fixed amount of time, after which I would run off to play. One day, I said that something very exciting was to take place on the farm during the time when we normally learned. My father allowed me to take a break from my learning to go and watch, with the understanding that as soon as the event had ended, I would return to my studies. He felt that by not allowing me to go and watch, I might harbor a negative feeling toward the learning that "interfered" with my fun.[10]

One year, the Agudath Israel annual convention fell on the same Shabbos as the bar mitzvah of one of Reb Reuven's sons. As chairman of the Moetzes Gedolei HaTorah and the convention's keynote speaker, Reb Moshe could not miss the convention. It was decided that the bar mitzvah boy would be called to the Torah on Thursday at Tifereth Jerusalem, and following *Shacharis*, close family members would participate in a modest *seudas mitzvah*. The boy would be called up again on Shabbos and a *kiddush* would be held, but Reb Moshe would be at the convention at that time.

10. From an interview with Reb Reuven conducted by Rabbi Rafael Berlson, published in the Hebrew *Yated Ne'eman* and later in *Mipihem shel Rabboseinu*.

Years later when someone recalled this episode, Reb Reuven was asked, "Didn't you feel bad that your father did not participate in the Shabbos festivities?"

Reb Reuven replied, "Of course, everyone wants to have the bar mitzvah boy's grandparents at his *simchah*. But I was able to accept my father's absence with the knowledge that he loved me and he simply had no choice but to be away at that time." Reb Reuven cited the above episodes from his childhood as proof of his father's love.[11]

REB MOSHE'S CONDUCT WAS SO DOWN-TO-EARTH AND NATURAL THAT IT took some time for his children to realize that their father was someone very special. In Reb Reuven's words:

Seemingly Regular

As a child, I always looked at my father as a regular person. I assumed that this is how all fathers were. I played marbles next to his desk and that was perfectly fine with him.

He would take me to shul and on the way, we would pass a fence that was made of a row of metal bars. Every time I passed it, I needed to touch *every* single bar. If I missed one, I would go back and start all over again — as my father stood patiently waiting for me to finish. One day, a man said to me, "Reuven, it's not right to keep your father waiting." My father replied, "Leave him — he needs to play."

As I grew older, I began to realize that my father was someone special. Quite possibly, it had to do with the fact that my rebbeim would often say to me, "Ask your father what he holds about this."

When I came home from Telshe for Yom Tov at age 15, I told my father that I would like to begin addressing him in the third person. He was not happy about it. "It is not necessary," he responded. "True," I countered, "but a mitzvah it is, nonetheless." "I see that you mean it sincerely," he replied, "so I will accept it," meaning he was not altogether happy about it, but he would permit it.

As Reb Reuven approached his 20th birthday, Reb Moshe wrote him a letter of guidance along the path of life:

> … *Most important of all is the study of Torah and to toil in Torah … One needs to ponder well each [Torah] topic to arrive at its true meaning. Then Hashem Yisborach will help you to grow great in*

---

11. From *In the Footsteps of the Maggid* by Rabbi Paysach Krohn.

Torah and to know each topic with clarity — and this will lead you to practice [all the Torah's commandments correctly].

… Your whole goal in this world should be to toil in Torah all your days. Then, I am certain that Hashem will assist you and send you an abundance of material blessing, which is all a gift from Hashem …

You must also train yourself in the way of good middos, particularly with regard to anger, from which one must distance himself very much. For anger and arrogance are both traits from which one must stay far away. If you will have a strong will to train yourself in this area, Hashem will help you …[12]

There is no better way to teach than by example. How fortunate were the Feinstein children and the Tifereth Jerusalem talmidim to have had a role model who embodied every good quality one could hope to find in a human being.

But it was not only the talmidim of his yeshivah who looked to Reb Moshe as their rebbi, their guide for life. Every *ben Torah,* young and old, viewed him as such.

IN THE SUMMER OF 1982, A GROUP OF 13-YEAR-OLD YESHIVAH BOYS FROM CAMP Torah Vodaath (in Highland, New York), accompanied by their counselor,

The Visitors set out on a twenty-five-mile hike to Camp Staten Island, where they hoped to visit Reb Moshe. It was common knowledge that Reb Moshe was not well and was allowed few visitors. The group did not call the camp in advance of their journey, but instead hoped that when they would arrive there and tell of the sacrifice they had made in coming, they would be permitted to see him.

It was a hot, sunny day, and by mid-afternoon the group — which had set out very early in the morning — had covered only thirteen miles. The counselor feared that some of the boys could not continue for much longer. Not about to see their efforts wasted, he hired taxis to take the group the rest of the way.

When they arrived at Camp Staten Island, the story of their journey was related to the grandson who was attending Reb Moshe. Though Reb Moshe was officially not seeing anyone that day, his grandson did not have the heart to disappoint the weary campers. He asked them to wait in front of the bungalow's screened porch, where he would bring Reb Moshe. In this way the boys would at least get a chance to see him.

---

12. *Igros Moshe, Yoreh De'ah III,* #96.

With Rebbetzin Feinstein at their bungalow in Camp Staten Island

When Reb Moshe heard what they had gone through to come, he exclaimed, "Such *mesiras nefesh!*" Before he could say more, his Rebbetzin entered and, upon hearing of the boys' self-sacrifice, suggested that her grandson bring them to the back door of the bungalow where Reb Moshe would greet them individually. He shook each boy's hand, asked him his name, and gave his blessing. He then instructed his grandson to get food for them from the camp's dining room and make sure that they went for a swim before returning home — by car! Reb Moshe then wished the boys well, and told them not to undertake such an arduous trip ever again.

> Rabbi Yisroel Belsky recalled an incident that illustrates the special love which all *bnei Torah* felt for Reb Moshe. One summer, a meeting of rabbanim at which Reb Moshe would be presiding was to take place in Camp Agudah. As the time for Reb Moshe's arrival approached, the entire camp lined the path to the entrance of the camp grounds. It began to rain. Everyone ran to their rooms, got umbrellas, and returned to their places to wait. They were not aware that Reb Moshe's driver had made a wrong turn. He arrived one and

half hours late. Yet, no one moved from his place, despite the steady rain, until the beloved *gadol hador* had arrived.[13]

THE ABOVE ANECDOTES ILLUSTRATE THE FEELING THAT *ALL* STUDENTS OF Torah, young and old alike, had for Reb Moshe. However great the physi-

Everyone's Father

cal distance may have been between them, Reb Moshe was still *their* guide, *their* rosh yeshivah, *their* rebbi. This was indicative of Reb Moshe's status as *gadol hador* and the "father of all yeshivos."

Torah students understood that when they had the privilege of being with him, they were in the presence of a spiritual grandeur that gave light to Jews everywhere. It was this understanding that influenced scores of yeshivah students in the New York area to rise early every so often and take the subway to East Broadway for a chance to observe Reb Moshe as he *davened*, and perhaps even shake his hand and receive his blessing. It influenced elementary-school rebbeim to schedule buses to take their classes to Tifereth Jerusalem. It influenced hundreds of yeshivah students to press against police lines a few months before Reb Moshe's passing, in an attempt to catch a glimpse of him as he attended the wedding of a grandson.

Listening to the mishnayos recitation of a Pirchei Agudath Israel national contest winner.

---

13. Rabbi Belsky recalled that a large crowd of *bnei Torah* stood at night in the rain to attend the funeral of Rebbetzin Feinstein, in keeping with the teaching that אֵשֶׁת חָבֵר כְּחָבֵר.

Speaking to bnei Torah in Jerusalem during his visit in 1964

For his part, Reb Moshe was exuberant whenever he heard of a new undertaking for the spreading of Torah and he rejoiced whenever being introduced to a Torah student. Once, when he was forced to reprimand a yeshivah student for a gross misdeed, Reb Moshe exclaimed, "I have a headache from chastising a student of Torah! It had to be done, but it does my health no good."

How Torah students the world over prayed, in the last two years of Reb Moshe's life, that his failing health be preserved. How they hoped that he would lead them in greeting *Mashiach*.

The *Ribono shel Olam* willed it otherwise.

Following Reb Moshe's passing, a student of a prominent American yeshivah told his father, "Since I was old enough to go to funerals of *gedolim*, I would hear speakers say that now we are like orphans. But I never felt like an orphan because I knew that Reb Moshe was still here. Now I am an orphan."

They both cried.

CHAPTER FIVE

Keys to Torah Greatness

IN 1947, REB MOSHE PUBLISHED THE FIRST OF HIS MANY WORKS — *Dibros Moshe* to *Masechta Bava Kamma.*[1] Rabbi Chaim Shmulevitz, legendary Rosh Yeshivah of Mirrer Yeshivah in Jerusalem,

Genius Recognized

examined its contents carefully and then told his talmidim, "A fabulous *gaon* has written this *sefer.* I was able to go through his questions. But his answers and expositions? They are so lengthy, it is incredible to what depths he has gone. He is truly among the *geonim* of this generation." Reb Chaim suggested to his talmidim that in studying a given topic in Gemara, they examine all of Reb Moshe's questions and observations on the subject, and then seek to find answers on their own.

Rabbi Nochum Partzovitz, a son-in-law of Reb Chaim and a *gaon* in his own right, added the following: "I met Reb Moshe when I was in

---

1. Reb Moshe viewed the publishing of one's Torah thoughts as a sacred obligation. In the preface to the first volume of *Dibros Moshe* he writes, "The benefit of publishing that which *Hashem Yisborach* has helped me to understand [in the words of our Sages] through much toil and effort ... is obvious ... It seems to me that one who has the ability to publish his *chiddushim* and does not has not fulfilled the mitzvah of teaching Torah to others in its fullest sense ..."

Rabbi Chaim Shmulevitz   Rabbi Nochum Partzovitz

America. He is much more than a *gaon* in learning. He is a *gaon* in *Bavli*, *Yerushalmi*, *Halachah*, *Aggadah*, *drush*, *chesed*, *tzidkus* … He is of a type that we simply do not find today, an אִישׁ מוּשְׁלָם (a complete and consistent person)."

> Rabbi Aharon Kotler is said to have commented after studying *Dibros Moshe* to *Bava Kamma* that every meaningful opinion and concept on the tractate is contained in the *sefer*.

"Reb Moshe was sent down from *Shamayim* to show us the greatness of *gedolim* of previous generations," Rabbi Shlomo Zalman Auerbach told Rabbi Simcha Bunim Cohen. And then he added, "Do you know anyone else who can author a *Dibros Moshe*?" When Rabbi Cohen described how Reb Moshe also found the time to attend everyone's wedding and lend an ear to every unfortunate soul, Reb Shlomo Zalman began to weep.

In his *hesped* of Reb Moshe, his illustrious nephew Rabbi Yechiel Michel Feinstein said:

> My uncle's greatness in Torah and *geonus* was of a different generation. While it is not for us to draw comparisons, in a certain sense, his method of learning and broad range of knowledge was of a kind that was seen in earlier generations in the days of Hagaon Rav Akiva Eiger

and the Chasam Sofer. This greatness can clearly be seen in his multi-volume *Dibros Moshe*.

Among great Torah scholars we find roshei yeshivah who give forth a wellspring of *chiddushei Torah* and clarification of *sugyos* in specific *masechtos*. We also find *poskim* who are well versed in the laws of *Shulchan Aruch* and can render judgment in *dinei Torah*. One scholar possesses that which the other does not.

My uncle was unique in that his knowledge was all-inclusive. He learned *kol haTorah kulah* (the Torah in its entirety) and knew it all. He was an expert in *Tanach*, fluent in the Six

With his nephew, Rabbi Yechiel Michel Feinstein, upon Reb Moshe's arrival in Eretz Yisrael for the Knessiah Gedolah in 1964

Orders of *Mishnah*, his entire life he was learning and reviewing *Bavli*, *Yerushalmi*, *poskim*, *Tosefta*, etc. His range of knowledge was of a different sort entirely, different than what we are accustomed to in our generation. It is not an exaggeration at all to say that his style of learning was more akin to that of the generation of Rav Akiva Eiger and the Chasam Sofer. The wide range of knowledge of the scholars of that generation was of a different kind; they studied all of Torah and they knew it. And this was how my uncle, zt"l, studied Torah.

REB MOSHE'S LEVEL OF TORAH GREATNESS CANNOT BE ACCURATELY described, for we cannot begin to fathom it. He knew all of *Shas* and

Phenomenal Memory

Shulchan Aruch along with many of their commentaries virtually verbatim, and had a flawless command of scores of other works, spanning the many centuries of *Rishonim* and *Acharonim*.

Once during a halachic discussion among rabbanim, Reb Moshe voiced his opinion. A young rav responded, "But the *Shach* says differently," and he proceeded to quote what he thought was the *Shach's* opinion. Reb Moshe did not respond and instead reiterated his *psak*. After the rav quoted the *Shach* a second and then a third time, Reb Moshe said, "This

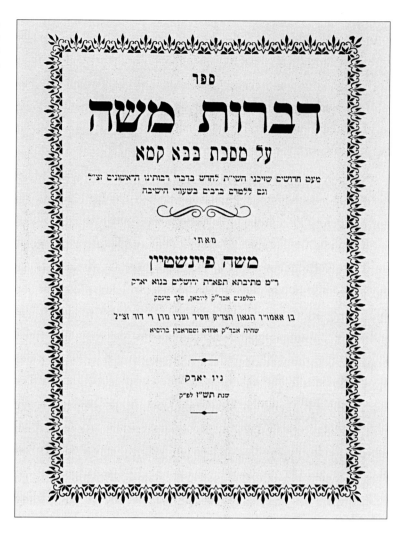

ספר

דברות משה

על מסכת בבא קמא

מעט חדושים שזכני השי"ת לחדש בדברי רבותינו הראשונים זצ"ל
וגם ללמדם ברבים בשעורי הישיבה

מאתי

משה פיינשטיין

ר"מ מתיבתא תפארת ירושלים בנוא יארק

וֶמלפנים אבד"ק לוּבאן, פלך מינסק

בן אאמו"ר הגאון הצדיק חסיד ועניו מרן ר' דוד זצ"ל
שהיה אבד"ק אוזדא וסטאראבין ברוסיא

ניו יארק

שנת תש"ז לפ"ק

is what the *Shach* says," and he proceeded to quote the lengthy *Shach* verbatim. The rav had misquoted it.

That he had been blessed with a phenomenal memory was also obvious from incidents unrelated to his learning.

Once, a *sofer* called to say that while checking a parchment of *tefillin*, he had inadvertently made a tiny hole in it. The parchment was still kosher, but the *sofer* wanted to know if he owed money for the damage. Three years later, this *sofer* called to ask whether or not a tiny drop of ink that had splashed on a *tefillin* parchment had rendered it invalid. Reb Moshe ruled that the parchment was valid but added, "This is the second time a mishap has occurred while you were inspecting *tefillin*. You need to be more careful."

Torah was Reb Moshe's lifelong pursuit, but he was always available for those who needed him.

Once, he learned that a 15-year-old student of his yeshivah had criticized someone else and in doing so had deeply wounded that person's feelings. Reb Moshe knew that while the boy had committed a wrong, his intention had been to correct what *he* thought was an error. Reb Moshe judged the boy too young to understand his mistake and therefore let the matter rest — for the time being.

Twelve years later, Reb Moshe was alone in a car with this young man, who was now 27. "You know," Reb Moshe began, "some years ago you made a certain remark …" He reminded the young man of the incident before beginning his gentle reproof.

☙ ☙ ☙

Whenever he was introduced to a yeshivah student, Reb Moshe would ask where the boy was studying. To one student he remarked that some ten years earlier, the boy's rosh yeshivah had enlightened him with an excellent interpretation of a comment by *Rashi*. Surely, he intended also to elevate that rosh yeshivah's stature in the eyes of his student.

To appreciate how amazing such incidents are, one must bear in mind that, in the words of one of Reb Moshe's closest associates, "The Rosh Yeshivah was the busiest man in the world." Countless numbers of people came to him each year in search of his halachic expertise, blessings, counsel, and comfort. Yet Reb Moshe did not forget anything or anyone.

THE THOROUGHNESS OF HIS KNOWLEDGE WAS PHENOMENAL. THE LATE Rabbi Shmuel Berenbaum, revered Rosh Yeshivah of Mirrer Yeshivah in

All-Encompassing
Brooklyn, once discussed with Reb Moshe a complex *sugya* in *Eizehu Neshech,* one of the most difficult chapters in *Shas.* Reb Shmuel presented a list of questions and Reb Moshe resolved them all, demonstrating a mastery of the topic down to its fine details. Reb Shmuel was amazed when in the course of conversation it emerged that it had been more than eight years since Reb Moshe had studied the chapter thoroughly.

On another occasion, Rabbi Moshe Baruch Newman accompanied Reb Shmuel to Reb Moshe's apartment, where the Mirrer Rosh Yeshivah raised a number of points in a difficult *sugya* in *Masechta Bava Kamma.* When they left the apartment, Reb Shmuel exclaimed, "סְ׳אִיז נוֹרָאוֹת׳דִיג" (It is awesome!) One can speak with Reb Moshe on any topic in *Shas* and he is fluent in all its fine details."

Reb Shmuel felt bound to Reb Moshe with bonds of *ahavas haTorah,* and would refer to him as "the *gadol hador*" and "*posek acharon.*" Often in his *shmuessen,* Reb Shmuel would use Reb Moshe as an example of "an *adam gadol.*"

> In the last weeks of his life, when he was suffering greatly from his illness, Reb Shmuel commented that he hoped that in the merit of his suffering, he would be permitted to "speak in learning" in the Next World with Reb Moshe and with the Ponevezher Rosh Yeshivah, Rabbi Elazar Menachem Shach.[2]

A group of senior yeshivah students was delving into a certain halachic subject. Slowly and deliberately, they studied the halachah as it is developed in the original sources, *Shulchan Aruch* and its commentaries. Finally, they opened the *Igros Moshe* and examined a *teshuvah* relevant to the topic. It seemed that Reb Moshe's opinion contradicted that of the *Pri Megadim* (a classic commentary to *Shulchan Aruch*). The students brought the question to their rosh yeshivah — and he was as surprised as they were. There was only one thing to do, he told the students. Soon, one of the yeshivah's scholars was on his way to East Broadway.

Reb Moshe welcomed the student and asked what had prompted him to come. The young man, pointing to the particular *teshuvah* in *Igros Moshe,*

---

2. See *Sefer Kisrah shel Torah* on the life of Rav Shmuel Berenbaum by his grandson, Rabbi Yosef Simcha Klein. Reb Moshe once referred to Reb Shmuel as "a *yungerman vas ken Shas* (a young man who knows *Shas*)."

With Rabbi Shmuel Berenbaum

said that he had found an apparent difficulty in it. Reb Moshe did not need to familiarize himself with the *teshuvah,* one of the thousands he had written on subjects that cover the entire range of Jewish law. Nor did he wait to hear the student's question. "Yes,'" came the instant reply, "it seems to contradict the *Pri Megadim.* However, there is really no contradiction at all, for ..."

Two outstanding talmidim of Tifereth Jerusalem spent days trying to unravel a difficult comment of *Kesef Mishneh* in *Hilchos Nizkei Mamon.* Finally, they went to ask the Rosh Yeshivah to shed some light on the matter. No sooner had one of them pointed to the comment than Reb Moshe said, "Yes, and the difficulty can be explained as follows ..."

> Some years ago, two *talmidei chachamim* found a number of difficulties with a *teshuvah* written by Reb Moshe some thirty years earlier on a complex Talmudic subject. The two were anxious to confront Reb Moshe with their questions, but first they spent days researching and studying all related material. When they finally felt very well prepared, they went to the beis midrash of Tifereth Jerusalem following *Shacharis,* as Reb Moshe was folding his *tallis.*
>
> He listened patiently to their arguments and then quickly refuted every one of them. Stunned, the two thanked Reb Moshe and turned to leave. As they walked toward the exit of the beis midrash, one

was overheard remarking to the other, "A *gaon* of *geonim;* the entire Torah is at his fingertips ..."

Those who were privileged to observe Reb Moshe as he put a *teshuvah* in writing were amazed to see him cite source upon source while rarely referring to a *sefer.* On the other hand, he took no question lightly. As the Sages teach, it makes no difference whether a question involves a penny or a huge fortune; the Torah must be interpreted accurately because it is the word of Hashem.

Reb Moshe's amazing power of reasoning and analysis is plainly apparent in his many volumes of *Dibros Moshe* on Gemara and *Igros Moshe* on Halachah. His longtime friend and neighbor, Rabbi Tuvia Goldstein, who was himself known as a *posek,* commented that we find various authors of the Mishnah and Talmud praised for the characteristic in which they were most outstanding. Rabbi Elazar ben Hyrkanos retained all that he learned, while Rabbi Elazar ben Arach was known for his sharpness of mind and power of understanding;[3] Rav Yosef was called *Sinai* because of his wide-ranging knowledge, while his contemporary Rabbah was called *Oker Harim* (the Uprooter of Mountains) because of his penetrating analysis.[4]

"What can we say," asked Reb Tuvia, "of someone who is most outstanding in both his breadth *and* depth of Torah knowledge? Such a person comes along but once in a generation. This was Reb Moshe."

> As Rabbi David Feinstein put it: "My father's greatness was not simply that he remembered all of the Torah, but that he could apply any relevant thing he ever learned all his life to any question that ever came to him."

NATURAL BRILLIANCE DOES NOT MAKE ONE INTO A *GADOL B'YISRAEL.* Conversely, many *gedolim* were born with average intelligence. Rather than

The Fruits of Diligence dwell on Reb Moshe's inborn genius and extraordinary memory, it is important for us to analyze his attainment of greatness and see how it applies to ordinary people.

Reb Moshe used to say that one can retain what he has learned even without the benefit of a very good memory. When a person views an unusual event, he can often recall it years later with perfect clarity. It does not take a good memory for one to remember something that made a deep

---

3. *Avos* 2:11.
4. *Berachos* 64a.

impression on him. Similarly, one who appreciates the inestimable value of Torah and savors every new Torah thought and teaching as priceless will find it possible to recall what he has learned. As the Chasam Sofer, a great Moshe of a previous era, used to say, "It is not that I have such a good memory. I invested so much time and hard work in mastering a Torah topic that it is a shame to forget it."

With Rabbi Avigdor Miller

We may venture to say that Reb Moshe's deep love for Torah, and his recognition that life had no meaning without it, were important factors in his ability to recall what he had learned with the freshness of one who had studied it that very day.

A yeshivah student who was very close to Reb Moshe once asked him directly how he had become so great in Torah. Realizing that the questioner was sincere, Reb Moshe suppressed his deep humility and gave the boy an honest answer. "Of course, one is fortunate to be blessed with a good head, but hard work and *hasmadah* (diligence) are crucial to success in Torah."

A father once brought his young son to Reb Moshe for a blessing. The father said proudly, "My son learns very well. In fact, his rebbi says that if he continues along this path he will grow up to become another Rabbi Moshe Feinstein!"

Reb Moshe responded sincerely, "I hope he will be even greater than I, but I must tell you that success in Torah does not come easily. The main thing is to love learning, work very hard, and not waste a minute."

In the 1950s, Reb Moshe and the legendary Rabbi Avigdor Miller spent their summer vacation in the same bungalow colony.[5] The bungalows were not equipped with phones; the only way to place or receive a call was via

---

5. In one of his famous Thursday-night lectures, Rabbi Miller said of Reb Moshe, "I *love* that man!"

the public pay phone. Thus, Reb Moshe's learning was not interrupted by frequent phone calls as was the case in the city. Rabbi Miller's illustrious son, Rabbi Shmuel Miller, recalls watching Reb Moshe learning uninterrupted for hours on end, which left a great impression on him.

AFTER REB MOSHE'S HEART ATTACK IN THE LATE 1970S, RABBI SIMCHA BUNIM Cohen was asked to sleep in the Feinsteins' apartment for one night. At **A Toraholic** 3:00 a.m., he heard voices in the bedroom. Reb Moshe wanted to get up for the day, while his rebbetzin wanted him to sleep longer. Reb Moshe stayed in bed a bit more; at 3:40, he was ready to begin writing his comments to *Masechta Gittin*.[6] Later, the Rebbetzin asked Rabbi Cohen if he had heard their conversation. When he replied affirmatively, she said, "Sometimes, I tell my husband: 'Rabbi Feinstein, you have already learned so much — you can rest a bit.' But he is like a drunkard with his liquor. A drunkard is always thirsty for another drink; my husband always wants more Torah."

The late Telshe Rosh Yeshivah, Rabbi Mordechai Gifter, observed that Reb Moshe was always "in the middle of learning." Even when he was engaged in some other activity, it was only a temporary interruption of his studies; Torah was his love, his comfort, his ambition. Whenever there was a half-minute to spare he would be glancing at his *sefer*. While he put away his *tefillin*, as he walked in the street, or sat at a wedding waiting for the *chupah* to begin, whenever he was involved in light activity, he was reciting *mishnayos* by heart. He was always adding to his thousands upon thousands of pages of writings.

With Rabbi Mordechai Gifter

Rav Gifter recalled arriving early for a meeting at Reb Moshe's home. While he and Reb Moshe waited for the other

6. Reb Moshe felt bad seeing that Rabbi Cohen was up for the day, for he assumed that he and his rebbetzin had woken him. Rabbi Cohen replied, "I am so excited at the thought of being able to look at the Rosh Yeshivah's *kesavim* (writings) that I find it hard to sleep."

participants, they both sat and studied. The Rebbetzin asked Reb Moshe to come eat lunch before the meeting began. He got up from the table without closing his gemara, although one should do so when he stops learning. He explained to Rav Gifter that he was not required to close his gemara because he would be returning to it the instant his meal was over, so he still had the status of being engaged in his studies.

Once, a granddaughter and her husband came to visit him and found him learning in his study, his back to the door. Not wanting to disturb him, the couple stood silently in the doorway, waiting for Reb Moshe to pause in his studies. Some time passed and Reb Moshe remained immersed in his learning. When the Rebbetzin came by and observed the scene she exclaimed, "If you are waiting for him to stop learning, you will be standing here all day!" Hearing this, Reb Moshe turned around to his grandchildren and said laughingly, "How I wish that you should never find me sitting idle."

Every Second Counts

ANYONE WHO WAS PRESENT AT TIFERETH JERUSALEM FOR *KRIAS HATORAH* was witness to an unforgettable lesson in how to utilize every available moment for Torah study. Until he reached his late 80s, Reb Moshe's procedure during the Torah reading was to study *mishnayos* until the first *oleh* would begin to recite the opening blessing, then rush to stand near the *bimah* and listen to the reading while a child held a *Chumash* for him, then rush back to his seat at the conclusion of the *aliyah* to resume his Mishnah study until the next blessing.[7]

Once, when Reb Moshe was called to the Torah reading, a talmid brought his volume of Mishnah to the *bimah*, so that he could study it between *aliyos*. Someone told the talmid that he was taking things too far and in the future should allow Reb Moshe to stand at the *bimah* without a *sefer*, like everyone else who was called to the Torah reading. When the talmid asked Reb Moshe about this, he was told to continue bringing the *sefer* to the *bimah*. No matter where one found himself, time was too precious to waste.

No one knows how many times Reb Moshe reviewed the Six Orders of the Mishnah, but that he knew them fluently was obvious. Once,

---

7. Someone asked Reb Moshe why he learned *mishnayos* every day. He replied, "*Mishnayos* is the foundation of *Torah she'b'al peh*. And I should not learn it every day?"

Listening to the Torah reading

while driving Reb Moshe to a wedding, Rabbi Yitzchak Frankel mentioned that while there is a *Masechta Megillah*, which focuses mainly on the Yom Tov of Purim, there is no such *masechta* on Chanukah. Reb Moshe responded, "But Chanukah is mentioned a number of times in *mishnayos*." He then began to turn his face back and forth from right to left, as if he were scanning the pages of a *sefer*, and announced, "There is mention of Chanukah in the sixth *perek* of *Bava Kamma*, and in …"

For most of his life, Reb Moshe slept between five and six hours a night, and took a short nap in the afternoon. As a student in Yeshivah of Staten Island, Rabbi Moshe Meir Weiss was privileged to attend to Reb Moshe for some time and once observed him arising from a nap. As Reb Moshe opened his eyes, he instinctively reached for a small *Tanach* that he took with him almost everywhere he went. He arose and then, carrying the *Tanach*, made his way to the sink that was in the room. He rested the *Tanach* on the sink's edge while opening the faucet and reaching for a washing cup. As he filled the cup with one hand, his other hand turned the pages of the *sefer* until he found the proper place. After washing his hands and face, he began — or rather resumed — learning without a moment's delay.

At *shalosh seudos* in Tifereth Jerusalem, Reb Moshe would recite the *Hamotzi* blessing, eat a small amount and then recite *Tehillim* until it was time for him to deliver his talk on the weekly *parashah*.[8] Once, some men interrupted the *shalosh seudos* to pose some questions relating to the death of a local beggar who had passed away that day. In between questions, when the questioner paused for a few seconds to recall his next question, Reb Moshe resumed his recital of *Tehillim*. A few seconds could not go to waste.

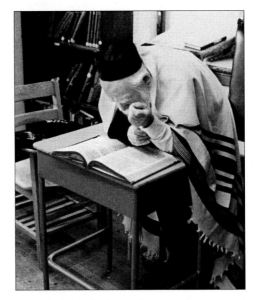

It was Reb Moshe's practice to review mishnayos as he wound his tefillin and put away his tallis at the conclusion of Shacharis.

IN THE EARLY 1970S, THREE *YESHIVAH BACHURIM* SHARED A CAR TO THE AGUDAH Convention with Reb Moshe, his brother-in-law Rabbi Isaac Small and

A Ride to Remember

Rabbi Moshe Rivlin, who served both Tifereth Jerusalem and Reb Moshe personally with great devotion. A *bachur* drove, his friend sat in the middle and Reb Moshe sat next to the window.

Rabbi Rivlin, who was seated directly behind Reb Moshe, had on his lap a *Chumash, Tehillim* and one or two other *sefarim*. As soon as they were comfortably seated, Rabbi Rivlin handed the first *sefer* to Reb Moshe. When Reb Moshe had finished using it and returned it, Rabbi Rivlin handed him the second *sefer*... This is how it went until Reb Moshe had completed his daily regimens in each of these *sefarim*. In the midst of all this, the driver had turned around to Rav Rivlin and asked if he could wipe the vapor off the window next to Reb Moshe so that he could see the right mirror. Without taking his eyes off the *sefer* which he was holding in his left hand, Reb Moshe wiped the window clean with his right hand.

After closing the last *sefer*, Reb Moshe asked, "Rav Rivlin, *vas iz nei'as* (What's new)?" Rav Rivlin withdrew some newspaper clippings containing current events and proceeded to read the headlines to Reb Moshe. When

---

8. He recited *Tehillim* as the others present ate and sang *zemiros*.

At a gathering in Los Angeles (left to right): Rabbi Yehudah Isaacson,
Rabbi Simcha Wasserman, Rabbi Usher Zilberstein, Reb Moshe, Rabbi Moshe Rivlin

that was finished, the *bachurim* asked if they could present their questions to Reb Moshe in Gemara and Halachah, and that is how they spent the remainder of that unforgettable trip.

HIS GRANDSON, RABBI YOSAIF ASHER WEISS, COMMENTED, "WHEN HE WOULD come to the yeshivah [of Staten Island] before *Shacharis*, you could see

Never Enough Time

that he had his time mapped out, minute by minute. Not a moment would go to waste."

Reb Moshe once remarked, "In America I have heard people say, 'I have plenty of time!' I wish they could give me some of that time — I never have enough of it!"

To talmidim, a daily reminder of Reb Moshe's love of Torah and value of time was watching him rush to his seat in the beis midrash with the zeal of a child who was rushing to claim a much-cherished prize.

In explaining the proper attitude a student of Torah should have towards learning, Reb Moshe would offer a *mashal*:

Someone is sitting in the beis midrash and has before him a long and potentially difficult *Tosafos*. He is expecting a phone call at the yeshivah pay phone in five minutes. It would be impossible for him to complete this *Tosafos* in five minutes, so he closes his Gemara five minutes early and heads for the phone to await his call.

Someone who is truly devoted to Torah study, said Reb Moshe, would never do this. He understands that it is worthwhile to start the *Tosafos* now, even if he will have to begin it anew after the phone call. He also knows that there is a possibility the caller will be late and he *will* have ample time to complete the *Tosafos*.

True dedication to Torah means developing an attitude that the greatness of Torah study does not allow for even a moment to be

Addressing an assembly. Seated at left are the Rebbes of Boyan and Bluzhev.

wasted. It also means making a commitment that one's fixed learning sessions are sacred; except for extenuating circumstances, nothing should be allowed to interrupt one's *limud haTorah*.

Reb Moshe would say that he merited two miracles on a regular basis: He always fell asleep immediately no matter how weighty the problems he had dealt with that day; and he never fell asleep while learning no matter how little he had slept the previous night. Perhaps this was a reward for his lifelong commitment of not letting a moment go to waste.

THOUGH HIS MEMORY WAS INFALLIBLE, REB MOSHE DID NOT CEASE TO REVIEW all that he had mastered. He once remarked that many geniuses had fallen

Maximum Effort
far short of their potential in Torah study, for they were satisfied with having amassed more knowledge than most others and therefore made no effort to gain the maximum benefit from their G-d-given abilities. Reb Moshe was most certainly not this type of genius, for he used *every* bit of his mental and physical ability to its utmost.

It was *hasmadah* (diligence in study) and not brilliance that he valued more than anything. Once, he asked an older talmid to suggest a certain *bachur* as a *shidduch* possibility for the daughter of a distinguished *talmid chacham*. The talmid questioned whether the match was what the girl's father was seeking. "I know the *bachur*,"

Reb Moshe learning outdoors lost in thought

he said, "and he is not a *lamdan* (proficent in analytical Talmudic reasoning)."

Reb Moshe was visibly upset by this remark and rebuked his talmid. "How does one speak this way about a *bachur* who studies day and night...?" He repeated these words two or three times; the talmid carried out his mission.[9]

The time Reb Moshe devoted to study was outstanding as much for its quality as for its quantity. At the wedding of a son of Rav Mordechai Gifter, Reb Moshe got up to leave at 11:00 p.m., before the end of the meal. He apologized to Rav Gifter, explaining that he had to sleep a few hours because it was his practice to get up at 4:00 a.m. to learn for three hours before *Shacharis*. Only then, he said, was he able to study without interruption and achieve the maximum benefit from the time.

He would frequently cite the Vilna Gaon's teaching that Torah study without proper toil is equivalent to wasted time. "Praiseworthy is he whose *toil* is in Torah"[10] — only when one studies Torah with proper effort and concentration, using his G-d-given abilities to the fullest, has he performed this greatest of mitzvos properly.

During the Second World War, a number of great *talmidei chachamim* spent their summer vacation in Sea Gate. Among them were

---

9. From *Meged Givos Olam*.
10. *Berachos* 17a.

Rabbi Shlomo Heiman, Rabbi Yitzchak Hutner, Rabbi Dovid Bender,
and Reb Moshe.

One afternoon, Reb Moshe and Rav Shlomo Heiman sat for a
while "talking in learning." When their discussion concluded and Reb
Moshe left, Reb Shlomo turned to Rav Dovid Bender and said, "Do
you know why Reb Moshe is becoming a *gadol hador*? Because his
back never touches the back of his chair while he learns!"[11] To Reb
Shlomo, Reb Moshe's posture was indicative of greatness. He never
leaned back to relax as he learned. He always leaned forward, his
brow furrowed, straining to uncover the true meaning of the Torah's
holy words.

Decades later, Rabbi Binyomin Kamenetsky accompanied his father,
Reb Yaakov, to a meeting of senior roshei yeshivah where an important
topic was to be discussed. Reb Moshe expressed his opinion on the matter, as did others. When everyone else had spoken, Reb Yaakov rose and
explained why Reb Moshe's opinion was the correct one and should be
unanimously accepted. "The Rosh Yeshivah meant to say that ..." and he
continued to refer to Reb Moshe as "the Rosh Yeshivah" as he explained
and endorsed Reb Moshe's viewpoint.

On the way home, Reb Binyomin asked his father why he had repeat-

11. From *A Tale of Two Worlds — Rabbi Dovid Bender and Rebbetzin Basya Bender* by
Devorah Gliksman, published by ArtScroll/Mesorah.

*With
Rabbi Yaakov
Kamenetsky*

edly referred to Reb Moshe as "the Rosh Yeshivah" and not by name,
when there were other great roshei yeshivah present.

To Reb Yaakov the answer was simple. "Have you ever seen Reb Moshe
lean back in a chair?"

🦋 🦋 🦋

In *Darash Moshe,* Reb Moshe focuses on Moshe Rabbeinu's appointment of judges to assist him with the many cases that were brought to him
for adjudication. At the end of his life, Moshe reprimands *Bnei Yisrael* for
agreeing to this suggestion: *"You should have responded: 'Our teacher,
Moshe! From whom is it more appropriate to learn, from you or from
your students? Is it not better to learn from you, for you suffered over the
Torah!"*[12]

Reb Moshe poses an obvious question. Would it not have been even
better for *Bnei Yisrael* to have responded, "We want to learn from our
teacher, Moshe, for it is better to learn from the teacher himself than from
his students!" Why the stress on Moshe's "suffering over the Torah"? Reb
Moshe explained:

> *This serves to illustrate who is the quintessential rebbi from whom one
> needs to learn. He is the one who endured much suffering to know*

---

12. Rashi to *Devarim* 1:14.

every law with absolute clarity in the way that Hashem commanded in His Torah. He is the one who does not rely on his knowledge and wisdom, though he is very great; rather, he toils and expends great effort to ascertain the truth. Though he is blessed with great natural abilities and an outstanding memory, he never accepts what appears to be correct at first glance. Instead, he toils tremendously to know the truth.[13]

Fitting words for someone who never relied on his natural brilliance, but toiled relentlessly to plumb the full meaning of every word of Torah.

In the *battei midrash* of Mesivtha Tifereth Jerusalem and Yeshivah of Staten Island, talmidim study at desks or tables as opposed to the high *shtenders* (lecterns) found in many other yeshivos. It was Reb Moshe's feeling that *shtenders,* which a student can easily pull toward his chair as he leans back, can breed lethargy and hinder proper toil in Torah study.

Reb Moshe would encourage *chavrusos* (study partners) to toil equally, reading together, explaining the *Gemara* to one another, sharing in each other's insights, rather than have one student listening silently while the other reads the Gemara aloud. Difficulties should be written down for future reference; most will in all probability be resolved as the Gemara becomes clearer and its meaning begins to take form. With proper toil, success is inevitable.

While Reb Moshe stressed toil as a vital ingredient in learning, he also felt it important that Torah be studied in comfort, not to be confused with leisure. His approach is best demonstrated by his custom of studying outdoors in the summertime in his shirtsleeves, hunched forward in intense concentration — toil without discomfort.

REB MOSHE'S SELF-DISCIPLINE WAS ANOTHER FACTOR IN HIS GREATNESS. HE was an exceptionally well-organized person. His day was governed by a

Internal Clock

carefully arranged schedule that usually began at 4:00 a.m. and ended at around 11:00 p.m. He did not wear a watch and did not use an alarm clock, but somehow never overslept and was always on time for *tefillah.*

Someone close to Reb Moshe recalled that when they would be away from home together, he would sometimes say, "I'm going to nap now for half an hour." He would then lie down, without asking to be awakened. Without fail, he was always up half an hour later.

---

13. *Darash Moshe,* Vol. II, *Parashas Devarim.*

He would arise on Friday morning at 2:00 a.m. to prepare for his weekly *pilpul shiur*. Somehow his body knew that once a week it had to manage on less sleep.[14]

THE AVERAGE PERSON FINDS IT DIFFICULT TO RID HIS MIND OF PROBLEMS AND other thorny issues. Reb Moshe learned to become an absolute master

Concentration

over his thought process. He possessed an incredible power of concentration. Once, immediately after his Friday-morning *shiur*, he turned to Rabbi Elimelech Bluth, his talmid of many years, and said, *"Es tut mir vei di tzein* (My teeth are hurting)."* Rabbi Bluth took him to the dentist, who found that he had an abscessed tooth. The pain was excruciating, but one would never have known from watching Reb Moshe during the *shiur*.[15]

> Neither a loud noise, a bang on the table, or anything else could startle him. Often, he would look up to see if someone needed him — he could even hear a footstep on a carpeted floor — but always calmly. While he took to heart the suffering of others to the point that their pain was his pain, this in no way disturbed his total immersion in his studies after they had gone. Through the course of a day, Reb Moshe could be confronted with news of travail after travail. Those who were with him could see the distress on his face as he heard a piece of bitter news, and they could often hear him groan in anguish. But Torah, for which heaven and earth exist, still had to be learned. And by Reb Moshe's definition, learning meant that one apply himself to the fullest under all conditions.

Once, a couple whom he knew came to see him. The wife was terminally ill. Reb Moshe listened to them as they poured out their troubles, felt their pain, and offered his heartfelt blessing for a *refuah sheleimah*. The moment they left, he picked up his fountain pen and continued with his writing.

Someone who was present could not help but ask, "How is it possible for the Rosh Yeshivah to focus on his learning so quickly?" Reb Moshe

---

14. Rabbi Shneur Kotler once told a talmid that as a *yeshivah bachur* in Europe, he had learned to awaken himself at a specific hour without any assistance. He remarked that every person has the ability to discipline himself in this manner.

15. Once, Reb Moshe delivered his two-hour Friday *shiur* and mentioned at its conclusion that he was suffering pain in his foot. Out of *kavod* for his talmidim, he had remained standing despite the pain. When he was still in pain the following Friday, Rav Michel Barenbaum convinced him to sit for the *shiur* until the condition improved.

responded by quoting a Gemara: "זְמַן תְּפִילָה לְחוּד וּזְמַן תּוֹרָה לְחוּד" *(The time for prayer is separate from the time for Torah").*[16]

Many of the notebooks containing Reb Moshe's *chiddushei Torah* start and end in the middle of sentences. In a sense this sums up his entire life: a never-ending flow of Torah from a most unusual wellspring of thought.

Incredibly, he had the ability to resume his writing after an interruption, without pausing to collect his thoughts. Once, he put down his pen to hear the case of an *agunah* (a woman whose husband is missing and may be dead). Reb Moshe listened to the story, probed and considered the available evidence, and finally issued his *psak* as to whether or not the woman was permitted to remarry. The instant that the parties had left, Reb Moshe picked up his pen and without a moment's hesitation continued from where he had left off.

A man who had observed the entire scene could not believe his eyes. Unable to contain himself, he asked, "How could the Rosh Yeshivah deal with so delicate a question and not lose track of what he had been thinking of before?" Reb Moshe replied simply, "I have worked on this."

Rabbi Dovid Birnbaum was present when a group of rabbanim presented Reb Moshe with a difficult question involving the precise language of a *get* given under unusual circumstances. After the question had been presented, Reb Moshe immediately took pen in hand and began to write the *get's* text. Then the doorbell rang, and a couple came in to discuss a *shalom bayis* matter. Reb Moshe put his pen down and spoke to the couple. The moment they turned to leave, he began to resume writing the *get* without having to collect his thoughts or even read what he had written thus far.

In Rabbi Reuven Feinstein's words:

> My father's *ahavas Yisrael* was so great that he would stop writing even in the middle of a word if someone needed to speak with him. And his *ahavas haTorah* was so great that he was able to continue writing that word without a moment's pause as soon as the person turned to leave.

On another occasion, Reb Reuven reflected:

> The greatest thing I saw from my father was how he could write *teshuvos* in Halachah for ten consecutive hours and not grow weary. He recalled everything from memory. On those occasions when he

---

16. *Shabbos* 10a.

Galley from a volume of Dibros Moshe with Reb Moshe's penned corrections

did need to look up something, he opened the *sefer* while standing and perused it for about a minute. If in the middle of writing a *teshuvah* someone entered to ask a *she'eilah* (halachic query), he would interrupt his writing and turn his attention to his visitor. The conversation could last five minutes … ten minutes … the moment it was finished, he would immediately resume his writing from the place where he had left off! Generally, when resuming writing, a person needs to pause and collect his thoughts. My father, however, was different.[17]

His ability to resume writing without pause was very important to him. He told his brother-in-law, Rabbi Isaac Small, that a paramount factor in his success was the ability to stop in the middle of a subject and return to it many hours later exactly where he had left off, without needing to refresh his memory by review.[18]

He also had the ability to do two things at once. He could, for example, answer a question on the phone and at the same time correct galleys of a forthcoming *sefer,* a task that requires a great degree of concentration. Rabbi Nissan Alpert recalled many conversations during which Reb Moshe listened and responded regarding weighty matters, but, under his breath, would review *mishnayos* while others were speaking.

IT IS INTERESTING THAT WHILE HE WAS BEST KNOWN FOR HIS *IGROS MOSHE* ON Halachah, in his own mind, Reb Moshe placed greater emphasis on his

Devoted to His Mission

Dibros Moshe to Gemara. Following her husband's passing, Rebbetzin Feinstein recalled the tremendous self-sacrifice Reb Moshe had endured in composing his *Dibros Moshe,* of which fifteen volumes were published in his lifetime and many more remained in manuscript form. The Rebbetzin remembered well her husband's boundless joy when he would receive a letter pertaining to something he had written in *Dibros Moshe.*

Many of his *chiddushim* had to be reconstructed after being destroyed in Russia. Yet this did not deter Reb Moshe, who viewed the writing of his *chiddushei Torah* as an important part of his mission on this world.

His writing was not only an end, but a means as well.

Rabbi Elimelech Bluth was once present when Reb Moshe did not have an immediate answer to a difficult question. He said, "I will commit my thoughts on the matter to writing. Perhaps things will become clear as they are written."

---

17. From an interview by Rabbi Raphael Berelson published in the Hebrew *Yated Ne'eman* and later in *Mipihem shel Rabboseinu.*

18. His notebooks were outstanding for their orderliness. Each had a table of contents in the front that listed the many chapters contained within by title. Often, Reb Moshe would revise a chapter and insert new material. He would always note which parts had been written earlier and which had come later.

THE TORAH COMMANDS US קְדוֹשִׁים תִּהְיוּ, *YOU SHALL BE HOLY.*[19] RAMBAN explains that to be holy means not to overindulge in that which the Torah

Holy and Pure

permits. In *Pirkei Avos,* we learn that one of the qualities needed to acquire Torah [*i.e.* to make it a part of one's essence] is מִיעוּט תַּעֲנוּג, *limited physical pleasure.* Overindulgence in physical pleasures precludes true growth in Torah.

Rabbi David Feinstein recalled:

> My father, *zt"l,* avoided all forms of indulgence and luxury. If he came to my house and my wife served pareve ice cream, he would take a bite to be polite and compliment her — but that was all. He did not finish the portion. He avoided sweets.
>
> Once during *shalosh seudos* in yeshivah, someone noticed that my father's chair was somewhat broken. He offered to bring my father a better chair, but my father declined the offer. He said that he did not want to get used to luxuries.

As mentioned in a previous chapter, as a young rav, Reb Moshe subsisted for three years on poor-tasting food. Only someone to whom physical pleasures held little importance could manage this. Reb Moshe was not enticed by the pleasures of this lowly world. It was Torah from which he derived pleasure and which he pursued with a burning passion.

In an essay on the mission of a teacher of Torah, Reb Moshe wrote:

In our land [America], due to the abundance of material blessing that Hashem has bestowed on it, there is a desire, a great craving, for the pleasures of this world in all areas — they call this "a good time." This ruins a person very much, for he accustoms his yetzer (inclination) to desire things for which he has no need, and this corrupts his middos until he becomes like a wild beast...

This is something over which Torah teachers must keep watch,

---

19. *Vayikra* 19:2.

and regarding which they must teach their talmidim how to conduct themselves. They should tell them about the shamefulness of baalei taavah and of the praise of deriving pleasure from good deeds, which is an eternal pleasure ...[20]

Reb Moshe learned this point from a verse in the Torah. Hashem assures us that if we go in the Torah's ways, there will be an overabundance of food. "...Threshing will overtake vintage for you, and the vintage will last until the sowing ..."[21] The very same verse promises, "You will eat bread to satiety," which Rashi explains to mean that one will need to eat only a little bit and he will feel full.

Why is such a *berachah* necessary? If there is an overabundance of food, then there is no need to feel full after eating only a little. One can eat to his heart's content and will still have plenty left over.

The answer, said Reb Moshe, is that to a G-d-fearing Jew, it is not a blessing for him to eat to his heart's content. Hashem does not want us to become gluttons. He does not want us to be steeped in physical indulgence. If He blesses us with an abundant crop, we should use it, says Reb Moshe, for mitzvos, to obtain that which we need to maintain good health, and for other constructive purposes.

Once, Reb Moshe and a prominent *talmid chacham* became involved in a lively Torah discussion. At one point, the scholar withdrew a pack of cigarettes, helped himself to one, and offered one to Reb Moshe.[22] He responded, "מִיּוֹם עָמְדִי עַל דַּעְתִּי (From the day I was mature enough to understand), I never put something into my mouth purely for the sake of pleasure."

When the Lakewood Mashgiach, Rabbi Nosson Wachtfogel, related the above in a *shmuess*, he burst into tears. "This is a level akin to that of Rabbeinu HaKadosh,"[23] he cried. "A different breed of '*gadol*.'"[24]

Reb Moshe was also careful to keep far away from anything that contradicted the purity necessary for spiritual growth. In a conversation with

---

20. *Igros Moshe, Yoreh De'ah* III, #71.
21. *Vayikra* 26:5.
22. This was at a time when the dangers of cigarette smoking were not widely known.
23. I.e. Rabbi Yehudah HaNasi, the *Tanna* who compiled the Six Orders of the Mishnah. The Gemara relates that just before he died, Rabbi Yehudah HaNasi lifted his ten fingers towards heaven and declared, "*Ribono shel Olam!* It is clear and known to You that I have labored with my ten fingers in the Torah and that I have not derived personal pleasure [in worldly matters] from even [the toil of] my smallest finger" (*Kesubos* 104a).
24. *Leket Reshimos* on *Tefillah*.

Rabbi Avraham Golombeck,[25] Reb Moshe grew emotional as he said, "With one glance at a newsstand, one can lose all he gained in a week's learning." Then he said, "And now I must calm myself down, because soon I must deliver a *shiur*."

HIS KEDUSHAH WAS APPARENT THROUGHOUT HIS LIFE IN A VERY OBVIOUS way. Flying insects which were found in abundance and annoyed every-

**An
Invisible
Net**

one else did not bother Reb Moshe. Rebbetzin Feinstein told her son, Reb Reuven, that in Russia on a summer day, Reb Moshe would sit under a tree writing his *chiddushim*. All around him, people were swatting the flying creatures that were attacking them, but none came near Reb Moshe.

In their early years in America, Reb Moshe and his family would vacation in Toledo, Ohio, at the home of his brother-in-law, Rabbi Nechemiah Katz. The first time Rabbi Katz found Reb Moshe learning in the back yard, he was surprised. That summer, the mosquitos were everywhere, and it seemed impossible to immerse oneself in learning while swatting the insects at the same time. After observing Reb Moshe for a couple of minutes, Rabbi Katz realized that there were no mosquitos in his vicinity. It was as if an invisible net were surrounding him, preventing the insects from coming near.[26]

---

25. Late *Mashgiach Ruchani* of the Philadelphia Yeshivah.
26. Related by the current Rav of Toledo, Rabbi Yehudah Garsek, who heard it from Rabbi Katz.

Years later in the Catskill Mountains, a talmid was sitting with Reb Moshe on his porch and both were served cups of tea. The talmid could not drink his tea because some of the gnats swarming around him had landed in his cup. But none were found in Reb Moshe's cup.

When Rabbi Yisroel Belsky observed a similar phenomena, he asked Reb Moshe about it. Reb Moshe smiled and replied with the verse, בִּרְצוֹת ה' דַּרְכֵי אִישׁ, גַּם אוֹיְבָיו יַשְׁלִם אִתּוֹ, *When Hashem favors a man's ways,*

even his enemies will make peace with him.[27] In one interpretation, the Midrash defines "enemies" as insects.[28]

IN *PIRKEI AVOS,*[29] RABBI MEIR TEACHES, "WHOEVER ENGAGES IN TORAH STUDY for its own sake merits many things." Among those rewards is an unusual level of success in one's learning:

Divine Assistance

The Torah gives him … analytical judgment; the secrets of the Torah are revealed to him; he becomes like a steadily strengthening fountain and like an unceasing river.

As Reb Moshe's dedication to Torah was of the highest degree, he was granted great *siyata diShmaya* (Divine assistance) in his learning. This is obvious simply from the depth and breadth of his enormous store of *chiddushei Torah* and *teshuvos.*

When Reb Moshe once visited Rabbi Ephraim Greenblatt, the two became involved in a halachic discussion, and Rabbi Greenblatt expressed surprise over the *psak* he had seen in a certain *sefer.* Reb Moshe said, "I too am surprised. In fact, I hold that what this author has forbidden is actually permissible."

---

27. *Mishlei* 16:7.
28. See *Yalkut Shimoni.* In *Sefer Melachim II* (2:9), the Shunamis woman referred to Elisha HaNavi as a "man of G-d." One reason for this, says the Gemara, is that she noticed that a fly never went near his table (*Berachos* 10b).
29. 6:1.

Later when the two were in Rabbi Greenblatt's study, Reb Moshe noticed the sefer *She'eilos U'Teshuvos Shoel U'Meishiv,* by the classic 19th-century *posek* Rabbi Yosef Shaul Nathanson. He reached for it while saying, "Just yesterday, someone told me that a *psak* of mine differs with that of the *Shoel U'Meishiv.* I would like to see if this is so." Reb Moshe then opened the *sefer* randomly and there, staring back at him, was the *first* question which Rabbi Greenblatt had put to him. The *Shoel U'Meishiv's* ruling concurred with Reb Moshe's.

Rabbi Greenblatt was amazed. "This is *siyata diShmaya,*" he said. Reb Moshe tried to make light of the matter. "It can happen sometimes …," he replied. Rabbi Greenblatt recalls that during his days in Tifereth Jerusalem, Reb Moshe would very often open a *sefer* to the exact page he was seeking.[30]

❦ ❦ ❦

One Shabbos morning, Reb Moshe invited Rabbi Simcha Bunim Cohen to learn *Teshuvos Chasam Sofer* with him. He commented that although he sometimes disagreed with the opinions of *Acharonim* (Later Commentators) including the Chasam Sofer, he had particular awe of the Chasam Sofer. "He was so great," said Reb Moshe, "he merited what no one else did. He was Rav of a renowned city, a rosh yeshivah, the greatest *posek* of his time — he merited a special *siyata diShmaya.* Though I do disagree with him at times, it is with difficulty that I do so."

By the testimony of his illustrious peers, as documented in the following chapter, Reb Moshe was the *posek hador.* He too merited a special *siyata diShmaya.* He too was a great rosh yeshivah, whose *shiurim* on all areas of *Shas* were incredible in their breadth and depth.

It follows, then, that when approaching a *psak* of Reb Moshe, one must do so with awe and trepidation.

---

30. When the average person opens a gemara and seeks a specific *daf,* he keeps his eyes focused on the page number on top as he turns the pages. One talmid recalls watching Reb Moshe focus his eyes on the *bottom* of the *daf,* recognizing each page by the final words of *Tosafos.*

CHAPTER SIX

Posek of the Nation

WITHOUT A DOUBT, REB MOSHE ACHIEVED HIS GREATEST RENOWN in the area of Halachah. His *Igros Moshe,* in which thousands of his responsa spanning the full range of Torah law are collected,

Universal Acceptance was acclaimed as a classic decades before his passing. The Steipler Gaon, Rabbi Yaakov Yisrael Kanievsky, said that Reb Moshe was the leading authority of the era. Rabbi Shlomo Zalman Auerbach of Jerusalem, who until his passing in 5755 (1995) was recognized as one of the greatest *poskim* of his time, declined to eulogize Reb Moshe, saying, "Who am I to eulogize him? I studied his *sefarim;* I was his talmid."

It happened that Rabbi Yaakov Kamenetsky sent one of his closest disciples to Reb Moshe to ask him about a complicated issue, saying, "Only Reb Moshe has shoulders broad enough to rule in this matter. But if he tells you that you are permitted to follow a lenient course, your conscience should not bother you at all. If he says so, it is permitted by the Torah."

A prominent chassidic rav ruled a certain act permissible, unaware that Reb Moshe had ruled to the contrary. One day, the two met and debated the matter. The rav was not convinced of Reb Moshe's reasoning; nevertheless, from then on, when asked what the halachah was, the rav would respond, "Reb Moshe forbids it." He also instructed his own household to abide by Reb Moshe's *psak.*

With Rabbi Aharon Kotler at a wedding

The Torah giants of the previous generation showed similar reverence for Reb Moshe. When he was well into his 90s, Rabbi Eliyahu Lopian, legendary Mashgiach of Yeshivah Knesses Chizkiyahu, insisted on attending the Knessiah Gedolah held in Jerusalem in 1964, so that he could fulfill the mitzvah of standing up for Reb Moshe.

Rabbi Aharon Kotler, who until his passing in 1962 was the recognized leader of the American yeshivah world, declared Reb Moshe to be the leading halachic authority of his generation. Reb Aharon once could not contain his surprise upon hearing a *psak* that had been recently issued by Reb Moshe. Nevertheless, he said, "The halachah is like him at all times. If the *posek hador* says that the halachah is so, then we must listen to him."

In 1971, the great *gaon* Rabbi Yisrael Zev Gustman made known his plans to move from New York to Jerusalem and reestablish his yeshivah there. Rabbi Elimelech Bluth was very close to Rav Gustman and expressed a desire to join him. "Whatever for?" Rav Gustman asked. "Here you have Reb Moshe, the *amud hahora'ah* (pillar of *psak halachah*)!"

Yet another *gadol* of yesteryear, Rabbi Yaakov Yechiel Weinberg, author of *Seridei Eish,* once compared Reb Moshe to Rabbi Yitzchak Elchonon Spector, the *posek hador* of a century ago, in explaining why he had the authority to dispute a ruling of the Chasam Sofer while other *poskim* did not.

❀ ❀ ❀

Rabbi Ben Zion Abba-Shaul   With Rabbi Ovadiah Yosef

When the great Sefardic rosh yeshivah and *posek* Rabbi Ben Zion Abba-Shaul visited America for the first time, he met with Reb Moshe and the two entered into a lengthy Torah discussion. Rabbi Abba-Shaul emerged from that meeting amazed at Reb Moshe's greatness in Torah. At Reb Moshe's funeral in Jerusalem, Rabbi Abba-Shaul rent his garment as one does for his *rebbi muvhak* (primary Torah teacher), and he instructed his talmidim to do the same.[1]

He once commented, "Reb Moshe's greatness can be seen in the fact that he took upon himself to answer any person who called him on the phone. He did not refuse anyone who had a question for him. It is hard to imagine how such a commitment is possible!"[2]

When the great Sefardic *gaon* and *posek* Rabbi Ovadiah Yosef visited New York, he *davened Shacharis* one morning in Tifereth Jerusalem. At the conclusion of *Shacharis,* Rav Yosef greeted Reb Moshe, kissed his hand (according to Sefardic custom), and the two entered into a halachic discussion.

❦ ❦ ❦

1. From an article by Rabbi David Sutton in *The Jewish Observer* and later published in *Torah Leaders* (ArtScroll/Mesorah Publications).

When a family member reminisced about Rabbi Abba-Shaul's meeting with Reb Moshe, he remarked that Reb Moshe's respect for the *Chacham* was evident in that he escorted him all the way to his car. Rabbi Abba-Shaul remarked humbly, "I'm sure he would have done that for any visitor from Eretz Yisrael."

2. From *Gedolei Yisroel — Portraits of Torah Greatness* by Rabbi Mattis Goldberg (Feldheim Publishers).

Rabbi Yosef Sholom Elyashiv

Rabbi Chaim Ganzweig is *Mashgiach Ruchani* at Mesivtha Tifereth Jerusalem and a talmid of Reb Moshe. He recalled: "When I visited Rav Shlomo Zalman Auerbach, זצ״ל, and, יבלח״ט, Rav Yosef Shlomo Elyashiv, שליט״א, I was astonished at the degree of *bitul* (deference) that these two Torah giants had towards the Rosh Yeshivah."

> Rav Elyashiv once related that he first realized Reb Moshe's stature in 1956, when Rabbi Aharon Kotler visited Eretz Yisrael. Rav Elyashiv, who by that time was already among the leading *poskim* in Eretz Yisrael, was anticipating Reb Aharon's arrival so that he could discuss with him a difficult and sensitive halachic case. When Reb Aharon was told the case's details, he surprised Rav Elyashiv by saying, "There is only one person in the world who can rule on this *she'eilah*." Reb Aharon immediately placed an overseas call (which was quite expensive in those days) to Reb Moshe and remained on the phone with him for forty-five minutes.[3]

Recently, when the venerable Rav Elyashiv, who today rules on the most difficult *she'eilos* from around the world, was asked why he does not pub-

---

3. From an article by Rabbi Michel Shurkin published in *Yated Ne'eman* in commemoration of Reb Moshe's fifth *yahrzeit*.

lish his *teshuvos*, he responded with classic humility: "Who am I to write a definitive *teshuvah* which becomes Torah for all generations after it is published? ... *Chas v'shalom!* ... Rav Moshe Feinstein — he had the ability to *pasken* (issue halachic rulings) for all generations, he had the ability to write exactly what needed to be written, but as for me ...?"[4]

Rabbi Tuvia Goldstein, late Rosh Yeshivah of Yeshivah Emek Halachah and a respected *posek*, was a longtime neighbor of Reb Moshe on FDR Drive and enjoyed a close relationship with him. When a son was born to his children, Rabbi and Mrs. Mordechai Goldstein of Ramat Beit Shemesh, they wanted to name the baby Moshe. However, a relative who was struggling with a serious illness asked that they name the child Raphael. She explained: In her family there was a tradition that naming a baby Raphael would bring to the family the healing powers of the *Malach Raphael*.

The parents decided to present their dilemma to Rav Elyashiv. The *gaon* asked Rabbi Goldstein whether Raphael was a family name. Told that it was not, Rav Elyashiv reacted uncharacteristically, rising from his chair and declaring forcefully, "Rav Moshe Feinstein *is* the *Malach Raphael*!" The baby was named Moshe.

MR. EPHRAIM ZALMAN MARGULIES WAS A DISTINGUISHED *ASKAN* WHO RESIDED in London. At one point, his livelihood involved extensive dealings in

Reb Shlomo Zalman Ghana, which is part of the British Commonwealth. When the Prime Minister of Ghana visited London and was invited to dine with the Queen, Mr. Margulies was invited to the dinner as well.

A few days before the dinner, Mr. Margulies began the observance of *shivah* upon the death of a close relative. This situation presented serious questions: Should Mr. Margulies attend the dinner with the Queen? And if so, should he shave and wear formal attire?

These questions were first presented to Rav Shlomo Zalman Auerbach, who responded, "Only Rav Moshe Feinstein can rule on such a *she'eilah*."

Rabbi Simcha Bunim Cohen once asked Reb Shlomo Zalman a question concerning a difficult *psak* of the *Magen Avraham*.[5] After Reb Shlomo Zalman offered a solution, Rabbi Cohen told him that he

---

4. From *HaShakdan* on the life of Rav Elyashiv, *shlita* (Jerusalem 5770). A recently published collection of *teshuvos* of Rav Elyashiv was gleaned from letters in halachah he had written to others.
5. Classic commentary to *Shulchan Aruch, Orach Chaim*.

Rabbi Shlomo Zalman Auerbach

had posed this question to many rabbanim; some were not familiar with the issue, while others had offered solutions that seemed somewhat forced. But when Rabbi Cohen had merely broached the subject with Reb Moshe, he immediately expounded on the *Magen Avraham,* pointed out the difficulty, and presented a most satisfying solution.

"What is the surprise?" Reb Shlomo Zalman responded. "We are all infants when compared to him!"

While Reb Moshe and Reb Shlomo Zalman never met in person, they discussed halachic issues by phone many times. A special relationship of mutual love and admiration existed between them. Interestingly, both were world-renowned *poskim* and great roshei yeshivah who delivered *shiurim* regularly.

Once, when Rabbi Yosef Buxbaum, Menahel of Mechon Yerushalayim and a neighbor of Reb Shlomo Zalman, was planning a trip to America, Reb Shlomo Zalman asked a favor of him:

"I have written, but not publicized, a *psak* that is at variance with that of Reb Moshe. Please show it to Reb Moshe and say that I am requesting permission to publicize it."

"And what if he does not grant permission?" asked Rabbi Buxbaum.

"Then I will not publicize a word of it," the *gaon* replied.

When Rabbi Buxbaum presented the request to Reb Moshe, he smiled and responded, "He needs to ask my permission? …Permission is granted!" Reb Moshe then added, "People do not appreciate his [Reb Shlomo Zalman's] true worth — he is a *gadol hagedolim.*"[6]

---

6. From *Torah Mesameches: The Incredible Life of Rabbi Shlomo Zalman Auerbach* (Hebrew) by Yosef and Rus Eliyahu.

Reb Shlomo Zalman published his *teshuvah* (*Minchas Shlomo,* Vol. I, #8), with the following introduction: "Inasmuch as a *psak* regarding this matter is found in the renowned *Sefer Igros Moshe* (Orach Chaim 4:80) from the renowned *gaon* and *tzaddik,* may Hashem lengthen his days and years with good and pleasantness, and this matter relates to Biblically prohibited labor on Shabbos, I am publicizing this essay after receiving permission for this from the aforementioned *gaon.*"

When Reb Moshe turned 80, the Hebrew *Hamodia* published an article about him in honor of the occasion. It was Reb Shlomo Zalman's practice to flip through the paper each day and read the headlines. When he noticed the heading of the article on Reb Moshe and its accompanying photo, he mistakenly thought that Reb Moshe had passed away. He began to cry, *"Oy, Reb Moshe is nisht da ..."* ("Oh, Reb Moshe is no longer here ..."). When a relative told him that this was not so, Reb Shlomo Zalman rejoiced. He then did something which he never did — he read the entire article on Reb Moshe. Upon finishing he remarked, *"Ashrei ha'am* (Fortunate is the nation) to have a *posek* like Reb Moshe."[7]

When a discussion centered around the term *Sar HaTorah* (Prince of Torah), which is sometimes used to describe an outstanding Torah luminary, Reb Shlomo Zalman said, "To be worthy of that title, one must be able to decide contemporary halachic issues directly from the *sugyos* in the Gemara. In our generation, Reb Moshe is the *Sar HaTorah.*"[8]

DURING HIS STAY IN ERETZ YISRAEL, REB MOSHE WAS VISITED IN HIS HOTEL room by Rabbi Shlomo Shimshon Karelitz, Rav of Petach Tikvah and one

A Heated Debate of the great *poskim* of the time. Prior to the visit, a complicated question regarding a woman's marital status had been the subject of dispute among the foremost *poskim* of the day. A primary purpose of Rav Karelitz' visit was to debate this matter.

Reb Moshe at the Knessiah Gedolah

And debate they did. Torah is the very essence of life to great Torah personalities, and when they engage in the *milchamtah shel Torah* (battle of Talmudic debate) they can argue as if their very life depends on it. The discussion between Reb Moshe and Rav Karelitz became heated as

---

7. From an article on Reb Shlomo Zalman in the English *Hamodia.*
8. *Chiko Mamtakim* by Rabbi Eliyahu Noe, Vol. II, p. 34.

each strove to prove his point and refute the other's view. A chambermaid listening from outside the closed door later said, "When I heard the shouting coming from Rabbi Feinstein's room, I was sure that they were pulling at each other's beards!"

After close to an hour of dialogue, a hotel representative knocked on the door to say that Reb Moshe had other visitors. The Chevron Rosh Yeshivah, Rabbi Yechezkel Sarna; the Tchebiner Rav, Rabbi Dov Beirish Weidenfeld, and other *gedolim* had been waiting more than half an hour and apparently did not want to interrupt the discussion. Upon hearing this, Rav Karelitz brought the "battle" to a close. As they took leave of each other, Reb Moshe asked Rav Karelitz to commit his opinion to writing and send it to him in America so that he could examine it further.[9]

Rav Karelitz once commented to Rabbi Yonah Ganzweig:[10] "I disagree with the *Igros Moshe* on many points, but I bow my head [in submission]; since the time of the Chasam Sofer there has not been anyone who can decide halachic issues directly from the Gemara as Reb Moshe does."

IN HIS PREFACE TO IGROS MOSHE, REB MOSHE HUMBLY EXPLAINS HOW ONE has the right to propound new halachic rulings in this generation, even

Genesis of a *Posek*
though we are so far below the level of wisdom of earlier generations that one should fear that his opinions are not in accordance with Torah truth. It was such a fear, writes Reb Moshe, that caused many Torah luminaries of the past to abstain from *psak,* "and certainly [this should apply] to those of little worth like me, who has neither Torah nor wisdom in proper measure …"

Still, Reb Moshe continues, one who is fit to rule in matters of Halachah is permitted and even obligated to do so, " … after he has toiled and strained to clarify the Halachah through [studying] *Shas* and *poskim* as much as his strength allows, with a serious sense of responsibility and with fear of Hashem … and, as *Rabbeinu Yonah* writes,[11] that one review until he does not forget a thing and until he has plumbed to the depths of the matter …"

Toiled and strained …as much as his strength allows …with a sense of responsibility and with fear of Hashem …that one review until he does not forget a thing …These guidelines say much for how Reb Moshe came to be the greatest posek of his day.

---

9. *Amudei Sheish — The Life of HaGaon Rav Shlomo Shimshon Karelitz* (Hebrew).
10. Rav Ganzweig served as a rav in Los Angeles for over forty years.
11. *Avos* 4: 12.

ספר

אגרות משה

אורח חיים

והם מה שחננו השי"ת להשיב לשואלים אותי מתלמידי וחברי דבר
ה' זו הלכת, וגם מה שבאתי בכתובים לגדולי תורה
להשתעשע בדברי תורה.

מאת

משה פיינשטיין

ר"מ מתיבתא תפארת ירושלים בנוא יארק
ומלפנים אבד"ק ליובאן, פלך מינסק

בן אאמו"ר הצדיק חסיד ועניו מרן ר' דוד זצ"ל
שהיה אבד"ק אזרא וסטראבין ברוסיא

נוא יארק
שנת תשי"ט לפ"ק

❋

Rabbi Chaim Ganzweig wrote that in appreciating the greatness of *Igros Moshe*, one must also recognize its connection to *Dibros Moshe* on *Shas*:

Every halachic decision of the Rosh Yeshivah, regardless of how seemingly simple or instantly rendered, was deeply rooted in *sugyos haShas* (the discussions recorded in the Talmud). There was no superficiality in his decisions. They were based on a deep awareness and understanding of all relevant Talmudic discussions and their ramifications. He did not rely on this opinion or that decision, nor did he automatically follow precedent; rather, the decision was the result of toil in, and depth of understanding of, the relevant Talmudic discussions at the source, following through the classic codes and the views of the great *poskim*.

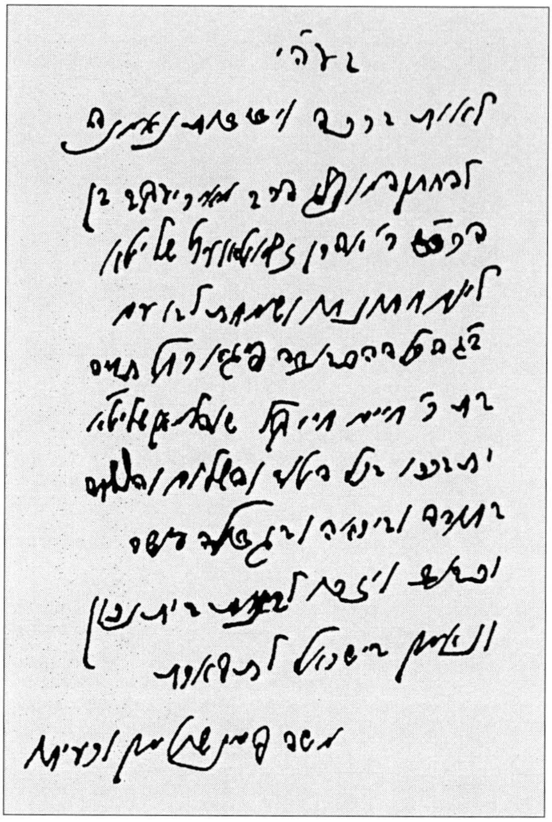

Reb Moshe's personal inscription in a volume of *Igros Moshe* which he would present to his close talmidim as a wedding gift.

The inscription reads:

בעה"י
לאות ברכה וידידות נאמנה
להחתן המופלג הרב מאיר יעקב בן
הרה"ג ר' אהרן זלאטאווייץ שליט"א
ליום חתונתו ושמחת לבו
עם ב"ג הכלה הכבודה פיגא רחל תחי'
בת ר' חיים חייקל שוהלמאן שליט"א
יתברכו בכל הטוב והשלום והצלחה
בתורה וביראה ובגדולה עושר
וכבוד ויזכו לבנות בית נכון
ונאמן בישראל לתפארת

משה פיינשטיין ורעיתו

In a similar vein, even a casual perusal of the *Dibros* will show that a question or answer was not said merely for its educational value as part of a *shiur*; rather, every facet of an argument or proposal had to have a valid halachic basis.[12]

Rabbi Ganzweig applied to Reb Moshe the words which the Chasam Sofer wrote of his own approach to *psak*: "One should tarry over every issue until it is as clear and refined as fine flour, then retain the information in the recesses of his mind so that it will be readily accessible when an occasion to use it arises."[13]

Rabbi Michel Shurkin, today a Rosh Yeshivah at Yeshivah Toras Moshe in Jerusalem, was a close talmid of Reb Moshe and a member of Tifereth Jerusalem's Kollel L'Hora'ah. As its name implies, a primary purpose of this kollel is to prepare young *talmidei chachamim* to be *poskim* for the

---

12. From a piece in *The Jewish Observer* published on the occasion of Reb Moshe's tenth *yahrzeit*.
13. Preface to *She'eilos U'Teshuvos Chasam Sofer*, *Yoreh De'ah*, concluding paragraph.

*At a Ganzweig
family simchah
(left to right at
head of table):
Meir Posen, Rabbi
Yonah Ganzweig,
Reb Moshe*

new generation. Rabbi Shurkin recalls that often Reb Moshe would present real-life *she'eilos* that had been presented to him for *psak*, and he would challenge the kollel members to plumb the depths of the *sugya* and render their own halachic ruling.[14]

Rabbi Shurkin describes Reb Moshe as a *lamdan* who, with great toil and *siyata diShmaya*, merited אֲסוּקֵי שְׁמַעְתָּא אַלִיבָּא דְהִילְכְתָא *to conclude legal [i.e. Talmudic] discussions in accordance with Halachah.*[15] Like many of the classic *poskim*, his proficiency as a *posek* was predicated on his incredible command of *Shas* and its commentaries. Perhaps this is why, as his rebbetzin recalled, Reb Moshe took special pleasure when he received queries regarding something he had written in *Dibros Moshe.*

In Rabbi Shurkin's words:

> Someone once remarked to me that he could not understand how someone who could attack a topic from every angle and at such length, as Reb Moshe does in *Dibros Moshe,* could rule with such clarity and often brevity, as he does in *Igros Moshe.* The paradox is only on the surface. Precisely because he had so thoroughly worked out every question was he able to rule with such clarity.

Another Torah giant of that era who knew Reb Moshe well once told Rabbi Shurkin, "Reb Moshe has a *mehalech* (clear approach) in every topic in Torah. He has mastered every subject with tremendous *yegiah*

---

14. From Rabbi Shurkin's *Meged Givos Olam.*
15. From *Yoma* 26a.

(toil) and *every diyuk* (deduction) that is possible to make anywhere in *Shas* is at his fingertips."[16]

As mentioned above, when practical *she'eilos* were brought to Reb Moshe, he often presented them to members of his kollel to see how they would rule on the matter. Sometimes the *yungeleit* would try to determine, based on their knowledge of Reb Moshe's method of *psak*, how he would rule. Often, they were surprised when Reb Moshe's *psak* was *the opposite* of what they had though it would be. Rabbi Shurkin explained why: "We did not plumb the depths of his thinking, because his ruling was not based on a 'first-glance opinion' or a gut feeling; it was based on a deep understanding of the relevant *sugyos* and the opinions of *Rishonim*."

SOMEONE ONCE EXPRESSED HIS AMAZEMENT AT HOW REB MOSHE RULED ON every sort of question that came to him, without doubt or concern that

With Hashem at His Side perhaps he had not analyzed the problem correctly. Reb Moshe told the person that he had accepted upon himself the yoke of *psak halachah* only in response to the needs of his generation. He then said, "From the time that I accepted this yoke upon myself, Hashem granted me a special degree of *siyata diShmaya*. At times when I have been asked to rule on extremely difficult and complex questions, it has been obvious to me that Hashem has illuminated my eyes."

At a gathering to preserve the sanctity of Eretz Yisrael. Left to right: Reb Yitzchak Hutner, Reb Mordechai Pinchas Teitz, Reb Moshe, Reb Yaakov Kamenetsky

16. From an article by Rabbi Shurkin in *Yated Ne'eman*.

Responsa to Rabbi Pinchas Mordechai Teitz regarding the permissibility of bringing a seeing-eye dog into a shul. It appears in Igros Moshe, Vol. I, #45.

That Reb Moshe merited such *siyata diShmaya* is certainly no cause for wonder. *Shiltei HaGibborim*[17] writes:

> When a man toils in Torah for its sake, then *Hakadosh Baruch Hu* illuminates his darkness so that he will not come to sin and will not rule against the Halachah …

It happened that a poultry plant was accused of using questionable methods for *kashering*. A stellar *beis din* of three was formed to rule on the case: Reb Moshe; the great *Nasi* of Ezras Torah Rabbi Yosef Eliyahu Henkin; and Rabbi Pinchas Mordechai Teitz, renowned Rav of Elizabeth,

---

17. To *Mordechai*, *Shabbos* 2:265.

With his son Reb David

New Jersey. The case was complicated and took some time to resolve. One day, Reb Moshe appeared fatigued. When Rav Teitz asked if he was not well, Reb Moshe replied that his health was good. The problem, he said, was the case at hand. The situation was complex and their *psak*, whatever it would be, would have major ramifications. Reb Moshe had been arising even earlier than usual to review the relevant sources and think the matter through. That was why he was fatigued.

Rabbi David Feinstein says that while his father did everything in a very natural and simple way, his sense of responsibility and fear of Hashem were obvious from his method of formulating a *psak*. In determining a halachah, he would leave no stone unturned, straining and struggling to adduce proofs to either side of the question. Reb Moshe's *teshuvos* are replete with proofs to back up their conclusions. This firm basis for his rulings was a source of pride to Reb Moshe, his son recalls.

> Reb David once sought to determine the basis for a certain halachah. After spending some time researching the matter, he then studied his father's *teshuvah* on the topic and saw that not a single source related to the question was missing from it. Reb David notes that his father was granted great *siyata diShmaya* in locating the necessary sources to any given question with amazing speed, and he had such total command of his fund of knowledge that he could unerringly relate to everything that had a bearing on the topic at hand.

In exhorting his talmidim to strive for greatness in Torah, which, he said, was within everyone's reach, Reb Moshe would name diligence and *siyata diShmaya* as the two prime ingredients for success. Diligence is in the hands of the individual, while *siyata diShmaya* is granted by the *Ribono shel Olam*, according to what the individual deserves.

REB MOSHE'S CONFIDENCE THAT HEAVEN GUIDED HIS DECISIONS ALONG THE
path of truth was visibly apparent. Once, he ruled that an *agunah* was per-

Confidence in *Psak*

mitted to remarry. After she did so, a story began to circu-
late that her husband was still alive — which would have
meant that her second marriage was a tragic mistake. The
woman's family was horrified, and those who were closest to Reb Moshe
were dismayed that he would be humiliated by an error with such tragic
consequences. The only one not daunted by the news was Reb Moshe. As
his grandson Rabbi Mordechai Tendler recalls, Reb Moshe remained confident that he had ruled according to Halachah and that Hashem would not
permit such a calamity to occur as a result of his *psak*. The rumor *had* to be
false.

In due time, Reb Moshe was proven right. The first husband was not alive.

Rabbi Meir Zlotowitz was present when a related incident was brought
to Reb Moshe. A Holocaust survivor claimed that she was permitted to
remarry on the basis of evidence that her husband had perished in the
concentration camps. Then, after more than twenty years, when she had
grown children of marriageable age, her first husband was found to be

*Letter from Reb Moshe to
Rabbi Tzvi Hirsh Kaufman,
requesting that he join
Rabbi Yaakov Twersky
in helping an agunah
of eight years.*

alive in Eretz Yisrael! The distraught woman had come with her rabbi from South America to seek Reb Moshe's guidance.

Reb Moshe asked the woman to tell her story. She told of how she had brought her case to a well-known rav in one of the Displaced Persons camps after the War. Based on available testimony and evidence, this rav had ruled it correct to assume her husband dead, and had given her a *heter agunah,* a document containing this decision. It was on the basis of this ruling that she had remarried. The rav had passed away not long after the War, and due to the chaotic post-War conditions, she had lost the document. Now she and her family were suffering indescribably from a mistake that was not theirs!

Reb Moshe asked her to repeat her story, and she did so. He asked her to tell it a third time. The atmosphere in the room was tense. Why was Reb Moshe tormenting the poor woman so? What could be added by another repetition of her sorrowful tale?

> Reb Moshe's brow was furrowed in intense concentration, while everyone in the room was silent. Then, abruptly, he rose, leaned across the table, and said agitatedly to the woman, "It cannot be! I knew the rav of whom you speak. He was a *gaon* and a *tzaddik,* and I do not even approach his ankles in Torah. I have permitted over 2,000 *agunos* to remarry and never did the first husband reappear. Now you are telling me that such a thing could have happened to that *tzaddik*? It is impossible! It cannot be!"

Heter agunah written after the Holocaust for a woman whose husband was killed in Auschwitz; signed by Reb Moshe, Reb Menachem Mendel Pollack (Szerence Rav) and Reb Elkanah Zoberman (Yardonover Rav)

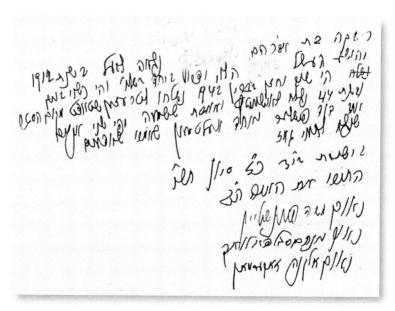

The people in the room were shocked that Reb Moshe, who was famous for his mild manner and compassion, could have spoken in such a way to a woman in distress. But their shock gave way to incredulity when the woman broke down in tears and admitted that her story was indeed false! She had been sure that her husband was dead — she had asked herself how he could possibly have survived. When she heard that a highly respected rabbi had passed away, she made up the story concerning the document, using that rabbi's name.

TO REB MOSHE'S MIND, A PERSON'S COMPLETE OBEDIENCE TO THE TORAH EVEN when it involved personal suffering was a source of very great merit. A

Greater Than a Blessing
young man, whose marriage had been childless for some time, came to ask whether it was permissible to undergo a certain medical test. Reb Moshe would not permit the procedure. The questioner became very upset and begged the Rosh Yeshivah to find some way to permit it. With love and concern, Reb Moshe took the young man's hand and said, "Often a childless couple will seek the blessing of a *tzaddik*. You should know that obeying Halachah is greater than any blessing." The man followed Reb Moshe's decision and did not undergo the test. The young man's wife eventually bore him a number of children.

Mr. Chaim Yehoshua Biderman was contemplating the purchase of a building in Brooklyn. The building had a laundromat from which the owner could earn a lucrative income. However, the laundromat was open on Shabbos. The tenants were Hispanic; no Jews would be using the

machines, and Mr. Biderman could have acquired a non-Jewish partner to whom all the Shabbos earnings would belong. However, he was not comfortable with this arrangement.

He consulted Reb Moshe, who discouraged him from making a purchase that involved *s'char Shabbos* (Shabbos earnings). Mr. Biderman listened to Reb Moshe and did not buy the building. That neighborhood soon deteriorated; it became dangerous to walk there even during daylight hours. Had Mr. Biderman made that purchase, he would have regretted it. His decision to follow a *gadol's* guidance regarding a potential business deal paid him great dividends.[18]

Once, the funeral of a wealthy individual was held on Chol HaMoed. The man had been a generous supporter of Torah. Reb Moshe was asked to deliver a *hesped* at the funeral, but he politely declined, stating the halachah that one does not eulogize on Chol HaMoed. A distinguished individual suggested that the man's support of Torah equated him with the scholars whom he supported, and there is leniency in Halachah to eulogize a *talmid chacham* on Chol HaMoed.[19] Reb Moshe did not respond; the halachah, as stated in *Shulchan Aruch*, spoke for itself.

ONCE, REB MOSHE URGED A TALMID TO ENTER THE RABBINATE AND UNDER-
take to decide questions of Halachah, but the young man felt he was not

Passion for Accuracy qualified, saying, "I have spent most of my time in yeshivah studying Gemara, not Halachah." Reb Moshe replied, "You have strained to understand Torah? You are truly fortunate! But you can still acquire the halachic knowledge you will need. Study each section of *Shulchan Aruch* with its primary commentary, and then review it again and again. Then you will know where all the major topics are discussed and you will be able to research individual questions as they arise."

Of course, there is a vast difference between knowing where to find existing answers to questions and offering one's own original rulings, as Reb Moshe did in thousands of cases, many of which required applying the Torah's unchanging statutes to areas of modern medicine and technology. Only by meeting the most exacting standards he had established for himself would he rule so often, on so many complex and delicate issues, with such certainty.

His memory was of utmost importance to him, because he could not undertake to decide complex and serious questions of Halachah unless he could be certain that he had not overlooked any sources.

> Once he and several rabbis were sitting in the large communal *succah* of the apartment complex in which he lived, when a Talmudic passage came under discussion. Reb Moshe said that it was explained in a commentary of *Tosafos* in *Sanhedrin*, while the others all agreed that the source was not in *Masechta Sanhedrin* but in *Makkos*. Reb

---

18. From a piece by Mrs. Faygie Borchardt in *Hamodia* magazine, Cheshvan 5771.
19. In fact, *Biur Halachah* (ch. 547 שמותר ד"ה) states that our custom is not to eulogize a *talmid chacham* on Chol HaMoed.

Moshe rose and rushed from the table. The others were surprised. True, he had completed his meal, but it was out of character for him to leave the table without saying *"Gut Yom Tov."*

Several minutes later he returned. He had crossed the courtyard and climbed the steps to his apartment to look up the Gemara. As he had thought, it was in *Sanhedrin,* but he simply could not wait until later to verify his recollection, because truth was his most important value, his most pressing concern. If his memory was challenged, then the source must be checked — now, not later.

❧ ❧ ❧

The following incident, related by Rabbi Yitzchok Yaakov Sekula, encapsulates some of the qualities that made Reb Moshe the *gaon baTorah* and *posek hador* that he was:

When Rabbi Sekula was a talmid at Bais Medrash Elyon in Monsey, he and his *chavrusa,* Rabbi Moshe Linchner, spent many days struggling to plumb the depths of a difficult *Tosafos* in *Masechta Zevachim.* A specific passage in the *Tosafos* was particularly obscure. The pair decided to drive to the Lower East Side and ask Reb Moshe to shed light on the matter.

When they entered the beis midrash in Tifereth Jerusalem, Reb Moshe was in the midst of delivering a *shiur* on *Masechta Sanhedrin*. As the *shiur* progressed, Reb Moshe cited a *Pri Megadim* that had a tangential connection to the topic. He cited the chapter in *Shulchan Aruch* in which the *Pri Megadim* is found and its *se'if katan* (sub-paragraph), ג"י.

An elderly *talmid chacham* attending the *shiur* called out, "It's ד"י."

Reb Moshe responded, "No, it's ג"י."

The man smiled and retorted, "It doesn't really make a difference, but it's ד"י."

Reb Moshe turned to a talmid and said, "Bring a *Shulchan Aruch*."

Reb Moshe opened the volume, found the *Pri Megadim* and announced, "It's ג"י. I am correct.

"I realize," Reb Moshe then said, "that you are all wondering why I have to prove myself right. You see, I have reviewed *Shulchan Aruch,* with all its *nosei keilim* (marginal commentaries), many, many times. I have memorized every *Pri Megadim, R' Akiva Eiger, Shach, Taz,* etc. When people ask me *she'eilos,* I rely on my memory and offer a *psak* without consulting any *sefarim.* However, when the day comes that I have begun to forget which *se'if katan* the *Pri Megadim* appears in, then I will no longer be able to rely on my memory, and I will be forced to consult *sefarim* before issuing a *psak.* That it was why it was so important for me to make sure that I was correct."

Reb Moshe then resumed his *shiur,* the kind of deep, intricate *shiur* upon which *Dibros Moshe* is based. Almost as soon as the *shiur* ended, the phone at Reb Moshe's seat in the beis midrash began to ring with halachic queries on all sorts of topics. Reb Moshe calmly responded to each question, clearly, succinctly, and without consulting any *sefarim.* He showed no sign of mental or physical fatigue that one would expect of one who had just completed such a *shiur.*

When the phone calls ended, Rabbi Sekula and Rabbi Linchner approached Reb Moshe with a *Gemara Zevachim* and pointed to the problematic passage in *Tosafos.* After a mere glance at the words and before the two could even begin to explain the difficulties they had encountered, Reb Moshe offered a brilliant explanation that made everything crystal clear.

Rabbi Sekula vividly recalls how stunned he and his *chavrusa* were. "The Rosh Yeshivah did not have to look over the *daf* or even the previous lines of the *Tosafos.* He looked at the passage that we had come to discuss, and immediately began to explain it." Truly, the Torah, in all its breadth and depth, was open before him.

MOSHE RABBEINU ADMONISHED THE JUDGES OF *KLAL YISRAEL,* לֹא תָגוּרוּ

מִפְּנֵי אִישׁ, *You shall not tremble before any man.*[20] Reb Moshe would cite

Fear No Man

Yam Shel Shlomo[21] which states that a judge must not back down from a Torah ruling even when threatened with death. To alter a halachah is to alter the Torah, G-d forbid, and this must be avoided regardless of the consequences.

Rabbi Michel Barenbaum recalled Reb Moshe's tenacity in standing by his decisions. Even on the rare occasions when a ruling was opposed rather forcefully in certain circles, both verbally and in writing, Reb Moshe remained unshaken. He was ready to back down if proven wrong, but until that time there could be no wavering from what he held to be truth.

> His passion for truth was apparent in one of the very first *dinei Torah* that he judged in America. The case involved the Agudath HaRabbanim, the Union of Orthodox Rabbis, an organization that was doing much to spread Reb Moshe's fame among the American Torah community and to help him become established. Reb Moshe ruled *against* the organization. Would this leave its directors with bitter feelings and damage Reb Moshe's relationship with them? There were those who said that his future in the American rabbinate was doomed. Perhaps, but this did not figure an iota in his decision. All that mattered was that truth be determined and justice be carried out. In fact, Reb Moshe did not suffer because of his decision; rather, he gained esteem for his noble character and courage.

During most of his career, he was constantly asked to rule in disputes between individuals, businesses, and institutions. People knew that a *din Torah* at which Reb Moshe presided would be decided fairly and correctly. At such sessions, he would listen to the arguments intently and respectfully, without revealing by word or expression that he could tell which side was being more truthful.

Some people misunderstood his evenhandedness; they thought he was being fooled. But, as he told Rabbi Meir Zlotowitz after a *din Torah* session, with an amused look on his face, *"zei meinin az zei naarin mir upp,"* "They think they are deceiving me." In private discussions he held with the parties to work out compromises, he had a way of defining which issues were most important to each side. He would say to a party in the dispute, "Tell me how you would want the result to be."

---

20. *Devarim* 1:17.
21. *Bava Kamma* 4: 7.

Left to right: Rabbi Yehuda Leib Seltzer, Secretary of the Agudas HaRabbanim; Rabbi Yisrael Rosenberg, Agudas HaRabbanim's president; Reb Moshe; and Rabbi Sholom Litwack

Rabbi Chaim Ganzweig recalled:

> When we observed the Rosh Yeshivah when he was asked [halachic] questions and rendered decisions, we tried to learn and understand his approach in the halachic decision-making process.
>
> The Rosh Yeshivah had an unusually clear understanding of people and human nature. He had an uncanny ability to sift out the truth and determine the genuine needs of the individual or the true issue of any situation, what was really important to the question at hand.
>
> … I believe that this was also a contributing factor to the sense that his *psak* was a true and real *psak*: There were no *negi'os*, no personal interests, in his dealings with people; only his love for people, peace, and truth dictated his actions.[22]

In a public forum, Reb Moshe said that a *posek* must approach a halachic query with a completely open mind, without any leaning towards leniency or stringency. It is the Torah that must decide the halachah, not one's personal feeling of what the halachah should be.

---

22. From an article in *The Jewish Observer* published on the occasion of Reb Moshe's tenth *yahrzeit*.

At the bris of Rabbi Chaim Ganzweig's son: Reb Moshe, as sandak, with Rabbi Ganzweig

THE TORAH STATES THAT THE OIL USED IN THE MENORAH HAD TO BE שֶׁמֶן זַיִת זָךְ, *pure, pressed olive oil.*[23] The oil had to be produced through

Crystal Clear pressing, not crushing. Crushing of olives produces sediment, and even if the sediment is removed from the mixture, such oil is unfit for the *Menorah*, though

it could be fit for the *Mizbei'ach* (Altar). Reb Moshe explained that the light of the Menorah represents the light of Torah. A teacher of Torah must communicate his lessons in a way that is crystal clear. In transmitting Torah to one's students, there is no room for ambiguity or any sort of confusion. Each lesson must be clear and pure, like the highest-quality oil, which never contained any sort of impurity.

Rabbi Reuven Feinstein said that this was Reb Moshe's approach in every aspect of Torah teaching. Whether he was delivering a *shiur,* rendering a *psak,* or inspiring his talmidim with a *shmuess,* the teaching was clear, complete, and accurate.

With his son Reb Reuven

---

23. *Shemos* 27:20.

NO QUESTION WAS TOO BIG OR TOO SMALL FOR REB MOSHE. HE COULD

Everyone's Posek

closet himself in a room for days researching and studying before deciding a life-and-death matter, a decision which the Surgeon General of the United States and a team of doctors awaited before going ahead with a delicate and dangerous operation. And he could listen just as carefully to the question of an educator regarding which text to use for an *Al Hamichyah* poster for children.

> One day, Reb Moshe's beis midrash phone rang. The caller told the talmid who answered it that he lived in the Bronx and had a question regarding the observance of a *yahrzeit*. The talmid, trying to be protective of Reb Moshe's precious time, told the caller that such a question did not require the Rosh Yeshivah's expertise; there were a number of distinguished rabbanim in the Bronx who could respond to it. When the talmid hung up the phone, Reb Moshe asked him what the call was about.
>
> Upon hearing what had transpired, Reb Moshe grew upset. "From now on," he said, "you must give me every phone call. Just because he told you he called about a *yahrzeit* does not mean it was really so. He may have called for a different reason but was embarrassed to say the truth."

A well-known rosh yeshivah related how, as a *bachur*, he personally witnessed Reb Moshe's sensitivity and concern when responding to a halachic question.

He had a medical problem and was uncertain as to how the therapy should be done on Shabbos. The *bachur* came to Tifereth Jerusalem and stood on line after *Shacharis* to ask his question. When his turn came, a few of Reb Moshe's talmidim were standing at his desk in order to listen and learn. But Reb Moshe immediately sensed that this *bachur's* question was of a personal and somewhat embarrassing nature. So he led the *bachur* to a bench behind his desk where they were out of earshot. The *bachur* described the nature of his condition and Reb Moshe rendered his *psak*. Their discussion ended and the *bachur* rose to leave. Reb Moshe smiled and wished him a *"refuah sheleimah,"* a *berachah* for which the *bachur* had forgotten to ask and which he gratefully accepted.

Rabbi Ephraim Greenblatt described Reb Moshe's complementary qualities of kindness and dedication to truth:

> There is so much to learn from his ways. He always greeted others with a cheerful countenance; the *Shechinah* seemed to rest upon

him. At the same time, he never showed favoritism to anyone. Once, he disqualified someone from testifying in a *din Torah*. He became ill from having done this, yet he did it because he perceived that this is what the Torah demanded.

… He delivered *shiurim* and authored *teshuvos* with the strength of a lion. Yet he would interrupt his writing to offer a *berachah*, a *tefillah*, to write a *hamlatzah* (letter of endorsement) and to respond to halachic queries — and immediately return to his gemara. In his *sefarim*, he honored others to whom he wrote by addressing them with exalted appellations.[24]

In a *teshuvah* Reb Moshe writes:

It is unnecessary for his honor to excuse himself for disagreeing with me. This is the way of the Torah, to clarify the truth, and G-d forbid for one who disagrees to remain silent … Therefore even if you view me as a man of stature, it is permissible to disagree and you are therefore obligated to state your opinion … but, in any case, with regard to the actual question, what I have written is correct …"[25]

SOMEONE CLOSE TO REB MOSHE WAS ONCE SENT TO ASK HIM A HALACHIC question — and to make an unusual request. "The Rosh Yeshivah should

The Role of Compassion

please forgive me," the emissary began, "but if I do not present the following request then I will not have properly fulfilled my mission. I was asked to tell the Rosh Yeshivah that the person wants a decision that is strict Halachah without any leniencies."

"I do not rule with leniencies," replied Reb Moshe. "I rule according to the law."

That is certainly true, but it is also true that often Reb Moshe arrived at a lenient *psak* when no other recognized *posek* felt able to. How could *he* do so?

In a written appreciation of Reb Moshe, Rabbi Chaim Pinchas Scheinberg, revered Rosh Yeshivah of Yeshivah Torah Ore in Jerusalem, cites a case from the *teshuvos* of the Kovno Rav, Rabbi Yitzchak Elchonon Spector. An *agunah* came to Reb Yitzchak Elchonon, the leading *posek* of that era, seeking his authorization to remarry. In Reb Yitzchak Elchonon's words:

---

24. *She'eilos U'Teshuvos Rivevos Ephraim*, Vol. V, preface 3.
25. *Igros Moshe, Orach Chaim I*, 109.

The doors of permissibility appeared closed ... but because of the weeping and anguished cries before me, my compassion was stirred for this suffering woman, and I was able to deduce a *heter* (leniency) in accordance with how Heaven guided me ...[26]

Reb Yitzchak Elchonon's compassion had driven him to strain his mind even more than was required of him until, somewhere in his vast storehouse of knowledge, he discovered what was needed for a lenient ruling. Had he not been so compassionate, he would not have taken the extra effort to rule as he did. True, his lenient ruling was made possible by his compassion, but it was not *based* on his compassion, for Torah truth can *never* be compromised, no matter what the consequences. The woman could remarry because Reb Yitzchak Elchonon understood that Halachah indeed permitted her to.

So it was with Reb Moshe. As Rabbi Michel Barenbaum expressed it, "Reb Moshe was the man of Halachah, but from studying his *teshuvos,* one can see his *chesed* and the concern he felt for others."

Rabbi Reuven Feinstein commented:

The Rosh Yeshivah never veered an iota from Torah truth. It is true,

---

26. *She'eilos U'Teshuvos Ein Yitzchak, Even Haezer I,* #24. From a piece published in a special edition of the *Am HaTorah* journal in memory of Reb Moshe and Reb Yaakov Kamenetsky.

though, that he did seek to find leniencies to help solve people's problems. There were many times when he searched and searched and could not find any basis to be lenient. Even then, the petitioner did not walk away dejected because he knew that the Rosh Yeshivah had tried his best, because he cared.

It was because he cared so much that he was often able to find a leniency. He made *everyone else's* pain his own in a very real sense. When a person came to him with a problem that touched on a halachic issue, my father's *ahavas Yisrael* and *nosei b'ol* (sharing another's burden) impelled him to leave no stone unturned in trying to find a valid *psak* that could help the person's situation. He used his flawless command of all of Torah to find firm basis to be lenient. And when he found such basis, his feeling for the other person provided the impetus for him to take responsibility for the *psak* and rule definitively on the matter.

…When someone claimed that my father tended to be a *meikil* (lenient one) in matters of *psak halachah,* he responded, "What does he mean by '*meikil*'? I studied the topic in depth and derived the practical halachah. Should I falsify matters and rule stringently when in fact the halachah is lenient?"

Reb Moshe would occasionally show a *teshuvah* he was preparing to other *talmidei chachamim.* One such *talmid chacham,* a renowned *adam gadol*, remarked, "Reb Moshe often brings proofs from far-flung *gemaros* that at first glance have nothing to do with the topic at hand. Only after delving into the topic well was I able to fully grasp his point."

Reb Moshe's knowledge of Torah was incomparable, and his *siyata diShmaya* in *psak* was unusual. These two factors permitted him the 'broad shoulders' needed to be lenient when others may have hesitated to do so.

Once, he involved himself in a very sensitive case and as a result was the target of verbal attack by one party. Someone asked Reb Moshe, "Why does the Rosh Yeshivah allow himself to get involved in such cases? He has nothing but aggravation from these matters!"

Replied Reb Moshe, "Had you seen the tears of the person who brought the problem before me you would not have asked such a question."

A young woman who was going through difficult times was scheduled to see Reb Moshe regarding a halachic matter related to her problem. The day after the appointment was made Reb Moshe told someone, "The thought of a *bas Yisrael* suffering so disturbed my sleep last night."

> Late one night, Rabbi Tuvia Goldstein received a phone call from Reb Moshe asking that he come upstairs to his apartment to discuss an urgent matter. A woman had phoned Reb Moshe with the following question:
>
> Her brother was dying of kidney failure. She wanted to donate a kidney to save his life, but she had been diagnosed with a serious medical condition and her doctor had advised her against donating the kidney — but she wanted to. Did Halachah permit her to go against the doctor's advice and donate the kidney?
>
> For two hours, Reb Moshe and Reb Tuvia discussed the matter. Finally, Reb Moshe ruled that she was permitted to donate the kidney.
>
> By the time Reb Tuvia returned to his apartment, it was past 2 a.m. A few minutes later, Reb Tuvia's phone rang again. It was Reb Moshe. "We have just ruled on a matter of *pikuach nefesh* (where a life is at stake). Now we must say *Tehillim*."

IN THE FORMATIVE YEARS OF HATZOLAH, THE WORLD-RENOWNED VOLUNTEER medical emergency service, it was Reb Moshe who established the hala-

A *"Machmir"* chic guidelines for responding to calls on Shabbos. At a meeting between rabbanim and Hatzolah coordina-
tors, a rav suggested to Reb Moshe that he was being lenient with regard

to *Hilchos Shabbos*. Reb Moshe rose and declared, "I am not a *meikil* in *Hilchos Shabbos*; I am a *machmir* in *pikuach nefesh* (saving a life)."

A short time later, Reb Moshe sent a message to Rabbi Heshy Jacob, coordinator of the Lower East Side's Hatzolah division, asking if he could become an official member of Hatzolah. Rabbi Jacob asked Reb Moshe's grandson, Rabbi Mordechai Tendler, to explain the request. Rabbi Tendler said, "Your work is *pikuach nefesh* and the Rosh Yeshivah would like to be a part of your work." Rabbi Jacob replied that as Hatzolah's supreme halachic authority, Reb Moshe surely was a member.

IT UPSET HIM GREATLY TO HEAR THAT SOMEONE HAD DISTORTED OR MISQUOTED one of his rulings, thereby deducing proof for a leniency that was false!

Dedication to Truth Someone once told Reb Moshe a story of how a famous 19th-century *tzaddik* would swallow steaming hot food without chewing it so as not to enjoy earthly pleasures. Reb Moshe replied that he could not believe that so great a *tzaddik* would do something that could be so damaging to his health. "But they say it's a true story!" the man insisted. "Yes," Reb Moshe responded, "and people also say things about me which are not true, although I am alive to deny it. So why is it hard to believe that a story about someone who passed away over one hundred years ago is, in fact, a fabrication!"

Reb Moshe's commitment to truth in his everyday life was unswerving; nothing in the world could ever cause him to stray from it. Undoubtedly this attribute was another important reason why Hashem, Whose seal is truth,[27] granted him the help needed to arrive at the truth in Halachah.

> His passion for truth went to unusual lengths. He always insisted on paying for the breakfast he ate in Tifereth Jerusalem. While the yeshivah administration felt that he was entitled to the breakfast — and a great deal more — Reb Moshe would not hear of it. He received a salary from the yeshivah for his services and he would not accept a penny more than had been agreed upon. Of course, when it came to making appeals, attending functions, or doing anything else to raise funds for the yeshivah, Reb Moshe was always ready to be of service, without the slightest notion of accepting payment for such voluntary services.

Through an error, the government began sending him Social Security

---

27. *Shabbos* 55a.

Reb Moshe being greeted in Miami upon his arrival for a fund-raising visit. At right is the late Rabbi Shmuel Labkovsky, who served as Executive Vice President of Tifereth Jerusalem in the 1960s.

checks before he was legally entitled to them. He returned the money, along with a note of explanation.

People often donated money to Tifereth Jerusalem so that *mishnayos* would be learned in memory of the deceased. As time went on, the membership of the *Chevrah Mishnayos,* which had always fulfilled such requests, dwindled. This prompted Reb Moshe to arrange his daily schedule in a way that allowed for additional *mishnayos* study, which he dedicated to the memory of those for whom money had been donated.

SIXTY-FIVE YEARS AGO, A MAN WHOSE SON WAS STUDYING FOR *SEMICHAH* (rabbinic ordination) at Tifereth Jerusalem loaned the yeshivah $20,000,

Personal Integrity

thereby rescuing it from financial disaster. As the time of his son's ordination approached, the man sent out printed invitations to a gala affair celebrating the event. Meanwhile Reb Moshe was told by someone that the man's son was not conducting himself as a student of Torah should. Reb Moshe investigated and found the allegations to be true. Fully aware of the consequences, Reb Moshe told the young man that he could not be awarded his *semichah.* The enraged father then demanded that his loan be repaid without delay. It was.

Reb Moshe expected students of Torah to live up to the Torah's high standards of truth and honesty. He once received an unusual phone call from a yeshivah student. The young man had become involved in a friendly argument with a friend. The two had bet that whoever would be proven wrong would not shave on the coming Erev Shabbos. The caller had lost the argument, and now he wanted Reb Moshe's help in finding a way to be released from his vow.

Instead of helping the caller, Reb Moshe chastised him. "Whatever happened to the command of מוֹצָא שְׂפָתֶיךָ תִּשְׁמֹר *(Guard that which escapes your lips)*[28]?" he demanded. "Is it proper for a student of Torah to utter a vow without a serious intention to honor it?" While Reb Moshe could have found a loophole for the student, he refused to do so. The young man would have to learn to weigh his words more carefully.

A YOUNG MAN PURCHASED A HOME THAT HAD BELONGED TO A 95-YEAR-OLD Jewish woman who had passed away. The seller of the house was the

The Hidden Treasure

woman's 70-year-old daughter, who had neither the desire nor the strength to clear out her mother's possessions from the house. She therefore stated that the house was being sold along with all its contents (furniture, clothing, etc.), and had this written into the contract of sale.

The young man planned to renovate the house before moving into it. One day, before the renovations began, his children were looking for something to do. The young man gave them the key of their new home, only a few blocks from where they were then living, telling them to go there and play. The happy children excitedly ran off.

They made their way through the house until they reached the master bedroom. The old woman's family had left the house virtually untouched since her death and her bed was still perfectly made, just as she had left it. This did not prevent the young man's little boy from climbing onto the bed and jumping on the mattress. Up and down he went until, suddenly, something popped out from underneath the mattress. It was a securely locked metal box.

Before telling his father of his find, the boy decided to find out what he had discovered, so he got a screwdriver and pried the lid open. He and the other children could not believe their eyes. The box was filled with cash,

---

28. *Devarim* 23:24.

bonds, and assorted jewelry, some of it studded with diamonds. They raced home with the box.

It was obvious to the young man that the contents in the box were worth tens of thousands of dollars. It was also obvious to him that the old woman had not told her children about the small fortune she was leaving behind. Were he to remain silent, they would never know, and even if they *were* to learn of his discovery, it was quite possible that they had no legal claim to the box, for did not the sales contract stipulate that the house was being sold *with all its contents?*

However, all this meant nothing to the young man; there was no question in his mind as to what he should do. He would not even consider keeping the box unless Halachah declared it rightfully his. The old woman had not been observant, nor was her daughter, but that did not matter. He *did* live by the Torah, and that meant that *everything* he did had to be governed by its teachings.

The young man called Reb Moshe and told him the story. Reb Moshe said that he needed some time to think the matter through and asked that the young man call back the next day. When the two spoke again, Reb Moshe was prepared with his *psak.*

"You must return everything," he said with finality. "The clause stating that the contents were being sold along with the house did not include cash contents. People sell furniture, clothing, or other commodities along with a house; they don't sell money with it. In this case, jewelry has the status of cash. There was never any intent to sell such things."

The young man complied with the *psak* and returned everything to the seller, with the suggestion that she donate some of her new-found fortune to charity.

ASIDE FROM BEING WELL VERSED IN THE LAWS OF STA"M,[29] REB MOSHE HAD practical skills as well. At times, he personally repaired problems that sur-

Practical Skills faced with regard to his yeshivah's *sifrei Torah.*

One summer, a yeshivah camp that had only one *sefer Torah* found one of its letters to be problematic. At 6:30 on a Monday morning, the *sefer Torah* was brought to the summer lodgings of Reb Moshe. As the men alighted from their car, they met Reb Moshe on his way to *Shacharis.* Reb Moshe led them to an outdoor table and had them open the *sefer Torah* and show him the problem. Rather than tell them whether or not the letter was *pasul,* Reb Moshe excused himself and

---

29. *Sifrei Torah, tefillin* and *mezuzos.*

Writing a letter in a sefer Torah presented to Tifereth Jerusalem by Herman Wouk

went to his bungalow. To their surprise, he returned with a quill and bottle of ink, and fixed the letter.

He knew when a repair required a more skilled hand. One summer in Camp Staten Island, when a recently purchased *sefer Torah* was being used, two problems were found on the very first Shabbos. After Shabbos, Reb Moshe said that he felt a *"mumcheh"* (expert) was needed for the repair. Among the yeshivah's talmidim was a *bachur* still in his teens, Yisroel Kohn, who had trained as a *sofer*. Reb Moshe agreed that Yisroel should make the repairs, after which Reb Moshe would examine his work to determine whether a more experienced hand was needed. It was not. For the rest of the summer, Yisroel was assigned the task of reviewing that week's *parashah* in the *sefer Torah* before Shabbos to make sure that all the letters were correct.

One day, Yisroel approached Reb Moshe with a *safrus*-related question. Reb Moshe responded by asking for a particular volume of his *Igros Moshe*. They sat down and Reb Moshe showed Yisroel a *teshuvah* that discussed this very question. Together, they learned the responsum's main points. Reb Moshe then said, "Now study the *teshuvah* in its entirety; then we will discuss it further."[30]

---

30. A few years later, Rabbi Kohn received a *ksav kabbalah* (letter of certification) in *safrus* from Reb Moshe. Reb Moshe designated Rabbi Elimelech Bluth to write the initial draft of the certificate, after which he reviewed it carefully before signing it.

REB MOSHE STRESSED THE SANCTITY OF THE *MINHAGIM* (CUSTOMS) OF *KLAL Yisrael*.[31] He was as fluent in the *minhagim* of Lithuania as he was in *Shas*

Minhagim   and *Shulchan Aruch.* To Reb Moshe, the fact that thousands of Jews of previous generations, whose leaders were *gedolim* and *tzaddikim*, had followed a certain practice was sufficient proof that this practice was correct. This does not mean that all of *Klal Yisrael* must follow this *minhag*; it does mean that the *minhag* surely conforms with Halachah. If it seems otherwise, it is for us to study the matter and reconcile it.

When Rabbi Michel Shurkin was a *bachur* and not yet a talmid of Reb Moshe, he brought his *tefillin* to a *sofer* who, seeing that he was left-handed, changed the form of the *yud* (the knot on the *shel yad*) from the standard one. It did not look right to Michel, so he showed the *tefillin* to Reb Moshe, who told him to find a *sofer* who was familiar with the *minhagim* in Europe. The *bachur* went to his rebbi, the legendary Rabbi Leib Malin, who recommended the Satmar Rav's *sofer*, Rabbi Aharon Pollak. Rav Pollak said that the *minhag* in Europe had been to tie the knot in the standard way even for one who was left-handed, and he promptly restored it to its original form.

In later years, when Rabbi Shurkin would have a *safrus*-related question that was not easily resolved, Reb Moshe would send him to an elderly *sofer* on the Lower East Side who was fluent in the *minhagim* of Europe. If the *minhag* seemed at variance with the opinion of *poskim,* Reb Moshe would plumb the depths of Halachah until he had found firm basis for the *minhag*.[32]

---

31. One Tishah B'Av after *Minchah*, Reb Moshe asked Rabbi Yisrael Shurin to accompany him to a cemetery, in keeping with the custom found in *Rema* (*Orach Chaim* 559:10). Though it was a very hot day, Rabbi Shurin could not dissuade Reb Moshe from observing this *minhag.*
32. From a piece by Rabbi Shurkin in *Yated Ne'eman.*

WHEN A PARENT PASSES ON, CHILDREN STRIVE THEIR UTMOST TO HONOR THEM in *every* way possible. For men, this includes leading the *davening* on

Priorities

weekdays. Sometimes, in their desire to carry out their obligations as children, people lose sight of what truly is the greatest source of merit for their parent's *neshamah*.[33]

Reb Moshe told his son, Reb Reuven, that when there is the possibility of *machlokes*, one should forgo his right to the *amud* even though the halachah gives him precedence. [34]

Reb Moshe taught by example to carefully evaluate what truly is the greatest source of merit for one's parent. Each year on *Parashas Zachor*, Reb Moshe was called to the Torah for *Maftir*. While it is customary in many shuls and yeshivos for the Rav or Rosh Yeshivah to be called to the Torah for this important *aliyah*, the primary reason why Reb Moshe received this honor was that his mother's *yahrzeit* fell in the following week.[35]

One year, an *aufruf* was held in Tifereth Jerusalem on *Parashas Zachor*.

---

33. During the year of mourning for his father, it happened only once that the *gaon* and *tzaddik* Rabbi Tzvi Kowalsky did not lead the weekday *davening*. He was already at the *amud* in Bnei Brak's famous "Itzkowitz shul" for that morning's last *minyan* for *Shacharis* when an elderly man who had *davened* with the previous *minyan* announced, "I can't walk home alone. Can someone please walk me home?"

Except for this man, everyone else in the shul had not yet *davened*. No one came forward to help the man. When he made his announcement a second time and no one responded, Rabbi Kowalsky left the *amud* and told the man, "Come, I will be happy to walk you home."

By the time Rabbi Kowalsky returned to the shul, someone else was leading the *davening*.

That night, Rabbi Kowalsky's father appeared to him in a dream. "I am *mochel* the *amud*," he said. "Just keep doing these sorts of mitzvos" (from *Ana Avda* on the life of Rabbi Tzvi Kowalsky).

34. It is common that when two men are in mourning for their parents, the congregation is divided into two *minyanim* so that each mourner can lead the entire *tefillah*. Reb Moshe said that there is no basis for this in Halachah; to the contrary, בְּרָב עָם הַדְרַת מֶלֶךְ, *In a multitude of people is a king's glory (Mishlei* 14:28) — the larger the *minyan*, the more honor to Hashem. Therefore, the *minyan* should not be split; instead, the second mourner should lead the *tefillah* from אַשְׁרֵי-וּבָא לְצִיּוֹן until the end of *Shacharis* (from a *teshuvah* published in the *Am HaTorah* journal, *Mahadurah Tinyana*, #12). In discussing this Reb Reuven Feinstein commented that there can be no greater source of merit for a *neshamah* than to follow the Halachah.

(Reb Moshe notes that the *minyan* should not be split even when the second room has an *aron kodesh* with a *sefer Torah*. Very often when the *minyan* is split, the second *minyan* is held in a small, cramped side room which is not conducive to proper *kavanah*. This is an additional reason not to split the *minyan*.)

35. "The custom is that a man who will observe a *yahrzeit* during the week is called up to the Torah-reading for *Maftir* on the preceding Shabbos" (*Mourning in Halachah* published by ArtScroll/Mesorah, citing *Birkei Yosef* and other sources).

Reb Moshe instructed the *gabbai* to call him to the Torah for another *aliyah* and to reserve *Maftir* for the *chasan*, though halachically the *yahrzeit* surely took precedence. He explained that the *chasan* and his family were celebrating a *simchah* and would be hosting a *kiddush* following *Mussaf*. It would be proper, then, to allow their celebration to be complete by calling up the *chasan* for the coveted *aliyah*.

TO REB MOSHE, ANYTHING STATED IN THE TORAH, IN THE WORDS OF *CHAZAL*, or decided by Halachah was an actuality, to be utilized in real life whenever applicable.

A Living Torah
Someone once came to Rabbi Shlomo Zalman Auerbach with a difficult question regarding the permissibility of a certain marriage. Hearing that the petitioner was soon leaving for America, Reb Shlomo Zalman advised him to pose the question to Reb Moshe. Reb Shlomo Zalman requested of the man that he also ask Reb Moshe what he felt were the halachic ramifications of the teaching, "We disrupt Torah study to escort the dead [to their final resting place] and to bring the *kallah* to the *chuppah*."[36]

> Reb Moshe was not feeling well at the time and was confined to bed. The man was admitted to his bedroom to present his questions. He posed the marriage question as Reb Moshe remained lying in bed. Reb Moshe responded to the complicated matter without hesitation, while still lying down. When the man posed Reb Shlomo Zalman's question regarding the Gemara, Reb Moshe sat up in bed and thought in silence before responding. His response reflected the seriousness with which he approached every teaching of *Chazal*.[37]

When Rabbi Ephraim Greenblatt's grandfather was hospitalized for an extended period of time, Reb Moshe visited him a few times accompanied by Rabbi Greenblatt who recalled: "My grandfather was unable to speak, so he wrote his halachic queries and the Rosh Yeshivah responded. The Rosh Yeshivah remained standing the entire time. He explained that the *Shechinah* rests above the head of the infirm, especially one who is a *tzaddik* and *talmid chacham*. Therefore, it is proper to stand."[38]

---

36. *Kesubos* 17a.
37. From *Sefer Halichos Shlomo*, Vol. I p. 163.
38. Before Pesach, Reb Moshe would send to Rabbi Greenblatt's grandfather the best of the matzos whose baking he had supervised.

Once, at an Agudath Israel convention, he was making his way to a meeting of Torah leaders when he suddenly stopped. There in front of him was a man praying the *Shemoneh Esrei*. There was no way for Reb Moshe to reach the doorway without passing in front of the man, something Halachah does not permit.

A while passed; the man was still *davening*. Someone who had accompanied Reb Moshe to the convention and was now standing next to him whispered that the hour was late. "What shall I do?" Reb Moshe responded. "There is a wall in front of me!" To Reb Moshe, passing before a man who was reciting *Shemoneh Esrei* was as impossible as walking through a wall, because Halachah declared it forbidden.

In 1968, Reb Moshe traveled with Rabbi Yisrael Eidelman, his talmid and Executive Vice-President of Tifereth Jerusalem, to the town of New Square in upstate New York to attend the funeral of Rabbi Yaakov Yosef Twersky, the saintly Rebbe of Skver.[39]

Unavoidable circumstances caused the start of the funeral to be delayed for some time, while thousands of mourners stood in the streets waiting. Had the organizers known that Reb Moshe was present and standing, they surely would have provided him with a place to rest. However, Reb Moshe, in his usual humble way, did not make his presence known and remained standing along with everyone else. A young Skverer *chassid* went into the Rebbe's home and brought Reb Moshe a chair, but he refused it. More

---

39. Both Reb Moshe and Reb Yaakov Kamenetsky held the Skverer Rebbe in the highest regard. Once, in the early 1970s, Reb Moshe was hospitalized, and Reb Yaakov came to visit him. When Reb Moshe mentioned that there had been some discussion about switching doctors, Reb Yaakov asked, "Has the Skverer Rebbe been consulted?" He was referring to the present rebbe, Rabbi Dovid Twersky. When Reb Moshe replied in the negative, Reb Yaakov said, "His father (Rabbi Yaakov Yosef Twersky) had a special *siyata diShmaya* in *inyanei refuah* (matters of healing). He gave that *siyata diShmaya* over to his son."

Skverer chassidim relate that a man who was suffering heart failure was told that only a relatively new dangerous procedure could save his life. Reb Yaakov advised him to seek the counsel of the Skverer Rebbe, R' Yaakov Yosef, who advised that he undergo the procedure. When the man reported back to Reb Yaakov, the *gaon* told him, "Heaven will not disappoint the Skverer Rebbe."

A few patients underwent the procedure that week; only this man recovered from it.

When Reb Moshe would spend Yom Tov with his son-in-law and daughter, Rabbi Moshe David Tendler, *shlita*, and Rebbetzin Sifra Tendler, ע"ה, he would travel to nearby New Square on erev Yom Tov to immerse in a *maayan* (spring). When this occurred on Erev Pesach, the Skverer Rebbe would be apprised of Reb Moshe's presence and he would send him a special gift — matzos baked on Erev Pesach whose baking the Rebbe had personally supervised.

*With Rabbi Yisrael
H. Eidelman*

time passed. Realizing how strenuous the standing must have been for Reb Moshe, then 73 years old, the chassid again offered him the chair.

Reb Moshe said, "One does not stand when others are sitting; one does not sit when others are standing." Once the person heard this, he did not make the suggestion again. He had thought that Reb Moshe had simply not wanted to trouble him, but now he understood that there was more to it than that. Reb Moshe's refusal was rooted in a teaching of *Chazal,* and if such was the case, he would not change his mind.

IN HIS EARLY YEARS AT TIFERETH JERUSALEM, A FIRE IN THE BASEMENT OF THE yeshivah caused the building's heating system to be temporarily shut down.

Devotion to His Calling The entire yeshivah took up temporary residence in a local shul. Only one person remained in the frigid yeshivah building, wrapped in his coat and scarf as he learned — Reb Moshe remained at his seat in the beis midrash so that those who had *she'eilos* to ask would have no trouble finding him.

Reb Moshe once arranged for a *get* to be written for a certain couple and then had a talmid act as the husband's emissary *(shaliach)* in delivering the *get* to his wife in the presence of the required two witnesses. The woman, however, was not Torah-observant and refused to accept the *get*. The emissary and witnesses returned to Reb Moshe, their mission unaccomplished.

Reb Moshe, accompanied by the emissary and witnesses, made his way up the four flights of steps leading to the woman's apartment, in a run-down Manhattan tenement. He was met at the door not by the woman, but by her father, who yelled at Reb Moshe to leave his daughter alone. Reb Moshe calmly insisted that he be allowed to speak with the woman. The angry father finally conceded and allowed the group to enter. Reb Moshe calmly and clearly explained to the woman what a tragic mistake she was making. She agreed to accept the *get*, whereupon the *shaliach* gave it to her and they left.

As they were walking down the steps, the talmid said, "Please forgive me, but when the Rosh Yeshivah presides over such cases doesn't he represent the Jewish court? Is it proper that he should belittle himself so by trekking up flights of steps to take such abuse? The Rosh Yeshivah is a *gadol b'Yisrael* — it is not fitting for him …"

"What?" Reb Moshe countered forcefully. "In such situations I should be concerned not to belittle myself? What about the honor of Hashem? What if the woman would, G-d forbid, have found a new husband without having accepted a *get*? The honor of Heaven would have been cast into shame! Can there be a greater disgrace than that?"

In a responsum, Reb Moshe writes, "I literally have no free time, even for a short while, because I must respond to those who ask in practical matters. Nevertheless, since his honor has raised a challenge to my words … I must respond, and may Hashem help me to clarify matters."

How much Reb Moshe did to merit that Divine assistance!

CHAPTER SEVEN

Leader of His People

Rabbi Meir said: Whoever engages in Torah study for its own sake merits many things ... from him people enjoy counsel and wisdom, understanding and strength ...[1]

OR MANY PEOPLE, ONE OF THE GREATEST EXPRESSIONS OF honor for Torah they ever witnessed was the sight of Reb Moshe entering a crowded auditorium to take his seat. He would rush to his place, with concentration etched on his face and his body bent forward. As soon as his presence was noticed, there would be total silence; people would jump up from their seats, lean, push, stand on chairs and contort their bodies to get a glimpse of him. To some, it was reminiscent of the accounts of the Chofetz Chaim entering the hall for the Knessiah Gedolah in Vienna in 1923, causing a hush to fall over the crowd as people strained to see him.

Greeting the Shechinah

The Telsher Rosh Yeshivah, Rabbi Chaim Dov Keller, recalls that when Reb Moshe would deliver his address at the annual Agudath Israel national convention, "You could hear a pin drop. One could gain *yiras Hashem* just by gazing at him."

Attending that convention each year was a man who did not attend sessions featuring Yiddish addresses, for he did not understand the

---

1. *Avos* 6:1.

Reb Moshe addressing the Agudath Israel convention (front dais left to right):
Rabbi Pinchas Menachem Alter (then Gerrer Rosh Yeshivah and later Gerrer Rebbe);
Rabbi Moshe Sherer; Reb Moshe at podium; and Rabbi Yaakov Kamenetsky

language. But whenever Reb Moshe — who spoke a quick, heavily accented Yiddish — was on the program, the man would come early to get a
front seat. When asked why, he explained, "I can't understand what Reb
Moshe says, but when he speaks, I feel that the *Shechinah* is coming to us
from him through his throat."[2]

Indeed, the Jewish soul has an instinct that enables it to recognize its
gedolim, to sense the throat through which the voice of the *Shechinah* comes
down to earth. In Reb Moshe, the nation recognized its living Torah scroll.

WHEN ASKED IF HE COULD COMMENT ON HIS FATHER'S WISDOM IN PRACTICAL
matters, Rabbi Reuven Feinstein said, "In the family, once we brought a
question to him and he offered his counsel, the matter
was settled. We had no further doubts about what to do."

**A Heavenly
Ring**

Reb Moshe's family knew that his ability to solve
any given problem was in no way limited to matters of Halachah. In the
Torah — of which it is says, "Delve into it and continue to delve into it, for

---

2. When Rabbi Reuven Feinstein was approaching 40, he told his father that after years
as a Rosh Yeshivah, he still felt uncomfortable speaking in public. Reb Moshe responded,
"And I am close to 80 and I still have אֵימָתָא דְּצִיבּוּרָא (lit. *fear of the congregation*). Actually,
it's a good thing; this way, one does not *ploider*" (a Yiddish word meaning to ramble on
without a cohesive theme).

everything is in it"[3] — lies the solution to all problems, the guidance for all matters. Not everyone has the vision to see all this in the Torah, but it is there nonetheless. Reb Moshe's total immersion in Torah study, along with his many other attributes, earned him the wisdom and necessary Divine assistance to advise people from all walks of life in all sorts of matters.

A widow was having difficulty with her daughter, a teenager. Someone arranged for the two of them to meet with Reb Moshe in his home. When the meeting was over, the woman said, "Reb Moshe did more for my daughter than the greatest psychologist in the world could have done. He spoke to her like a father to a daughter. She is a changed person."

A young man once came to Reb Moshe deeply troubled by some unpleasant news. He had been in poor health for a long time and had finally gone to a specialist to try to find the cause of his troubles. The doctor ran a series of tests and had just called with the results. He told the young man that he was suffering from a physical abnormality that could not be corrected; nothing could be done for him.

Reb Moshe listened as the young man continued to speak for a while longer and then said decisively, "The doctor is wrong. *Chazal* speak of the type of abnormality that the doctor claims you have. According to them, a person affected by this problem should have certain symptoms. I have observed you for the past few minutes and you have none of the signs mentioned by our Sages. The doctor is wrong. You have nothing to be concerned about. You will get better."

Reb Moshe was right — the young man recovered in due time.

SOMEONE ONCE ASKED REB MOSHE A QUESTION AND WAS NOT HAPPY WITH his response. "Is this *daas Torah* (the Torah viewpoint)?" the person asked.

Daas Torah
Reb Moshe replied simply, "I don't know anything else."

In a *teshuvah*, he wrote:

> It is obvious from his honor's letter that he thinks I am upset by his words of reproof. And I say: To the contrary, I am moved by the fact that men of spirit are to be found who are neither afraid nor ashamed to offer reproof.
>
> However, the truth is that whatever I have written and ruled is [based on] the authentic Torah thoughts of our teachers, the Rishonim ... His honor's challenges are based on a distorted outlook that is rooted in knowledge of secular thinking ...Thank G-d, I know noth-

---

3. *Avos* 5:6.

ing of them. … My outlook is based purely on Torah without any admixture of secular philosophy.[4]

His Torah approach could be utterly simple and at the same time enlightening. An Orthodox Jewish scientist once expressed dismay to him about the world population explosion and how this might affect "quality of life" in future generations. Reb Moshe smiled and responded, "When Kayin and Hevel lived, they also thought that the world was not big enough."

To someone who sought an understanding of how prophets communicated with Hashem, Reb Moshe explained:

> Picture someone holding a transistor radio, listening to a news report. Those sound waves are in the air available to anyone, but only someone with the proper apparatus can "tune in" and actually hear those sounds.
>
> The *shefa nevuah* (flow of Divine prophecy) was present until the end of the first Temple era. But to access that flow, one had to possess the necessary spiritual qualities. Moshe Rabbeinu was on a unique level that allowed him to access that Divine flow at any given time. Other prophets could access it only at specific times and under specific conditions. The rest of the population did not have the "apparatus" to access it at all.

An All-Encompassing Torah

HIS ABSOLUTE CONVICTION IN THE TRUTH OF EVERY WORD OF THE ORAL AND Written Torah was apparent time and again, as was his firm belief in the supremacy of Torah above all else and the teaching that "There is not a thing that is not alluded to in the Torah."[5]

To a talmid whose wife had given birth to a baby boy, Reb Moshe wrote that in wanting to express his wishes to the

---

4. *Igros Moshe, Even HaEzer,* Vol. II, #11.
5. *Zohar, Parashas Pinchas.*

parents, many blessings came to mind. However, our Sages have established a standard blessing for such an occasion: "Just as he has entered the *bris*, so may he enter into Torah, the marriage canopy, and good deeds." We can be sure, Reb Moshe went on, that if these particular blessings were chosen by our Sages, then there cannot be a blessing in the world that they do not represent.

As the years passed, more and more people would seek Reb Moshe's advice. He received them all with great respect and sincere warmth. Sometimes the questions were rather unusual. A young kollel scholar once asked Reb Moshe if it was proper for him to do janitorial work in his spare time. The money he earned would help him make ends meet and could extend his stay in kollel. Reb Moshe replied, "If you are concerned that such work might be degrading to the Torah's honor, you have nothing to worry about. It is no disgrace to do physical work for the sake of Torah study. However, your wife may be upset if you do such work. Do not undertake it without her consent."

Once, a man came to Reb Moshe complaining that his young son was very ashamed because he was quite short for his age. This was making the boy unhappy and the father could not find a way to pacify him. Reb Moshe, who was not well at that time, wanted to speak to the boy personally. In the meantime, he told the father, "Tell your son that Moshe Feinstein said that he knows some short people who can learn quite well!" Saying this, Reb Moshe, who was a very short man, smiled broadly.

REB MOSHE POSSESSED THE WISDOM TO KNOW NOT ONLY WHAT TO ADVISE, but also when it was proper to advise it. While a Purim *seudah* was in

A Time and a Place
progress in his home, two men came in to wish him well. Surrounded by family and friends, Reb Moshe greeted the visitors warmly. Before leaving, the two asked Reb Moshe's advice on a matter affecting a friend of theirs. Reb Moshe refused

to talk about it, saying, "I do not discuss someone's private matters in public."

Yet, on another Purim, his reaction in a similar setting was totally different. After the *Megillah* reading, Reb Moshe's home was filled with family, friends and *talmidim*, one of whom was experiencing difficult personal problems. Reb Moshe motioned to the young man to come into his study. "How are things?" Reb Moshe asked as soon as they were alone. While moved by Reb Moshe's genuine concern, the young man said that he did not want to take up the Rosh Yeshivah's time while his apartment was filled with guests. Reb Moshe answered, "I have time for my guests later; you have a problem now."

> His sensitivity when offering advice took on many forms. Once, a young man wrote a note to Reb Moshe, seeking his advice in a very delicate, personal problem. Upon receiving the note, Reb Moshe immediately took another piece of paper and wrote a response. The next day, he phoned the young man and asked that he meet him at Reb Moshe's apartment, where the Rosh Yeshivah climbed on a stool to take down an envelope which had been placed inside another envelope. "Here is the note that you sent me yesterday," he said. "I realize that it's very personal and I didn't want you to worry that some day in the future someone would read it. I am giving it back to you so that you can dispose of it yourself."

IN A WELL-KNOWN ADDRESS, REB MOSHE LAMENTED THE FACT THAT PEOPLE rarely come to seek guidance in the areas of giving *tzedakah* and the Torah

On Giving Tzedakah
education of their children. With regard to *tzedakah*, Reb Moshe said that times being what they are, people should not be satisfied with contributing one-tenth or even one-fifth of their earnings for the benefit of Torah institutions:

> In our days, this is not simply a matter of *tzedakah*. When one gives to strengthen Torah study, he is actually giving for his own sake and for the satisfaction he hopes to reap from his offspring. With regard to *chinuch* of one's own children, there is no limit (as to how much one should give) …
>
> It goes without saying, of course, that one must not only consult the Halachah with regard to how he should distribute his funds, but also in the way he goes about earning this money. A Jew must honor all laws pertaining to honesty, being careful to avoid all prohibitions against cheating and thievery.

At a meeting in Jerusalem during the 1964 Knesssiah Gedolah, on behalf of Kupat Rabbi Meir Baal Hanes – Kollel Polin; left to right: Rabbi Yitzchak Flasker (Sgan Rosh Yeshivas Sfas Emes); the Ozherover Rebbe, Rabbi Moshe Yechiel Epstein; Reb Moshe; Reb Moshe Deutsch (Kollel Polin's Honorary President); Reb Yeshayah Leib Levy; Rabbi Yaakov Shlomo Pardes; יבל"ח, Rabbi Fabian Schonfeld; להבחל"ח, Rabbi Yitzchak Yedidyah Frankel

A man once came to Reb Moshe and presented him with a generous donation for his yeshivah, which at the time was experiencing financial difficulties. Knowing the donor to be a man of means, Reb Moshe asked that he increase the donation to a specific sum. The donor replied that he would increase his contribution, but was unable to contribute as much as the Rosh Yeshivah had requested. He promptly wrote out a new check for an additional sum and handed it to Reb Moshe.

Some time later the Internal Revenue Service conducted a tax audit on the man's business. After negotiations between the IRS and the company's accountants, a settlement was reached requiring the man to pay a specific amount in back taxes. The amount was the exact difference between the man's total contribution to Tifereth Jerusalem and what Reb Moshe had requested of him.

The above incident is reminiscent of a story recorded in the Gemara.[6] Rabbi Yochanan ben Zakkai once dreamt that his nephews would suffer

---

6. *Bava Basra* 10a.

a loss of 700 *dinarim* in the coming year. Throughout that year, Rabbi Yochanan coaxed his nephews into contributing to the poor. By year's end, they had contributed a total of 683 *dinarim.*

On Erev Yom Kippur, the Roman government imposed upon them a tax of 17 *dinarim.* Rabbi Yochanan reassured them, "Do not fear; they will take only 17 *dinarim* from you," meaning that there would be no further tax.

"How do you know?" they asked him. Rabbi Yochanan related his dream to them.

They complained, "Why didn't you inform us of this [so that we would have contributed the full amount to the needy]?"

Rabbi Yochanan replied, "I felt that it would be better for you to give *tzedakah* only for the sake of a mitzvah!"

THE TORAH STATES REGARDING THE FARMER'S FEARS AS *SHEMITTAH* APPROACH-es: "And if you will say, 'What shall I eat in the seventh year?' ...I shall
Guaranteed Returns command My blessing ..."[7] Some commentators under-stand this question as showing a lack of faith on the part of the farmer. At *shalosh seudos* in his home in the spring of 5741 (1981), Reb Moshe said, "Today, I thought of a new *pshat* (expla-nation) in these words." He explained:

The farmer believes in Hashem's blessings and that only good can come from performing His mitzvos. However, he fears that he is personally unworthy and that even if he observes the laws of *Shemittah*, his personal shortcomings will deny him the blessings that he needs to survive without planting in the seventh year. Hashem therefore promises him, "If you observe *shemittah,* you will be the recipient of My blessings regardless of your failings in other areas. This mitzvah will guarantee you the material blessing that you need."

Reb Moshe added that this is the meaning of Rambam's statement, "No one ever becomes poor from giving *tzedakah*, and no evil or harm can come from giving *tzedakah.*"[8] A person may think: "How can I part with my money and give *tzedakah*? I am an unworthy sinner and am not deserving of Hashem's blessing in return." Rambam teaches us that such an attitude is false. One can never lose from giving *tzedakah.*

---

7. *Vayikra* 25:20-21.
8. *Hilchos Matnos Aniyim* 10:2.

AS MENTIONED ABOVE, IN THE 1950S, REB MOSHE ASSUMED RESPONSIBILITY FOR Tifereth Jerusalem's financial stability.[9] Thus, the tiresome and often thank-**Fund-** less burden of fund-raising fell upon his shoulders. As we shall **Raising** see, Reb Moshe also gave of his precious time to raise funds for other very worthy causes. His angelic personality shone through even in his solicitation of funds. A man recalled one such encounter:

> One evening, I answered the doorbell and there stood Reb Moshe and his assistant Rabbi Moshe Rivlin. We shook hands and I then escorted them upstairs to my dining room. My wife brought in glasses of tea and we began to talk. Reb Moshe had come to ask that I become a supporter of his yeshivah, and our discussion went on for some time.
>
> Finally, Reb Moshe rose to leave. It was then that my two young sons came over and asked Reb Moshe if he would pose with them for a picture. I was embarrassed and told them that it was wrong to ask such a thing of the Rosh Yeshivah, but he interjected, "No, no, there is nothing wrong at all. I would be happy to pose with them." I went and got my camera and Reb Moshe put one arm around each of my sons for the picture. He then wished me well and left.
>
> A few minutes later the doorbell rang again. I opened the door and was shocked to find Reb Moshe and Rabbi Rivlin standing there again. Reb Moshe explained that he had forgotten to thank my wife for the tea. He and Rabbi Rivlin climbed the stairs again (Reb Moshe was 74 at the time), thanked her, and then left.

One year, a *melaveh malkah* was held in a Manhattan neighborhood for the benefit of Tifereth Jerusalem. The event was a dismal failure, with less than twenty people in attendance, although Reb Moshe was scheduled to address the gathering. Some suggested that since almost no one was there his talk should be cancelled. However, to Reb Moshe it made no difference whether twenty people or two hundred people were present. Every Jew was important in his own right. Incredibly, Reb Moshe opened his address by excusing all those who had failed to attend, saying that the lateness of the hour coupled with other factors had made it difficult for them to come. He then delivered a *dvar Torah* with the fire and enthusiasm one would expect of a speaker standing before a huge crowd.

---

9. See Chapter Three.

On a fund-raising trip to Miami

In 1957, severe financial problems threatened to permanently shut down the Lower East Side's *mikveh.* At an emergency meeting it was declared an obligation upon all to help raise the necessary funds. Reb Moshe, accompanied by Rabbi Nissan Alpert, went knocking on doors soliciting donations. More often than not their efforts were rewarded with only a token contribution. One day, after completing their door-to-door rounds, they went to solicit at a shul where a board meeting was in progress. While acknowledging Reb Moshe's presence, the board members had the audacity to continue with their agenda until its completion before permitting Reb Moshe to address them. After he spoke, they presented him with a pitifully small contribution on behalf of their congregation.

As he left the shul, Reb Moshe noticed Reb Nissan's dejected look. He said, "The *Navi* Yechezkel was called ben (son of) Buzi, for he was willing to suffer disgrace for the sake of the Torah.[10] The disgrace we have suffered is in itself of benefit!"

---

10. The *Midrash* relates בּוּזִי, Buzi, to the word בָּזָיוֹן, *disgrace.*

With members of the Agudas HaRabbanim (left to right): Rabbi Noach Chadash (standing, facing Reb Moshe), Rabbi Ephraim Yolles, Reb Moshe, Rabbi Simcha Elberg, Rabbi Baruch Leizerowski and Rabbi Yaakov Neiman (standing at right). Standing behind Reb Moshe is Rabbi Meir Zvi Ginsberg.

REB MOSHE'S INVOLVEMENT WITH THE AGUDAS HARABBANIM REFLECTED HIS outlook that greatness in Torah is a requirement for leadership of *Klal Yisrael.* As soon as he arrived in America, Reb Moshe joined the organization. Historically, membership was limited to those rabbanim who possessed a wide-ranging knowledge of Gemara and Halachah.

Agudas HaRabbanim

Reb Moshe arrived in America at a time when the Agudas HaRabbanim was a primary force for Orthodoxy not only in the United States, but for European Jewry as well. During and after the First World War, when the yeshivos of Eastern Europe were suffering dispersion and deprivation, it was to the Agudas HaRabbanim that the Chofetz Chaim and Rabbi Chaim Ozer Grodzensky sent an urgent telegram, requesting financial assistance from American Jewry. The outcome was the founding of the Ezras Torah organization, which provides financial assistance to *bnei Torah* to this day.

When word of German atrocities against the Jews of Europe reached these shores, it was under the auspices of the Agudas HaRabbanim that great roshei yeshivah and rabbanim formed the Vaad Hatzalah (Rescue Committee).[11]

Well before he succeeded Rabbi Eliezer Silver as head of the Agudas HaRabbanim,[12] Reb Moshe was intimately involved in its activities. The

11. Later, other groups, most notably Zeirei Agudath Israel, played an important role in the Vaad's work.
12. Rabbi Silver was chairman of a presidium that included, at different periods, Reb

organization office's close proximity to Tifereth Jerusalem allowed for
important questions to be brought in person to Reb Moshe for his immediate response.

WHEN REB MOSHE CAME TO THE EAST SIDE, HE BECAME THE NEIGHBOR OF A
remarkable man and a remarkable organization. As mentioned above,

**Rav
Henkin** Ezras Torah was founded to provide for poor Torah scholars
and their families and for the great yeshivos everywhere in the
world.

Several years after it was founded, Ezras Torah came under the guidance of Rabbi Yosef Eliyahu Henkin, a rare *gaon* and *tzaddik*. Seldom
has a *tzedakah* institution been under the full-time supervision of one of
the greatest rabbis in the world.[13] Throughout his very long lifetime, Rav
Henkin was respected as one of the leading *poskim* in the United States.

Though Rav Henkin was much older than Reb Moshe, it was natural
for them to become close friends. They often consulted one another on
halachic questions. Once, on a frigid winter day, Reb Moshe approached

---

Aharon Kotler, Reb Moshe, Reb Yaakov Kamenetsky, Reb Dovid Lifshitz and Reb Pinchas
Mordechai Teitz. When Rabbi Silver passed away in 1968, Reb Moshe was appointed *Nasi*
(President) of the organization.

13. Rabbi Yisrael H. Eidelman's father, Rabbi Lipa Eidelman, was a rav in the Bronx. The
wife of one of his congregants was from Brisk. When the woman and her daughter were
preparing to visit Eretz Yisrael, Rabbi Eidelman suggested that they seek a *berachah* from
the Brisker Rav. When they carried out this suggestion, the Brisker Rav told them, "Why
do you need my *berachah*? In America, you have Rav Henkin!"

a talmid who owned a car and said, "Perhaps you can do me a favor? I want to discuss a *she'eilah* with Rav Henkin. Could you drive me there?"

Not always did they agree, but there was always great love and respect between them. In a *teshuvah,* Reb Moshe wrote how he and Rav Henkin had disagreed about the matter in question and written to one another, each attempting to disprove the other's points. The respect with which Reb Moshe writes about his great contemporary is a classic example of the love *tzaddikim* feel for one another even when they disagree.

Reb Moshe once said of Rav Henkin, "This man has not benefited an iota from the pleasures of this world."

Every Erev Rosh Hashanah, Reb Moshe would visit Rav Henkin to wish him *"a gut yahr"* and to "receive a *berachah* from an *adam gadol.*"

> Rav Henkin often asked Reb Moshe to make appeals for Ezras Torah, sometimes involving long walks on a Shabbos or Yom Tov. Reb Moshe never refused, out of respect for the holy cause of Ezras Torah and the great *gaon* who led it. Rav Henkin was at the head of Ezras Torah for nearly fifty years, until he passed away in his 90s. He used to keep a record of the time that he was busy responding to Torah questions while in his office — that was time that he "owed" to Ezras Torah, and he always stayed at his desk extra hours to make it up. He often refused to accept raises in salary, because he felt that the needy were more entitled to Ezras Torah's funds than he was.
>
> Even when he became blind in his old age, he continued to study Torah by heart and with others who read the Gemara aloud, and he

continued to run the affairs of Ezras Torah. In these ways, he and Reb Moshe were very similar: They put *Klal Yisrael* and service to Hashem ahead of everything.

Once, Rabbi Moshe A. Margolin, an esteemed member of the Ezras Torah *hanhalah,* came to Reb Moshe's apartment at Rav Henkin's request, at a time when Reb Moshe was ill. The Rebbetzin was visibly upset that Reb Moshe was not permitted to rest. Rabbi Margolin waited as Reb Moshe rushed into the kitchen and calmed her. "The *gaon* Rav Henkin called about Ezras Torah. How can I refuse him?"

WHEN ONE THINKS OF THE MAIN LEADERS OF THE AMERICAN YESHIVAH world from 1940 to 1986 two names come to mind: Rabbi Aharon Kotler

Go to Meet Moshe

and Rabbi Moshe Feinstein. They first came to know each other in Slutzk, where Reb Moshe studied and where Reb Aharon was the son-in-law of Rabbi Isser Zalman Meltzer, but it seems that Hashem wanted to bring them together to replant Torah Judaism in America.

When Rabbi Aharon Kotler was in Japan in 1940 along with other roshei yeshivah and their students who had escaped from German-occupied Europe, he debated whether to come to America or join his father-in-law, Reb Isser Zalman, in Eretz Yisrael. His goals were to save as many European Jews as possible and to replant Torah — in which continent should he work? As he frequently did where major decisions were involved, he cast the *goral haGra,* the method taught by the Vilna Gaon to find a Scriptural verse that would indicate what someone should do in a crisis. The indicated verse was, וַיֹּאמֶר ה' אֶל אַהֲרֹן לֵךְ לִקְרַאת מֹשֶׁה הַמִּדְבָּרָה, *Hashem said to Aharon, go toward Moshe to the wilderness.*[14] To Reb Aharon, this was a clear indication that he was to join the Moshe *par excellence* of his generation, Reb Moshe Feinstein, in the spiritual "wilderness," the term that was characteristically used to describe the United States in those years.[15]

The two leaders had enormous respect for one another, but they had different personalities and each had a role in which he was preeminent. It was as if they had divided the responsibilities for the future of Torah life. Reb Aharon was the dynamic, charismatic teacher and builder of Torah, who brought to America the concept that our most talented young

---

14. *Shemos* 4:27.
15. From *HaGaon HeChassid MiVilna* by Rabbi Bezalel Landau. Some question the veracity of this account.

With Reb Aharon

men should devote themselves exclusively to Torah study. Reb Moshe was out of the limelight, channeling his prodigious energies to serve as tireless leader of his own yeshivah and foremost *posek* of the nation. Reb Aharon was, so to speak, the Rosh Yeshivah of *Klal Yisrael,* while Reb Moshe was its *posek.*

As with Torah leaders of all generations, the idea of competition with each other in role or popularity did not exist between these two *geonim* and *tzaddikim.* A Torah scholar does not become a recognized leader through opinion polls or elections. His greatness in Torah, zeal for every mitzvah, and genuine concern for his people, combined with true humility and a revulsion for honor, catapult him into a position of leadership, often against his will.

A good example of the difference between Torah leaders and statesmen is the manner in which these two Torah giants traveled from place to place. For years, Reb Moshe would walk the mile or so distance from his home to the yeshivah. It was only in later years that he was always driven to yeshivah and accompanied wherever he went. Similarly, Reb Aharon could often be found traveling alone on a subway train or bus as he shuttled between his yeshivah in Lakewood, New Jersey, and his apartment in the Boro Park section of Brooklyn.

THE LOVE AND REVERENCE THE TWO *GEDOLIM* FELT FOR ONE ANOTHER IS AN inspiring lesson. Once, a student of Reb Moshe met Reb Aharon sitting on

Mutual Respect a train, recording his *chiddushei Torah* in a notebook. The two discussed a topic which the young man was studying, after which Reb Aharon asked his companion to relate some of Reb Moshe's recent halachic rulings. To one *psak,* Reb Aharon said, "This is a *chiddush* (original idea) and a correct one. The halachah is as Reb Moshe has said." The next day the talmid repeated the conversation to Reb Moshe. He beamed upon hearing that Reb Aharon agreed with his ruling.

In the summer of 1961, President John Kennedy invited leaders of 12 major Jewish organizations to a meeting in the White House to hear his explanation of a United States vote in the United Nations that was considered unfavorable to Israel. The meeting would take place on Tishah B'Av. One of those invited was Rabbi Moshe Sherer, who was representing Agudath Israel of America.

Rabbi Sherer presented three questions to Reb Aharon, with whom he was in daily contact regarding his *klal* work: 1) Should he attend the meeting on Tishah B'Av? 2) If he did attend, should he shave and wear shoes? 3) This would be his first meeting with a President of the United States. Does a president meet the criteria of a king for whom, *Chazal* say, a special blessing is recited?[16]

Reb Aharon told Rabbi Sherer that he must attend the meeting, that he must shave and wear shoes; he should put sand in his shoes to fulfill the requirement of mourning. As for the question regarding reciting the *berachah*, Reb Aharon said, "Ask Reb Moshe."

This incident illustrates another difference between Torah leaders and secular leaders. One would be hard-pressed to recall an incident where a political leader was asked an important question and suggested that the question be asked instead to one of his peers. However, Reb Aharon, the *gadol hador*, did not hesitate to suggest that a question posed to him be presented instead to Reb Moshe.

It was rare that Reb Aharon conferred *semichah* [rabbinical ordination] upon a talmid. Those of his talmidim who sought to be ordained were usually sent to Reb Moshe, who would accord special honor to these young men, for they were Reb Aharon's talmidim.

A talmid once came to Reb Moshe with a glowing letter of recommendation from Reb Aharon. Reb Moshe told the young man that since Reb Aharon thought so highly of him, he would be given *semichah* without a test; no test was necessary. The young man was taken aback, because he had mastered the *semichah* curriculum and would feel slighted to be ordained as a mere formality. Realizing that the young man was hurt, Reb Moshe suggested becoming study partners with the *semichah* candidate in the yeshivah for several weeks, and in that way the young man could prove his mettle. So it was.

---

16. See *Berachos* 58a.

Left to right: Reb Elimelech Gavriel ("Mike") Tress, Reb Moshe, Rabbi Moshe Sherer, Reb Yaakov Kamenetsky, Reb Aharon

One day, the young man overslept and rushed to the yeshivah without eating breakfast. Reb Moshe noticed that he seemed a bit weak. Had he eaten? No. Reb Moshe took him downstairs to the kitchen for breakfast. It happened again several days later. This time the kitchen was locked — and Reb Moshe insisted that the young man come home with him. That morning he ate a breakfast prepared by Reb Moshe himself — and he never overslept again.

> As Reb Aharon once prepared to leave for a visit to Eretz Yisrael, his talmidim were making plans to escort him to the airport. When Reb Aharon learned of this he let it be known that he would much prefer that everyone remain in the beis midrash rather than close their *sefarim* to see him off. The talmidim appointed a representative to call Reb Moshe and ask him what to do. He replied unequivocally, "Escort the Rosh Yeshivah. To honor Reb Aharon is to honor the Torah itself."

*Reb Aharon
on a visit to
Eretz Yisrael*

REB MOSHE VISITED LAKEWOOD A NUMBER OF TIMES TO VISIT HIS RELATIVES
there and participate in family celebrations. On these occasions, he was

**Memorable
Visits**

invited by Reb Aharon to deliver *shiurim* in the yeshivah's beis midrash. Those who were there still recall the
sight of Reb Moshe giving the *shiur* while Reb Aharon sat
to the right of the *Aron HaKodesh* concentrating intently on Reb Moshe's
every word. They also recall that some of Reb Moshe's *chiddushim* were
identical to some that Reb Aharon had said in previous *shiurim*.

Rabbi David Feinstein's *Shabbos sheva berachos* was held in Lakewood.
The wedding guests *davened* at Beth Medrash Govoha. After *Mussaf*, Reb
Aharon and Reb Moshe walked together, followed by all the Lakewood

talmidim and the wedding entourage. No one present will ever forget
the sight of these two *gedolim* arguing over a *sugya*, gesticulating as
they made their respective points.
Later that day, Reb Moshe delivered
a *shiur* in *Masechta Kiddushin* at the
yeshivah.

When Rabbi Reuven Feinstein
became engaged, he was a talmid at
Beth Medrash Govoha. Reb Moshe
wanted Reb Aharon to be *mesader
kiddushin*. However, the *kallah's*
family lived on the Lower East Side
and felt very close to Reb Moshe.
Reb Moshe's brother-in-law, Rabbi
Isaac Small, convinced Reb Moshe
to "make the *kallah* happy" and

*At a chuppah ceremony; Reb Aharon
is at right*

accept the honor of *siddur kiddushin*. Reb Aharon recited all seven *berachos*.

Once, Reb Aharon visited Tifereth Jerusalem to deliver a *shiur*. Reb Moshe escorted Reb Aharon to the beis midrash and motioned for him to enter the study hall ahead of him. Reb Aharon said, "Not in your yeshivah. Here, you must enter first."

"No, I cannot," Reb Moshe responded.

"Then," responded Reb Aharon, "we will walk in together," and that is what they did.

THE WORD "RESPONSIBILITY" IS ONE OF THE KEYS TO UNDERSTANDING REB Moshe and his mission. By nature, Reb Moshe was not a public man. He

The Moetzes

shunned the limelight, leadership, and controversy. His loves were Torah, teaching and defining Halachah, and committing his Torah thoughts to writing. Nevertheless, when he felt that his responsibility to *Klal Yisrael* required that he assume a public role, he did so.

Reb Moshe's selfless dedication to the spreading of Torah and to *Klal Yisrael* in general was apparent throughout his forty-nine years as a Torah leader in America. After World War II ended, a handful of great survivors formed the Moetzes Gedolei HaTorah (Council of Torah Sages) of Agudath Israel of America. The first chairman of the Council, Rabbi Reuven Grozovsky, and his colleague Reb Aharon, called on Reb Moshe to serve. In this way, he became involved in formulating a Torah approach for, and making major decisions on, matters affecting Jews the world over.

The authority of the Moetzes Gedolei HaTorah was based on the fundamental principle that Jews must follow the directives of Torah leaders even with regard to politics and other areas not mentioned specifically in the *Shulchan Aruch*. Reb Moshe explained the concept this way:

> There are people who maintain that *talmidei chachamim* are not qualified to decide political matters, that *gedolei Yisrael* should limit themselves to Torah and Halachah. Such people cannot be considered within the Torah camp. One might well say that disregarding the advice of a *talmid chacham* is far worse than violating a commandment. One who violates a commandment because he is too weak to resist temptation at least knows that his action is wrong. By contrast, one who ignores the advice of a *talmid chacham* denies that a Torah scholar's wisdom is superior. This is a far more serious breach.

After Reb Aharon passed away in 1962, Reb Moshe was drafted by his colleagues to assume the helm of *Klal Yisrael* and he became chairman of the Moetzes. Leadership meant a major change in Reb Moshe's life; indeed, it forced upon him roles that he had previously avoided.

WHAT HAD IMPELLED REB MOSHE TO ACCEPT THE CHAIRMANSHIP OF THE *Nesius* of Agudath Israel[17], and become so involved in day-to-day affairs

Turning Point

of Agudath Israel? And then, why did he accept the chairmanship of the Moetzes Gedolei HaTorah in addition, as well as the presidency of the Agudath HaRabbanim, Chinuch Atzmai and Ezras Torah, a leadership role in Torah Umesorah, and more?

> The turning point can be summarized in an almost unknown incident that was witnessed by Rabbi Meir Zlotowitz, who was standing only a foot away from Reb Moshe when it took place. Reb Aharon was in the hospital during his final illness, and Reb Moshe and his students were reciting *Tehillim* in the beis midrash of Mesivtha Tifereth Jerusalem. Suddenly someone entered the room with the tragic news that Reb Aharon was gone, and he motioned to indicate that it was no longer necessary to recite *Tehillim*.
>
> Reb Moshe looked across the room at the bearer of the news and asked quietly, "Is it all over?" The person nodded yes.
>
> Reb Moshe stood stock-still with shock and disbelief on his face. He mumbled these words to himself:
>
> "It can't be.
>
> "But, if it is true, it is the Will of the Creator.
>
> "This is how it must be.
>
> "If so, then it must be good."
>
> He repeated this monologue twice as if in a trance.

In retrospect it seems as if he could have been evaluating both the tragedy and his new responsibilities: *It can't be! But if this is Hashem's will, then it must be good, and we must accept it.* On the one hand, his personal struggle constituted *tziduk hadin,* an acceptance of the righteousness of the Divine judgment. But those who were close to Reb Moshe saw in it also that he was grappling with the Heavenly decree that would cast upon *him* much of the burden of leadership and responsibility that had been borne by Reb Aharon up until then. It was regarding this decree, too, that Reb Moshe could have said, "If this is Hashem's will then it must be good, and we must accept it."[18]

---

17. See further in this chapter.
18. Then he instructed the bearer of the news to tell the family that before anything was done, they should wait for him to arrive at the hospital. He literally ran out of the beis

ANOTHER MAJOR TORAH FIGURE WITH WHOM REB MOSHE HAD A SPECIAL RELA-
tionship was Rabbi Yaakov Kamenetsky, Rosh Yeshivah of Mesivta Torah

Reb Yaakov Vodaath. After Reb Aharon's passing, there were knowledgeable people who urged that the various positions of leadership
be divided between Reb Moshe and Reb Yaakov, but Reb
Yaakov would not hear of it. He insisted that Reb Moshe alone must lead
Klal Yisrael in America.

For twenty-three years following Reb Aharon's passing Reb Moshe and
Reb Yaakov worked closely and tirelessly in guiding the course of *Klal
Yisrael.* Our generation viewed them as our two wise fathers, who always
put their children's concerns ahead of their own.

Their love for each other was deep. Reb Moshe himself once said, "I
love Reb Yaakov and I am certain that he loves me as well; כַּמַּיִם הַפָּנִים
לַפָּנִים, כֵּן לֵב הָאָדָם לָאָדָם *(As a face sees its reflection in the water, so does
one man's heart reflect another's feelings).*"[19] When these words were
repeated to Reb Yaakov, he beamed with obvious pleasure.

When speaking before a group, Reb Yaakov once said, "When I was a
5-year-old boy, everyone in my town envied an old man of about 90, who
at age 5 had shaken the hand of Reb Chaim Volozhiner. I assure you that

*With Rabbi
Yaakov
Kamenetsky*

---

midrash and was driven to the hospital by his grandson, Rabbi Aryeh Don Greher. He
recalls, "I was *zocheh* to be the driver for the Rosh Yeshivah on many occasions. Always,
he would converse with me as I drove. The one exception was the day Reb Aharon passed
away. He was absolutely silent both to and from the hospital."
19. *Mishlei* 27:19.

in years to come your grandchildren will boast that they had the privilege of meeting Reb Moshe Feinstein."

From the late 1970s, when his health began to fail, Reb Moshe was forced to limit his attendance at important meetings. The Moetzes Gedolei HaTorah, which he headed, sometimes met in his home. Once, the meeting needed to be held at the Agudath Israel offices in Manhattan and it was felt that Reb Moshe's presence was crucial. Rabbi Elimelech Bluth drove Reb Moshe to the meeting. When Reb Moshe entered the meeting room, Reb Yaakov embraced and kissed him. Then he embraced Rabbi Bluth and blessed him with a special *berachah* in recognition of Rabbi Bluth's devotion to Reb Moshe.

> For most of Reb Moshe's years of illness, Reb Yaakov was still quite active, even speaking in public on numerous occasions. Reb Yaakov visited Reb Moshe regularly, until his own illness prevented him from doing so. During one of his last visits, Reb Yaakov said, "Reb Moshe, you must protect your health. We are two of the last ones left, and the young people need us."
>
> During another visit, Reb Moshe bemoaned the fact that his weakened condition was forcing him to sleep more than he had for most of his life. He remarked that, often, older people are able to manage on less sleep than they had in their younger years, but with himself the opposite was true.
>
> Reb Yaakov attempted to console Reb Moshe. He said, "People who sleep less in their old age can do so because their lifestyles slow down when they grow old. They strain their bodies less, so they need less sleep. But, you, Reb Moshe, have always engaged in mental strain more than physical strain. Even now you continue to strain your mind in study as you always did. You have not slowed down, so you need more sleep."

In the summer of 1984, after having partially recovered from a stroke, Reb Yaakov visited Reb Moshe. The next day, Reb Moshe remarked to someone how upset he was at seeing Reb Yaakov unwell.

One day, Reb Moshe received word that Reb Yaakov's condition had worsened. At his *minyan's* Torah reading, he instructed the *gabbai* to recite a *mi shebeirach* for him. However, no one present could recall the name of Reb Yaakov's mother (when praying for the sick, one always uses the mother's name). Reb Moshe then told the *gabbai*, "It is

Their last meeting, in the summer of 1984 in Reb Moshe's bungalow at Camp Staten Island

enough to say 'Reb Yaakov' — the *Ribono shel Olam* knows who Reb Yaakov is!"

BEGINNING WITH 1983, AN ANNUAL TESTIMONIAL DINNER WAS HELD IN REB Moshe's honor, with the proceeds of the affair going to Tifereth Jerusalem.

In Reb Moshe's Honor
In 1983 and again in 1984, Reb Moshe came a few hours before the dinner and received visitors in a private suite. It was a physical strain for him, but he considered it his duty to honor supporters of Torah who made the effort to come to help his yeshivah. Guests at the dinners treasure the unforgettable moments when Reb Moshe entered the ballroom or rose to speak, though it was clearly very difficult for him. Nearly a thousand people shot to their feet in silent reverence in an inspiring display of honor for Torah and the *gadol hador*.

In 1985, despite his strong desire to come, he was unable to do so.

Each of those years, Reb Yaakov came to the dinner. In 1983 he spoke and paid a moving tribute to Reb Moshe. He quoted the teaching of the Sages that if we are like mortals, then the earlier Sages are like angels compared to us. We should realize, Reb Yaakov told the audience, that Reb Moshe's greatness is equivalent to that of the luminaries of earlier generations.

In 1985, Reb Yaakov was very weak after a stroke, and his family pleaded with him not to attend the dinner, but he insisted that he must go in Reb Moshe's honor, especially since Reb Moshe himself was unwell.

At the Tifereth Jerusalem dinner in Reb Moshe's honor; Reb Yaakov is seated alongside Reb Moshe; Rabbi Yisrael H. Eidelman is in the background

Rabbi Matisyahu Salomon, then Mashgiach Ruchani of the Gateshead Yeshivah, addressing the 1984 Tifereth Jerusalem dinner, the last that Reb Moshe attended

As Reb Yaakov made his way from the elevator to the dais, he was forced to stop every fifteen or so steps and sit. He made a brief speech and left shortly thereafter, again pausing to rest frequently on his way out. On the way home, he sat slumped in the car, barely able to sit up. Reb Yaakov's coming had been an extreme sacrifice, for the honor of the man with whom he had shepherded the nation for 23 years.

They passed away only two weeks apart. It seemed incredible, yet to some it magnified what they had both meant to *Klal Yisrael* during these

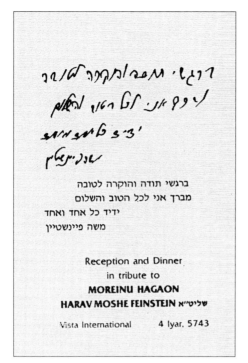

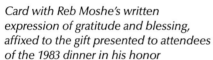

ברגשי תודה והוקרה לטובה
מברך אני לכל הטוב והשלום
ידיד כל אחד ואחד
משה פיינשטיין

Reception and Dinner
in tribute to
MOREINU HAGAON
HARAV MOSHE FEINSTEIN שליט״א

Vista International   4 Iyar, 5743

Card with Reb Moshe's written
expression of gratitude and blessing,
affixed to the gift presented to attendees
of the 1983 dinner in his honor

Jack Levenson greeting Reb Moshe
at the Tifereth Jerusalem dinner
reception

last decades — they who were "beloved and pleasant in their lifetime and in their deaths were not parted."[20]

GENERALLY, MOETZES MEETINGS ARE PRIVATE AFFAIRS; *GEDOLEI YISRAEL* serve their people modestly, selflessly, and prefer not to be in the headlines. One meeting, however, garnered much attention.

Meeting the Prime Minister

On a visit to the United States, Israel's Prime Minister Menachem Begin met with the Moetzes Gedolei HaTorah in Reb Moshe's home. It was a fruitful meeting. Begin showed genuine respect for the *gedolim,* wore a large yarmulka in honor of the occasion,[21] and conversed in Yiddish rather than Ivrit. In Reb Yaakov's words, with Begin one felt he was talking with a *Yiddishe mentsch.*

---

20. From *II Shmuel* 1:23.
21. At the White House signing of the Israeli-Egyptian peace treaty in 1979, Begin placed a yarmulka on his head before quoting from *Tehillim* in his speech. Rabbi Moshe Sherer viewed this as a great *kiddush Hashem* (from *Rabbi Sherer: The Paramount Torah Spokesman of Our Era* by Yonoson Rosenblum, published by ArtScroll/Mesorah).

Meeting with Prime Minister Menachem Begin in Reb Moshe's home.
Clockwise from left: Rabbi Moshe Sherer, Reb Yaakov, Reb Yitzchak Hutner,
Reb Moshe, Prime Minister Begin

Before the prime minister arrived, Israeli security agents searched Reb Moshe's apartment for possible explosives or weapons. As one of the agents looked underneath the dining room table, Moetzes member Rabbi Yitzchak Hutner remarked, "He is looking for explosives there? *There* are the explosives!" and he pointed to the multi-volume *Igros Moshe.*[22]

Some time after that meeting, a crisis arose in Eretz Yisrael over archeological digs that had unearthed human remains. Reb Moshe penned a letter to the prime minister expressing his concern over the matter. He received the following response:

> To his honor, Moreinu v'Rabbeinu hana'aleh (our exalted guide and teacher) HaRav Moshe Feinstein, President of the Agudas HaRabbanim of the United States and Canada:
> Moreinu v'Rabbeinu hana'aleh,
> I open by asking forgiveness for the significant delay in my response to his important letter. Many pressing matters, as well as the Yom Tov

---

22. In the yeshivah world, a great *chiddush* in Torah is sometimes referred to as *"a bumba"* (a bomb).

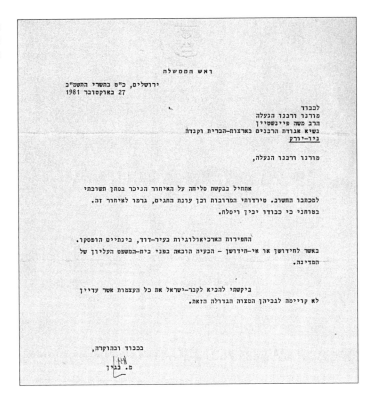

ראש הממשלה

ירושלים, כ"ט בתשרי התשמ"ב
27 באוקטובר 1981

לכבוד
מורנו ורבנו הנעלה
הרב משה פיינשטיין
נשיא אגודת הרבנים בארצות-הברית וקנדה
ניו-יורק

מורנו ורבנו הנעלה,

אתחיל בבקשת סליחה על האיחור הניכר במתן תשובתי
למכתבו החשוב. טירדותי המרובות וכן עונת החגים, גרמו לאיחור זה.
בטוחני כי כבודו יבין ויסלח.

החפירות הארכיאולוגיות בעיר-דוד, בינתיים הופסקו.
באשר לחידושן או אי-חידושן – הבעיה הובאה בפני בית-המשפט העליון של
המדינה.

ביקשתי להביא לקבר-ישראל את כל העצמות אשר עדיין
לא קריימה לגביהן המצוה הגדולה הזאת.

בכבוד ובהוקרה,
מ. בגין

season, brought about this delay. I am confident that his honor will understand and forgive.

The archeological digs in the City of David have ceased for the time being. Regarding whether or not they should resume — this matter has been brought before our country's High Court.

I have requested that all remains should receive a proper Jewish burial, if this great mitzvah has not yet been accomplished.

With honor and esteem,
M. Begin

ANOTHER MEETING AMONG GEDOLIM, ONE THAT WAS KEPT PRIVATE, REVEALS much about their greatness.

A Private Meeting
When Rabbi Moshe Mandel was a *bachur* in his teens, he was asked to accompany Reb Moshe to a meeting at Agudath Israel headquarters in New York. When they arrived there, Reb Yaakov and the legendary *Nasi* of Mirrer Yeshivah, Rabbi Avraham Kalmanowitz, were already there. The three were to meet to discuss the spiritual rescue of young Sefardic immigrants in Eretz Yisrael who were being forcibly separated from their parents and robbed of their heritage.

Left to right:
Reb Avraham
Kalmanowitz,
Reb Yaakov
Kamenetsky,
Reb Moshe

When Reb Moshe and his young companion entered the room, the three *gedolim* showed the *bachur* a seat and invited him to remain in the room while they met. The *bachur*, however, was not comfortable with this arrangement, so he sat right outside the room, where he was able to hear snatches of their conversation. Twice, he heard someone say, "And what would Reb Aharon have said?" Rav Aharon Kotler had already passed away. These three luminaries, each a living *sefer Torah* in his own right, were not satisfied offering their own view of the situation. They wanted to understand what to their minds Reb Aharon would have said.

When the meeting ended, Rav Kalmanowitz remarked to Moshe Mandel, "I am old and sick, but we must do what we can for the sake of *Yiddishe kinderlach*."

BEFORE REB AHARON'S PASSING, REB MOSHE HEADED THE *NESIUS* (PRESIDIUM) of Agudath Israel, while serving as a member of the Moetzes.[23] When Reb

Agudath Israel and Rabbi Sherer
Aharon passed away and Reb Moshe was appointed to succeed him as the Moetzes chairman, the Agudah leadership requested that he remain at the *Nesius'* helm as well, surely a strain on his precious time and energy. As Rabbi Moshe Sherer, the late revered President of Agudath

---

23. Simply put, the Moetzes charts the course of Agudath Israel, through formulating policies according to Torah, while the presidium guides the diversified activities of Agudath Israel for the benefit of Jews throughout the world.

Members of the Moetzes conferring (l to r): Reb Yaakov Yitzchak Ruderman, Reb Yaakov Kamenetsky, Reb Moshe, Reb Boruch Sorotzkin

Israel of America, recalled, Reb Moshe responded, "If you feel that it is important for the Agudah, then I will remain."

Even before Reb Moshe's appointment as Chairman of the Moetzes, Rabbi Sherer frequently sought his counsel on issues of major importance, especially in matters of Halachah. A talmid from the 1950s recalled that already in those years, Rabbi Sherer would often come to Tifereth Jerusalem to speak with Reb Moshe.

Rabbi Sherer's close relationship with Reb Moshe actually began in 1943, with Rabbi Sherer's marriage to Debby (Devorah) Fortman. His father-in-law, Rabbi Shimshon Zelig Fortman, had grown up in Starobin, where Reb Moshe's father, Reb David, was Rav. Rabbi Fortman and Reb Moshe were friends from their youth. Like Reb Moshe, Rabbi Fortman studied in Slutzk under Reb Isser Zalman Meltzer, where he became *chavrusos* with Reb Elazar Menachem Shach. When, for a time, the yeshivah in Starobin was temporarily without a Rosh Yeshivah, Reb David Feinstein brought the *bachur* Shimshon Zelig Fortman back from Slutzk to fill the post until a permanent rosh yeshivah could be found.

The Sherer family drew even closer to Reb Moshe through Rabbi Sherer's many years of devoted service to *Klal Yisrael*. When Rabbi Sherer's son, R'

With Rabbi Moshe Sherer

At the wedding of Mr. and Mrs. Bernard Baker. The kallah's father, Dovid Paley, was a Starobin native. Left to right: Reb Moshe; Reb Shimshon Zelig Fortman; the chasan; Rabbi Avraham Chinitz, a maggid shiur at Mesivta Torah Vodaath

Shimshon, became engaged, Reb Moshe was already past eighty and not in the best of health. Reb Moshe had been forced to curtail his schedule somewhat and the only weddings he attended were family weddings. The Sherers and their *mechutanim* came to Reb Moshe's apartment to receive his *berachah*. When someone mentioned that it was understood that the Rosh Yeshivah would not be able to attend the wedding, Reb Moshe

At the wedding of Rabbi Shimshon Sherer; standing (beginning second from left):
Rabbi Aharon Felder, Rabbi Moshe Sherer (background), Rabbi Anshel Finkl,
Rabbi Naftali Neuberger, the chasan

replied that the Sherers were family and he definitely would attend. He
did, serving as *mesader kiddushin*.

❦ ❦ ❦

Rabbi Shimshon Sherer recalls the great *kavod* his father accorded
Reb Moshe and other senior roshei yeshivah at Agudah conventions.
On Motza'ei Shabbos, when the keynote session was held, Rabbi Sherer
would personally escort each of the senior roshei yeshivah into the convention hall. Rabbi Sherer would wait until the thousands of seats were
almost filled, and then send a message to each rosh yeshivah, informing
him of how many minutes remained until Rabbi Sherer would be at his
door. When R' Shimshon was a young teenager, he was given the privilege of conveying this message to the roshei yeshivah. When Reb Moshe
welcomed Shimshon into his room, he withdrew a box of matches which
the hotel had supplied and told the boy, "I was not close enough to be
yotzei the *berachah* of *Borei Me'orei HaEish* at *Havdalah*.[24] Please hold

---

24. *See Shulchan Aruch, Orach Chaim 298:4.*

two lit matches together so that I can make the *berachah*." Shimshon did as instructed, and then Reb Moshe took two lit matches and instructed Shimshon to fulfill the mitzvah as well.

AFTER REB MOSHE'S PASSING, RABBI SHERER WROTE:

Wonder of the Generation

As one who is involved with *klal* work and who knows how difficult the burden of the community can be, I would always wonder how Reb Moshe found the time to do so much. ... For years, I could not comprehend how one individual had the strength to learn and write so much Torah, to respond to so many *she'eilos* from rabbanim and *dayanim*; to participate in so many, many gatherings; and at the same time to find time to deal with the problems, big and small, of so many individuals.

I am personally familiar with only a small portion of that which passed through his study. And yet I venture to say that even if Reb Moshe would not have been the preeminent *gaon, posek* and *marbitz Torah* that he was, his *chesed* and boundless *ahavas Yisrael* alone would have distinguished him as the *mofes hador* (wonder of the generation).[25]

Rabbi Sherer offered two examples of Reb Moshe's boundless *chesed* which he personally witnessed:

Five years before Reb Moshe's passing, I visited him together with Yosef Mendelevich, who had been released from a Soviet prison only a short time before.

Mendelevich had revealed a secret to me. He was greatly distressed that he had been freed while so many other Jewish prisoners, whose names were not so well known, were still languishing in prisons behind the Iron Curtain. Therefore, he had begun a hunger strike. He would not eat or drink until at least some other Jews had been set free. "Today is the second day of my fast," he said, and I knew that he was very serious about this.

I had arranged for Mendelevich to visit Reb Moshe in a few days. However, after hearing about his hunger strike, I immediately phoned Reb Moshe. I could perceive that Reb Moshe was shaken by my words. "Bring him here right away," he instructed.

I will never forget Reb Moshe's reaction when Mendelevich told

---

25. This quote and the ones that follow are from an article by Rabbi Sherer in *Dos Yiddish Vort*, Iyar-Sivan 5746 (1986).

A meeting of the Moetzes Gedolei HaTorah and rabbanim in Reb Moshe's home.
Clockwise from left: Reb Moshe; the Bluzhever Rebbe; Rabbi Sherer; Rabbi
Elya Svei; Rabbi Chaskel Besser; Rabbi Shmuel Bloom; Rabbi Avraham Pam; the
Bostoner Rebbe, Rabbi Moshe Horowitz; Rabbi Yaakov Yitzchak Ruderman

him of his fast. He was not satisfied to inform him with a definitive
psak that such a fast was contrary to Halachah. Hearing that it was
already more than a day since Mendelevich had begun fasting, Reb
Moshe, despite his weakness, rose from his chair with alacrity, hurried into the kitchen, and asked the Rebbetzin to prepare eggs for
their guest.

"Here, in my house, you will break your fast," he told him. Reb
Moshe sat with Yosef Mendelevich until he had finished eating all that
he had been served.

Thus I had witnessed for the umpteenth time that to Reb Moshe,
Halachah was not something abstract to be proclaimed from the
podium. Rather, it was a way of life that he personally taught others
to incorporate into their lives. And I had once again seen that to Reb
Moshe, *chesed* was not a mitzvah that was to be discharged by others.
Rather, he needed to perform it personally, despite his advanced age.

The second example of Reb Moshe's *chesed* also happened in his
final years. Reb Moshe called Rabbi Sherer and told him that he had a
problem which only he could help with. A young woman had called Reb

Moshe's home and, with no one else available at the time, Reb Moshe had answered the call himself. The caller explained that she had been orphaned of her father many years earlier, and just recently her mother had passed away. She was getting married and it would add greatly to her *simchah* if Reb Moshe would attend the wedding. Reb Moshe had agreed, despite his advanced age and poor health, but in her excitement, the young woman had forgotten to tell him her name and where she was getting married. Reb Moshe had called Rabbi Sherer in the hope that he could locate the wedding hall and the *kallah*.

Rabbi Sherer would relate this story to his offspring as a classic illustration of the greatness of *gedolei Yisrael*.[26]

In writing of Reb Moshe, Rabbi Sherer cited the verse that describes the reaction to the passing of Aharon HaKohen: "They wept for Aharon thirty days, the entire House of Israel."[27] Rashi writes that men and women alike wept over Aharon's death because, as one who loved and pursued peace, he earned the love and admiration of all. There is a type of Torah leader who touches the heart of every Jew in a very personal way, and when he passes on, everyone feels a very personal loss. Reb Moshe was such a leader.

In Rabbi Sherer's words:

> In recent times, no Torah leader was as deeply etched in the hearts of Torah Jews as Rabbi Moshe Feinstein. The name "Reb Moshe" was uttered by thousands upon thousands with awe and love. And this is no cause for wonder. For no leader in recent times so faithfully served all of Torah Jewry, men and women, young and old, people of all backgrounds and customs, as did Reb Moshe, *zt"l*.

RABBI SHERER NOTED THAT IN *PSAK HALACHAH*, REB MOSHE WAS SEEN BY SOME as a *"meikil"* (one who is lenient).[28] However, there was one area where he certainly was a *"machmir"* (one who is stringent) — where

When Lives Are at Stake
Jews were spiritually endangered. As many stories illustrate,[29] Reb Moshe loved every Jew, regardless of his or her level of mitzvah observance. It was precisely because of this love that it distressed him to see so many of our brethren led astray by movements

---

26. From the biography of Rabbi Sherer by Yonoson Rosenblum, published by ArtScroll/Mesorah.
27. *Bamidbar* 20:2
28. See Chapter Six.
29. See Chapter Eight.

Reciting Tehillim at the 1958 Agudath Israel convention (l to r):
Rabbi Yehudah Altusky, Rabbi Mendel Chodorow, Reb Moshe, Boyaner Rebbe,
Rabbi Eliezer Silver, Kapyshnitzer Rebbe, Sadiger-Pshemishel Rebbe,
Rabbi Binyamin Zev Hendeles

that promote a Judaism devoid of commitment to the 613 mitzvos. Therefore, Reb Moshe left no room for compromise in his opposition to Orthodox groups or rabbanim joining organizations that included members of the Conservative or Reform rabbinate. His *Igros Moshe* contains numerous *teshuvos* where he takes a strict approach to issues such as joining a *minyan* in a building of a Conservative synagogue, or allowing a conversion to be conducted by a *beis din* in which Conservative rabbis are participants.

Rabbi Yaakov Heftler observed the week of *shivah* for his mother at the bedside of his father, who was hospitalized. The only weekday *minyan* in the area was held in a small room of a Conservative synagogue building. The majority of the *minyan* (in which only men participated) were members of the local Orthodox shul, who were unable to assemble a weekday *minyan* in their shul.

Reb Moshe told Rabbi Heftler that he should not join that *minyan* though this meant that he would not be able to recite *Kaddish* for his mother during *shivah*.[30]

❧ ❧ ❧

Once, a yeshivah opened in a city with a large Jewish population, but only a small percentage of the people were Orthodox. The closest *mikveh*

---

30. From a piece by Rabbi Heftler in the *Kol HaTorah* journal.

was quite a distance away, and the rosh yeshivah felt it imperative to build a *mikveh* locally. Realizing that the local Orthodox community did not have the means for such a project, he approached the local Conservative rabbinate and asked if they would ask their congregants to support the project. The rabbis responded positively, and it appeared that construction would soon begin.

The rosh yeshivah then visited Reb Moshe to present halachic questions regarding the actual construction. Reb Moshe asked how the project was being funded. When the rosh yeshivah responded, Reb Moshe said forcefully, "No! You cannot take one cent from them! If you do, then they will use the *mikveh* for *geirim* whose conversions are not in accordance with Halachah. It is better not to build the *mikveh* than to build it in such a way. Hashem will help you to find other avenues of support."

Later, it was suggested that the rosh yeshivah call on the Satmar Rav, Rabbi Yoel Teitelbaum, whose chassidim are great *baalei tzedakah* and who personally distributed huge amounts of charity each year. Upon hearing the rosh yeshivah's request, the Rav asked why the community could not fund the project. When the rosh yeshivah related his encounter with Reb Moshe, the Rav promised his support. He raised $75,000 for the project, and the *mikveh* was built.[31]

IN A FAMOUS AGUDAH CONVENTION ADDRESS, REB MOSHE CALLED UPON every man and woman to live a life that would bring glory to Hashem and

A Nation of Teachers

His Torah:

We should be aware that we influence others in more ways than formal teaching. Our very actions serve as learning experiences for others. If we carefully follow the mitzvos and study Torah, our fellow men take note and follow our example. Thus, we ask Hashem every day that we be granted the ability לִלְמֹד וּלְלַמֵּד לִשְׁמֹר וְלַעֲשׂוֹת וּלְקַיֵּם אֶת כָּל דִּבְרֵי תַלְמוּד תּוֹרָתֶךָ בְּאַהֲבָה, *to learn and to teach, to safeguard, to do and to uphold all the words of Your Torah's teachings with love.* Not all of us are teachers, *talmidei chachamim* or *poskim*, but we all teach by virtue of our actions.[32]

In a piece appearing in *The Jewish Observer*,[33] Rabbi Sherer reacted to the publication of a book written by a secular Israeli journalist which spoke

---

31. From *Meged Givos Olam*.
32. *The Jewish Observer*, November 1974.
33. Published in 1993.

Reb Moshe addressing the 55th annual Agudath Israel dinner

of *chareidi* Jews in very derogatory terms. After refuting and protesting the book's descriptions, Rabbi Sherer made the point that it is the obligation of every Torah Jew to raise the banner of Torah and bring glory to Hashem's Name, and he buttressed his point with the above *vort* of Reb Moshe.[34]

RABBI SHERER ENJOYED AN UNUSUALLY CLOSE RELATIONSHIP WITH NEW YORK Governor Hugh Carey and was among his closest confidants.[35] Soon after

Governor Carey

Carey's election as governor in 1974, a bill was presented before the New York State Assembly regarding the definition of "death." The bill would have allowed for the pulling of the plug on a patient who was breathing with the aid of a respirator. Rabbi Sherer contacted Reb Moshe, who confirmed that pulling the plug in such a situation would constitute murder, and he urged Rabbi Sherer to do everything possible to stop passage of the legislation. The governor was informed of Reb Moshe's view and the legislation was aborted. The gov-

---

34. See the Rabbi Sherer biography, pp. 191-193. Rabbi Sherer himself epitomized a life of *kiddush Hashem* — every moment of his day. In the words of author Yonoson Rosenblum: "As carriers of the banner of *Klal Yisrael,* united by Torah, the first and foremost important task of Agudath Israel was lifting the image of the Torah Jew. Agudath Israel as an organization, and each employee of the organization, Rabbi Sherer insisted, must always be guided by a consciousness of the *kiddush Hashem* implications of every action. Every time they entered a meeting, Rabbi Sherer would say, 'We are going into this meeting as *sheluchim* (emissaries). We have to make sure that a *kiddush Hashem* comes out.'"
35. See Chapter Thirteen of the Rabbi Sherer biography.

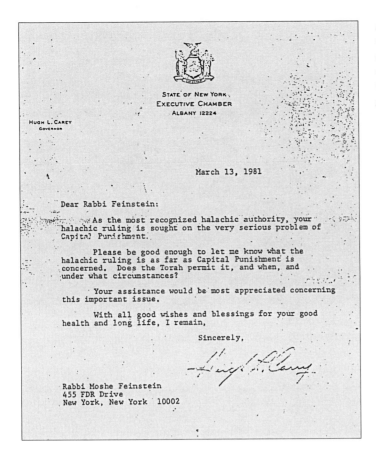

Letter from Governor Carey to Reb Moshe seeking his "halachic ruling" on capital punishment

STATE OF NEW YORK,
EXECUTIVE CHAMBER
ALBANY 12224

HUGH L. CAREY
GOVERNOR

March 13, 1981

Dear Rabbi Feinstein:

As the most recognized halachic authority, your halachic ruling is sought on the very serious problem of Capital Punishment.

Please be good enough to let me know what the halachic ruling is as far as Capital Punishment is concerned. Does the Torah permit it, and when, and under what circumstances?

Your assistance would be most appreciated concerning this important issue.

With all good wishes and blessings for your good health and long life, I remain,

Sincerely,

Rabbi Moshe Feinstein
455 FDR Drive
New York, New York 10002

ernor's office made no secret of the fact that his decision was based on "the opposition of the Orthodox Jewish community."

In 1981, when the issue of capital punishment was under discussion, Governor Carey sent a letter to Reb Moshe seeking the Torah's view on the matter. He wrote, "As the most recognized halachic authority, your halachic ruling is sought on the very serious problem of capital punishment ..." Reb Moshe responded with a lengthy exposition on the topic which was subsequently published in *Igros Moshe*.[36]

As Chairman of the Moetzes, Reb Moshe would regularly attend the annual Agudath Israel dinner. One year, he was not feeling well and was planning not to attend. However, he received a phone call from Rabbi Sherer informing him that Governor Carey would be attending and that it was important for the Rosh Yeshivah to attend, if at all possible. Rabbi Elimelech Bluth accompanied Reb Moshe to the dinner and wasted no

36. *Choshen Mishpat*, Vol. II, #68. Reb Moshe wrote the exposition in Hebrew and his son-in-law, Rabbi Moshe David Tendler, translated it into English for the governor to read.

At the Agudath Israel Dinner (l to r): Reb Shneur Kotler, Rabbi Chaskel Besser,
Rabbi Aharon Felder (background), Reb Moshe, Mendy Shayovich, Mr. Lowinger,
Rabbi Sherer, Governor Hugh Carey, unidentified, Reb Yaakov Yitzchak Ruderman

time in escorting him to a comfortable chair, where he remained seated.
Rabbi Sherer brought the governor to where Reb Moshe sat, introduced
him, and mentioned that the Rabbi had made a special effort to attend
in the governor's honor. Reb Moshe wanted to rise, but clearly was not
feeling up to it. In Yiddish, he spoke of *"kvod malchus"* (the need to show
honor for the government). When Rabbi Sherer attempted to translate,
the governor interrupted. "There is no need to translate," he said. "I am
humbled and flattered."

AGUDATH ISRAEL'S EFFORTS TO SPREAD THE STUDY OF TORAH THROUGH THE
learning of *Daf Yomi* brought Reb Moshe much joy. After the Holocaust,

The Eighth Siyum HaShas in which tens of thousands of *Daf Yomi* students perished, the completion of the seven-and-a-half-year cycle of study was largely unnoticed until the *siyum* in 1975. At that time, Agudath Israel rented the 1,200-seat Manhattan
Center to celebrate the event. For the next *siyum*, in 1982, the 5,000-seat
Felt Forum at Madison Square Garden was reserved.

The late Rabbi Chaskel Besser was a distinguished rav and longtime
member of Agudath Israel's *Nesius*. For many years, he headed the
Agudah's *Daf Yomi* Commission. Prior to the 1982 *siyum*, he and Rabbi
Yaakov Goldstein visited Reb Moshe in his apartment:

Reb Moshe addressing the seventh Siyum HaShas of the Daf Yomi

We were cognizant of his poor state of health, and aware of the concern which this caused his family, particularly his Rebbetzin. Therefore, our intention was to ask Reb Moshe to greet the gathering via a pre-recorded tape.

However, as soon as he heard of the plans for a grand celebration, he whispered to us, "Why a tape? I will attend personally!" He repeated this a few times. He added that while he realized he was not up to delivering an address, he wanted to join the masses in this gathering *lichvod haTorah.*

He asked us not to publicize that he planned to participate, because as a rule, he no longer attended public gatherings. "However, at this event I will be present," he reiterated.

He was prepared to come. However, he did not feel well on the day of the *siyum* and was not able to attend.[37]

REB MOSHE'S SENSE OF RESPONSIBILITY TOWARD *KLAL YISRAEL* KNEW NO bounds. When meeting with people involved in *klal* work he would often

For *Klal Yisrael* ask, "How can I help?" His time, every second of it, was very precious, but if it was used for *Klal Yisrael's* sake, then it was being spent wisely.

---

37. From a piece by Rabbi Besser in *Dos Yiddish Vort,* Iyar-Sivan 5746 (1986).

One year, on the fast of Tzom Gedaliah, Reb Moshe sat at a phone, placing call after call to inform key people of a development in an important matter. After a few hours of calls, he wearily leaned his head on the palms of his hands.

Someone said, "The Rosh Yeshivah appears very tired; perhaps he should rest a bit."

Reb Moshe responded, "Whom else should we call?"

He never allowed his commitment to one organization to conflict with his obligation to another. He once called the office of a well-known benefactor to request a donation for Chinuch Atzmai (Torah Schools for Israel), the independent network of more than two hundred yeshivos and Bais Yaakovs in Eretz Yisrael. However, the man was not in at the time. That night the man greeted Reb Moshe at the annual Torah Umesorah dinner. "I understand that the Rosh Yeshivah called today. Is there some way that I can be of help to the Rosh Yeshivah?"

"I am sorry," replied Reb Moshe, "but we are here for the benefit of Torah Umesorah. I will call you again tomorrow about the other matter." The man was amazed by Reb Moshe's words. The next day, the two did speak, and the result was a $50,000 donation for Chinuch Atzmai.

This sense of responsibility prevented him from ever undertaking tasks that he could not carry out properly. Many organizations involved in

When Reb Moshe spoke, listeners of all ages listened with rapt attention.

very important work for Jewry sought Reb Moshe as their leader, but he refused. He endorsed their work, always made himself available for guidance and decision-making, but would not serve as their president or chairman. To serve in such capacities meant assuming responsibility for all that went on within an organization. Reb Moshe knew that his other obligations would not allow him the necessary time to assume yet another such role. To assume such a position and *not* meet the responsibilities that came with it were out of the question, as far as Reb Moshe was concerned.

IN THE EARLY 1950S, THE RECENTLY FOUNDED CHINUCH ATZMAI WAS EXPERIENCing its first financial crisis. Future Knesset member Rabbi Shlomo Lorincz

Chinuch Atzmai spent a winter in America as representative of the organization. Most evenings that winter, he accompanied a delegation of the foremost *gedolim* in America on fund-raising visits to the homes of Jews in the tri-state area. Delegation members included Reb Aharon Kotler, Reb Moshe, Reb Yaakov Kamenetsky, and the *Admorim* of Kapyshnitz and Novominsk.

The work was difficult. There were few affluent Orthodox Jews in America at that time, and many donations were needed to raise anything substantial. Most nights, the delegation began its visits at 8 p.m. and ended

At a chuppah ceremony (left to right): the chasan, Novominsker Rebbe (Reb Nochum Perlow), Reb Aharon, Reb Moshe, Kapyshnitzer Rebbe, the present Novominsker Rebbe is standing just behind Reb Aharon.

at around 11. On many nights, these *gedolim* did not return to their respective homes until midnight.

Rebbetzin Feinstein was not happy with this arrangement. Reb Moshe would arise before dawn to study and write until *Shacharis*. She was concerned that these nightly excursions would adversely affect his health. Privately, she asked Rabbi Lorincz to find a way to bring her husband home by 10:30. Rabbi Lorincz did try, but he was not successful. Reb Moshe insisted that it was a *zechus* to be a full partner in this mitzvah and he would not return home until the nightly visits had been completed.[38]

ONE OF THE POSITIONS THRUST UPON REB MOSHE AFTER THE PASSING OF REB Aharon was that of *Nasi* (President) of Chinuch Atzmai. When Reb Moshe

As Nasi became *Nasi*, it was another time of crisis for Chinuch Atzmai. Energetically, he reorganized the entire organization, recruiting all the major roshei yeshivah to become actively involved. There were regular meetings, all of which he attended. He supervised policy-making, fund-raising, and the budget. Not a day went by that he was not in personal contact with Rabbi Henoch Cohen, Chinuch Atzmai's executive director, and Rabbi Yosef Tannenbaum, his chief colleague. He wanted

Delivering an address on behalf of Chinuch Atzmai

information about activities in Eretz Yisrael, American fund-raising, the day's mail, the bank balance, plans for the annual dinner and mail campaigns — everything!

He devoted countless days and nights to personal visits to raise funds for Chinuch Atzmai, and he personally guaranteed bank and private loans even though he knew that this would jeopardize the campaigns of Tifereth Jerusalem. To Reb Moshe, the cause of Torah was higher than that of any individual institution, even his own. This was especially true concerning Chinuch Atzmai because Reb Moshe, like Reb Aharon before him, felt that

---

38. From *BiMechitzasam shel Gedolei Yisrael* by Rabbi Shlomo Lorincz, Vol. II.

Greeting Reb Aharon Kotler at a Chinuch Atzmai Dinner; in the center is Rabbi Yosef Dov Soloveitchik

the future of Torah Jewry in Eretz Yisrael depended on the success of Chinuch Atzmai.

Rabbi Yisrael Eidelman recalled:

> When the Rosh Yeshivah spoke at a Tifereth Jerusalem fund-raising event, he never spoke about his yeshivah specifically. He spoke about Torah and the great *zechus* of being a Torah supporter.
>
> I was present when a wealthy individual came to the Rosh Yeshivah and said, "I have $100,000 that I want to give to one institution. What does the Rosh Yeshivah suggest that I do with it?"
>
> My eyes lit up, for at that time the yeshivah was in the midst of a financial crisis. The Rosh Yeshivah, however, told the man, "Give it to Chinuch Atzmai." After the man left, the Rosh Yeshivah turned to me and said, "I know that you are wondering why I didn't tell him to give the money to us. After all, in the *matzav* (situation) that we are in, we certainly need the money. This is true, but Chinuch Atzmai needs it even more. And Chinuch Atzmai is *Klal Yisrael's mosad* (institution)."

In May 1967, when Egypt and its Arab allies threatened to invade Israel, the roshei yeshivah proclaimed a day of fasting and *tefillah*. The fast day was a few days before the Chinuch Atzmai dinner, and immediately after *Minchah*, Reb Moshe and Reb Yaakov went to visit people to help ensure the success of the dinner — even though both men were in their 70s and still fasting.

At the annual Chinuch Atzmai Dinner in 1963 (l to r): Stephen Klein, Irving Bunim, Reb Moshe, and יבל״ח Zev Wolfson. Reb Yaakov Yitzchak Ruderman and Reb Chaim Mordechai Katz are seated in background.

Left to right: Reb Shneur Kotler, Reb Moshe, philanthropist Irving Stone and יבל״ח Rabbi Henoch Cohen

As the head of Chinuch Atzmai, Reb Moshe was loyal to its employees and encouraged them to use their own initiative. As he told Rabbi Henoch Cohen, who requested authorization for an office expense, "That is your job. If you feel it is necessary, buy it."

When Rabbi Cohen was first asked by Reb Aharon to work for Chinuch Atzmai full time, he had doubts. He had a lucrative business opportunity and felt that it might be better to become a businessman who would be an active volunteer in community affairs. He consulted Reb Moshe, who said, "Henoch, in the time of the Gemara, people were so great that they could be roshei yeshivah and still support themselves by some occupation. For example, Rav Yitzchak gave *shiurim* even though he was a blacksmith. But nowadays, we can't do both. If someone wants to serve *Klal Yisrael* in the most effective way, he must give it his full concentration. If you truly want to serve our nation, you should do it full time. *But*," Reb Moshe concluded, "you must make a living. You have the right to request a proper salary."

He gave similar advice to Rabbi Tannenbaum when another institution tried to lure him away from Chinuch Atzmai with a position at a much higher salary. Rabbi Tannenbaum consulted Reb Moshe, who felt that it was not right for him to be approached by others. However, Reb Moshe urged him to request that Chinuch Atzmai grant him an increase. To their great credit, however, neither Rabbi Cohen nor Rabbi Tannenbaum requested anything close to what they could have earned elsewhere. One who lives in proximity to people like Reb Aharon, Reb Moshe, and Reb Yaakov realizes that there are far more important goals in life than the size of one's paycheck.

Torah Umesorah

DURING THE TIME THAT RABBI YAAKOV KAMENETSKY SERVED AS CHAIRMAN of the Rabbinical Board of Torah Umesorah (The National Society for Hebrew Day Schools), Reb Moshe was a very active board member. He attended meetings and was a featured speaker at the organization's annual convention. Most important, he was often consulted when sensitive issues required a *psak halachah*.[39] And he was amazingly knowledgeable in the affairs of day schools around the country, as illustrated by the following incident:

Many years ago, three day schools in three West Coast cities were seeking a new menahel (Hebrew principal). Torah Umesorah asked the renowned *mechanech* Rabbi Shmuel Kaufman (today of Detroit) if he would be interested in any of the positions. He responded that he would first consult with Reb Moshe, as he did regarding any important matter. Someone expressed surprise that one would consult Reb Moshe regarding schools with which he probably was unfamiliar. Rabbi Kaufman responded that if Reb Moshe did respond to his question, his answer could most certainly be relied upon.

It was summertime, so Rabbi Kaufman traveled to where Reb Moshe was vacationing to discuss the matter in person. As soon as Rabbi Kaufman stated the purpose of his visit, Reb Moshe asked him to name the three schools. When he did, Reb Moshe immediately responded, "School A is a small school and the parents run it. As menahel, you will be powerless; your opinion will mean nothing. School B presents you with an excellent opportunity to spread Torah. However, you have a wife and children to

---

39. See, for example, *Igros Moshe, Yoreh De'ah*, vol, IV, #28.

support. Do not accept the position unless you have determined that the school is financially sound and will be able to pay you a decent salary in a timely fashion." Reb Moshe made no mention of the third school.

Rabbi Kaufman reported Reb Moshe's response to the Torah Umesorah office, and they promised to look into the matter. They were amazed by their findings. The first school was, indeed, a small school in which the menahel took orders from the parents. The second school was a good institution but was experiencing financial trouble and could not be counted on to make good on a salary commitment. The third school had already hired a new menahel.[40]

Deference to Other Gedolim

HIS RESPECT FOR OTHER TORAH LEADERS SOMETIMES CAUSED HIM TO abstain from offering his view on a matter. As a rule, Reb Moshe would not render decisions on issues and events that concerned the Torah community of Eretz Yisrael. He insisted that such decisions were to be made only by the Torah leadership of that land.

With the Ponevezher Rav, Rabbi Yosef Shlomo Kahaneman

40. From the *Kol HaTorah* journal.

Once, when he was asked to participate in a meeting whose outcome could have had a bearing on matters in Eretz Yisrael, Reb Moshe phoned Reb Elazar Menachem Shach, friend of his youth and senior Rosh Yeshivah in Eretz Yisrael, to be sure that Rav Shach would not object. Often, Rav Shach would call Reb Moshe before making a statement on an important issue, to be sure that Reb Moshe did not oppose his view.

His high regard for the *tzaddikim* of Eretz Yisrael was not limited to their expertise as leaders of the community. In a letter, he wrote:

> *It is my practice to respond in writing only regarding divrei Torah that the writer finds difficult and feels that I, through the kindness of Hashem, am able to resolve. Then, I am obligated to offer my opinion and clarify the matter. Regarding conferring berachos and offering tefillos, there are many yirei Hashem in Eretz Yisrael whose prayers are surely pleasing to Hashem — so what have I to do with this? However, as your pain is great, I will respond ...*[41]

TORAH LEADERS ARE REFERRED TO IN THE TORAH AS "עֵינֵי הָעֵדָה, THE EYES OF THE nation." They, with their clear Torah perception, often have a very different

Overlook Your Differences

view of matters than do others. Those who benefited from Reb Moshe's guidance in their own work for *Klal Yisrael* often saw this for themselves, as the following episode illustrates:

Two men had worked together on an important project and had achieved much success. Then a time came when they did not see eye to eye on certain things, and one of them suggested that the partnership should come to an end. A few days later the man who had initiated the break-up received a call from Reb Moshe, who had learned of what had transpired. After hearing the man's feelings on the matter, Reb

---

41. *Igros Moshe, Orach Chaim*, Vol. IV, #47.

Moshe said, "I understand what is bothering you. Certainly you have a valid point, but you must weigh the consequences of your decision. The two of you have accomplished so much for *Klal Yisrael* and there is so much more that you can still accomplish *together*. There is no doubt in my mind that you are much more effective as a team than as individuals. For the sake of *Klal Yisrael,* I think you should overlook your differences and continue working together."

The man heeded Reb Moshe's advice, and — with his partner — went on to add many new achievements to his credit.

Once, a man who had successfully represented Torah organizations in places of government found himself in a dilemma. He had been granted a meeting with a group of United States senators in Washington, D.C., to discuss a matter of prime importance to the Torah community in Eretz Yisrael. The meeting had been scheduled for Erev Rosh Hashanah and there was a real possibility that he would not have enough time to return home for Yom Tov. Should he cancel the meeting?

Again, it was Reb Moshe who placed a call, after being informed of the man's doubts. "I *pasken* (rule) that you *must* attend the meeting, even if you will have to remain in Washington over Yom Tov. You will be going there for the sake of Hashem, the Torah, and *Klal Yisrael*, and your personal considerations should not deter you from going."

IN 1965, PRESIDENT LYNDON JOHNSON WAS SEEKING THE PASSAGE OF HIS Elementary and Secondary Education Act, which would have provided

"Go With Truth" federal funds to all elementary and secondary schools, including parochial schools. Rabbi Amos Bunim, Torah Umesorah's associate chairman of the board at that time, went to Washington to lobby for the bill, which would have provided desperately needed help for yeshivos and day schools around the country. In the course of his meetings with Catholic lobbyists for the bill, Rabbi Bunim learned of the so-called "three-letter rule": that Catholic divinity schools whose credits were recognized by three Catholic universities were eligible for federal funding such as student aid loans, work study programs, and much more.

Rabbi Bunim realized that this was the key for the yeshivos to achieve a significant gain from President Johnson's education bill. Without such accreditation, the gains from the bill, as far as yeshivos were concerned, would be minimal.

For this dream to become a reality, Rabbi Bunim would have to meet with the head of the Catholic Education Committee and enlist his help in

Left to right: Irving Bunim, יבל"ח his son Amos and Reb Moshe

this matter. Did Halachah forbid such association with Catholic religious leaders for even so lofty a purpose? Rabbi Bunim took his case to Reb Moshe, who was very enthusiastic about the development.

Reb Moshe said, "You can meet with him, as long as you meet with him in a place that is not church-oriented." In the months that followed, Rabbi Bunim became almost a member of Reb Moshe's household. As the project progressed from stage to stage, careful planning was required and new questions of Halachah arose. Reb Moshe was always ready to offer his *psak,* advice, and encouragement in a long and often frustrating affair.

Finally, the entire plan was worked out. It had Reb Moshe's full approval and blessing. Now came the hardest part — winning the government's agreement to accredit yeshivos.

The key man in achieving success was Dr. Samuel Halperin, who had been designated by President Johnson to represent the White House before Congress to gain passage of his education bill. Dr. Halperin had in fact enlisted Rabbi Bunim's help in convincing members of Congress that a significant percentage of American Jewry wanted the bill passed. Now, Rabbi Bunim arranged for a Sunday afternoon meeting at Dr. Halperin's home.

*Letter from Reb
Moshe to
Dr. Halperin
for his efforts
to help the
yeshivos*

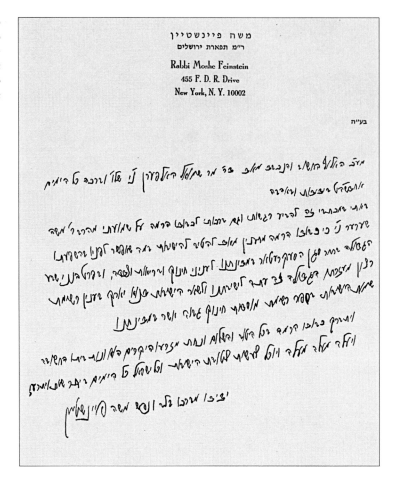

Reb Moshe's instructions in dealing with government people still ring in Rabbi Bunim's ears. "You are going on a mission for the sake of Hashem. Go with truth. Speak truth, and Hashem will be with you."

The meeting on that Sunday afternoon lasted four hours. Rabbi Bunim presented his case well, but Dr. Halperin, though sympathetic, said he could not hope to be of assistance. He was, as he put it, "the busiest man in Washington," as he was working day and night for passage of the president's bill. Perhaps in a few months he would have some time …

"Go with truth. Speak truth and Hashem will be with you."

"Do you know what Purim is about?" Rabbi Bunim suddenly asked. When Dr. Halperin said he was familiar with the holiday, Rabbi Bunim came straight to the point. He reminded him that when the Jews were threatened with annihilation, Mordechai told Esther that it was possible she had been made queen *only* so that she could help her people at that time. Mordechai had warned:

First page of a letter of hakaras hatov from the Telshe Rosh Yeshivah, Rabbi Mordechai Gifter to Rabbi Amos Bunim, which opens, "I always carry with me the inner feeling that the Torah world owes you a great debt of gratitude."

> *If you persist in keeping silent at a time like this, relief and deliverance will come to the Jews from another place, while you and your father's house will perish. And who knows whether it was just for such a time as this that you have attained a royal position.*[42]

Because Esther accepted the challenge, the Jewish nation was saved.

Rabbi Bunim now stared at his host. "Dr. Halperin, in all your years in government, this is probably the first time that you've been given an opportunity to do something for the eternity of the Jewish people. And this may be the very reason that you were placed where you are. G-d will find another way if you refuse to help. But the loss, Dr. Halperin, will be yours."

With those words, Rabbi Bunim rose to leave for an appointment with the Israeli Ambassador. An obviously moved Dr. Halperin rose with him and insisted on driving him to the appointment. Rabbi Bunim reluctantly

---

42. *Esther* 4:14.

accepted the offer, on the condition that they not discuss the project any further. As the two parted from each other, Dr. Halperin said, "I'll never forget Mordechai."

The next day, Dr. Halperin phoned Rabbi Bunim, saying that he had been unable to sleep the entire night. He would do anything necessary to gain recognition for the yeshivos.

Rabbi Bunim then met with Rep. James H. Scheuer of New York, powerful chairman of the House Education Committee. He was one of the most respected men on Capitol Hill. The conversation did not go well. Rep. Scheuer objected to the proposal on philosophical and constitutional grounds, but he was an intelligent and open-minded person who was willing to listen. Again, Rabbi Bunim combined logic with passion, and Scheuer became a powerful ally. Thanks to his support, Halperin was able to convince the Office of Education to recognize the yeshivos.

From that time on, Rabbi Bunim made a point of sending a gift to Dr. Halperin before every Yom Tov. He sent hand-baked matzah before Pesach, *mishloach manos* for Purim, a menorah for Chanukah, and so on. The thank-you notes he received were all signed, "Mordechai."

Two years later, Rabbi Bunim received a phone call from Dr. Halperin. He said, "I've made a decision that I want you to know about. For the last two years my conscience has bothered me. After making a contribution toward the eternity of my people, I should at least ensure that my offspring have a connection to eternity. Now, I'm finally doing something to change this. I'm taking my daughter out of public school and enrolling her in an Orthodox day school."

On the day of Reb Moshe's passing, Rabbi Bunim called Dr. Halperin and informed him of the tragic news. Dr. Halperin then revealed for the first time that he had received a warm letter of thanks from Reb Moshe for his efforts on behalf of Torah institutions. "Now I will treasure that letter more than ever," he said.

The outcome of the above story has been many millions of dollars in government aid to yeshivos over the last forty-five years. Rabbi Bunim makes it clear that all this could never have happened without the guidance and encouragement of Reb Moshe.

From top: with Rabbi Avraham Yoffen, with Rabbi Henoch Leibowitz, (bottom left) with the Bluzhever Rebbe (Rabbi Yisrael Spira), (bottom right) with the Bostoner Rebbe (Rabbi Moshe Horowitz)

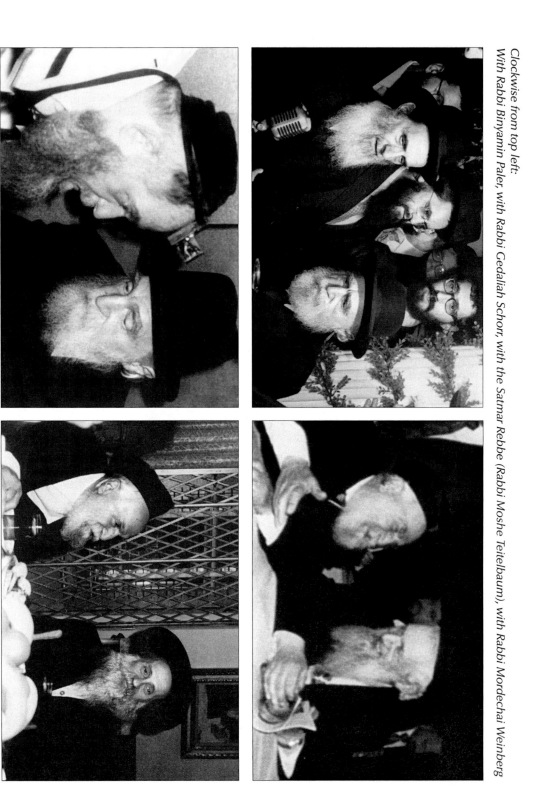

CHAPTER EIGHT

The Beauty of His Ways

*A Jew should study Scripture and Mishnah, serve Torah schol-
ars, deal honestly in business, and speak pleasantly to his fellow
man. What will his fellow man say of him? "Fortunate is his
father who taught him Torah! Fortunate is his teacher who taught
him Torah! Woe to those who do not study Torah! He who studies Torah — how beautiful are his ways and how proper are his
deeds." To him the verse applies: And He said to me: "You are
My servant Israel, through whom I will be glorified."*[1]

(Yoma 86a)

IN 1964, REB MOSHE LED THE AMERICAN DELEGATION TO THE FIFTH
Knessiah Gedolah, the world convention of Agudath Israel
held in Jerusalem.[2] Great honor was accorded him by roshei yeshivah, lay
leaders and scores of *bnei Torah* who traveled to the

**The Essence
of Greatness**

airport to greet him. The crowd burst into a song of
welcome as Reb Moshe appeared at the door of the
plane, and government officials were on hand to wave him through cus-

---

1. *Yeshayahu* 49:3.
2. This was his only visit to the Holy Land. One reason why he never returned there was
that during his visit, he was able to receive only a fraction of the scores of petitioners who
wanted to meet him. Reb Moshe did not want to be in a situation where he had to close
his door to someone who needed him (preface to *Igros Moshe*, Vol. VIII).

Arriving at the Knessiah Gedolah in 1964. Left to right: Rabbi Shlomo Lorincz, Reb Moshe, Rabbi Yechiel Michel Feinstein, Rabbi Isaac Small

toms. All this honor did not affect him. It was as if they had come to honor someone else.

> During that visit, Reb Moshe called on the Tchebiner Rav, Rabbi Dov Beirish Weidenfeld, one of the great Torah leaders and *poskim* of his time. The Rav accorded Reb Moshe unusual honor, and when the visit came to a close he escorted him for a lengthy distance. Upon returning to his apartment, the Rav said that aside from Reb Moshe's greatness in Torah, he was amazed by his superlative *midos* and simple manner. He concluded, "*Dos iz dos gantza sheinkeit* (This is the essence of his beauty)."[3]

Someone once asked Reb Moshe in what merit he had become so revered by all. He replied, "All my life I never knowingly caused hurt to another human being."

Reb Moshe possessed all the wonderful attributes that the Torah seeks in a person. His *every* word and deed was governed by the Torah. His kindness, humility, sensitivity, and other superlative *middos* were living

---

3. From *Sar HaTorah* on the life of the Tchebiner Rav (Hebrew), published by Feldheim.

illustrations of the Torah's command that we emulate the ways of Hashem, and of the many mitzvos *bein adam lachaveiro*.[4]

AVOS D'R'NOSSON[5] STATES: "EVEN IF A PERSON CANNOT GIVE HIS FRIEND ANY-thing tangible, if he greets him pleasantly, it is as if he has given him all the gifts in the world."

Respect for All

Someone who knew Reb Moshe for many years remarked, "I never met another man who could make people feel so important simply by the way he looked at them."

He greeted everyone with respect and good cheer. One man recalled how Reb Moshe had once failed to notice him and walked by without greeting him. About ten steps later, Reb Moshe turned around and came back, greeted the man, and then, to make up for his oversight, spent some time conversing with him.

> The high-rise apartment complex in which the Feinsteins resided had its own park behind the building. On a nice day, the park benches were full of elderly Jewish couples, of whom only some were obser-vant. Often, when returning to his apartment, Reb Moshe would opt to enter the building through the back, which required him to walk through the park. He would walk past the benches slowly, greeting everyone with a warm *"Shalom Aleichem."* Someone once sug-gested that it would be more convenient to use the building's front door. Reb Moshe disagreed: "When else do I have the opportunity to greet so many Yidden who survived the War?"[6]

Once, Reb Moshe and his family were driven home from a function by a total stranger. As they got into the car, the driver whispered to someone, "What am I going to talk to the Rosh Yeshivah about? I can't speak with him in learning!"

His anxiety last but a few moments. Reb Moshe engaged him in friendly conversation, asking him about his family, livelihood, and other topics with which the man felt comfortable.

---

4. He once told Rabbi Simcha Bunim Cohen, "All bad actions are an outgrowth of bad *middos*." He suggested that one half-hour before bedtime, one should review in his mind all his actions and words of that day to see what required correction.

5. Chapter 13.

6. For decades, the Lower East Side was inhabited by numerous beggars and others who were atypical. On his long walk from his home to Tifereth Jerusalem each Shabbos, Reb Moshe wished every such person a warm *"Gut Shabbos."*

Reb Moshe noticed that the man was taking a route that was not the one generally used, and he asked him about it. The driver explained that the traffic lights on this street were synchronized, which made the trip a bit faster. When they reached Reb Moshe's apartment, he thanked the man and added, "I have learned something good; now I will tell others that there is a better route to take!" The driver beamed with pleasure.

A simple, elderly neighbor came to Reb Moshe's apartment on Pesach for *davening*. Reb Moshe greeted the man and asked, "So how was the fish this Yom Tov?" Reb Moshe knew that the man was unlearned, and this was a topic that he would appreciate.

☙ ☙ ☙

At the Pioneer Hotel each summer, a *shiur* was delivered between *Minchah* and *Maariv*. One evening when Reb Moshe was a guest there, a learned businessman was asked to deliver the *shiur*. As he walked up to the podium to speak, Reb Moshe was the only one who rose to his feet to honor the man who would be teaching them Torah.[7]

When Rabbi Berel Wein first moved to Monsey, he prayed at the shul of Reb Moshe's son-in-law, Rabbi Moshe David Tendler. One evening, Rabbi Tendler was out of town, and Reb Moshe was present. In Rabbi Wein's words:

> There were about twelve people there. Most of them came in off the street to say *Kaddish*. Between *Minchah* and *Maariv* there was a short break and Reb Moshe would not allow it to be frittered away. So he took a *Chumash* from a shelf and began teaching from it to the small crowd. He read each verse and then translated it into Yiddish

---

7. From a piece by Rabbi Yaakov Heftler in the *Kol HaTorah* journal.

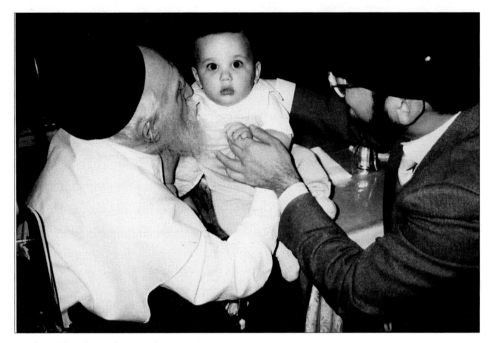

With Rabbi Shmuel Greenberg and son

with such a simple quality. He didn't say any deep Torah thoughts, no deep analyses from the commentators; just the plain words. *Vayomer — un er hot gezokt* (and he said). But he spoke in such a way that he wasn't talking down to anyone. Great people have that ability to talk to everyone: children, teenagers, adults.[8]

Rabbi Shmuel Greenberg related:

In the world at large, the more prominent someone's position, the less accessible he is and the more distant one feels even when meeting him face to face. It was impossible not feel great *yiras hakavod* in the Rosh Yeshivah's presence. Yet at the same time, one felt so much warmth, love, and closeness.

In the summertime, when I was a young boy, the Rosh Yeshivah would take me along when he checked the bungalow colony's *eruv*. He would point out the way in which the *eruv* was constructed and explained to me what a *tzuras hapesach* is.

When I got older and spent my summer in a learning camp, I had an opportunity one day to leave camp for a few hours and visit with Reb David [Feinstein] and his family. I dialed the number and the

---

8. From *Vintage Wein* by Dr. James David Weiss, published by Shaar Press.

Rosh Yeshivah answered the phone. When I explained why I was calling, he said, "No one else is here right now; they have all gone away. But you can come visit me!"

When I was studying in beis midrash, I would come to the Rosh Yeshivah for *Shabbos Shuvah* and *Shabbos HaGadol*, so that I could hear his *derashah*. As we walked through the hallways of his apartment complex, everyone — including the mailman — exchanged friendly greetings with him. There were no barriers; everyone felt his love and kindness.

One year, Mesivtha Tifereth Jerusalem wished to honor a Sefardic supporter at its annual dinner. Rabbi Yisrael Eidelman dialed the gentleman's phone number and gave Reb Moshe the phone. In Yiddish, Reb Moshe asked the man to accept the honor for the benefit of the yeshivah. When Rabbi Eidelman took back the phone so that he could translate Reb Moshe's words, the man said, "There is no need to translate. The Rosh Yeshivah speaks *sfat halev* (the language of the heart) and I understood what he wanted. It is my privilege to be honored by his yeshivah."

ONE SUMMER DURING HIS STAY IN THE CATSKILL MOUNTAINS, REB MOSHE WAS being seen by a doctor who was a Holocaust survivor. The doctor's wife,

Numbers Tell the Story

who served as his nurse, was a survivor as well. They were far removed from the world of the yeshivos, but they knew that Reb Moshe was a renowned rabbi.

During that summer, their nephew, Yitzchak Herschkopf, came to visit them for a week. One day, the woman said to her nephew, "We have one patient who is a celebrity, Rabbi Moshe Feinstein. He has an appointment here tomorrow. Would you like to meet him?"

Yitzchak was excited beyond words. He had studied at Talmudic Academy of Manhattan and one of his rebbeim was Reb Moshe's son-in-law, Rabbi Moshe David Tendler, who often quoted Reb Moshe in class, and always with great reverence.

The next morning, he donned his Shabbos clothes and seated himself in the doctor's waiting room. A few minutes later, Reb Moshe entered, accompanied by a family member. The boy's aunt entered the room and spoke to and treated Reb Moshe as though he were her close friend, in an affectionate but wholly irreverent manner. It was obvious that she simply had no idea of the proper way to address a Torah scholar, especially one of Reb Moshe's stature. Her nephew was shocked and embarrassed.

With his son-in-law, Rabbi Moshe David Tendler

As soon as she left the room, Yitzchak began to apologize for his aunt's behavior — but Reb Moshe quickly put his finger to the boy's lips to silence him. "She has numbers on her arm," he said softly. "She is holier than I am." To Reb Moshe, anyone who had endured the concentration camps was a *kadosh* and deserved special respect.[9]

MR. TIBOR KUPFERSTEIN OF BROOKLYN RELATED THE FOLLOWING:

The Friendly Passenger

In the 1960s, on a Motza'ei Shabbos in the Catskill Mountains, I joined a friend for *melaveh malkah*. As I rose to leave, my friend said to me, "I was supposed to drive someone back to the city tomorrow morning at 6:30, but my plans changed and I will be staying in the mountains for another day. Could you perhaps do this favor instead of me?"

I was happy to oblige. The next morning, I picked up a nice, elderly man who wore a high, rectangular-shaped yarmulka and held his hat in his hand. As we began the drive, my passenger, who was seated alongside me, initiated a friendly conversation:

"What is your name?"

"Kupferstein. And yours?"

---

9. Adapted from the memoirs of Dr. Isaac Steven Herschkopf.

"Feinstein. Where are you from?"

"Budapest. And you?"

"Luban. Do you have a family?"

"Yes, *baruch Hashem*."

"I, too, have children, *baruch Hashem*. And what is your occupation?"

"I'm a manufacturer of heavy metal. And yourself?"

"I'm a rebbi in a yeshivah."

We continued conversing like two old friends, engaging in small talk on a variety of topics. At some point, my passenger suggested that we share a *dvar Torah,* and I readily agreed. He then began a deep discussion about the *neshamah* and its purpose on this world.

As we approached the George Washington Bridge, my passenger said to me, "I hope you won't mind joining my rebbetzin and myself for a cup of coffee. I'm sure that she would be happy to have you as our guest." I accepted his gracious offer. He directed me from the bridge to the Lower East Side and soon we arrived at his address on FDR Drive. After parking the car, I made my way upstairs to his apartment. We sat at the table, the three of us, enjoying some home-baked cake with our coffee. The rabbi's wife thanked me for taking her husband home from the mountains.

Three days later, my friend phoned and asked me how the trip went. "Very good," I replied. "I enjoyed that rabbi's company immensely. He is a very intelligent and interesting person."

My friend laughed. "You don't have to tell me that Rabbi Moshe Feinstein is a very intelligent person!"

Coming from Budapest and a chassidic environment, I was not too familiar with the Lithuanian yeshivah world. I had heard of Rabbi Feinstein but had never seen him. I knew that he was someone very, very great.

For the next two weeks, I had difficulty sleeping. I had had no idea who this passenger was. Rabbi Feinstein had lowered himself to engage in conversation that he felt someone like myself would appreciate. I actually wept out of concern that I might have said something wrong. Perhaps I had made a joke or comment that was not appropriate when speaking to someone of his stature!

To this day, I become emotional when I think of that experience.

The Mishnah states: "Who is honored? One who honors people, as it is written, 'For I will honor those who honor Me, and those who shame Me will

In 1969, Reb Moshe visited Montreal and was honored at a special gathering held in the mayor's office. In this photo, Reb Moshe is seated in the mayor's chair with the mayor standing directly behind him. To the right of Reb Moshe is the late Rabbi Pinchas Hirschprung, Av Beis Din of Montreal. Rabbi Moshe Rivlin is at far right.

be degraded.'"[10] Rav Chaim Volozhiner explains that to honor an important person shows nothing about one's own character. It is an honor and a privilege to be allowed to honor a dignitary. However, one who honors בְּרִיּוֹת, *all* people, shows that he recognizes the *tzelem Elokim* in every human being. And therefore Hashem declares, "I will honor those who honor Me."

Rav Michel Barenbaum applied this insight to Reb Moshe, who honored young and old, Jew and non-Jew, and earned the love and veneration of Jews of all shades and stripes.

RABBI EPHRAIM GREENBLATT RECALLS WALKING REB MOSHE TO SHUL IN THE morning when he visited Memphis, Tennessee. He wished good morning to every man, woman, and child whom he passed on the way. As he was walking down the street, a youngster ran in front of him to take a picture. One of Reb Moshe's escorts told the "photographer" not to annoy the Rosh Yeshivah, to which Reb Moshe responded, "Let him take the picture. He enjoys it, so let me give him some pleasure."

Giving Children Pleasure

---

10. *Avos* 4:1.

Reb Moshe with the boys for whom he signed autographs

In the early 1970s, a Queens shul held a fund-raising affair benefiting Mesivtha Tifereth Jerusalem. Many neighborhood boys were in attendance, eager to meet Reb Moshe. One boy approached Reb Moshe with a pledge envelope and asked, "Can I have the Rosh Yeshivah's autograph?" Reb Moshe smiled and obliged. Within moments, a line of boys had formed, all of them holding envelopes. When the shul's rav, who was chairing the event, realized what was happening, he hurried over to stop it. "The Rosh Yeshivah is the *gadol hador*, not a baseball player!" he said. "You cannot bother him for autographs!"

"*Vos iz* (What is wrong)?" asked Reb Moshe. "*Zei zenen Yiddishe kinderlach* (They are Jewish children)." For the next ten minutes, he signed his name, and then posed for a picture with the boys.

When Rabbi Yehoshua Blum's youngest son was becoming a bar mitzvah, it was arranged for the Blum family to visit Reb Moshe in Camp Staten Island to receive his *berachah*. When the family entered Reb Moshe's bungalow, one of the children took out a camera and prepared to snap a photo of Reb Moshe. Rabbi Blum, however, objected, telling the children that to stand in front of the Rosh Yeshivah snapping pictures was not respectful.

Rebbetzin Feinstein saw that something was amiss and asked Mrs. Blum

what the problem was. As soon as she heard, the Rebbetzin turned to Reb Moshe and said, "Rabbi Feinstein, the children want to take your picture, but their father feels it is not respectful."

Reb Moshe smiled, seated himself, gathered the children around him, and asked that one of the parents take the picture.

> One day, Reb Moshe was in a hurry to leave yeshivah after *Minchah* to chair a meeting of the Moetzes Gedolei HaTorah. Those who assembled for *Minchah* were told that no one could speak with the Rosh Yeshivah at the conclusion of the *davening*. The moment *Minchah* ended, Reb Moshe hurried out of the beis midrash to a waiting car. As he neared the car, a young boy holding a camera approached to take his picture. Reb Moshe stopped and smiled for the boy. However, a well-meaning talmid told the boy that the Rosh Yeshivah was in a rush, and this caused the boy to nervously fumble the camera and snap a hurried photo. Reb Moshe entered the car and it pulled away — only to stop seconds later at Reb Moshe's insistence. Reb Moshe alighted and said to the boy, "I don't think the picture will come out good. Take it again!" The boy was overjoyed.

One Chol HaMoed, a boy of bar-mitzvah age traveled by train to the Lower East Side for *Shacharis* at Tifereth Jerusalem — and the opportu-

Conferring his berachah upon young visitors

nity to request a *berachah* from Reb Moshe after *davening*. However, he was disappointed when *davening* ended. It was announced that the Rosh Yeshivah was not feeling well, and therefore no one was to ask him anything or even offer his hand in greeting.

As Reb Moshe prepared to leave the beis midrash, the boy had an idea. If he could not meet Reb Moshe, at least he could serve him in some way. He hurried to the back of the beis midrash and held the door open as the Rosh Yeshivah made his way down the aisle.

As Reb Moshe approached the door, he noticed the boy and realized that he was not from the neighborhood. When he reached the door, he handed his *tallis* bag to someone and offered the startled boy his hand, smiled, and said, *"Yasher koach!"*[11]

Some fifty years ago, a parade to strengthen Shabbos observance was held on a weekday in the Lower East Side. Hundreds of children were to march behind cars in which rabbanim and roshei yeshivah would ride.

When Reb Moshe arrived at the parade departure point, the children

---

11. Adapted with permission from *Visions of Greatness* by Rabbi Yosef Weiss (CIS Publications).

With the Manchester Rosh Yeshivah, Rabbi Yehudah Zev Segal, who once remarked that Reb Moshe's sterling personality made visiting with him a spiritual delight.

had already assembled. When someone showed Reb Moshe a waiting car, he said, "What? I should ride in a car while the children walk? If they are walking, I am walking."

The other rabbanim and roshei yeshivah joined Reb Moshe in leading the parade on foot.[12]

ॐ ॐ ॐ

The late Rabbi Zeidel Epstein was a great disseminator of Torah and *mussar,* first in America and later in Jerusalem as *Mashgiach Ruchani* of Yeshivah Torah Ore. For a number of years, he lived on the Lower East Side and grew very close to Reb Moshe.

One summer the Feinsteins and the Epsteins spent their summer vacation in the same bungalow colony. When little Boruch Epstein completed *Sefer Bereishis,* Reb Zeidel and his rebbetzin made a *"siyum"* party, to which they invited some neighbors. They did not invite Reb Moshe because they felt uncomfortable bothering a man of such stature whose every moment was so precious. Reb Moshe happened to pass by their bungalow when the celebration was in progress and asked what the commotion was about. Moments later, Reb Moshe entered the bungalow and said to Reb Zeidel, "You're making a *simchah* and you did not invite me?"

---

12. From an article by Rabbi Yaakov Heftler in the *Kol HaTorah* journal.

Reb Moshe sat down and remained for a while, as he offered *berachos* to the young "guest of honor" and his family.

MR. LOUIS M. FRIEDMAN WAS A GENEROUS SUPPORTER OF MESIVTHA TIFERETH Jerusalem. In addition to the money he donated, Mr. Friedman would

Preserving Their Dignity outfit the yeshivah's neediest students each year before Pesach. At that time, a large truck would pull up in front of the yeshivah building loaded with new, first-quality suits, shoes, shirts, ties, caps, socks, underwear, and *tzitzis* to make some 100 children happy.

One year, to honor Mr. Friedman for his clothing distribution, the yeshivah's administration organized an assembly in its beis midrash which was to be followed by a dinner in the lunchroom. The beis midrash was crowded with Jews from the Lower East Side. The poorer boys, who were to be outfitted, sat in a section to the left, women sat in the ladies' section to the right, while the center was filled with the Board of Directors, members, parents, and local people. In the back were tables heaped high with the clothing that Mr. Friedman had donated.

The president of the yeshivah spoke, praising Mr. Friedman profusely. Before ending, he turned to the boys and suggested that they show their appreciation by rising in honor of Mr. Friedman. The boys looked at one another sheepishly, embarrassed to stand up in front of so many people and thereby acknowledge their poverty.

Their embarrassment lasted for but a moment. Sensing the boys' discomfort, Reb Moshe instantly stood up. Some men, seeing the Rosh Yeshivah stand up, also stood up. The Board of Directors stood up. The women stood up. Everyone else stood up. The boys, now having nothing to feel ashamed of, all stood up as well. Even Mr. Friedman, who was a modest man, felt embarrassed at being the only one left sitting. He too stood up, giving the impression that everyone was rising in honor of some other Mr. Friedman.

Louis M. Friedman

Once, a young boy greeted Reb Moshe in the house of a mourner during the *shivah* period. Reb Moshe did not acknowledge the greeting. Later, after leaving the house, Reb Moshe asked someone to go back inside and find the boy. When the child came outside, Reb Moshe extended his hand and warmly greeted him. "I'm sorry that I could not greet you before, but this is not permitted in a mourner's house."

❀ ❀ ❀

One Friday afternoon, a woman on the Lower East Side was preparing chicken for Shabbos when she noticed something unusual on one piece that might possibly have rendered it *treif*. She put the piece into a bag and asked her eight-year-old son to quickly run to Tifereth Jerusalem where Reb Moshe could often be found following his Friday *shiur*.

When the boy arrived in the building, he asked a man in the lobby where he could find Rabbi Feinstein. The man shouted at the boy, "How can you bother the Rosh Yeshivah on a Friday afternoon? Doesn't he also have to make Shabbos? People don't let him live, not on the weekdays, not on Shabbos."

The frightened boy turned around and ran out of the building and down the street. Soon he heard someone running behind him. It was Reb Moshe, who took him by the hand, smiled, and said, "He meant well, but he didn't realize that if you are coming now, it is probably with a question that has to do with Shabbos. Come back with me, and let us see what the problem is."

Once inside the building, Reb Moshe examined the piece of chicken, then went over to a bookcase and withdrew a *Shulchan Aruch, Yoreh*

De'ah. He sat down with the eight-year-old boy and showed him where this question is discussed. He ruled that the chicken was kosher and explained his reasons to the child until he was sure that the boy could repeat them to his father, who was a *talmid chacham*. The boy, who only minutes before had felt so demoralized, went home with the memory of a lifetime of having been given a private *shiur* by the *gadol hador*.

REB MOSHE ONCE SAT AT HIS DESK IN THE FRONT OF THE BEIS MIDRASH WHILE a middle-aged scholar sat in the back studying alone. The door of the beis

Honor for Scholars

midrash swung open and in walked a stranger, looking for a way to pass the time. Noticing the man studying on the back bench, the stranger attempted to "quiz" him on what he was learning, challenging him to explain the Gemara's questions and answers. In a flash, Reb Moshe was there. "Excuse me," he said, "but I can assure you that this man is a great *talmid chacham*; there is no need to test him."

He once listened as someone made a disparaging remark about a certain *talmid chacham*. Reb Moshe's normally calm demeanor underwent a sudden change. He looked straight at the speaker and said with barely suppressed anger, "I am prepared to testify that [for making such remarks] one is *pasul l'eidus* [unfit to serve as a court witness]!"

When the Lower East Side's Bialystok Shul celebrated a milestone anniversary, Reb Moshe was a featured speaker. Upon arriving at the event, he told the shul's Rav, the late Rabbi Yitzchok Singer, "I am going to be *mesader kiddushin* tonight at a wedding; I must leave from here as soon as I finish speaking."

Reb Moshe completed his *derashah* and then began making his way down the aisle towards the door. As he did, Rabbi Singer ascended the podium and began his address. Reb Moshe had not known that Rabbi Singer was the next speaker. He abruptly turned around and returned to his seat. Reb Moshe did not want the members of the shul to think that in his eyes the Rav's *derashah* was not important. He remained for the duration of the address and arrived late at the wedding.

Reb Moshe once visited Baltimore to attend a family wedding. Some local supporters of Tifereth Jerusalem took advantage of Reb Moshe's visit to hold a fund-raising meeting that was graced with his presence. Attending the meeting was Rabbi Yaakov Yitzchak Ruderman, Rosh Yeshivah of Ner Yisrael in Baltimore and one of the generation's senior Torah sages. Rabbi

*With Rabbi
Yaakov
Yitzchak
Ruderman*

*Mayor
D'Alessandro
of Baltimore
presenting
Reb Moshe
with "the key
to the city"
at a City Hall
reception*

Ruderman had taken time from his own schedule to attend, primarily in tribute to Reb Moshe and, indeed, Reb Moshe was accorded great honor throughout the course of the meeting.

It was obvious to everyone that Reb Moshe felt very uncomfortable at receiving such honor in the presence of Rav Ruderman. Reb Moshe began his address by saying, "I do not understand why I am being accorded so much honor. Surely it is not me as a person to whom this honor is being shown. Perhaps it is because I have learned some Torah ..."

Once a stranger came to his home for *Shacharis* and Reb Moshe greeted him. Then he asked his grandson, Rabbi Mordechai Tendler, who the man was. Hearing that he was a rav in Argentina, Reb Moshe said, "A rav in Argentina deserves a different '*Shalom Aleichem.*'" Reb Moshe felt that someone who is *moser nefesh* to spread Torah in a distant land deserves recognition for his efforts. He went over and greeted the man again, this time with a touch of excitement.

HIS RESPECT FOR OTHERS SOMETIMES TOOK ON A MORE SUBTLE FORM.

When Rebbetzin Feinstein would bring women guests to the dining
Gracious Host room table while Reb Moshe was sitting there studying, he would immediately acknowledge the guests and close his *sefer,* so that no one would feel ignored by him. He would not necessarily join the conversation, but the *sefer* would remain closed nonetheless. His son Reb Reuven recalled his father saying that it is good for one to memorize a portion of Mishnah or Gemara, so that he will be able to study from memory at times when it is inappropriate or impossible to study from a *sefer.* When one studies from a *sefer* he is, in effect, ignoring everyone and everything present. However, when one reviews Torah in his mind, it is not obvious to anyone. No one who ever sat at Reb Moshe's table ever felt a reluctance on Reb Moshe's part to converse. In this way, no one was ever slighted.

> An aged *talmid chacham* whom Reb Moshe knew for many years once came to visit him. Reb Moshe began a conversation, but soon noticed that his visitor was not well enough to respond. Reb Moshe stopped speaking and sat in silence with his long-time friend. Seeing an opportunity to discuss Torah with Reb Moshe, a young man who had accompanied the visitor began asking questions in Halachah. However, Reb Moshe did not acknowledge the questions and continued to sit in silence. He felt it disrespectful to discuss Torah in front of his visitor, who, unfortunately, could not take part in the conversation.

On the morning of April 8, 1981, Jews all over the world gathered to recite *Bircas HaChamah,* the blessing for the sun that is recited once every 28 years.[13] The preferred time to recite the blessing is at sunrise, and so,

---

13. After that *Bircas HaChamah*, Reb Moshe remarked, "If only everyone approached every mitzvah with the *hislahavus* (fiery zeal) with which they have approached this mitzvah."

early that morning, scores of Jews converged on FDR Drive, so that they could fulfill this rare mitzvah together with Reb Moshe.

Rabbi Aharon Felder, a Rav in Philadelphia and a talmid of Reb Moshe, drove to the East Side for the event and was waiting outside Reb Moshe's apartment door at 4:00 a.m., together with his young son. Rabbi Felder dared not knock at that hour (though Reb Moshe usually rose around that time), but someone in the apartment opened the door for some reason and, seeing Rabbi Felder, ushered him inside.

Reb Moshe greeted his talmid warmly, invited him and his son into his dining room, and had a glass of tea brought for his guest. Then Reb Moshe disappeared into the kitchen and as Rabbi Felder sipped his tea, he could hear the repeated sounds of cabinet doors being opened and closed. After a few minutes, Reb Moshe returned to the dining room with some sugar cubes in his hand which he presented to Rabbi Felder's son. "I am sorry," he said, "but the Rebbetzin is not up yet and I can't find the candies. I hope you will like these cubes."

> Once, Reb Moshe asked his talmid, Rabbi Yitzchak Selengut, to come to his apartment to discuss something. Rabbi Selengut entered the apartment building accompanied by his eight-year-old daughter. When the elevator opened in the lobby, Rebbetzin Feinstein stepped out. She told Rabbi Selengut: "Please do not disturb the Rosh Yeshivah now. He has not eaten breakfast yet, and I prepared hot cereal for him." Rabbi Selengut replied that he had to go upstairs because the Rosh Yeshivah had asked that he come at this time; however, he would tell the Rosh Yeshivah that their discussion could wait until after breakfast.
>
> Reb Moshe welcomed his guests, and Rabbi Selengut said that he would wait until the Rosh Yeshivah had eaten. However, instead of returning to the breakfast table, Reb Moshe began searching in the kitchen for something to give Rabbi Selengut's daughter. He found some cookies, gave them to his young visitor, and then returned to eat his cereal. Moments later, he rose abruptly, went to the breakfront and bent down to open a bottom cabinet, as he explained, "I just remembered that this is where the Rebbetzin keeps the candies." He gave the little girl some candies and then resumed his meal.

A young man from Gateshead, England, was visiting New York and wanted to meet Reb Moshe. This was in Reb Moshe's last years when a daily *minyan* for *Shacharis* was held in his dining room. The visitor called

the person in charge and received permission to be part of the *minyan* on a specific day.

He arrived quite early and decided to knock on the door softly. Reb Moshe opened the door and the young man felt terribly uncomfortable when he realized that the Rosh Yeshivah was the only one in the apartment who was awake at that hour.

But he did not feel that way for long, as Reb Moshe welcomed him warmly. Hearing that his visitor studied in the Gateshead Yeshivah, Reb Moshe said, "I met your Rosh Yeshivah, Rav Leib Gurwitz, at the Knessiah Gedolah in Yerushalayim." He then led the young man to the window, motioned toward the horizon, and launched into a discussion on how to determine the time of *alos hashachar* (dawn) and *hanetz hachamah* (sunrise). By the time *Shacharis* began, the young man felt as if he had known Reb Moshe for a long time.

One year a few days before Pesach, a beggar with tattered and stained clothing approached Reb Moshe and asked, "Can I be Rav Feinstein's guest for the *Seder*?"

Reb Moshe asked, "And where were you last year for the *Seder*?"

"By my sister," the beggar responded, "but she died this year."

"I will ask my rebbetzin," said Reb Moshe. "Come back tomorrow and I will tell you what she said."

Rabbi Michel Shurkin witnessed this exchange. After Pesach when Rabbi Shurkin met the beggar, he asked him where he had spent the *Seder*. The beggar's face lit up and he replied: "What a beautiful Pesach! One cannot find another person as good-hearted as Rav Feinstein!"[14]

THROUGH HIS OWN CONDUCT REB MOSHE TAUGHT THAT THE MENTALLY ILL MUST also be treated with dignity. One day, his *shiur* in Tifereth Jerusalem was inter-

Everyone Counts

rupted by a man who sat reviewing the *sidrah* in a loud voice. A student went over to the man and told him that he was disturbing the Rosh Yeshivah's *shiur*. However, the man, seemingly oblivious to what he had been told, continued his chanting as before. A couple of students then suggested to Reb Moshe that they escort the man out of the beis midrash. "No," came the reply. "He doesn't know what he is doing. I will speak louder." And so the *shiur* continued, with Reb Moshe speaking as loudly as he could, while the man went on with his chanting, undisturbed.

---

14. From *Meged Givos Olam.*

Nor was his respect for people limited to Jews. There was an elderly gentile who worked as a janitor in Tifereth Jerusalem. He spoke little English and no one paid much attention to him. One day, suffering from a toothache, he walked around with a kerchief tied around his face. When Reb Moshe met the janitor in the hallway he stopped and spoke to him in Russian for a few minutes. When the conversation ended, the man walked away with the biggest smile that anyone ever remembered seeing on him.

Once, a neighbor who was to take Rebbetzin Feinstein to the doctor rang the doorbell to announce his arrival. When Reb Moshe opened the door and greeted the man, the driver joked, "In Europe they would say, 'The wagon-driver [baal agalah] is here.' In America we say, 'The car is waiting.'" Reb Moshe made no comment and went to call the Rebbetzin. He returned and led the driver to his study, while they waited for the Rebbetzin to get ready. Reb Moshe said, "Your comment illustrates a sad fact about this country. In Europe, no one would ever say, 'The wagon is here.' It was always 'The wagon-driver is here.' The emphasis was on the person. But, here in America, it is 'The car is here.' An individual is not given the respect he deserves."

> As an eloquent address in English was being delivered, Reb Moshe kept his eyes focused on the speaker the entire time. Afterward, someone close to him asked if he had understood the speech.
> "Not really," he replied.
> "Then why was the Rosh Yeshivah looking at him the entire time?" the person asked.
> Reb Moshe replied, "That is the respect a speaker deserves."

A shul celebrating the dedication of its new building asked Reb Moshe to be the keynote speaker. Also on the program was a local politician who was known to be somewhat long-winded. Aware that time was very precious to Reb Moshe and that he probably would not understand the speech, someone whispered to him, "The politician will be introduced soon. If the Rosh Yeshivah wants, he can go into the rabbi's study and learn during that time."

"And embarrass the man?" Reb Moshe retorted. "I will remain in my seat. While he speaks, I will review in my mind the shiur that I will deliver in yeshivah on Friday."

In his final years, Reb Moshe once yawned during shalosh seudos in his home on Shabbos Shirah. He felt the need to apologize to everyone.

"There is a lot of Rashi in this week's *parashah*, so I arose from my nap earlier than usual. That is why I am tired."

RABBI CHAIM TWERSKY, A DISTINGUISHED BORO PARK RAV, SERVED FOR MANY years as the chaplain at Maimonides Medical Center. Once, he addressed

"A Real Rabbi!" a group of nurses and in the course of his remarks mentioned Reb Moshe's name. "Oh!" exclaimed a gentile nurse named Shirley. "I know Rabbi Feinstein. He's a *real* rabbi!"

Rabbi Twersky could not imagine how the woman could know Reb Moshe and told her that she must be confusing him with someone else. No, Shirley insisted, there was no mistake. She was speaking of the famous Rabbi Feinstein. She had been the nurse for one of Reb Moshe's newborn great-grandsons, at whose *bris* Reb Moshe had served as *sandak*. As he was being wheeled out following the *bris*, Reb Moshe made a point of turning around in his wheelchair to say good-bye to the nurse. This show of respect had made an indelible impression on her.

This same nurse called Reb Moshe's family after his passing to express her condolences. "I remember how the Rabbi smiled and wished me a good day," she recalled. "I could *see* that in his *eyes* I was important."

> The mitzvah of *eglah arufah* (decapitated calf) involves a case where a murder victim is found between cities in Eretz Yisrael and the murderer's identity is not known. A ceremony is performed as an atonement for the Jewish people, and as part of that ceremony, a verse beginning with the words, *"Please forgive Your nation, Israel … "* is said. *Chazal* tell us that this verse was said by Kohanim. Why doesn't the Torah inform us of this?
>
> Reb Moshe explained that the Kohanim are known to be those who effect atonement for *Klal Yisrael*. This is their sacred task in the *Beis HaMikdash*. Therefore, there is no need for the Torah to identify the Kohanim as those who utter a verse asking for atonement. It is obvious.
>
> Reb Moshe drew a lesson from this. A Jew's behavior should be so exemplary in all situations that when people hear that something outstanding was done, they should automatically associate that action with this individual.

When this gentile nurse heard Rabbi Twersky discussing a renowned "Rabbi Feinstein," she immediately associated the name with the kind, elderly sage who had made a point of showing her recognition.

AFTER CONCLUDING A MEETING, REB MOSHE AND REB YAAKOV KAMENETSKY stood outside a waiting car discussing who would sit in front next to the driver and who would sit alone in the backseat. Reb Yaakov took the front seat. After Reb Moshe alighted from the car, Reb Yaakov explained to the driver, "We were discussing who would be getting off first. That person, we decided, should sit in the back. Were he to sit in the front, you would be left alone in the front when he left the car, with your remaining passenger in the back. It would have looked as if you were nothing more than a chauffeur."

Not a Chauffeur

Once, Reb Moshe and Reb Yaakov attended a *bris* in Kew Gardens. Mr. Yitzchak (Jerry) Jacobs was at the *bris* and had arranged to drive Reb Moshe home. At the *seudah's* conclusion, Reb Moshe asked

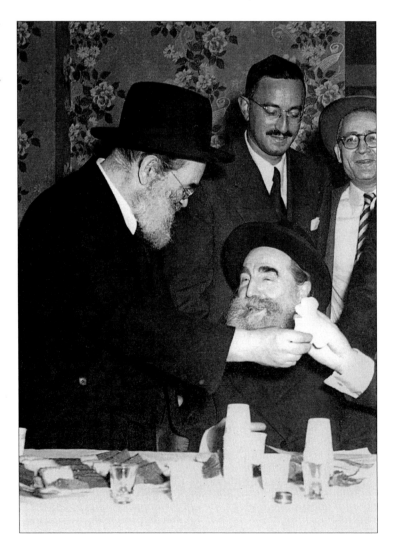

With Reb Yaakov at a wedding; Louis J. Septimus (with mustache) in background

Mr. Jacobs, "Would it be all right if Reb Yaakov came along with us and you dropped him off at his home in Willamsburg?" Mr. Jacobs was more than happy to oblige. Reb Moshe then asked, "Would you mind if I sat in the back with Reb Yaakov?" Apparently, there was something important that these *gedolim* needed to discuss. Of course, Mr. Jacobs did not mind. When Reb Yaakov alighted from the car, Reb Moshe got out and moved to the front seat.

Reb Moshe's recognition of each person's self-worth translated into practical advice. When a distinguished *bachur* asked if he should seek a wife who was the daughter of a rav or rosh yeshivah, in keeping with the teaching that one should marry a *bas talmid chacham*, Reb Moshe replied, "Today, there are many *baalei batim* (laymen) who are *talmidei chacha-mim,* and this too meets the criteria of *bas talmid chacham.*"

An unusual incident in which Reb Moshe was indirectly involved points to the stature of even *"pashute" Yidden* ("simple" Jews):

A *bachur* who was close to Reb Moshe was asked by a friend if he could possibly bring him one of Reb Moshe's yarmulkas. The friend explained his request:

> His father was in the construction business and owned a hard hat which he wore whenever he was on site. One day, he realized that for the past two weeks, his hard hat had mistakenly been exchanged with that of a non-Jewish worker. When the mistake was rectified, the worker told the Jew, "You should know that during the two weeks that I wore your hat, I had a very hard time getting a curse out of my mouth. I just found it hard to curse."
>
> The friend continued, "My father is a *pashute Yid* (simple Jew). If his hard hat can make it difficult for a non-Jew to curse, then I can only imagine the benefits one can gain from wearing Reb Moshe's yarmulka!"
>
> When this story was repeated to Reb Moshe it elicited no surprise, and he gave the *bachur* one of his yarmulkas as a gift.

MANY YEARS AGO, A PROMINENT RAV GAVE A WEEKLY COURSE IN HOMILETICS TO students of Tifereth Jerusalem. One evening, he walked into the beis

Apologies and Deference

midrash before going up to the third floor where the class was held. He noticed Reb Moshe sitting in his usual seat up front and quickly went over to greet him. In his haste, the rav failed to notice that *Maariv* was in progress and

Reb Moshe was in the middle of reciting the *Shema*. When the rav realized his error, he turned around hurriedly and went up to his class.

A short while later there was a knock on his classroom door. It was Reb Moshe. He apologized profusely to the rav for not responding to his greeting. He explained that although the halachah does permit such a response, he could not break the accepted custom of not answering greetings while reciting *Shema*. Now, Reb Moshe greeted the rav warmly and spent several minutes speaking with him before leaving.

❧ ❧ ❧

One snowy evening, a young man was loading his family into a car on a Lower East Side street when he noticed Reb Moshe trudging through the snow on his way to a meeting in Tifereth Jerusalem. The man quickly went over and offered Reb Moshe a ride, which he graciously accepted. The car was crowded; at one point a three-year-old girl sitting in the back with Reb Moshe cried out, "I'm being squished!"

When the car pulled up in front of the yeshivah, Reb Moshe thanked the young man, then turned to the three-year-old and said, "Excuse me for 'sqvishing' you."

Once, Rabbi Yitzchak Selengut drove Reb Moshe home as Rabbi Selengut's daughter, a little girl, sat in the backseat. Reb Moshe alighted from the car, walked a short distance, and then returned to the car. "I forgot to say 'Goodbye' to your daughter," he explained to his talmid.

❧ ❧ ❧

When Rabbi Yisroel Kohn was a *bachur*, he spent a Shabbos in his parents' bungalow when their colony was honored with Reb Moshe's presence. It was the Shabbos of Reb Moshe's annual appeal there on behalf of Tifereth Jerusalem. Sunday morning, Yisroel hoped to return to Camp Staten Island in the car that was to take Reb Moshe back to camp. However, all seats were already reserved, and he had to find some other means of transportation.

That night back in camp, Yisroel met Reb Moshe in the dining room. Reb Moshe asked how he had returned to camp and was upset that the trip had not been convenient. "Why didn't you come in our car?" he asked. "You could have sat in the front between me and the driver!" It did not occur to Reb Moshe that Yisroel would not have wanted to inconvenience the Rosh Yeshivah. Reb Moshe felt a need to mollify the *bachur* and handed him two plums as a "gift."

As a *bachur,* Rabbi Michel Shurkin traveled every day from Brownsville in Brooklyn to study under Reb Moshe in Tifereth Jerusalem. One day, Reb Moshe approached him and asked if he could deliver galleys of a forthcoming volume of *Dibros Moshe* to the printer, whose office, Reb Moshe thought, was in the neighborhood in which his talmid resided. Michel was only too happy to oblige.

The next day, Reb Moshe approached Michel and apologized; he did not realize that the printer was located in East New York, some distance from Brownsville. He insisted on giving his talmid the fare for the bus he had taken to get there, and never again did he request this favor of him.[15]

FOLLOWING REB MOSHE'S PASSING, A NOTED ROSH YESHIVAH EXPRESSED concern that he had caused anguish to Reb Moshe by resisting his counsel

Tolerance for All
in a personal matter. Rabbi David Feinstein replied, "My father never felt hurt by such things. He considered everyone like his own child. A parent makes allowances for his children's shortcomings."

A gentleman from northern New Jersey started to become observant when he was past the age of 60. He told a friend that he felt despondent because, when his time was over, he would have to face the Heavenly Court without having amassed any Torah knowledge. The friend suggested that he drive to the Yeshivah of Staten Island from time to time — surely one of the students would be glad to teach him. So it was. He went to the yeshivah once a week for an hour of learning. He found it very difficult, because he had no Torah background and was not of an intellectual bent; however, after four years he glowed with pride at having mastered his first *"blatt gemara."* One of the students told the story to Reb Moshe, who said that for this man, a single *blatt* was as much of an accomplishment as for a scholar to complete an entire *masechta.* The Rosh Yeshivah asked the talmidim to celebrate the occasion with a *seudas mitzvah* which he, too, would attend.

The *seudah* was festive indeed, with Reb Moshe adding his own words of blessing and congratulation. With tears in his eyes, the "guest of honor" rose to thank everyone for making his life so much more meaningful. He said, "Now I am not afraid to die."

❀ ❀ ❀

As mentioned in the previous chapter, Reb Moshe wrote forcefully and unequivocally against the doctrines and practices of those movements

---

15. From *Meged Givos Olam.*

within Judaism that are unfaithful to Torah. It pained Reb Moshe to see so many of his fellow Jews being led astray from the path of truth, and he saw it as his obligation to rule on any question involving a breach in Halachah. But this in no way diminished his love for individuals who blindly engaged in the practices he condemned.

One Erev Yom Kippur a few years before his passing, Reb Moshe was wheeled into an elevator of his apartment building. Outside waited a car that was to take him to the Yeshivah of Staten Island, where he would observe the fast. In the elevator stood a Jew whose head was bare. The man bent down towards Reb Moshe and with a touch of hesitation said, "A happy new year, Rabbi." Reb Moshe looked up and with genuine warmth wished the man the same. Reb Moshe's sincerity moved the man to bend down again and say, "And a healthy year, too, Rabbi." With his sparkling eyes, Reb Moshe looked back at the man and said, "May you also be blessed with a healthy year, one filled with success and *nachas* from your children. And may you live to witness *Mashiach's* arrival."

> Reb Moshe's blessing moved its recipient deeply. As Reb Moshe was wheeled to the car, the man turned to Rebbetzin Shelia Feinstein (wife of Reb Reuven) and said, "It is obvious that I am not religious — my head is not even covered — yet, to the Rabbi, I am a 'Somebody'!"

With Rabbi Mordechai Tendler (left) and Rabbi Aryeh Don Greher (behind Reb Moshe), Gershon Spiegel, Rabbi Shmuel Bloom, Rabbi Yitzchok Kaplinsky

When they were in the car, Reb Moshe's daughter-in-law related what the man had said. Reb Moshe explained his show of warmth to the man in one short sentence — "*Uber ehr iz a Yid*" ("But he is a Jew").

In the words of his grandson, Rabbi Aryeh Don Greher, "Every *gadol* has his own path. The Rosh Yeshivah's face shone with וְאָהַבְתָּ לְרֵעֲךָ כָּמוֹךְ *(Love your fellow as yourself)*."

HE WOULD ACTIVELY SHOW HIS REGARD FOR THE CUSTOMS OF OTHER Orthodox sects. Before his health began to fail in his later years, Reb

Another's Minhag

Moshe would make annual appeals for his yeshivah in the Lower East Side shuls. On the Shabbos morning of an appeal, Reb Moshe would *daven* in that shul. One of these shuls was the *"Nine un Ninetziger Shtiebel,"* whose members were chassidim. When he entered the *shtiebel*, Reb Moshe would ask for a *gartel*, the additional belt worn by chassidim during *tefillah*, so as not to appear different from the members of the *minyan*.

In his last years, his weakened health confined him to his home, and a daily *minyan* was held in the dining room of his small apartment. At one point, the *minyan* was also convened on Friday nights. In another wing of the building lived a chassidic rebbe, who for a long time had a Friday-night *minyan* in his home. Reb Moshe became aware that his own *minyan* was drawing people away from that of the Rebbe, so he disbanded it.[16] When Pesach arrived, the Rebbe transported his *minyan* to Reb Moshe's apartment so that he could *daven* with a *minyan* on the *Seder* night. Though it was not Reb Moshe's custom to recite *Hallel* at *Maariv* on the *Seder* night, he insisted that it be done, in deference to the Rebbe, who observed the custom.

Among those who were privileged to have a close relationship with Reb Moshe is Mr. Yissochor Hasenfeld, whose chassidic roots drew him close to the Satmar Rav, Rabbi Yoel Teitelbaum, and other chassidic *gedolim*. Appreciating the *zechus* of assisting a *gadol* of Reb Moshe's stature, Mr. Hasenfeld funded the publication of a number of volumes of *Dibros*

---

16. For a period of time, Reb Moshe *davened* at the Rebbe's *minyan*. One Friday evening, Reb Moshe had *yahrzeit* and was to serve as *shliach tzibur* for *Minchah*. Though the custom was that every *shliach tzibur* donned a *gartel,* the Rebbe told the *mispallelim* that it would not be proper to ask Reb Moshe to don one. When Reb Moshe walked up to the *amud*, he turned around to face the *minyan* and said with a smile, "The *minhag hamakom* is to wear a *gartel*; please give me a *gartel*."

Yissochor Hasenfeld (l) and Dov Levy (r) escorting Reb Moshe into the ballroom at the 1983 Tifereth Jerusalem dinner held in his honor. Rabbi Michel Barenbaum is at right.

Moshe, in addition to his support of Tifereth Jerusalem. When asked about his relationship with Reb Moshe, Mr. Hasenfeld traced its beginnings to an incident that occurred many years ago:

> He was part of a group of chassidic laymen living in the Lower East Side who wanted to make some improvements to the neighborhood's community mikveh. The mikveh was certainly kosher for use, but for its status to be *l'chatchilah* (ideal) according to the opinions of renowned chassidic *poskim*, certain changes in the way it was filled had to be made. A meeting was held whose participants included Reb Moshe, the Boyaner Rebbe, local rabbanim, and the laymen who had initiated the meeting. While Reb Moshe was of the opinion that the mikveh in its current state was *kasher l'chatchilah*, he sided with those who wanted changes made so that everyone would be comfortable using the mikveh — and his opinion prevailed. This attitude, of showing respect for the feelings and needs of others whose background was different than his own, stamped Reb Moshe as "everyone's *gadol*."[17]

---

17. Before a yom tov or a family *simchah*, Mr. Hasenfeld would visit Reb Moshe to receive his *berachah*. It happened prior to Rosh Hashanah in the last years of Reb Moshe's life

With his genuine love for *every* Jew and deep understanding of the importance of peace, throughout his long life Reb Moshe remained above dispute and strife. It made no difference to Reb Moshe if someone was a chassid, *misnaged,* Sefardi or Ashkenazi — if the person was a Jew he had Reb Moshe's love and concern. Everyone was welcome in his home, and as a result, his name is revered wherever true Torah values are respected.

Small wonder that on a Motza'ei Shabbos in 1968, Reb Moshe received a phone call from the Satmar community asking that he pray for the recovery of the Satmar Rav, who earlier that day had suffered a crippling stroke.

He had a close relationship with the great chassidic rebbes who lived in his Lower East Side neighborhood.

UNTIL THE LATE 1960S, THE BOYANER REBBE, RABBI MORDECHAI SHLOMO Friedman, lived on the Lower East Side, not far from Tifereth Jerusalem.

The Boyaner Rebbe
Each year on his way home from *Maariv* on the first night of Rosh Hashanah, Reb Moshe would stop at the Boyaner Rebbe's home to exchange greetings for a good year.[18] Later, when the Rebbe's health worsened, he moved in with his children on the Upper West Side. From then on, Rabbi Moshe Zev Feierstein, a talmid of Reb Moshe[19] who is a Boyaner chassid, would drive Reb Moshe to the Rebbe before Rosh Hashanah and Pesach so that the two *gedolim* could exchange *berachos.*

Once, Reb Moshe emerged from the Rebbe's room, his face radiant. *"Baruch Hashem,"* he exclaimed, "the Rebbe said that the *dor* (generation) needs me and therefore I should have *arichas yamim v'shanim* (longevity) — *aza berachah* (what a *berachah*)!"

The Rebbe's esteem for Reb Moshe was obvious. On one occasion, he spoke glowingly to Rabbi Feierstein of Reb Moshe's towering greatness as a *posek.*

---

that Mr. Hasenfeld received a phone call from a grandson of Reb Moshe: "My grandfather requested that you prepare a paper with the [Hebrew] names of your family members." While writing a *"kvittel"* is common practice when visiting a chassidic rebbe, it was the first time Mr. Hasenfeld ever presented one to a Lithuanian *gadol.*

Another time, Mr. Hasenfeld went to the Lower East Side in the early-morning hours. Afraid that he might wake someone up by knocking on the door, he slipped a piece of paper under Reb Moshe's door with a request for a *berachah.* As he made his way to the elevator, Mr. Hasenfeld heard footsteps behind him. It was Reb Moshe, inviting him to come inside.

18. The Rebbe was seven years older than Reb Moshe.
19. See the end of Chapter Nine.

Reb Moshe and the Rebbe both attended a meeting of *gedolim* at Agudath Israel headquarters in Manhattan; Rabbi Feierstein drove them home. The Boyaner Rebbe's home was the first destination. When the Rebbe alighted from the car, Rabbi Feierstein alighted as well and began to escort him up the steps — but the Rebbe stopped him. "No, don't walk with me — take the Rosh Yeshivah home," he instructed his chassid.

When the Rebbe passed away in 1971, Reb Moshe advised Rabbi Feierstein to accompany the *niftar* to Eretz Yisrael for the burial on Har HaHazeisim. "He was a great man," said Reb Moshe.

ALSO RESIDING ON THE LOWER EAST SIDE WAS ANOTHER CHASSIDIC GIANT OF that era, the Kapyshnitzer Rebbe, Rabbi Avrohom Yehoshua Heschel. The

The Kapyshnitzer Rebbe

Rebbe enjoyed a close relationship with a number of Lithuanian *gedolim*, including Reb Aharon Kotler and Reb Moshe.

Once, a proposal that touched on an important area of Halachah was presented to the Rebbe. He endorsed the project enthusiastically and even wrote a letter of endorsement. However, as soon as he became aware that Reb Moshe opposed the project on halachic grounds, the Rebbe withdrew his endorsement.

Both the Rebbe and Reb Moshe would go the East River for *Tashlich*. Sometimes they would meet there and would take the opportunity to con-

With the Kapyshnitzer Rebbe, Rabbi Avraham Yehoshua Heschel

With the Kapyshnitzer Rebbe, Rabbi Moshe Mordechai Heschel, son and successor of R' Avraham Yehoshua. He was a talmid of and received semichah from Reb Moshe. At right is Rabbi Yaakov Yitzchak Ruderman.

verse on important matters. In the Rebbe's later years, someone would carry a chair for him to sit on, as the walk from the car to the river was difficult for him. Once, he and Reb Moshe met and the chair was brought for the Rebbe to sit down. However, he would not sit since there was no chair for Reb Moshe.

Reb Moshe's practice was to eat his Succos meals in the *succah* of his son-in-law, Rabbi Eliyahu Moshe Shisgal, before he, too, moved to the high-rise apartments on FDR Drive. One Erev Succos, it rained with such intensity that Rav Shisgal's *succah,* which had no protective covering, was not usable for the Yom Tov meal that night. Although it had stopped raining, the table and benches were drenched and water dripped from the *s'chach.* Reb Moshe, his son-in-law, and a third *talmid chacham* who usually joined them for the Succos meals made arrangements to eat in the *succah* of the Kapyshnitzer Rebbe, whose *succah* had been protected by a strong cover.

That night, as the three made their way to the *succah,* the Kapyshnitzer Rebbe was already seated in his *succah,* surrounded by his chassidim. When the guests entered his *succah,* the Rebbe said, "*Chazal* tell us that rain on Succos is not a good omen. However, for me it *is* a good omen, for it has brought me such exalted guests!"

THE SKOLYE REBBE, RABBI DOVID YITZCHAK ISAAC RABINOWITZ, DEVELOPED A close relationship with Reb Moshe from the Rebbe's years on the Lower

The Skolye Rebbe

East Side when he first arrived in America and from summer vacations they spent together in New Hampshire. The Rebbe was a legendary *masmid* and a *gaon baTorah.* Among his many written works are one on *Masechta Berachos* and another on the 613 *mitzvos,* bearing *haskamos* (approbations) of Reb Aharon Kotler, Reb Moshe, the Steipler Gaon, and other luminaries.

His *sefer* on *Masechta Berachos* contains an exchange of letters of Torah discussion between the Rebbe and Reb Moshe. The Rebbe's letter, which initiated the exchange, concludes with:

> *I ask of his glorious honor to send me an explanation of the Rosh's words that will resolve the question.*
>
> *At this point, I feel compelled to state that each time I study his honor's revered work, Dibros Moshe, I realize that his honor's strength of Torah is as powerful as that of an awesome lion; he ascends mountains and descends to valleys, splitting great waters with his Torah strength. He is for us a beacon of light.*
>
> *I beseech our Master in Heaven to grant his honor long life and peace ... I remain, his friend who loves him and is bound to him in love forever ... Dovid Yitzchak Isaac ben HaGaon HaKadosh Maran Boruch Pinchos, zt"l.*

*With the
Skolye
Rebbe*

The salutation of Reb Moshe's response reads: "May life and peace rest upon my friend, the renowned rav and *gaon, tzaddik yesod olam, Sinai* and *Oker Harim.*"[20] The letter closes with, "I remain, his friend who loves and reveres him exceedingly and who blesses him always, Moshe Feinstein."

BECAUSE REB MOSHE WAS REMOVED FROM ALL PETTINESS AND STRIFE, HE WAS often asked to mediate in disputes between quarrelling parties. He once

For the Sake of Peace

stayed up throughout the night in an attempt to resolve an angry dispute — despite the fact that some of the people involved were treating him with less than the respect he deserved.

Someone once began to complain about the practices of certain zealots who were in the habit of making known their displeasure with others in an ugly manner. The person had only started to speak when he noticed tears in Reb Moshe's eyes. He abruptly changed the subject.

Reb Moshe once said:

> *Chazal* tell us, "The *yetzer hara,* the evil eye, and a hatred of people can take a person from this world."[21] Now, isn't "hatred of people" included in *"yetzer hara"*? What else can cause baseless hatred of others? This, however, is precisely the point that *Chazal* are making. Often, one develops a hatred for someone else, mistakenly thinking

---

20. *Sinai* alludes to the breadth of his knowledge; *Oker Harim* (one who uproots mountains) refers to its depth. See *Berachos* 64a.
21. *Avos* 2:16.

that his feelings stem from the *yetzer tov*! The other person's customs or opinions differ from his own, and this — he thinks — is sufficient grounds for hatred. Beware — it is not! One need not agree with everything that others do or even *understand* everything that others do, but he must respect them nonetheless. Receive every person with a cheerful face and give others the benefit of the doubt — this should be a Jew's path in life.

When, on another occasion, Reb Moshe spoke on a similar theme, someone asked, "But isn't it hard to be like that?" Reb Moshe replied, "With regard to sin, *Chazal* say, 'Once he has sinned and repeated it (the sin), it becomes to him like something permissible.'[22] Habit has a powerful effect. The same is true with proper behavior. The more a person does that which is correct, the easier it becomes."

IN AN ADDRESS DELIVERED IN LUBAN IN 1926, REB MOSHE DWELLED ON THE Torah's view of truth and how it relates to peace:

Truth and Peace   The Mishnah lists truth and peace as concepts upon which the world stands,[23] and derives this from a *pasuk*.[24] Elsewhere, *Chazal* cite this teaching and conclude that where truth is found, peace is found.[25]

It would seem that being truthful often leads to strife, Reb Moshe asked. And do we not find that one may alter the truth in order to preserve peace?[26]

The answer to this, Reb Moshe explained, is that we have a misconception of what *emes*, truth, is. He explained this with a *mashal*:

> Reuven did something that upset Shimon very much. In his distress, Shimon expressed the anger he felt towards Reuven in the presence of others. Levi, being a man of "truth," tells himself: "It is only right that Reuven should know what Shimon said about him."[27] Levi then informs Reuven of Shimon's comment,[28] the result being that Reuven and Shimon are now bitter enemies.

---

22. *Yoma* 77a.
23. *Avos* 1:18.
24. *Zechariah* 8:16.
25. *Derech Eretz Zuta.*
26. See *Rashi* to *Bereishis* 18:13.
27. Reb Moshe commented that this sort of righteous indignation is often the cause of *lashon hara*.
28. In doing so, Levi has been guilty of speaking *rechilus*, that is, *lashon hara* that causes ill will between Jews.

Said Reb Moshe: Aside from the full-scale feud that Levi has caused, his entire approach is rooted not in truth but in falsehood. If he was really concerned with truth, he would realize that if Shimon was so hurt that he felt a need to lash out against Reuven, then it is possible that, indeed, Reuven had wronged him. Levi should have approached Reuven privately and discussed the matter with him. If, in fact, Reuven acted incorrectly, then he should apologize to Shimon. And if Reuven is a man of truth then he will not seek to retaliate upon learning what Shimon said about him. Rather, he will remind himself that

man begins as a tiny speck and is destined to return to dust. One who is truly humble will not feel a need to respond to insults.

And if Shimon has blown matters out of proportion, then Levi should sit down with him and attempt to quell his anger. If the disagreement is about money, then a man of truth will tell himself that one's earnings are decreed in Heaven and no one can take away what is rightfully intended for someone else.

This is the meaning of "truth" by the Torah's standards.[29] The quest for genuine truth leads to peace.

THE SHAMEFUL REBELLION LED BY KORACH AGAINST MOSHE RABBEINU stands for all time as a symbol of a dispute that was not for the sake of

His Deepest Desire Heaven.[30] The Torah relates that after Korach and his people were swallowed up in the ground, Moshe and Aharon were confronted by the multitudes who accused them, "You have killed the people of Hashem!"[31]

---

29. In altering Sarah Imeinu's words when she declared, "After my old age I will become youthful? — and my husband is old!" Hashem plumbed the depth of Sarah's intent. In no way did she mean to denigrate Avraham; she merely was expressing her disbelief that at that stage in their lives they could have children. However, on the chance that the statement "and my husband is old" might have caused Avraham a bit of hurt, Hashem omitted it from her statement.
30. See *Avos* 5:20.
31. *Bamidbar* 17:6.

How could the people have made such a baseless accusation? They had seen Moshe warn Korach that if he would not cease his rebellion, then he and his followers would be swallowed up — and that is exactly what happened. How could Moshe be faulted?

Reb Moshe explained: The people knew very well that Korach had brought about his own demise. Their complaint was that Moshe and Aharon should have prayed to Hashem that the lives of Korach and his people be spared. They reasoned that his rebellion would have waned with time, as the nation witnessed more miracles performed by Moshe and the sublime ways of Aharon as *Kohen Gadol*.

Hashem knew otherwise. Strife, said Reb Moshe, even if it is rooted in baseless claims, can cause much greater destruction than the most serious sins. The first *Beis HaMikdash* was destroyed because of the Three Cardinal Sins and was rebuilt after 70 years, because the people recognized the evil of their ways and repented. The Second *Beis HaMikdash*, however, was destroyed because of *sinas chinam* (baseless hatred) and the *machlokes* it spawned — and, said Reb Moshe, paraphrasing the words of our Sages, "This *yetzer hara* still dances among us." People are very slow to recognize the tragedy of strife and to extricate themselves from it. This is why there was no choice but to remove an unrepentant Korach and his followers from this world.

Reb Moshe perceived the destructiveness of *machlokes*. Someone was once asked to participate in a meeting that dealt with a dispute between two parties. The person was reluctant to attend, but he felt that he would be looked down upon if he did not participate. He consulted with Reb Moshe, who told him, "Go and hide," meaning "make yourself unavailable on that day."

It happened that a group of young *talmidei chachamim* were invited to open a yeshivah in a small community where a yeshivah already existed. These young men were concerned that opening their yeshivah might lead to friction within the community. Reb Moshe advised them not to open the yeshivah, saying, "It could lead to *machlokes*, and one must flee from *machlokes* as from a fire." When the young men responded that apparently there was a great need for such a yeshivah, Reb Moshe responded, "Whatever the situation is now, it will be worse if there will be a *machlokes*." His advice was heeded, and eventually these scholars were invited to join the original yeshivah, and the community flourished.

When a particular *machlokes* erupted within the Torah community, Reb Moshe remarked privately, "*Mashiach* should have already come, but this *machlokes* has caused that it should not happen."

Once, a man involved in a feud told Reb Moshe regarding his adversary, "That man is a *rasha* (wicked person)!"

Reb Moshe replied softly, "The *Ribono shel Olam* loves the biggest *rasha* more than you and I love the biggest *tzaddik*."

In his personal life, he did everything possible to maintain peace and avoid bad feelings. It happened that one of the rebbeim in Tifereth Jerusalem retired and came to Reb Moshe somewhat agitated, saying that he wanted a certain amount of pension money from the yeshivah. Reb Moshe, to whom other yeshivos would come to settle monetary issues with rebbeim, would not rule on this matter himself. As an *ish hashalom*, he wanted to make sure that the rebbi would leave without complaints. He replied in a friendly tone, "Who says that we are not going to give you money? If you agree, we can go together to Rabbi Feivelson (a rav and neighbor of the yeshivah) and we will give you whatever he says to give."

When parties would come to him for a *din Torah*, Reb Moshe always tried his best to make peace between them, though this was often quite difficult.

Following Reb Moshe's passing, Rabbi Reuven Feinstein said, "My father's deepest desire was to bring peace to Jewish life. If he could speak to us now, that is what he would tell us."

How wonderful it would be if his desire were realized.

CHAPTER NINE

Family and Extended Family

EB MOSHE FULFILLED THE DICTUM "HE [A HUSBAND] SHOULD honor her [his wife] more than himself" in its fullest sense. A year before his passing, when hospitalized with an illness that had caused

Concern for the Rebbetzin

him to drift in and out of consciousness, Reb Moshe was informed by a grandchild that he would soon be going home, where a male nurse would administer necessary treatments.

"The *Bobbe* must give her consent," Reb Moshe responded, knowing that the presence of a stranger in the apartment would inconvenience his rebbetzin. While his own weakened condition required the nurse's care, this did not mean his wife's feelings could be ignored.

For her part, where Reb Moshe's health was concerned, Rebbetzin Feinstein would do whatever the situation warranted, even things that seemed out of character for a woman of her stature.

It was Reb Moshe's practice to deliver an address on the *yahrzeit* of his beloved son-in-law, Rabbi Eliyahu Moshe Shisgal. One year, when Reb Moshe's weakened heart was regulated by a pacemaker, his address had been going on for quite some time when the door of the beis midrash

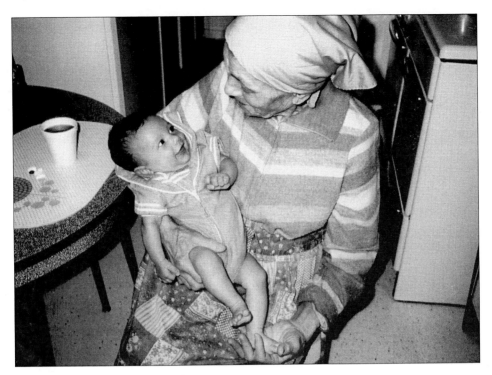

The Rebbetzin with a young visitor

opened and in walked the Rebbetzin, to insist that he had spoken long enough. He motioned to her that he was nearly finished, and brought his talk to a swift conclusion.

For a time, some of the fund-raising for Mesivtha Tifereth Jerusalem was done by people making telephone calls from Reb Moshe's small apartment. The reason for this novel arrangement was that often the solicitor felt that Reb Moshe should express his appreciation and blessings to the donor, and if the solicitor had easier access to Reb Moshe, much time would be saved and much more could be accomplished. The caller had only to take a few steps to Reb Moshe's study and briefly interrupt his learning to have him pick up the phone and speak for a few moments.

Reb Moshe appreciated the reasoning behind this arrangement, but he put a halt to it soon after it began. Reb Moshe was concerned for his rebbetzin, for he felt that she had become a prisoner in her own home. With the yeshivah occupying her living room and with her husband at his desk in the study, the Rebbetzin was confined to her kitchen and bedroom — a situation that Reb Moshe would not permit. Instead, a private line was installed in the yeshivah through which the solicitor could contact Reb Moshe at home to speak to a donor any time.

As with every mitzvah, Reb Moshe was extremely meticulous in reviewing the weekly *parashah* twice with *Targum,* as prescribed by Halachah.[1] Even during a period in his later years, when weakened eyesight forced him to study with the aid of a magnifying glass, he would strain to review the *parashah.*

One Friday night, as Reb Moshe was reviewing the *parashah,* the Rebbetzin announced that the *seudas Shabbos* was ready to begin. Reb Moshe closed his *Chumash* in the middle of a *pasuk,* so as not to keep her waiting even for a moment.

> Often, Rebbetzin Shelia Feinstein would come to take her mother-in-law to a women's function for Tifereth Jerusalem. If she arrived in the early evening, there would be a place mat on the table with a setting for Reb Moshe and a small pot on the stove. Before leaving, the Rebbetzin would remind Reb Moshe to turn on a low flame to warm his supper. When they returned a few hours later, the place mat was put away and the pot, dish, and cutlery had been washed and dried.
>
> Once, the Rebbetzin took ill and was confined to bed. Rebbetzin Shelia came to the apartment to tend to her parents-in-law's needs and found Reb Moshe in the kitchen drying glasses. "Why is the *shver* doing this?" she asked. "We would have done it — that's what we're here for!"
>
> "I know," Reb Moshe replied, "but I was afraid that your mother-in-law would get out of bed for something and upon entering the kitchen would feel bad that things are not in order as they usually are."

HIS GRANDSON RABBI MORDECHAI TENDLER, WHO WAS ALMOST INSEPARABLE from Reb Moshe in his final years, relates that Reb Moshe would urge him

A Model Marriage
to return his wife's phone calls at the earliest possible time. Reb Moshe would also not allow his grandson to remain with him past the time he was expected back home, saying, "It is more important that you be home when your wife expects you than for you to remain here with me."

To a young man who complained that his wife became upset if he

---

1. He also reviewed Rashi's commentary to fulfill the mitzvah in the optimum manner.

With her first great-great granddaughter, September 1988

did not call her during the day, Reb Moshe responded with amazement, "But of course you should call her during the day. I always call the Rebbetzin."

For most of their married life, Rebbetzin Feinstein had the difficult task of safeguarding her husband's health and at the same time allowing him to keep up his strenuous schedule of learning, teaching, and leading *Klal Yisrael*. She carried out her responsibilities with grace, dignity, and kindness.

In the words of Rebbetzin Sarah Mermelstein, whose family lived downstairs from the Feinsteins for over a decade:

> The story of Rebbetzin Feinstein's life is the story of Reb Moshe. She was the epitome of a devoted and conscientious wife. As a young bride of 21 and until Reb Moshe's passing in 1986, she constantly

guarded his physical needs to perfection, kept an immaculate home, and maintained an exact mealtime schedule, not wasting his precious minutes.

To me, her most compelling attribute was her total lack of pretension. Thousands of individuals passed through her door; she remained uncurious as to their personal stories, yet wholly concerned for their problems. She would treat the important and the simple with equal care. Without fanfare, she warmed hearts and unceremoniously heaped good will upon so many.[2]

One afternoon, Rabbi Yisrael Eidelman came to Reb Moshe's house to drive him to yeshivah,where he would deliver a special *shiur* for married men. The rebbetzin answered his knock. "The Rav is not going," she said. Reb Moshe had not been feeling well, and the Rebbetzin wanted him to rest. But Reb Moshe felt that he was well enough to deliver the *shiur* and that its importance overrode whatever discomfort it might cause him.

As Reb Moshe donned his coat, the rebbetzin said, "You shouldn't go." While Reb Moshe appreciated his rebbetzin's concern, he made it clear that he was up to the task and that he must go. When the rebbetzin realized how determined Reb Moshe was to go, she accepted his decision and did not say another word.

Rabbi Eidelman recalls witnessing this a number of times. The Rebbetzin worried about her husband's health and did everything in her power to safeguard it. At the same time, when she saw that Reb Moshe was determined to keep to his regular schedule, she respectfully deferred to his decision.[3]

The esteem in which the Rebbetzin held Reb Moshe is illustrated by a comment she once made.

A *chasan* who was close to the family wanted to go to Eretz Yisrael for the summer prior to his wedding. His parents were strongly in favor of the idea. Reb Moshe, however, seemed opposed. When the *chasan* told

---

2. From an appreciation in *The Jewish Observer* subsequently published in *Torah Luminaries* (ArtScroll/Mesorah Publications).

3. Reb Moshe lived by the requirement to guard one's health, just as he lived by every halachah in *Shulchan Aruch* and every teaching of *Chazal*. Rabbi Shlomo Freifeld would relate how one of his own talmidim, Avi Small, a great-nephew of Reb Moshe, spent Shabbos with the Feinsteins in order to tend to Reb Moshe's needs. This was towards the end of Reb Moshe's life when his weakness required that he be taken by wheelchair from room to room in his apartment. After the Shabbos meal, Avi wheeled Reb Moshe to his bedroom for a nap. A few feet before reaching his bed, Reb Moshe asked Avi to help him to stand up so that he could walk to his bed, for the Gemara teaches that following a meal, one should not lie down without first walking a minimum of four *amos* (from *Reb Shlomo: The Life and Legacy of Rabbi Shlomo Freifeld* by Rabbi Yisroel Besser, published by Judaica Press).

Rebbetzin Feinstein of his dilemma, she said, "If the Rosh Yeshivah says that you should not go, you should be afraid not to listen to him." The Rebbetzin offered to present the young man's dilemma to Reb Moshe, who was in his final years and was not well. Later that day, Reb Moshe told the *chasan* that he was opposed only to his going away for an extended period; a ten-day trip would be fine. This satisfied everyone.

LIKE ANY COUPLE, REB MOSHE AND HIS REBBETZIN HAD THEIR LIGHT MOMENTS together. Someone recalled being present on a Motza'ei Shabbos as Reb

Light Moments Moshe and Rebbetzin Feinstein prepared to leave for a *melaveh malkah*. "You must change your shirt, Rabbi Feinstein," the Rebbetzin said, referring to her husband formally, as she always did when anyone but relatives was present.

"Change my shirt?" Reb Moshe responded. "Whatever for? The Shabbos shirt that I am wearing is nice and clean." With a twinkle in his eye, Reb Moshe turned to the man who was to drive them to the affair. "Tell me," he said, "does one normally change his shirt before attending a *melaveh malkah* or not?"

Not sure how to reply, the person said, "At times yes and at times not!"

Reb Moshe laughed and went to change his shirt.

Before leaving for a wedding, the Rebbetzin could often be heard to remark, "Rabbi Feinstein, your frock is simply sparkling!"

On one occasion, Reb Moshe seemed in an unusual hurry to leave for a wedding. "What is the rush, Rabbi Feinstein?" the Rebbetzin asked. "Enough pictures of you have already been taken!"

In a light moment, the Rebbetzin told a talmid who was a frequent visitor to their home, "To know how to learn like my husband — you'll probably never know. But to be a gentleman like him — that you can be!"

WHEN RABBI DOVID WEINBERGER RESIDED ON THE LOWER EAST SIDE HE WAS asked to deliver a *shiur* on the *parashah* one Friday night in the apartment

"This Is Her Gadlus" complex where his in-laws and the Feinsteins resided.[4] At the Friday-night *seudah*, Rabbi Weinberger mentioned that he had forgotten to bring with him a certain *sefer* written by one of pre-war Europe's great Torah personalties which he wanted to quote from during the *shiur*. His father-in-law, Rabbi Nissan Alpert, did not own the *sefer* but suggested that Rabbi Weinberger knock on Reb Moshe's door and ask to borrow it.[5]

---

4. See further in this chapter about the closeness between these families.
5. An *eruv chatzeiros* had been made, making it permissible to carry within the building.

Rebbetzin Feinstein answered Rabbi Weinberger's knock. He explained why he had come and the Rebbetzin told him to go into the study and take whatever *sefer* he needed. Meanwhile, Reb Moshe was in the dining room reviewing the *parashah* and was not aware that he had a visitor.

The light was off in the study, but the outdoor lights provided some illumination through the window. Rabbi Weinberger could not find the *sefer*. He left the study and as he was leaving the apartment, he turned towards the kitchen to say *"Gut Shabbos"* to the Rebbetzin. "Did you find the *sefer* you needed?" she asked. When Rabbi Weinberger replied in the negative, the Rebbetzin told him to accompany her to the dining room. She explained the problem to Reb Moshe and when Rabbi Weinberger named the *sefer* he needed, Reb Moshe replied, "I don't know if I have it, but if I do it's on the right side on one of the top shelves." Reb Moshe was 88 years old and ill, so rather than search for the *sefer* himself as he would have done in earlier years, he suggested that Rabbi Weinberger do so.

Rabbi Weinberger returned to the study and again left empty-handed. When Rebbetzin Feinstein saw that he had not found the *sefer,* she insisted, over his protests, that he come back with her to the dining room.

"If you could not find it," said Reb Moshe, "then I probably don't have it."

Rebbetzin Feinstein was upset. "How could you not have this *sefer*?" she asked. "It was written by Rav _____ and you don't have it?"

Now Reb Moshe was a bit upset. "If someone would have sent me the *sefer* I would have it.[6] No one sent it to me so I don't have it."

Rabbi Weinberger left feeling terrible for having taken Reb Moshe's valuable time and for causing both him and his rebbetzin to become upset. He resolved to ask forgiveness at the earliest opportunity.

Shabbos afternoon, prior to *Minchah* at Reb Moshe's private *minyan*, Rabbi Weinberger apologized. Reb Moshe smiled and said that it was not necessary. "This is the *gadlus* (greatness) of the Rebbetzin," he explained. "What do we have in this apartment? — a few *sefarim*. And we could not even do this *chesed* by lending you the *sefer* you needed. This is why she felt bad."

> Once, during a *shiur* in *Hilchos Shabbos* in Tifereth Jerusalem, Reb Moshe brought proof to his halachic ruling from something the Rebbetzin had been doing in the kitchen on Shabbos since their marriage. "If the Rebbetzin does this," he told his talmidim, "she surely has a *mesorah* (family tradition) that it is correct to do so." Almost half a century later, a talmid recalled this incident as yet another indication of the esteem in which Reb Moshe held his rebbetzin.

As a guest at their Shabbos table, Rabbi Weinberger saw yet another dimension of the beautiful relationship between Reb Moshe and his rebbetzin. Rabbi Weinberger's wife had gone away with the children to a family *simchah*, while he had remained at home for a *simchah* in the shul where he served as Rav. When Rabbi Weinberger requested to eat the Friday-night *seudah* with Reb Moshe and the Rebbetzin, she arranged for him to eat with her son Reb David and his wife. Toward the end of the meal, Reb David said, "My mother said to tell you that you are invited to my parents for *shalosh seudos*."

At *shalosh seudos*, Rabbi Weinberger went into the kitchen and offered to help the Rebbetzin serve, but she would not hear of it. "You are our guest," she said, "and it is a *zechus* for me to serve you."

There was a *minyan* for *Maariv* in Reb Moshe's dining room. Before *Maariv*, Rabbi Weinberger watched in awe as Reb Moshe learned the week's seven *blatt* of *Daf Yomi*.[7] After *Maariv*, when Rabbi Weinberger

---

6. Reb Moshe received scores of *sefarim* in the mail, from authors and others who had published *sefarim* and would send their books out of respect and in an attempt to cover publication costs.

7. A number of times, Reb Moshe turned to the back of the gemara to learn *Rosh* and *Maharsha*.

thanked the Rebbetzin, she replied, "I wanted to have you as our guest last night. But on Friday night, we eat whitefish. Because of [the prohibition of] borer[8] my husband extracts the bones from the fish after the piece is in his mouth (rather than taking the bones out with a fork while it is on his plate). I think he would be uncomfortable doing this in front of a guest. At shalosh seudos, we eat gefilte fish, so it's not a problem."

Rabbi Weinberger still marvels at the Rebbetzin's sensitivity for her husband's feelings.

> During summer vacations, Reb Moshe and his rebbetzin would sometimes go for walks together. Reb Moshe would have with him the Tanach that he carried with him everywhere he went. When either he or his wife had something to discuss, Reb Moshe would keep the Tanach closed, with his finger at the place he was up to, and speak with his rebbetzin for any length of time. When the conversation had run its course, Reb Moshe would open the Tanach and study, until Rebbetzin Feinstein had to speak with him again, upon which the Tanach would be closed …
>
> This perhaps best sums up the relationship of this unique couple. The Rebbetzin was her husband's willing helpmate in assuring that every moment of his life revolved around his avodas Hashem, especially his Torah study. Reb Moshe, while being the most diligent Torah scholar imaginable, was sincerely sensitive to his wife's feelings and needs at all times.

REB MOSHE HAD ONLY ONE SURVIVING SIBLING IN THE UNITED STATES, HIS sister Rebbetzin Chana Small of Chicago. They were very close, and they

Reb Moshe's Sister shared many character traits. Her respect for him was boundless; she used to refer to him as "my brother, the tzaddik," and her husband, Rabbi Isaac Small, had an extremely warm relationship with Reb Moshe.

Rebbetzin Small always went out of her way to judge people favorably, even when they did not seem to deserve such sympathy. When she was not well, and particularly during her terminal illness, she used to say that she was suffering because of this or that shortcoming of which she had been guilty, the same sort of soul-searching that was so pronounced in Reb Moshe.

> When Rebbetzin Small was suffering for five years with a lingering, very painful illness, Reb Moshe made a point of calling her regularly. During

---

8. Lit. separating (in a proscribed manner); one of the 39 prohibited Shabbos labors.

one of these calls, a grandchild overheard her say, "Moshe, *daven* for me." She listened to his response and then said, "Moshe, since we were young we all knew that the One Above listens to your prayers."

Toward the end of her life, Rebbetzin Small slipped into a coma. When she had been comatose for four days, her doctors suggested to the family that they "pull the plug." There was virtually no hope that she would ever be conscious again, they argued, and even if she were to come out of the coma briefly, her brain could no longer function. The Small children asked Reb David and Reb Reuven to consult Reb Moshe on what they should do.

Reb Moshe was in very delicate health and his sons felt that it would be dangerous to give him such tragic news, but they told the Small family that he had never permitted such a procedure.

Soon after that call, Reb Moshe was reminiscing about his siblings and he mentioned the names of those who were no longer living; *"Uber Chana leibt nach"* ("But Chana is still alive"), he said. That very day, she awoke from her coma and became completely lucid. Her children and grandchildren visited and carried on conversations with her. For the first time she was able to meet a grandson's new bride. For the next seven days she was completely conscious, and then she passed away.

Family portrait of Reb Moshe with (counterclockwise) his son-in-law Reb Eliyahu Moshe Shisgal זצ״ל; יבל״ח his son, Reb David; his daughter-in-law Rebbetzin Malka; his daughter Rebbetzin Sifra Tendler ע״ה; his Rebbetzin ע״ה; יבל״ח his daughter Rebbetzin Faya Shisgal; his daughter-in-law Rebbetzin Shelia Feinstein; his son Reb Reuven; and his son-in law, Reb Moshe David Tendler.

Her son says of her, "She was a Feinstein. She suffered terribly, but she always tried to act cheerful and keep us from knowing how much pain she was in."

Yes, she was a Feinstein.

AS INVOLVED AS REB MOSHE WAS WITH THE NEEDS OF *KLAL YISRAEL*, HE NEVER neglected his obligations to his own children. Rabbi Reuven Feinstein

With His Offspring
recalled that as the youngest in the family, he was always seated next to his father at mealtime. The children were taught both through word and example that the needs of others came before their own. Yet, no matter how many guests joined the Feinsteins at their table, Reb Moshe always kept his young son next to him.

> There was not a more loving grandfather. He would cuddle his grandchildren and play with them. They adored him and loved to sit on his lap or roll a ball back and forth with him. On Yom Tov, he would take his young grandsons under his *tallis* for *Bircas Kohanim* and would move his *siddur* over so that they could follow along.

When Zeidy was around, the grandchildren were calm and happy, even after a long and cramped automobile trip. Reb Moshe's family and others who were close to him say that it was difficult to feel awestruck in his presence because his manner of doing things was so plain and simple. He never gave the slightest impression that he was different from anyone else. Nevertheless, even a very young great-granddaughter, while feeling quite content sitting on her great-grandfather's lap, would refer to him as "our *Tzaddik*." And his children recall feeling even as youngsters that there could be no one better to emulate than their father.

He would call and ask how a grandchild was faring in school, or how well he or she was recovering from a cold. When a nine-year-old great-grandson began to study Gemara, his parents encouraged him to call Reb Moshe and read some Gemara for him. The boy felt somewhat shy about doing this but was finally convinced to place the call. Then, the child thought of a problem. "How will Zeidy be able to follow what I'm saying without a gemara in front of him?" His parents laughed and convinced the young scholar that it would not be a problem. The boy called and told Reb Moshe the exciting news. Reb Moshe congratulated his great-grandson and then the boy proceeded to read from a gemara. After a couple of lines, he stopped to take a breath. Thinking that the boy had gotten stuck on a word or two, Reb Moshe continued the Gemara for him. When he hung up the phone, the boy exclaimed with astonishment, "Zeidy knew it by heart!"

All the children, grandchildren, and great-grandchildren were called by Reb Moshe and the Rebbetzin on their birthdays. The family would reciprocate by calling Reb Moshe every 7 Adar to wish him well on his birthday. Those who lived in the New York area would come to the Lower East Side to do this in person. This was so accepted a practice in the Feinstein family that when one grandchild was once unable to get through on the phone, she received a call that night from Reb Moshe, who was concerned that something was amiss.

The family emphasizes, however, that these were not simply "Happy Birthday" calls, but opportunities for them to express their fervent hopes and blessings that their father and grandfather merit another year of life in good health, and receive his blessing in return.[9]

---

9. Some of Reb Moshe's other "children," namely his talmidim, had their own way of marking his birthday. For a number of years, a group of students from Yeshivah of Staten Island would travel to the East Side on 7 Adar to present Reb Moshe with a loose-leaf containing *chiddushei Torah* written by the yeshivah's talmidim. Reb Moshe would glowingly accept this unique gift and leaf through the entire collection in the presence of the talmidim.

WITH GRANDCHILDREN AND GREAT-GRANDCHILDREN

REBBETZIN MALKA FEINSTEIN, WIFE OF REB DAVID, SAYS, "THE ROSH YESHIVAH was a father to me even before I became his daughter-in-law."

Warm and Devoted   As a child, she knew him and the Rebbetzin as friends of her parents, and had no idea that he was a great man as well. One day, when she was 13 years old and living in the Williamsburg section of Brooklyn, she came home from school for lunch. The door was unlocked — not unusual in those days — but her mother was not home. She took her lunch herself and then noticed a note saying that if the key was not in its usual place, she should not go back to school in the afternoon. She was puzzled, so she tried to call her brother, who was studying in Mesivta Torah Vodaath. He could not be found, but a friend of his came to the phone and told her that her mother and brother had gone somewhere together.

By now she was frightened and she felt she had to call someone for help and advice. The family had dozens of close friends, but somehow, instinctively, the person she thought of to call was Reb Moshe. Even a young teenager felt that sort of closeness to him. He calmed her and told her to stay home until she heard from him. Before long, she looked out the window and saw Reb Moshe and the Rebbetzin coming down the street. He had called the slaughterhouse where her father was a *shochet*, and learned that he had suffered a heart attack at work and had not survived the trip to the hospital.

Immediately, Reb Moshe and the Rebbetzin had crossed the Williamsburg Bridge and went to stay with the worried child in her time of fear and tragedy. Later, he left to take part in her late father's *taharah* [ritual cleansing and preparation for burial].

She recalls another incident that illustrates his thoughtfulness. The second summer after her marriage, she and her husband were in the city for the summer while Reb Moshe was in the Catskill Mountains, where summer bungalows did not have telephones. One day she received a postcard from Reb Moshe telling her that he had been in New York for a day, but had not had an opportunity to call her. He was therefore writing to apologize. He signed the card, *"dein tatte"* ("your father").

In her words:

> As a father, father-in-law, and grandfather, the Rosh Yeshivah was so warm, devoted, and natural that nothing he did seemed extraordinary. His relationship with his grandchildren was that of a typical *zeida*, one of mutual love.
>
> When my daughter was three years old, someone bought her a tea set. When the Rosh Yeshivah and the Rebbetzin would visit us,

this little girl would play a game, pretending she was making tea and bringing the Rosh Yeshivah a cup. He would accept the cup from her, pretend he was drinking, and then return the cup.

When she was in second grade, the students were asked to write a composition about their grandparents. There were a number of girls from distinguished lineage and some of them wrote of their grandfathers' position as rav or rosh yeshivah. My daughter wrote that sometimes, when she was together with her father and grand-father, and would express a desire to eat the Shabbos *seudah* at her grandparents' house, "My father says, 'No,' but my zeidy says, 'Yes.' "

My sister had a summer home in Swan Lake; for a number of years, my in-laws would go there for summer vacation. There was a room in the back where the Rosh Yeshivah learned, but in the afternoon when the sun on that side was strong, he would move to a porch in the front. One summer, my sister had a newborn and she put the baby on the porch while the Rosh Yeshivah sat and learned. Someone was assigned to sit inside and listen for when the baby cried — but it didn't cry! Finally, the person went outside and found the Rosh Yeshivah rocking the baby.

When a great-grandchild was born — and not the first one — the Rosh Yeshivah made a special trip from the Lower East Side to Washington Heights to see the baby. Around a week later, on his way to the Catskills for summer vacation, he had the car make a stop in the Heights to visit mother and child again.

The Rosh Yeshivah and the Rebbetzin visited us often; it was always a pleasure and an honor, never a burden. One year, the Rebbetzin took ill before Purim, so my in-laws came to us for the entire Pesach. They continued this practice for the next ten years, until the Rosh Yeshivah's illness made it too difficult for them to leave home. At the *Seder*, the Rosh Yeshivah sat at the head of our table, involving his grandchildren in the story of *yetzias Mitzrayim*.

When questions involving *chinuch* came up, we would consult with the Rosh Yeshivah. Our son, Mordechai, was slightly younger than the age for kindergarten, which in those days was the beginning class at school. I was apprehensive about sending him, so we asked the Rosh Yeshivah. He said not to worry, we should send him to kindergarten at the start of the school year. With the passage of time it became clear that this decision was correct.

In the Catskill Mountains, summer 1957

One Erev Shabbos, I received a phone call from Reb David: the Rebbetzin was not feeling well and the Rosh Yeshivah asked that I come over to get the house in order for Shabbos. Their apartment was always immaculate and the Rosh Yeshivah knew that it would upset the Rebbetzin to go into Shabbos with things not in order.

When I arrived there, the Rebbetzin said that it was not necessary for me to have come; she would do whatever needed to be done. (Apparently, she did not want to burden her daughter-in-law.) The Rosh Yeshivah said, "Let her do it. She is young (and can handle the additional chores), she is our daughter, and she will get the job done." The Rebbetzin acquiesced.

As I said, to the Rosh Yeshivah and the Rebbetzin, I was a daughter, not a daughter-in-law.

MRS. YOCHEVED (GREHER) FRIEDMAN IS A GREAT-GRANDDAUGHTER OF REB Moshe.[10] Growing up in the same building as Reb Moshe and his reb-

A Great-Granddaughter's Perspective

betzin, she and her siblings were especially close to their great-grandparents:

We often went downstairs to visit. Always, we found the Rosh Yeshivah involved with Torah, either learning from a *sefer* or writing his *divrei Torah*. But if we needed his attention, he was always available.

We knew he was a *gadol*: when he entered the room, we would stand up in respect. At the same time, there was not a more loving, caring grandfather. When we were small, we would play in his study with the fountain pens with which he wrote his *sefarim*. On our Hebrew birthdays, we would come to receive his *berachah*. When my older sister became engaged only a few weeks before his passing,

---

10. Her mother is a daughter of Rav Eliyahu Moshe Shisgal and his rebbetzin תבל״ח.

she showed him her engagement ring. The Rosh Yeshivah examined and admired it as would any excited grandfather.

In his last years when the Rosh Yeshivah was not well, my sisters and I took turns spending the night in my great-grandparents' apartment should an emergency arise. Each night, two of us slept in the Rosh Yeshivah's study. We were given instructions to make sure that he was in bed at 9 p.m. because even then, when he was not well, he was up for the day at around 4 a.m.

We did our job faithfully. At 9:00 sharp we would inform him of the time. Often, he would look up from his *sefer* with a smile and say, "Just a few more minutes." He so badly did not want to stop learning.

We knew that at around 4:30 each morning he would come into the study to get his *sefarim*. He would tiptoe in so as not to awaken us. Then he would go to the kitchen or dining room to learn.

The Rebbetzin was a regal woman in every way. Her apartment was always immaculate, as is befitting the home of a *talmid chacham*. She appreciated nice things and we always wanted her approval for what we purchased. Anytime we bought a new dress, we brought it downstairs to show to her.

Over the years, we spent countless hours in their apartment. Never did we hear either one raise a voice, and never did a bad word pass between them.

AS A TALMID OF TIFERETH JERUSALEM AND A NEPHEW OF RABBI REUVEN Feinstein, Mr. Beinish Kaplan was considered "family" in the Feinstein home. Even after he moved to Los Angeles, he maintained a

Far, Yet Near

very close relationship with Reb Moshe and the entire Feinstein family. He recalled:

The Rosh Yeshivah was always so warm to me. Whenever I would call from Los Angeles, he would inquire about each family member individually. When I would come to New York and visit him, he would insist, despite my protests, on accompanying me to the elevator when I left.

I had the privilege of joining him for the *Seder* for a number of years. Listening to him fulfill the mitzvah of *sipur yetzias Mitzrayim* was an unforgettable experience.

In the 1970s, I opened a clothing firm and negotiated with a famous manufacturer of designer clothing to obtain a license to use their label on our products. The deal would require a very significant monetary investment on my part. I came to New York to work out final details and sign a contract. My first stop was at the Rosh Yeshivah's home to receive his *berachah* for the success of this venture.

Before he would confer his *berachah,* the Rosh Yeshivah wanted to know *every* aspect of the deal; what the contract would state, how much I would be investing, what I hoped to gain from the deal, etc. He questioned me for an hour and his questions were more penetrating than those of the licensing lawyer whom I had engaged. When he was satisfied that the deal made sense, he conferred his heartfelt *berachah* and assured me that it would turn out "very good." It did.

Providence arranged that I should be in New York at the time of his passing so that I could assist with the funeral arrangements. I merited to accompany his *aron* to Eretz Yisrael and participate in his burial on Har HaMenuchos.

AS MENTIONED ABOVE,[11] RABBI NISSAN ALPERT WAS AMONG REB MOSHE'S greatest and most beloved talmidim. Reb Moshe and his rebbetzin were the

A Special Relationship

shadchanim who arranged the match between Reb Nissan and his rebbetzin, the former Zelda Scheinberg, daughter of the revered Rosh Yeshivah and *posek*

At the wedding of Rabbi and Mrs. Nissan Alpert:

Seated (left to right): unidentified, Reb Michel Barenbaum, Reb Eliyahu Mordechai Maza, Reb Moshe, Nissan Alpert, Kapyshnitzer Rebbe, Reb Shabsie Alpert, Reb Yisroel Kaplinsky

Second row (left to right): Avrohom Berman, Mr. Trauring, David Feinstein, Mordechai Dickstein, unidentified, Heshy Lercher, Mr. Berezin, Moshe Yehuda Goldstein

Third row (left to right): unidentified, Mendel Rubin, Chaim Nachman, Yitzchak Selengut, unidentified, Herbert Adler, Avraham Amsel, Efraim Dickstein, Louis Palgon, Aaron Palgon, unidentified, Stanley Lieber

---

11. See Chapter Three.

Rabbi Chaim Pinchas Scheinberg of Jerusalem. For many years, the Alperts resided in the same apartment complex as the Feinsteins and their windows faced each other. Rebbetzin Alpert recalls that the hardest part of moving to Far Rockaway when her husband became a rav there was moving away from Reb Moshe and his rebbetzin.

The Feinstein dining room had a picture window and the curtains were often open, so it was possible to observe Reb Moshe as he learned at the table on Shabbos. Each year on Chanukah, Rebbetzin Alpert would watch Reb Moshe kindle the Chanukah *lecht*. When he was finished lighting, he would remain bent over, staring at the flames for some time.

❧ ❧ ❧

Mordechai Alpert was in Yeshivah of Staten Island's first ninth-grade class. He was not yet bar mitzvah, and going to live away from home would require some adjustment. On the first day of yeshivah, Rebbetzin Alpert drove her son to Staten Island. Reb Moshe planned to be at the yeshivah that day and was an honored passenger in the Alperts' car.

Like Rebbetzin Alpert, other parents who brought their sons that day planned to stay to help them unpack and get settled. However, the yeshivah's administration made it clear that they felt it best for the boys if the parents would leave and allow their sons to acclimate themselves to their new surroundings. When Reb Moshe was ready to return home, he and Rebbetzin Alpert entered the car while Mordechai stood a few feet away watching them.

After Reb Moshe was seated comfortably, he gazed out the window and saw the boy's face. Mordechai, who was noticeably younger than the other ninth-graders, looked somewhat sad and perhaps a bit apprehensive. Some leeway was needed at that moment, Reb Moshe decided. He told Rebbetzin Alpert, "Mordechai looks upset. I think you should get out of the car and remain until you know that you are leaving him happy." She followed these instructions and saw that the few extra minutes she spent with her son had their desired effect.

❧ ❧ ❧

When Rabbi Dovid Weinberger became engaged to the Alperts' daughter, Adina, the *chasan* and *kallah* were not certain where to make their first home. Rabbi Weinberger planned to continue learning at Yeshivah Chofetz Chaim in Forest Hills, so Queens was one possibility. The Alperts, however, resided on the Lower East Side in the same apartment complex as Reb Moshe, where rentals were comparatively inexpensive, certainly a consideration for a young *kollel* couple. And Rabbi Weinberger knew that he had much to gain from living in close proximity to his illustrious father-in-law, Rabbi Alpert.

During the engagement, Rav Alpert brought his future son-in-law to Reb Moshe for a *berachah*. When the topic of apartments came up, the *chasan* explained their dilemma. After he enumerated the reasons for living on the Lower East Side, Reb Moshe said, "And [another reason to live here is because] I live here!"

Rabbi Weinberger seized the opportunity. "If I live here, would it be all right to stop in once in a while?" Reb Moshe replied, "My door will be open to you, in the merit of your father-in-law, who is like one of my children." This decided matters; the Weinbergers lived on the Lower East Side until Reb Moshe's passing.

THE SUDDEN PASSING OF YESHAYAH MENDEL ALPERT, A *TALMID* OF Mesivtha Tifereth Jerusalem and Yeshivah of Staten Island, and son of Reb

Shaya Alpert

Nissan Alpert, was a very personal loss for Reb Moshe.

Already as a young boy, Shaya stood out among his peers. His *middos* and *yiras Hashem* were unusual.

As a 15-year-old, he learned in the evenings with a young great-grandson of Reb Moshe. The boy's father, Rabbi Aryeh Don Greher, later told Rebbetzin Alpert that he chose Shaya as an older *chavrusa* for his son because of the way Shaya *davened* when just 9 years old. He wanted such a boy to serve as an example for his son.

They would learn together at night in Reb Moshe's apartment. Reb Moshe and his rebbetzin came to appreciate Shaya's special qualities. Once, when Rebbetzin Feinstein was away overnight for medical reasons, Shaya was asked to spend the night in the Rosh Yeshivah's apartment. He took the responsibility very seriously and set up a bell system in case of emergency.

> As mentioned, the Feinsteins and the Alperts lived in the same high-rise apartment complex on Manhattan's FDR Drive. On the morning of Erev Pesach, Shaya would make the rounds of elderly Jewish residents in the building and offer to burn their *chametz* for them. Many would give the boy their *chametz* and hand him a tip for the service he was rendering. A dollar was considered a generous tip.
>
> Reb Moshe fulfilled this mitzvah himself. However, in his later years after he took ill, he would designate Shaya as his *shaliach* (agent) to burn his *chametz*.

One year, after the burning was completed, Shaya returned to his family's apartment and rang the doorbell. "My shirt smells from smoke so I don't want to come inside," he told his mother. "I would appreciate it if you could bring me a clean shirt so that I can change in the hallway."

He then handed his mother an envelope containing his "tip money;" the total was $84. "Mommy," the young teenager said, "please take this money and buy yourself a dress for Yom Tov."

Rebbetzin Alpert was at a loss for words. Finally, she said, "Did the Rosh Yeshivah give you his *chametz* to burn?"

"Yes," Shaya replied. "He also gave me a five-dollar tip. I didn't want to take it, but the Rosh Yeshivah said that if I didn't take it, he would not let me burn his *chametz.*"

When Shaya passed away, Reb Moshe was almost 90 and in poor health. The funeral was held in the beis midrash of Tifereth Jerusalem. It was feared that attending the funeral, which would surely affect Reb Moshe deeply, might cause serious damage to his health, and therefore he was not informed about it. But somehow he found out about the funeral. While it was in progress, the phone rang in the office of the yeshivah. It was Reb Moshe, asking to speak to his son, Reb Reuven. When Reb Reuven picked up the phone, Reb Moshe's words left no room for doubt. "Come and get me, *now.*"

As Reb Nissan Alpert was in the midst of his *hesped*, the door of the beis midrash opened and in walked Reb Moshe, escorted through the crowd by a police officer. "Look, Shaya," said Rav Alpert, "the Rosh Yeshivah has come to be *melaveh* (escort)." When Rav Alpert concluded his words, Reb Moshe ascended the pulpit and delivered a moving *hesped.*

AMONG REB MOSHE'S GREATEST AND CLOSEST TALMIDIM WAS THE LATE RAV and *posek* Rabbi Avraham Blumenkrantz. Rabbi Blumenkrantz' family

Rabbi Avraham Blumenkrantz emigrated from Colombia when he was 11 years old. When he turned bar mitzvah, his parents enrolled him in Mesivtha Tifereth Jerusalem, where he quickly distinguished himself as a dynamic, budding *talmid chacham.* As a candidate for G.O. president, Avraham delivered an address in heavily accented English filled with *divrei Torah* that left the students spellbound. He won the election by a landslide and founded a school newspaper that contained both Torah essays and material relevant to secular studies. A few short years later, R' Avraham was serving as Reb Moshe's

At the wedding of Rabbi and Mrs. Avraham Blumenkrantz; seated (left to right): Reb Michel Barenbaum, Reb Moshe, the chasan

personal attendant, learning *psak halachah* from him at every step and expanding his own scope of Torah knowledge.

When Reb Moshe traveled, Rabbi Blumenkrantz traveled with him. When Reb Moshe addressed the high school or elementary school students, Rabbi Blumenkrantz was there to present an English translation of the Rosh Yeshivah's words. On at least one occasion when a group of *kollel yungeleit* from another yeshivah came to receive *semichah* from Reb Moshe, he instructed that they first be tested by Rabbi Blumenkrantz. When people would come to Reb Moshe to ask which kind of electric shavers were halachically acceptable, he would motion to Rabbi Blumenkrantz and say, "Speak to that *yungerman* in the corner."

> For all his prominence and personality, Rabbi Blumenkrantz, like Reb Moshe's other talmidim, never lost his awe of the Rosh Yeshivah. And once, when he feared that Reb Moshe mistakenly thought he had addressed him in a disrespectful manner, Rabbi Blumenkrantz was devastated.
>
> It happened one day that he entered the beis midrash and called out, "Good morning, Moshe," to a good friend. Without looking up

from his writings, Reb Moshe responded, "Good morning." Rabbi Blumenkrantz blanched and ran from the beis midrash. Outside in the hallway, he burst into tears and could not calm down. A friend, Rabbi Aaron Gold, approached Rabbi David Feinstein, and told him what had happened. Reb David went over to Rabbi Blumenkrantz and said, "There is no reason to be upset. First of all, I don't think my father even realized who had said 'Good morning'; he was focused on his writing. Second of all, even if he did know that it was you, my father never had a *k'peidah* (grievance) against anyone in his entire life." These words succeeded in calming Rabbi Blumenkrantz.

When Rabbi Blumenkrantz' father, a distinguished rav, passed away, Reb Moshe came for *nichum aveilim* and told his talmid, "The time has come for you to *pasken she'eilos* (decide halachic queries), even the most difficult."

When he was in his early 20s, Rabbi Blumenkrantz was appointed to his first position as rav. Soon after, Reb Moshe taught him a lesson which he carried with him for the rest of his life. A reputable kashrus organization called Rabbi Blumenkrantz and asked that he announce in shul that a particular food establishment which bore the kashrus certification of an Orthodox rav was, in fact, not kosher. Reb Moshe told his talmid that he was not permitted to make such an announcement without first contacting the *rav hamachshir* (certifying rabbi) to hear his side of the story. Otherwise, he would be guilty of *kabbalas lashon hara*, accepting an evil report as fact without first determining its veracity.

As mentioned above, Reb Moshe stressed the importance of parents instilling in their children a feeling of joy and pride in being a Torah Jew, and that no sacrifice was too great for the privilege of living a Torah life. Both in public and in private, Rabbi Blumenkrantz' very essence projected this feeling.

Once, as Rabbi Blumenkrantz was walking down the street, a young ruffian rolled down his car window and shouted, "Hey, Jew!" Rabbi Blumenkrantz smiled and responded, "You're jealous?"

RABBI SIMCHA BUNIM COHEN MERITED A CLOSE RELATIONSHIP WITH REB Moshe. The Cohens lived a block away from the Feinsteins, but until he was past bar mitzvah, young Simcha Bunim had no inter-

"He Was Very Nice to Me" action with Reb Moshe. One Shabbos afternoon, he decided to *daven Minchah* in Tiddereth Jerusalem. Reb Moshe noticed him and came over to greet the *bachur*, ask his name and where he lived. Simcha Bunim stayed for *shalosh seudos* and

Seated left to right: the Mattersdorfer Rav (Reb Shmuel Ehrenfeld); Reb Moshe;
Reb Chaim Kreiswirth

Maariv. After *Maariv,* Reb Moshe told him, "Don't walk home. I go home by car. You can come with me."

At that time, Simcha Bunim kept a diary. He wrote in it, "Reb Moshe was very nice to me, so I am going to go back there again." Thus began a relationship that continued until Reb Moshe's passing.[12]

Rabbi Cohen is a grandson of Rabbi Shmuel Ehrenfeld, the late Mattersdorfer Rav. The Rav had lived on the Lower East Side for many years and he and Reb Moshe knew each other well. In a letter of *haskamah* to a *sefer* written by Rabbi Cohen in memory of his grandfather, Reb Moshe wrote: "I knew your grandfather from the day he arrived in this country. I recognized him as a great *gaon* as befitting someone from such an illustrious family, and as a *marbitz Torah* to the multitudes ... All *gedolei Yisrael* recognized him as a great *gaon* ... "

When Rabbi Cohen was a young *bachur,* the Mattersdorfer Rav sent him to Reb Moshe with a question regarding *Hilchos Tefillin.* Simcha Bunim, who was then learning in Brooklyn, took the subway early in the morning with the hope of asking the question to Reb Moshe in yeshivah before *Shacharis.*

---

12. Often, Simcha Bunim would do grocery shopping for the Rebbetzin. He once observed as Reb Moshe stood on a chair and put the groceries away in the kitchen cabinets.

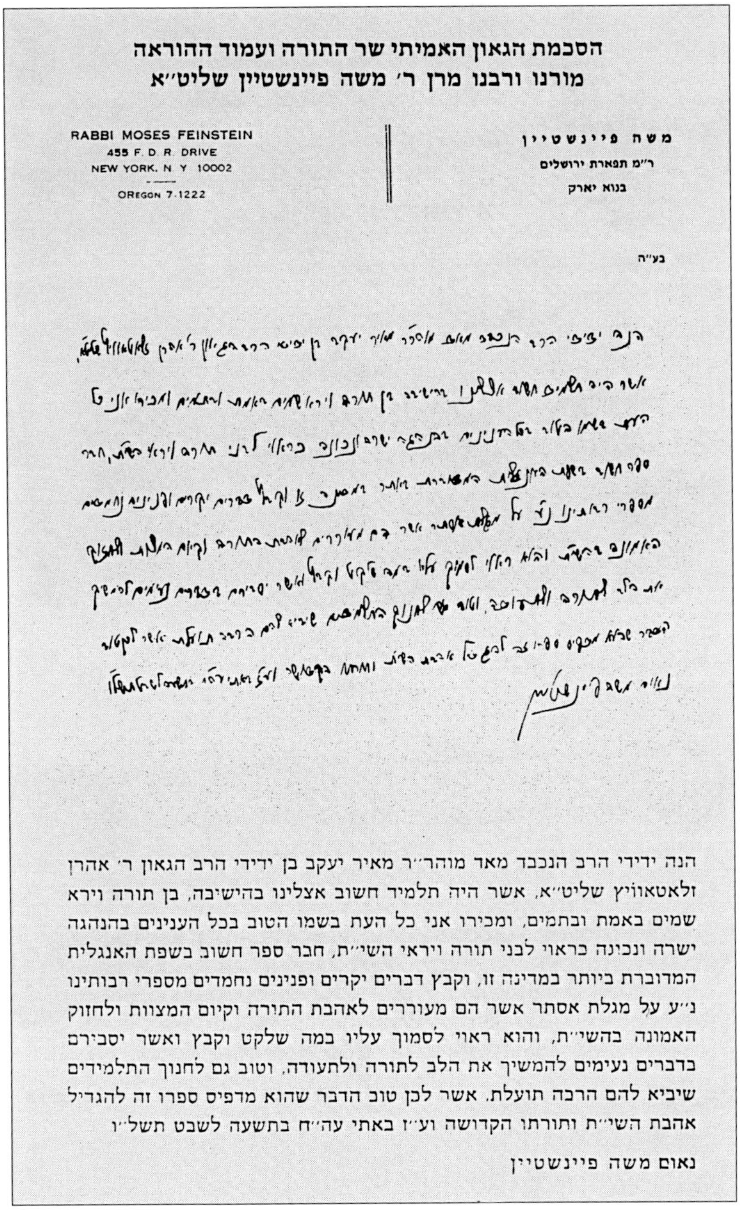

הסכמת הגאון האמיתי שר התורה ועמוד ההוראה
מורנו ורבנו מרן ר' משה פיינשטיין שליט"א

RABBI MOSES FEINSTEIN
455 F. D. R. DRIVE
NEW YORK, N. Y 10002
OREGON 7-1222

משה פיינשטיין
ר"מ תפארת ירושלים
בנוא יארק

בע"ה

הנה ידידי הרב הנכבד מאד מוהר"ר מאיר יעקב בן ידידי הרב הגאון ר' אהרן זלאטאוויץ שליט"א, אשר היה תלמיד חשוב אצלינו בהישיבה, בן תורה וירא שמים באמת ובתמים, ומכירו אני כל העת בשמו הטוב בכל הענינים בהנהגה ישרה ונכונה כראוי לבני תורה ויראי השי"ת, חבר ספר חשוב בשפת האנגלית המדוברת ביותר במדינה זו, וקבץ דברים יקרים ופנינים נחמדים מספרי רבותינו נ"ע על מגלת אסתר אשר הם מעוררים לאהבת התורה וקיום המצוות ולחזוק האמונה בהשי"ת, והוא ראוי לסמוך עליו במה שלקט וקבץ ואשר יסבירם בדברים נעימים להמשיך את הלב לתורה ולתעודה, וטוב גם לחנוך התלמידים שיביא להם הרבה תועלת. אשר לכן טוב הדבר שהוא מדפיס ספרו זה להגדיל אהבת השי"ת ותורתו הקדושה וע"ז באתי עה"ח בתשעה לשבט תשל"ו

נאום משה פיינשטיין

Reb Moshe's letter of approbation to Rabbi Meir Zlotowitz' work on Megillas Esther which was the inaugural volume of the ArtScroll Series.

When he arrived at Tifereth Jerusalem, Reb Moshe was already wearing his *tallis* and *tefillin* and was writing at his desk in the beis midrash. So absorbed was Reb Moshe in his thoughts that for a long time he did not realize that someone was standing in front of him. Finally, Simcha Bunim rubbed his shoes on the floor and the noise caused Reb Moshe to look up. "Could it wait until after *Shacharis*?" he asked. The *bachur* nodded affirmatively; he did not say that he had come on behalf of his grandfather.

Reb Moshe greeting Rabbi Simcha Bunim Cohen at right; behind Reb Moshe are Rabbi Mordechai Tendler (partially hidden) and Rabbi Avraham Fishelis ל״ז. יבל״ח Rabbi Elimelech Bluth is at center

The moment *Shacharis* was over, it was announced that the Rosh Yeshivah was not feeling well and would not be available for petitioners. Two weeks later, Simcha Bunim returned to the yeshivah hoping to speak to Reb Moshe. Before *krias haTorah*, he felt a tap on his shoulder. "You were here two weeks ago," said Reb Moshe. "What was it that you needed to ask?"

In relating this story, Rabbi Cohen reflected: Reb Moshe had so much on his mind; he never ceased thinking thoughts of Torah, he carried the burdens of *Klal Yisrael* on his shoulders, and scores of petitioners came to him each week. Yet, he did not forget that a 15-year-old boy had not been able to ask him a question two weeks earlier.

❧ ❧ ❧

When Rabbi Cohen turned 18, he was unsure whether or not to travel to Eretz Yisrael to learn in the Mirrer Yeshivah. Among his reasons to remain in America was his closeness to his grandfather, the Mattersdorfer Rav, and to Reb Moshe. "I will miss the Rosh Yeshivah," Simcha Bunim said to Reb Moshe. "I will be alive when you return," Reb Moshe assured him. Simcha Bunim went to Yeshivas Mir and studied under the legendary *gaon* Rabbi Nochum Partzovitz.[13]

---

13. The first time Rabbi Cohen returned home for Yom Tov, he wasted no time in going

After almost two years in Eretz Yisrael, Simcha Bunim thought that it might be time to return to America. Reb Nochum did not think so, but he suggested that Reb Moshe decide the matter. Simcha Bunim made an audio recording of himself, expressing all the reasons for and against a return to the States, and he arranged for the cassette to be delivered to Reb Moshe.

Reb Moshe sent his response[14] on a cassette and added thirteen minutes of personal *chizuk* to his *talmid*. Simcha Bunim brought the recording to Reb Nochum and played it for him. Reb Nochum was astounded at Reb Moshe's level of humility and kindness, and he wept from emotion. "Such an *adam gadol* speaks on a tape to a *bachur*?" he cried. "Reb Moshe Feinstein speaks on a tape?"

FOR OVER TWENTY-FIVE YEARS, RABBI MOSHE ZEV FEIERSTEIN HAD THE PRIVIlege of driving Reb Moshe to *Shacharis* at Tifereth Jerusalem.

His Morning Ride Rabbi Feierstein learned in the beis midrash of Tifereth Jerusalem in the 1950s and received *semichah* from Reb Moshe. During that period, Reb Moshe moved from his apartment on Henry Street, which was around the corner from the yeshivah, to FDR Drive some distance away. As a *bachur*, Rabbi Feierstein drove each morning from his parents' home in Crown Heights to the Lower East Side. Upon learning that his talmid owned a car, Reb Moshe asked if he could pick him up on his way to *Shacharis*. Each morning, Reb Moshe would greet Moshe Zev warmly when he entered the car and wish him a good day when they reached the yeshivah.

Moshe Zev's wedding was on a Thursday night and Reb Moshe was to be *mesader kiddushin*.[15] Before the wedding Moshe Zev told him, "I know that the Rosh Yeshivah gets up at two in the morning to prepare the Friday *shiur*. The Rosh Yeshivah does not have to stay for the *seudah*. He can leave right after the *chuppah*." While Reb Moshe appreciated his talmid's understanding, he did remain for a short time after the *chuppah*, probably as a sign of *hakaras hatov*. Rebbetzin Feinstein and her sons remained for the entire wedding.

After the wedding, Rabbi and Mrs. Feierstein settled in the Lower East

---

to see Reb Moshe. Reb Moshe greeted him with an apology: "I could not respond to your letter because I was not well." Rabbi Cohen told him, "It is hard to be away from the Rosh Yeshivah," to which Reb Moshe responded with a smile, "We will enjoy each other's company these few weeks."

14. He said that Simcha Bunim should remain in Eretz Yisrael for another *zman*.

15. The Boyaner Rebbe recited all the *sheva berachos* at the Feiersteins' *chuppah*.

Side. Even after becoming a rebbi in Far Rockaway and later Williamsburg, Rabbi Feierstein continued to drive Reb Moshe to Tifereth Jerusalem. He would arrive at yeshivah well before *Shacharis* and sit at his desk in the beis midrash writing his *chiddushim* until it was time to prepare for *davening*.

During those car rides, Reb Moshe made himself available for anything Rabbi Feierstein wanted to discuss. Family matters, questions related to his teaching, a request for a *berachah* — Reb Moshe amiably provided whatever his talmid needed. If Rabbi Feierstein had nothing to discuss, Reb Moshe would recite *mishnayos* from memory.

> One morning, Rabbi Feierstein's old jalopy would not start. He hailed a cab and went to pick up Reb Moshe. On the way to the yeshivah, Rabbi Feierstein told Reb Moshe what happened. "The car has gone almost 100,000 miles," he added. "I think it's time for a new one."
>
> "What for?" Reb Moshe responded. *"Der Eibershter vet helfen* (The One Above will help), it will go another 100,000."
>
> Rabbi Feierstein continued to drive the car until the odometer registered 210,000 miles! During those years, the car needed only minor repairs.

Once, Rabbi Feierstein went to Reb Moshe's apartment to receive his *berachah* before departing for Eretz Yisrael for the wedding of one of his children. At the end of the visit, Reb Moshe walked Rabbi Feierstein to the elevator and kissed him. Rabbi Feierstein asked if the Rosh Yeshivah could share a "parting *vort*" with him. Reb Moshe told him the following:

> In *Parashas Vayishlach,* as Yaakov Avinu beseeches Hashem for protection from Esav, he says, "וְאַתָּה אָמַרְתָּ הֵיטֵב אֵיטִיב עִמָּךְ, *And You [Hashem] said, 'I will do good with you.'*" Why is Hashem's goodness expressed in the double form, הֵיטֵב אֵיטִיב? Reb Moshe explained: A fundamental of Jewish faith is that whatever Hashem does is for the good. Yaakov was saying that Hashem had assured him that the goodness in his life would be such that he would *readily perceive it.*
>
> With this *vort,* Reb Moshe was expressing the wish that his talmid should merit this blessing in his own life.[16]

IN THE 1970S, THE FEIERSTEINS SPENT THEIR SUMMERS AT CENSORS' BUNGALOW Colony in the Catskills. Two hundred and fifty families, a mix of chassidim and Lithuanian-yeshivah families, enjoyed weeks of relaxation in a Torah atmosphere. The colony's owner, Mr. Wolf Censor, organized a summer "*cheder*" for the boys with structured Torah classes from first to eighth grade.

The Summer Appeal

One summer, Mr. Censor phoned Reb Moshe and said that if the Rosh Yeshivah would spend Shabbos in the colony, he could make an appeal for his yeshivos on Shabbos morning. Reb Moshe contacted Rabbi Feierstein and asked if he could be his guest. The Feiersteins happily prepared their bungalow's main bedroom for their honored guest. Reb Moshe led the Shabbos *seudos* in the bungalow. After the Friday-night meal, he said to Rabbi Feierstein, "Please show me where the coffee is. I get up early and I don't want you to have to get up." Rabbi Feierstein showed Reb Moshe the coffee, but at the same time was determined to arise early in case Reb Moshe needed something. Rabbi Feierstein did arise early but he found

---

16. Rabbi Avraham Pam said that this concept is alluded to in the text of the prayer we say at the *seudah* of the first night of Rosh Hashanah: שֶׁתְּחַדֵּשׁ עָלֵינוּ שָׁנָה טוֹבָה ... יְהִי רָצוֹן מִלְּפָנֶיךָ וּמְתוּקָה, *May it be Your will, Hashem ... that You renew for us a good and sweet year.* The word מְתוּקָה (sweet) expresses the hope that the טוֹבָה (good) of the coming year be such that we can perceive its sweetness.

One may wonder how Yaakov merited the fulfillment of this blessing, when his life was filled with so much travail, as related in the Torah. Perhaps the answer is that the above-cited verse continues with the blessing of children. Yaakov Avinu was the only one of the *Avos* who merited that all his sons were *tzaddikim.* This is the greatest of all blessings and one that Yaakov could easily perceive.

Reb Moshe already dressed and learning. Before *Shacharis*, he learned all seven *blatt* of that week's *Daf Yomi* and reviewed the weekly *parashah*.

It was an unusually uplifting Shabbos, as a spirit of Torah and *kedushah* permeated the atmosphere. Wherever Reb Moshe went, a crowd followed him. At the Friday-night and Shabbos-morning *seudos*, men crowded into the Feiersteins' bungalow to hear Reb Moshe's *divrei Torah*. The appeal before *Mussaf* was enormously successful.[17] *Shalosh seudos* for the entire colony was held in the shul.

The most memorable event took place on Sunday around noon, after the *cheder* had completed classes for the day. Reb Moshe addressed the hundreds of children, telling them that a Jew must invest effort in all three branches of *avodas Hashem* — Torah, *avodah (tefillah),* and *gemilas chasadim*. And how, asked Reb Moshe, does a young boy engage in *chesed*? "If you see that your friend does not understand the Gemara, don't wait for him to ask for help. Go over to him and offer to explain the Gemara. This is a great form of *chesed*."

When his address ended, a band began to play and, with the children carrying torches, Reb Moshe was escorted to the car that would take him back to Camp Staten Island. What was planned as a brief escort turned into a half-hour parade, with young and old singing and dancing as though at a *hachnasas sefer Torah*. The visit of Reb Moshe, a living *sefer Torah*, would forever remain etched in the memories of those who were privileged to have been there.

A few days later, the Feiersteins received a phone call from Camp Staten Island. As a token of gratitude, Rabbi and Mrs. Feierstein and their children were invited to the camp to have dinner with Reb Moshe and his family.[18]

RABBI YITZCHAK SELENGUT, WHO STUDIED UNDER REB MOSHE IN THE 1950S, expressed the sentiments of scores of talmidim:

A Talmid's Recollection The Rosh Yeshivah was always learning, teaching, and writing; he had his 'finger on the place' of every topic in *kol haTorah kulah*. When he wanted to show you something in a *sefer*, he would find the right page with such ease because he knew exactly where everything was.

Halachic *she'eilos* from everywhere were coming to the Rosh

---

17. On Sunday morning, Rabbi Feierstein, accompanied by two young men from Camp Staten Island, made the rounds of the bungalows to collect the pledges.

18. Reb Moshe returned the next summer for another Shabbos appeal. After that his health began to fail; for a number of years his son Reb Reuven went in his stead.

Inspecting hadassim on the Lower East Side; Rabbi Chaim Krinsky is at right and next to him is Rabbi Meyer Lazar.

Yeshivah's door. *She'eilos* involving emerging technology had to be dealt with and the Rosh Yeshivah patiently took the time to learn how each new device operated. Then he analyzed and issued his *psak*, a decisive *psak* that everyone could rely upon.

Yet, at the same time, he gave so much time for *chesed*. How the Rosh Yeshivah found the time to do so much is beyond understanding. He went to everyone's wedding, to the *bris* of every son of every talmid. I recall a major snowstorm when few were venturing out of their homes, yet the Rosh Yeshivah did leave his home for a talmid's *chasunah*. He accepted every request that he address a gathering — and he didn't leave after he had concluded his address. Out of respect for the other speakers, he stayed until the program was concluded.

When speaking with the Rosh Yeshivah privately, one never felt pressure to hurry. To the contrary, the Rosh Yeshivah would engage in "small talk" to put you at ease and make it easier for you to express yourself.

He possessed enormous sensitivity and empathy; he immediately perceived the other person's feelings in any given situation.

When he walked in the street, he took the time to greet everyone. Erev Succos, as he walked down East Broadway to his apartment, people were constantly stopping him along the way to show him their *arbaah minim* and ask if they were kosher. He had time for everyone.

When he saw someone searching among the shelves for a specific *sefer*, he would come over to ask, *"Vos zuchtz du?"* ("What are you looking for?") and then help the person find the *sefer*. All this was part of his *avodas Hashem* and his desire to fulfill the *retzon Hashem*.

IN A PIECE PUBLISHED AFTER REB MOSHE'S PASSING, THE LATE RABBI Yisrael Shurin wrote:

A Summer Neighbor I recall days gone by when we spent the summer together in a bungalow colony and I paid careful attention to Reb Moshe's ways. He arose early each morning to study Torah and to supervise a non-Jew's milking so that all of us would have milk to drink. Then, he sat and recited that day's *Tehillim* with a sweetness that tugged at one's heart, with sincerity and *hishtapchus hanefesh* (outpouring of emotion).

After that, we would walk together to *Shacharis*. Reb Moshe would recite *mishnayos* by heart as he walked, and one could tell that as he recited them, he was reviewing in his mind the *sugyos* of *Gemara* on each *mishnah*.

At two o'clock every afternoon, Reb Moshe would open a cot and take a nap outdoors for forty-five minutes. One day, I noticed that the cot was open but Reb Moshe was sitting and learning. When I asked him why he was not resting he replied, "Your little boy (who was around three) came over to me and said that he would like to rest on my bed. So I got off the bed and put him on it." Then he added with a smile, "Your little boy has caused me to learn more Torah!"

I went over to the bed and found my son enjoying a peaceful nap.

During that summer, I observed Reb Moshe writing lengthy *teshuvos* without consulting a single *sefer*. One of these *teshuvos* was seventeen pages long.

Throughout the day, rabbanim and admorim (chassidic rebbes) would come to ask him halachic questions. He greeted everyone with a cheerful countenance. He did the same for simple Jews, even rising to his full height when he greeted them. He greeted others even before they had greeted him, especially on Shabbos, when he wished *"Gut Shabbos"* to young and old.

His conduct made him beloved to everyone with whom he came in contact.[19]

---

19. Adapted from a Hebrew article in *Olomeinu*, Adar 5748 (1988).

CHAPTER TEN

A Giant of Thoughtfulness

"A distinguished Rav once asked me, 'Why does the Rosh Yeshivah give a personal letter of recommendation to every person who asks him for one? It cheapens the value of his signature! People pay little attention to these letters. It is not fitting for him!'

"It seems to me that this was the Rosh Yeshivah's basic approach to matters: If a Jew comes asking for something, one must respond first with chesed — a desire to help him and grant him whatever he seeks ... "

(Rabbi Nissan Alpert, at the funeral of Reb Moshe)

REB MOSHE'S DEDICATION TO ANYONE WITH WHOM HE CAME in contact is the subject of countless stories. He rarely declined to officiate at a wedding ceremony or to serve as *sandak* at a *bris milah.*

Always Available It is customary for a father not to honor the same person as *sandak* twice, unless he is a person of exceptional stature. Often, Reb Moshe was asked to be *sandak* for every son in a family, but in such cases he would sometimes refuse if he felt the honor belonged to

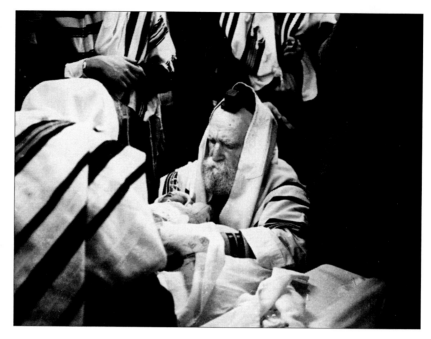

a grandfather. Once, when he accepted a second such invitation, due to his humility he remarked to the father in jest, "Being *sandak* is a *segulah* for wealth, which is why one who has already had this honor should give

Preparing a kesubah at a wedding

others a chance at gaining good fortune. Well, my being *sandak* at your first child's *bris* did not make me wealthy. So I guess it is all right for me to be *sandak* again."

At times, he would officiate at three weddings on the same night. Rabbi Nissan Alpert once escorted Reb Moshe on one such night. He recalled how taxing the evening was on the Rosh Yeshivah; still, Reb Moshe never entertained the thought of cutting down on such excursions. He once remarked, "I don't know why people feel it is so important that I attend their *sim-chos*, but if they feel this way, then I cannot refuse them."

Dancing with a chasan

THE WEDDINGS OF HIS TALMIDIM WERE OF PARTICULAR IMPORTANCE TO HIM. One Friday morning, someone met him in New York's Port Authority Bus

Special Weddings Terminal, waiting with Rabbi Moshe Rivlin to board a bus for the annual convention of Agudath Israel. The person could not believe that a car had not been provided to take the Rosh Yeshivah to the convention. Rabbi Rivlin explained, "Certainly a car was provided. The Rosh Yeshivah was to be driven to the convention last night, following the *chuppah* at a talmid's wedding. The car was there waiting after the ceremony had ended, but the Rosh Yeshivah said, 'How can I leave without dancing with the *chasan*?' He insisted that the car, which was to pick up other roshei yeshivah, not wait for him; he would find other means of transportation."

ONE DID NOT HAVE TO BE CLOSE TO REB MOSHE TO MERIT HIS PRESENCE AT a wedding. One young man — a total stranger to Reb Moshe — asked that

For One and All he attend his wedding to ensure that the *kesubah* be written in accordance with Halachah. He came.

A rav who had been designated as *mesader kiddushin* at a wedding was shocked when he saw Reb Moshe there. The rav could not imagine how *he* could officiate in the presence of the Rosh Yeshivah. He inquired of the father, "How could you ask me to officiate when you knew that Reb Moshe was coming to the wedding?" The father replied honestly

Reading the kesubah at a chuppah

that he was unaware that Reb Moshe was going to attend and, in fact, was still not sure why he had come.

The rav then asked Reb Moshe why he had come. "This morning," Reb Moshe said, "in the elevator of my apartment building I met a neighbor who told me that his granddaughter was getting married tonight and it would mean a lot to him if I would attend. That is why I am here."

> There was an *agunah* who for years received much *chizuk* (emotional support) from Reb Moshe. Finally, she received her *get* and later became engaged. She insisted that only Reb Moshe could officiate at her *chuppah,* and Reb Moshe accepted this honor. Then he suffered a heart attack and was hospitalized when the wedding day arrived. The *chasan* and *kallah* came to his bedside; there, in the presence of a *minyan,* is where their *chuppah* was held.

He was always scrupulous about bringing joy to orphans. Seldom would he stay to the end of a wedding, but he would almost always stay late at the wedding of an orphan. Rabbi Moshe Rivlin once asked Reb Moshe to accompany him to visit a wealthy man on behalf of Tifereth Jerusalem. Reb Moshe replied that the time of the appointment coincided with the wedding of an orphan girl, to which he had been invited. "I don't know the girl, but she came to me the other day and said that she would be grateful if I came to her wedding. You will have to visit that man alone."

On at least one occasion, Reb Moshe brought great joy to a *chasan* and *kallah* on their wedding day without attending their wedding! It happened that as a new couple was leaving the catering hall at the conclusion of their wedding, they realized that someone had misplaced their *kesubah*. Attempts at locating it were unsuccessful. Mindful of the halachah that a husband and wife must be in possession of a *kesubah* at all times,[1] the *chasan* phoned Reb Moshe. Reb Moshe, who had met the *chasan* a few times and remembered him, said that the couple should come to his apartment directly from the hall.[2]

Reb Moshe filled in a new *kesubah*. Then he and Rabbi Moshe Rivlin signed as witnesses, and the document was given to the new couple. Reb Moshe then asked his rebbetzin to bring out cake and drinks for a *"l'chaim."* He and Rabbi Rivlin offered their heartfelt *berachos* for a long and happy life. Reb Moshe rose, and as the Rebbetzin and the *kallah* stood together on the side enjoying the scene, the three men joined hands as they sang and danced in honor of the *simchah*.

Once, a blizzard blanketed the streets of New York with almost two feet of snow. A wedding to which Reb Moshe had been invited was to take place that night in the Bronx. It took a few phone calls before Reb Moshe could find someone who was able to dig out his car and was willing to attempt the drive under such difficult conditions. The next day, Reb Moshe told someone, *"Aza mitzvah!* (What a mitzvah!) Only a third of those invited showed up. When I walked in, the *chasan* and *kallah* were *so* happy!"

☙ ☙ ☙

While Reb Moshe usually accepted the honor of *siddur kiddushin* when asked, there were times when particular circumstances caused him to refuse. In the 1960s, a man who would visit Reb Moshe from time to time came to inform him that his son, a Lakewood talmid, was getting married. The *chassan's* father came to inform Reb Moshe of the upcoming wedding. "However," he went on, "I did not send the Rosh Yeshivah an invitation because I do not want the Rosh Yeshivah to make the effort to attend."

---

1. *Even HaEzer* 66:3.
2. He told the *chasan* that he had dealt with such scenarios before.

With Rabbi Shneur Kotler

To everyone's surprise, Reb Moshe arrived at the *kabbalas panim*.[3] He told the *chasan's* father, "I know that Reb Shneur (Kotler) is coming to be *mesader kiddushin*. If Reb Shneur says that I should be *mesader kiddushin*, I will not accept it. If necessary, I will walk out."

Reb Shneur was then a relatively young man; it was only a few years since he had succeeded his father, Reb Aharon, as Rosh Yeshivah of Beth Medrash Govoha. Reb Moshe felt that it was particularly important at that point in time for Reb Shneur to be accorded the honor of being *mesader kiddushin* as the *chasan's* Rosh Yeshivah.

Reb Shneur arrived at the wedding and as soon as he saw Reb Moshe, he took the *chasan's* father aside and said, "I cannot be *mesader kiddushin* in Reb Moshe's presence. He must be *mesader kiddushin*." Before the *chasan's* father could tell Reb Moshe anything, Reb Moshe told him, "Most probably Reb Shneur told you that he cannot be *mesader kiddushin*. Tell him that if that is the case, I will walk out." Upon receiving this message, Reb Shneur relented.

---

3. Aside from his incredible *middas hachesed* (attribute of kindness), halachic considerations may also have been a factor in Reb Moshe attending the wedding. See *Sefer Halichos Shlomo* (from Rabbi Shlomo Zalman Auerbach), Vol. I p. 163.

REB MOSHE DID NOT REQUEST PAYMENT FOR OFFICIATING AT WEDDINGS, writing *gittin,* or providing other services that required halachic expertise.

Distributing Charity
Many people gave him money in any case, often very large sums. Over the years, tens of thousands of *tzedakah* dollars passed through his hands, but he always turned the money over to Tifereth Jerusalem or another *tzedakah.* He supported his family with his modest salary as Rosh Yeshivah.

He established his own private charity fund, which he called *"Tzorchei Amcha"* ("The Needs of Your People"), and kept a ledger with an exact accounting of where each dollar went. Someone who used to watch Reb Moshe apportion his fund said that it was done with the same consideration and forethought as when he ruled on halachic matters.

> Often he would sit with a pile of charity envelopes that had come in the mail and place a specific amount in each. Always, he would refer to his ledger to see how much his last donation to that particular organization or individual had been. Among the organizations Reb Moshe sent to were American institutions for the physically handicapped and mentally ill. He felt it an obligation to respond to such requests to show that religious Jews — and rabbis in particular — respected the work of these causes.

In Reb Moshe's home there was a large jar filled with quarters. Before leaving for a public function, the Rebbetzin would reach into the jar and give her husband a handful of coins so that he could give something to every solicitor he would meet at the door. In general, Reb Moshe never refused a request for *tzedakah.* Even if a number of children would solicit for the same cause in shul, Reb Moshe would give each of them something. This he did for *chinuch,* so that children would learn not to refuse the requests of others when they grow older and are in a position to give.

> One morning, Rabbi Yosef Brick brought his four-year-old son, Yehoshua, to Tifereth Jerusalem for *Shacharis.* The boy brought with him a *tzedakah pushka* and through the course of the *davening* made the rounds of the beis midrash. After *Shacharis,* Reb Moshe smiled at the little boy and said to his father, *"Er hot mir gantz gut areingezogt!"* ("He told me off quite well!"). This is what had transpired:
>
> Reb Moshe had to step out of the beis midrash soon after *davening* had commenced. The little boy approached him with his *pushka,* but Reb Moshe had no coins on his person. As Reb Moshe started to walk away, the boy said to him, "Do you know that it is a big mitz-

vah to give *tzedakah?*" Reb Moshe immediately asked someone to
lend him a few coins which he put into the *pushka*. Apparently, Reb
Moshe felt that not to do so might give this little boy the impression
that it was not important to give *tzedakah*.

When a needy individual would ask him for a donation, Reb Moshe
would listen to the person's story with complete attention. Then, he would
turn around, so that the supplicant would not see him counting out the
money. Along with the donation came something that meant more to
many than the money — Reb Moshe's warm smile and good wishes.

One day, Dr. Melvin Zelefsky was to drive Reb Moshe home after
Minchah in Tifereth Jerusalem. As they were walking out of the beis
midrash, Reb Moshe noticed a homeless fellow from the neighborhood who had come into the beis midrash from the cold and was
sitting on a back bench. Reb Moshe abruptly turned around and
returned to his desk at the front of the beis midrash. He turned to
face the front wall so that those behind him could not see what he

was doing, withdrew his wallet, took some money out of it and held it in his clenched fist so that it would not be visible. He then proceeded to the homeless man, and as he greeted him with a warm smile and a handshake, slipped the money into his hand.

Reb Moshe and the Rebbetzin lived frugally on his small salary. Not only were their needs so simple that they managed quite well, but they even contributed very generously to *tzedakah* causes. So large were Reb Moshe's contributions in proportion to his income that the Internal Revenue Service questioned his income tax return regularly. Virtually every year, he, his accountant, or a member of the yeshivah staff would appear at an IRS office audit to show proof of Reb Moshe's contributions.

HIS FIRST MEETING AS CHAIRMAN OF THE MOETZES GEDOLEI HATORAH WAS scheduled at Agudath Israel headquarters soon after his *shiur* and *Minchah*

The Essence of Charity in Tifereth Jerusalem. A car was waiting for him outside the yeshivah and as soon as *Minchah* ended, the students surrounded their Rosh Yeshivah to escort him out without a moment's delay, since other Moetzes members would already be in the conference room waiting for him. As he was about to get into the car, a poor man asked him for charity. Reb Moshe reached into his pocket and gave the man a few coins, but the beggar wasn't finished yet. He began a conversation with Reb Moshe, while the waiting driver and students grew more and more impatient. A few attempted to tell the poor man that Reb Moshe was in a hurry, but Reb Moshe waved them away. After ten minutes, Reb Moshe excused himself, shook hands with the beggar and finally got into the car.

One of the students was bold enough to ask his rebbi why he had not simply given the man the money and said he had no time to talk.

Reb Moshe said, "You must understand that to that man the conversation meant more than the money. My mitzvah of *tzedakah* included showing him that I care about what he thinks and that I am not too busy to speak to him."

> Reb Moshe's older son, Reb David, remarked about him, "My father never wasted a minute, but if a poor or troubled person — or even a *nudnik* — took an hour to pour out his heart, my father could spare an hour."

There were mornings when women came to Tifereth Jerusalem before *Shacharis* to ask Reb Moshe a question. When he noticed them waiting in the lobby, he would not wait for them to approach him. Instead, he would hurry over to them and ask, "Do you need me?"

His younger son, Reb Reuven, recalled that *chesed* was an integral part of his parents' home. When he was a 5-year-old, Reb Reuven would regularly help an old woman carry firewood up the stairs to her tenement apartment. No one ever told him; it was simply the natural thing to do because he had always seen his parents and older siblings performing such acts as a matter of course. Reb Moshe and the Rebbetzin knew that the most effective way to teach was by example.[4]

> When young Reuven got older, he was entrusted with the mitzvah of delivering the cooked *kaparos* chickens, along with challos baked by his mother, to poor families on the Lower East Side. At the Pesach *seder* for many years, Reb Moshe and his rebbetzin hosted a number of poor, lonely people from the neighborhood. One year, everyone was gathered around the *Seder* table except for one elderly woman who had not arrived. Reb Moshe would not begin the *Seder* without first sending his son to her apartment to find out why she had not come. When he returned with her, the *Seder* began.

Helping others was so naturally a part of their parents' home that it is difficult for the Feinstein children to recall stories that left an impression. People tend to recall unusual events, not everyday occurrences. One incident, though, stands out in Reb Reuven's mind.

When already Rosh Yeshivah at Yeshivah of Staten Island, Reb Reuven came to Tifereth Jerusalem to discuss a pressing yeshivah matter with his father. Before he had a chance to begin, a well-dressed woman entered Reb Moshe's office and began to pour out her troubles. It soon became apparent that the woman was somewhat deranged. She imagined that "aliens" were chasing her and she wanted Reb Moshe to hear her "harrowing experiences." She went on speaking for half an hour. At that point, Reb Reuven — for his father's sake — was going to tell the woman that the Rosh Yeshivah now understood her plight well. Reb Moshe stopped him,

---

4. In commenting on the Torah's account of Rivkah Imeinu giving water to Eliezer's camels, Reb Moshe notes that when she responded to Eliezer's entreaty, she did not *offer* to water the camels, but simply watered them. This was in contradiction both to his prayer, which mentioned an explicit response on her part, and to Eliezer's repetition of the incident. Reb Moshe explains that Rivkah's kindness was so great that she took it for granted that another's needs should be provided for, whatever they were. That his camels had to be watered was so obvious to her that it was unnecessary for her to announce her intention to do so *(Igros Moshe, Orach Chaim II, #52)*.

Reb Moshe's illustrious sons

saying, *"Zee hot keinem nisht ihr ois tzuheren azeleche zachen"* ("She has no one who will listen to her tell of such things.")

The woman continued speaking *for another hour and a half!* She finally left, only because nightfall had come, which was "when the aliens came out."

A certain woman used to call Reb Moshe a few times a day with halachic questions. Often she would call two or three times just to be sure that she had heard the answer correctly the first time. Someone was tempted to take the phone and explain to her that she was wasting the Rosh Yeshivah's precious time. "No," insisted Reb Moshe. "She is a nervous woman and cannot help herself."

Mr. Daniel Sukenik recalled that concerned men and women from the Lower East Side used to tell Reb Moshe about their dreams and ask him to interpret them and convene a *beis din* for *Hatavas Chalom* [Amelioration of Dreams] to counteract possible ill effects. Even though he might have felt that their fears were groundless, he would listen patiently and discuss the dreams with them because no one else cared to be bothered.

❁ ❁ ❁

For many years, Rabbi and Mrs. Moshe Zev Feierstein lived with their children in a two-bedroom apartment on the second floor of a high-rise apartment building. It happened that they were offered a three-bedroom apartment on a fifth floor. With their family growing, this seemed to be an ideal opportunity, except for one factor. The Feiersteins were very involved with *hachnasas orchim*, especially *meshulachim* from Eretz Yisrael. Was it right to make these tired, overburdened individuals trek up five flights of stairs on Shabbos?

When Rabbi Feierstein presented this question to Reb Moshe, he responded, "You should take the apartment. As far as your guests, when you walk up the steps with them, distract them with some interesting conversation so that they will not find the stair-climbing so difficult. And in case you think that such 'shmoozing' is *bitul Torah*, do not worry. To ease a Jew's discomfort is not *bitul Torah*."

PEOPLE WOULD SOMETIMES ASK REB MOSHE TO PURCHASE A *LULAV* AND *esrog* for them. Though he had no time to spare, he never refused such

Any Sort of Favor
requests. When asked why, he replied, "How can one refuse a Jew who seeks a favor?"

Rabbi Chaim Twersky recalls that he once drove Reb Moshe from New York to his vacation spot in the Catskills. The trip was exhausting, and Rabbi Twersky stopped off at his own bungalow first so that Reb Moshe could rest before completing the trip. As usual, the first thing he did was call the Rebbetzin to tell her his schedule and make sure she was

Examining esrogim in preparation for Succos

all right. Word spread quickly that Reb Moshe was there, and people came to pay their respects. A few people from a neighboring bungalow colony asked if he would be willing to check their *eruv*, a sometimes strenuous task in a sprawling colony. As was his nature, the tired Reb Moshe agreed, but his host Rabbi Twersky intervened and refused to permit it.

> A woman once appeared at Reb Moshe's door, asking to speak to the Rosh Yeshivah. When told that the Rosh Yeshivah was busy, the woman insisted that she needed Reb Moshe to translate a letter she had received from her sister in Russia. The man at the door was stunned. "The Rosh Yeshivah cannot be bothered with such things!"
>
> "What do you mean?" retorted the woman. "He has been translating my letters for twenty years!"

In commenting on this incident, Rabbi Shlomo Freifeld, late Rosh Yeshivah of Yeshivah Sh'or Yoshuv, said:

> Reb Moshe did not help her with those letters because he was a "nice guy." As a matter of fact, when the situation required it, he could be as tough as nails. He helped her because he determined that this is what the Torah seeks in a person — and those who were in his proximity were influenced to be this way as well.[5]

IN SPEAKING OF REB MOSHE, RABBI MICHEL BARENBAUM RELATED:

Rav Naftali Amsterdam, a prime disciple of Rav Yisrael Salanter, once **To Make** sought Reb Yisrael's counsel on a disagreement between **Someone** himself and his wife. His wife was insisting that it was time **Happy** he bought himself a new suit, while he felt that such a purchase was wholly unnecessary. Reb Yisrael replied, "There is a level of *chesed* where one understands the need for a given item and sees to it that someone else has that item. And then there is a higher level of *chesed*, where one provides someone with that which he personally sees no need for at all."

The *chesed* of Reb Moshe, said Reb Michel, was of the higher level.

Rabbi Aaron Gold came from Philadelphia to study at Tifereth Jerusalem in the 1960s. Usually he spent Shabbos in Willamsburg, but one Shabbos he remained at the yeshivah in honor of a friend's *aufruf* and was invited to join Reb Moshe and his rebbetzin for the daytime *seudah*.

Shabbos morning at the *kiddush* in yeshivah, Aaron waited at the door

---

5. From the audio series *Rabbi Freifeld — Achieving Greatness.*

of the dining room until the Rosh Yeshivah was ready to leave. He watched as Reb Moshe donned his coat and began walking towards the door, but then was stopped by a chassidic Jew who said something to him. Reb Moshe hesitated for a moment, then removed his coat, sat down by a table, recited a *berachah*, broke off a small piece of cake and ate it before donning his coat a second time.

On the way home, he told his talmid, "That chassidishe Yid asked if I would partake of a piece of cake so that he could taste the *shirayim* (leftovers). This is not our custom, but it is the custom of chassidim. I didn't want my refusal to *shter* (disturb) his Shabbos, so I took a piece of cake."[6]

REB MOSHE DID NOT WAIT TO BE ASKED when he saw that his help was needed. Once, the elderly *shamash* in Tifereth Jerusalem needed help in

Without Being Asked
placing the *s'chach* on the yeshivah's *succah*, and asked if the Rosh Yeshivah could send a few students to assist him. Instead of honoring the request, Reb Moshe climbed onto a ladder and put up the *s'chach* himself.

Rabbi Shlomo Freifeld recalled:

> I was a summertime neighbor of Reb Moshe; we would sit on the lawn together. Reb Moshe was the greatest *masmid*. In the hottest summer days, he would sit there with his *sefarim* learning and learning.
>
> One day, a man was sitting on the lawn with his grandson. The little boy dropped his ball and it rolled down the hill into a ditch. Somehow, Reb Moshe noticed this. In a flash, he jumped from his seat and ran down to the ditch to fetch the ball. The grandfather was both grateful and upset.
>
> "Rosh Yeshivah," he said, "*vas tut ihr?* (what are you doing?) I would have gotten the ball myself!"
>
> Reb Moshe replied softly: "But didn't you once suffer a heart attack?" Reb Moshe's recollection was correct, and the appreciative grandfather understood.

---

6. At an Agudath Israel convention, Reb Moshe was preparing to make *kiddush* for himself and his rebbetzin. Noting this, a group of chassidim placed before him a large tray of cake so that Reb Moshe could recite *kiddush* for them as well, and they could then partake of his *shirayim*. Of course, he obliged.

One Yom Tov at Yeshivah of Staten Island, a *chassidishe bachur* waited outside Reb Moshe's private room as he and his family completed their *seudah*. When the door opened, the *bachur* asked if he could partake of the Rosh Yeshivah's *shirayim*. Reb Moshe smiled and remarked, "Today, even Litvishe rabbanim have chassidim!"

One Erev Yom Kippur after *Minchah,* as the beis midrash of Tifereth Jerusalem was quickly emptying out, Rabbi Nathan Lomner observed an interesting sight. In the back of the room sat Reb Moshe and the *shamash,* emptying *tzedakah* plates (that are customarily placed in shuls on that day) into envelopes, so that the monies could later be distributed to the various organizations for which they were intended. When Reb Moshe noticed Rabbi Lomner watching him, he said, "He (referring to the *shamash*) also must go home and eat before the fast."

Another Erev Yom Kippur after *Minchah,* Reb Moshe and Rabbi Lomner were walking home together when Reb Moshe suddenly said, "Let's visit the aged Rav of Boyan [not to be confused with the Boyaner Rebbe] who is bedridden. It's Erev Yom Kippur and probably no one has time to visit him today."

Sure enough, when they entered the Rav's bedroom they found him lying in bed with no one at his side. Reb Moshe sat down and chatted with him as if he had all the time in the world. Finally, he rose and blessed the now smiling Rav with a complete recovery and a good year, and then left.

For a time, he would detour on his way home from *davening* on Shabbos mornings to visit a chronically ill man. He once commented to someone walking with him that this mitzvah was especially important, for people who are ill for a long time tend to become forgotten as time passes.

A man was once hospitalized at Beth Israel Hospital in New York when he received the surprise of his life. In walked Reb Moshe, whom he did not know personally, to visit. In explanation, Reb Moshe said that earlier that day he had been told that an elderly Jewish man, who was also a patient at Beth Israel, had no visitors. Once Reb Moshe had come to see that man he decided to visit other patients as well.

ONE MORNING AS HE WAS BEING DRIVEN HOME FOLLOWING *SHACHARIS* AT his yeshivah, Reb Moshe asked his driver to stop at the home of an

The Ultimate Sacrifice
elderly widow so that he could bring her some money. When they arrived at the building, the driver offered to get out of the car and deliver the money. Reb Moshe, however, insisted on climbing the stairs of the building and fulfilling this mitzvah himself.

Reb Moshe's insistence was not merely a reflection of his wonderfully kind nature. Everything he did was dictated by Torah. He may have wanted to deliver the money personally because *Chazal* teach, "It is a greater

Being welcomed upon his arrival in Los Angeles

mitzvah through oneself than through an emissary."[7] And quite possibly, he felt that the woman would derive pleasure from the fact that he had taken the time to visit her.

Once, someone accompanied him to Los Angeles on a fund-raising trip. The schedule was gruelling. One day, after hours of fund-raising, Reb Moshe said that there was an elderly rav some distance away who would appreciate a visit from him. He asked that his companion arrange for a meeting. The person responded, "The Rosh Yeshivah has had a hard day and has barely had time to learn — wouldn't he prefer to spend the next couple of hours in front of a Gemara?"

> Reb Moshe replied, "The Torah says that you should love the *Ribono shel Olam* בְּכָל מְאוֹדֶךָ, with all your wealth. For many people, their money is their wealth. For me, my Torah is my wealth. It's what is most precious to me. And I am prepared to sacrifice it if a situation requires that I tend to some other mitzvah."

_____
7. *Kiddushin* 41a.

WHEN RABBI NISSAN ALPERT WAS STILL A STUDENT, REB MOSHE ASKED HIM FOR a favor. He had received a letter from a needy person asking for financial

Doing It Right

help before Pesach, but had misplaced the letter. All he remembered was that the sender was a Belzer chassid who lived on Rivington Street. "Nissan, come with me to Rivington Street and let's try to find him."

They went, but failed; Rivington Street was crowded with Jews of all sorts in those days. Reb Moshe was distressed but there was nothing he could do. On Erev Pesach, Reb Moshe came to the Alpert apartment and asked for Nissan. He had found the letter and wanted to deliver the money immediately; a poor family's Yom Tov would be much more festive if they knew there was some cash on hand. Would Nissan accompany him?

The two went to the Rivington Street address and delivered the money. On their way back, it started to rain. Reb Moshe told Nissan to hurry home; he, Reb Moshe, had to make a detour to buy a trivial item. Nissan wanted to go along, but Reb Moshe insisted that he not walk unnecessarily in the rain. It seemed strange to Nissan that his Rosh Yeshivah should need to make such a purchase on Erev Pesach, and to walk two blocks in the rain to buy it, but he did not dare ask why.

Several weeks later, Nissan found an opportunity to satisfy his curiosity. He told Reb Moshe that he had been wondering about the Erev Pesach purchase and thought he had solved the mystery. Reb Moshe asked to hear the solution. "The Rebbetzin probably would not have wanted the Rosh Yeshivah to deliver the money himself on such a busy day; so the Rosh Yeshivah said he was buying something. In order not to break his word, the Rosh Yeshivah had to buy that item even though it was raining." Reb Moshe smiled and nodded.

While the hectic pace of Erev Pesach might have caused the Rebbetzin to prefer having Reb Moshe at home, she too was a paragon of *chesed*. As Rebbetzin Sarah Mermelstein[8] wrote:

> Upon my parents' arrival from Europe in the aftermath of World War II, the Rebbetzin went apartment-hunting with my mother. The boorish landlord inquired of the Rebbetzin gruffly, "Who will pay the rent if they are unable?" In a most friendly tone, she replied that

---

8. Rebbetzin Mermelstein is the daughter of the great *gaon* and *posek* Rav Tuvia Goldstein, who, as mentioned elsewhere in this volume, was extremely close to Reb Moshe.

Holding six-month-old Aharon Machlis

she would gladly undertake the payment for my parents, whom she did not know at all.[9]

For many years, the Rebbetzin would walk the streets of the Lower East Side carrying a bag which served as a Tifereth Jerusalem *pushka*, as she collected badly needed funds for the yeshivah. Raising funds in this manner was not beneath her dignity, for she understood well that the world exists in the merit of Torah study and that assisting in its support is a privilege, not a burden.

On a hot summer evening in 1965, New Yorkers experienced a blackout that left them hot and in the dark. Outside the apartment complex on FDR Drive, emergency personnel worked to keep the situation under control. Rebbetzin Feinstein stood by an open hydrant, filling pitchers with water and offering drinks to thirsty firemen and others.

The Rebbetzin's goodness never waned; even as Reb Moshe's health deteriorated and she was preoccupied with caring for him, she still took every opportunity to bring joy to others.

In 1981, she was walking near her apartment building on FDR Drive when she met a neighbor, Mrs. Malkie Machlis, who was wheeling her six-month-old son, Aharon. The Rebbetzin invited the young mother to come upstairs with her infant so that he could receive the Rosh Yeshivah's *berachah.* "And bring along a camera," she added, "so that you can take a picture."

Mrs. Machlis arrived with her baby and Reb Moshe conferred his *berachah.* She felt uncomfortable taking out the camera — but the Rebbetzin took care of that. "Did you bring a camera?" she asked. "Give the baby to the Rosh Yeshivah to hold, and take a picture!" Mrs. Machlis complied, and that picture remains one of her family's most prized possessions.

---

9. From an appreciation in *The Jewish Observer* subsequently published in *Torah Luminaries* (ArtScroll/Mesorah Publications).

REB MOSHE WOULD NOT ALLOW HIS DEEP HUMILITY TO STAND IN THE WAY OF an act of kindness. Mr. Joseph Friedenson, editor of *Dos Yiddishe Vort,*

"I Wrote It to Help You" Agudath Israel's Yiddish-language monthly, related how some forty-five years ago he had called Reb Moshe for a favor. The Rosh Yeshivah's Shabbos address at that year's Agudah Convention had been transcribed after Shabbos by someone who had not been feeling well that weekend. The transcript was short and lacking in content. Could the Rosh Yeshivah give Mr. Friedenson some details of what he had said?

Reb Moshe did not understand the request. "What is wrong if my *drashah* is short? I did not say anything new … It is sufficient to write that I exhorted the gathering to strengthen themselves in Torah learning, *tzedakah* … "

Mr. Friedenson explained that his readers would consider it an affront on his part if he were to publish only a brief synopsis of Reb Moshe's address alongside much lengthier transcripts of other speeches. Upon hearing this, Reb Moshe's attitude immediately changed. Of course he would help. No, it would not be necessary for Mr. Friedenson to come see him. He would write out the address and mail it to Mr. Friedenson.

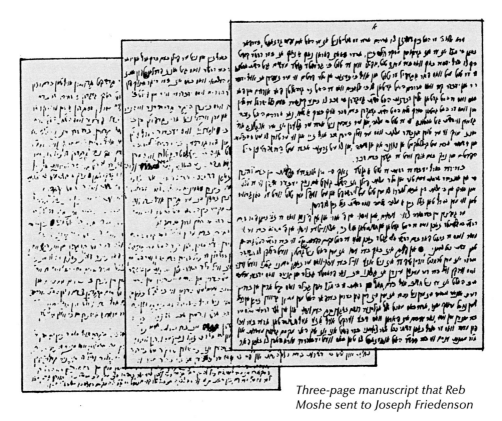

Three-page manuscript that Reb Moshe sent to Joseph Friedenson

Mr. Friedenson said that it would be sufficient for Reb Moshe to send him a few notes in Hebrew; he himself would write the article. "No," Reb Moshe said, "I'll write it in Yiddish, just as I used to write to my mother, and send it to you."

Reb Moshe's three-page, closely written address arrived the next day. Mr. Friedenson called to thank him and said he would publish it word for word if Reb Moshe wished.

Reb Moshe would not hear of it. He said, "I wrote it out to help you, but you should print whatever you see fit. You are an editor and you know better."

AT TIMES, REB MOSHE'S CHESED WAS DONE SO SUBTLY THAT IT COULD GO almost unnoticed. Many years ago, a young man entered the beis midrash

Subtle Chesed of Tifereth Jerusalem seeking to discuss an urgent matter with Reb Moshe. To his dismay, he was told that the Rosh Yeshivah was at his apartment preparing to leave the city for a few days, but if he hurried, he might meet the Rosh Yeshivah on his way out.

The young man ran the three-quarters of a mile to Reb Moshe's house at top speed. He was met at the apartment's door by two students carrying out some of Reb Moshe's luggage. No, it was impossible to see the Rosh Yeshivah now; he would be leaving in a matter of moments.

Just then Reb Moshe noticed the young man, still panting to catch his breath. He invited his visitor to have a seat in his study, while he busied himself gathering some *sefarim* to take along on his trip. For the next few minutes, Reb Moshe spoke to the young man in idle conversation, without pausing to allow his visitor to speak. "I'm going away for a few days … it's good to get away once in a while … I'll have more time to learn than I usually do … " Only after the young man had fully recovered from his dash to the apartment did Reb Moshe ask him why he had come.

❧ ❧ ❧

In his last years, Reb Moshe would *daven* the latter part of *Neilah* outside the beis midrash at Yeshivah of Staten Island, because he was too weak to stand as the fast neared its end and he would not sit in a beis midrash while the *Aron HaKodesh* was open, as is the custom during *Neilah*. On one Yom Kippur, he was joined in the hallway by a 15-year-old student who felt so weak that he sat with his head resting on his arms. Then, during those awesome moments, when the fate of every Jew is sealed for the coming year, Reb Moshe went over to the boy, put his hand on his shoulder, and said, "Don't worry, only a little while longer."

While he was quick to help others, Reb Moshe always sought not to inconvenience anyone. For many years, he spent Succos in the home of his daughter Sifra, ע״ה, and יבל״ח, his son-in-law, Rabbi Moshe David Tendler.[10] Reb Moshe would sleep in the *succah* and get up to learn before dawn, as he did all year long.[11] During her father's later years, Rebbetzin Tendler used to arrange a line of chairs so that he could support himself on them as he walked from his bed to get his morning coffee and to go to the room where he learned. Every morning, the family found the chairs neatly placed around the table, and everyone thought that some other family member had done it. The "family member" was Reb Moshe himself, who wanted to spare everyone else the bother of putting the chairs back where they belonged.

During the last several summers of Reb Moshe's life, his daughter-in-law Rebbetzin Shelia Feinstein helped care for Reb Moshe in Camp Staten Island. He would sit and learn at a table on the lawn and she would sit nearby in case she was needed. From time to time he would ask how she was or inquire about the children or something else. She realized that he was interrupting his learning only so that she should not feel ignored, and it made her uncomfortable that she was interfering with his concentration. She wanted to serve him but she did not want him to stop learning because of her, so she said, "It makes me happy just to watch you learn." "And it makes me happy that you want to sit nearby to help me," he responded.

Then she hit on a plan. She set up an intercom between his table and her bungalow so that he could have his privacy, while she would be available at a moment's notice. But he never called for her, for fear that she was busy and he would be disturbing her.

Early every Shabbos morning in camp, he would sit on his porch and chant the weekly Torah reading with the *trop* [cantillation]. She remarked to her friends that she loved to listen to her father-in-law chanting the *parashah*. The next Shabbos morning, he was not on the porch. Alarmed, she ran to his bungalow to find out if anything was wrong. He was reviewing

---

10. Rabbi Tendler is a rosh yeshivah at Yeshivas Rabbi Yitzchak Elchonon and Rav of the Monsey Community Synagogue.

11. One Succos there was a severe windstorm in Monsey on the first night of Succos, and many *succos* and much *s'chach* were blown down. Most of the *s'chach* in Rabbi Tendler's large *succah* was blown down, but all the *s'chach* over Reb Moshe's bed remained in place.

the *parashah* at the kitchen table. Why was he not on the porch as usual? He explained that he had overheard her telling her friend that she used to hear him every Shabbos morning. Apparently the sound of his voice was waking her up, and she was entitled to sleep later on Shabbos. With difficulty she convinced Reb Moshe that she was always up in any case, and that he would be doing her a favor by chanting the *parashah* on the porch, where she could enjoy listening to him.

ONCE, REB MOSHE SUMMONED RABBI YISRAEL H. EIDELMAN, THE YESHIVAH'S executive vice president, to his home. "Yisrael Hersh," he said, "it is a long

Subtle Chizuk

time now that our rebbeim have not received a raise in salary. I think it is time they got one, but the burden will fall on you, so I want to know how you feel about it." Rabbi Eidelman replied that of course the raise should be given.

Years later, he remarked, "The sensitivity that the Rosh Yeshivah showed then, how he took my feelings into consideration, carries me to this day."

Rabbi Eidelman is the *baal tefillah* for Yamim Noraim at Yeshivah of Staten Island, where Reb Moshe would spend Yom Kippur. One Motza'ei Yom Kippur after Rabbi Eidelman returned to his home in Brooklyn, the phone rang. It was Reb Moshe. Rabbi Eidelman recalls thinking, "Why is the Rosh Yeshivah calling? We just saw one another a short while ago and we will see each other in the morning!"

*With his grandson
Rabbi Mordechai Tendler*

Reb Moshe said, "We received a check for the yeshivah from Mr. _____ for $18,000. I know that you put in effort to get this donation, so I wanted you to know right away that your efforts bore fruit."

HIS APPRECIATION TOWARD THOSE WHO ASSISTED HIM IN ANY WAY KNEW NO bounds. His grandson Rabbi Mordechai Tendler was with him for many

Appreciation years as a talmid, companion, and protector, at a time when Reb Moshe's strength had to be conserved and his generous openness to all had to be curbed. Reb Mordechai became *S'gan Rosh Kollel* of Beth Medrash L'Torah V'Horaah in Tifereth Jerusalem. He distinguished himself for his single-minded devotion to his grandparents and he undertook the unpopular but essential task of protecting Reb Moshe from the incessant demands upon his time and strength. Those close to Reb Moshe often noted his special appreciation for his grandson's efforts.

Other grandchildren helped as well in caring for Reb Moshe in his last years, as did talmidim of Tifereth Jerusalem and other local *yeshivah*

Walking with his grandson Dovid Beinish Feinstein in Camp Staten Island

bachurim. Often, he would fondly kiss those who came to his aid and would occasionally present them with one of his *sefarim* — personally inscribed — as a token of appreciation.

In the summertime, when his younger assistants would leave for summer camps, Reb Moshe would be sure to send them personal regards at every opportunity. Once, he noticed one of his "boys" in a crowd of people that surged forward to greet him. Unable to get near the *bachur,* Reb Moshe smiled and waved at him.

When one of his attendants was hospitalized with appendicitis, Reb Moshe telephoned him every day.

> He felt a deep appreciation toward all who served his yeshivah in any capacity. This included the yeshivah's cooks, Mr. and Mrs. Herman Jaeger, who performed their chores with true dedication.
>
> Someone once answered the public telephone in the hallway of Yeshivah of Staten Island. The caller was none other than Reb Moshe, asking to speak to the Jaegers. The yeshivah's annual Chanukah celebration had taken place the night before and by the time it was over, the Jaegers had left. Reb Moshe was calling to thank them for having made the *simchah* so beautiful.
>
> Mr. and Mrs. Jaeger were very devoted to the students of the yeshivah in general, but their dedication to the Rosh Yeshivah was

boundless. During the summer they made a special arrangement with a fisherman to bring them fresh-caught fish, which they prepared for Reb Moshe's Shabbos meals. He, in turn, showed his gratitude in many ways. He once wrote them a personal letter of appreciation, which was mounted on a plaque and which they always treasured. A few weeks before his passing he asked to see them. Although his doctors did not want him to shake hands with anyone, he insisted on shaking hands with Mr. Jaeger, as he thanked and blessed the Jaegers for the last time.

The yeshivah's devoted cook, Herman Jaeger

It is remarkable that Rabbi Aharon Kotler and Rabbi Reuven Grozovsky also went out of their way to show their respect and gratitude to the cooks of their yeshivos. Our truly great people do not categorize a person according to wealth or position, but according to his essential worth as a *tzelem Elokim* and *ben Yisrael*.

HE SHOWED APPRECIATION TO ANYONE WHO ASSISTED HIM IN ANY WAY. ONE year as he prepared to leave the annual Agudath Israel convention, some-

Gratitude to All

one came to tell him that all gratuities for him and other rabbanim had been paid for by the Agudah. Reb Moshe thanked the person, but said that he still had to personally thank everyone who had assisted him in some way during his three-day stay at the hotel. He then proceeded to seek out those individuals and thank them.

In his later years, Reb Moshe would recite *Tashlich* on a weekday at the East River.[12] Special permission was obtained to drive him closer to the river than was legally permitted. One year when Rabbi Heshy Jacob called the local police captain for permission, the captain replied that he would send a police escort to accompany the Rabbi.

---

12. In earlier years, he would walk to the river on Rosh Hashanah.

Reciting Tashlich

After Reb Moshe completed his prayers, one of the four officers who had accompanied him said, "My mother told me that whenever I meet an elderly person of any religion, I should ask for a blessing. Can the Rabbi bless me?" Reb Moshe obliged, blessing the young man that he should be *oleh l'gedulah* (rise to prominence).[13] The other officers then came forward to receive individual blessings. The first officer then asked Rabbi Jacob, "Would it be okay if someone took a picture of us with the Rabbi so that I could show it to my mother?" When this request was conveyed to Reb Moshe, he said that it must be granted out of *hakaras hatov* (gratitude) and because the officer wanted the photo for *kibud em* (to honor his mother). The officers stood respectfully behind Reb Moshe and the photo was taken.

A LITTLE BOY ONCE ENTERED THE BEIS MIDRASH OF TIFERETH JERUSALEM CRYing profusely. When someone asked him what was wrong, he explained

For a Child's Sake that his rebbi had refused to allow him into class because he had forgotten to bring a quarter for a notebook. Before anyone else could make a move, Reb Moshe was there, having heard the boy's tale from his place in the front of the room. He held out a quarter for the boy and told him to take the money and return

---

13. The officer eventually became a deputy inspector in the police department.

Feeding his great-grandson Mordechai Eisenberg

to class. When Reb Moshe saw the boy's reluctance to accept the gift, he gently took him by the hand, led him up the three flights of stairs to his classroom, handed the rebbi the quarter and left.

Occasionally, students from the elementary grades would wander into the beis midrash during their recess. Generally, their presence would be acknowledged only if they were causing a disturbance and needed to be quieted. One day during recess, two boys entered the beis midrash, stood in the back and became involved in an argument. The talmidim had not even noticed — until Reb Moshe rushed down the aisle as if something urgent had come up. As everyone's eyes followed him, Reb Moshe approached the two boys, asked what they were arguing about, and resolved their dispute.

One Shavuos morning, a 14-year-old stood at the *amud* at Reb Moshe's *minyan*, reciting the morning *berachos* that cannot be recited if one is awake the entire night. When the boy did not say the *berachos* in the prescribed order, someone pointed this out to him. Reb Moshe was the one who told the boy that he did a fine job and had no reason to feel bad.

❧ ❧ ❧

Zalman Margulies presenting Reb Moshe with a scroll at the 1983 Tifereth Jerusalem dinner tendered in Reb Moshe's honor. Rabbi Yaakov Kamenetsky and Rabbi Michel Barenbaum are seated alongside Reb Moshe. Standing behind Mr. Margulies are (l to r): Rabbi Yisrael H. Eidelman, Eliyahu Chaim Zelinger and Joseph Gruss

The noted *askan* Mr. Zalman Margulies of London arrived in New York for a family wedding. He arranged for his family and two distinguished rabbanim to visit Reb Moshe in his apartment. Youngest among the group was 11-year-old Menachem Stern.

Soon after they were welcomed in, the curious boy entered Reb Moshe's study to look around. He was excited to see a beautiful photo of Reb Moshe, wrapped in *tallis* and *tefillin* as he looked into a *sefer Torah,* under the glass sheet that covered Reb Moshe's desk. Menachem took out his camera and took a photograph of the photo. Just then Reb Moshe entered the study. He smiled and said, *"S'iz a shod di gelt!* (It's a shame to waste the money [on developing the photo])." Reb Moshe moved aside the glass, took out the photo and presented it to the boy as a gift.

When the guests were seated around the dining room table, only Menachem was left standing without a seat. Before anyone realized what

Photo under glass that Reb Moshe presented to Menachem Stern as a gift

was happening, Reb Moshe sprang to his feet, went into the kitchen, brought his 11-year-old guest a chair, and seated him alongside himself. When a talmid brought tea for the adults, Reb Moshe took Menachem into the kitchen and poured him a cup of milk.

They're All His Children

RASHI CITES A TALMUDIC DISPUTE REGARDING THE *"EISHEL"* THAT AVRAHAM Avinu planted in Be'er Sheva;[14] according to one opinion it was an inn for guests, and according to the other it was an orchard from which Avraham took fruits to serve his guests. Reb Moshe said that these two interpretations complement one another. The inn represents the *chesed* that should be a part of one's life as he strives to do for others. The fruit-bearing orchard represents one's children, who must be imbued with the desire for *chesed* that he sees in his parents.[15]

When Rabbi Reuven Feinstein was a child, a student of the yeshivah offered to treat him to an ice cream. The youngster said no, he could not accept a treat unless his friends got one, too. Years later, his "benefactor" told him about the ice cream he was never given. Reb Reuven did not remember the incident, but said that in his parents' household they were brought up that way by example; it was perfectly normal that no one accepted a favor or a treat that was not available to others.

Indeed, that was an old Feinstein tradition. In Luban, as well as in many European cities, it was customary that weddings took place on Friday afternoons. On the Friday that Reb Moshe and his rebbetzin

---

14. *Bereishis* 34:33.
15. From *Sefer Kol Rom* by Rabbi Avraham Fishelis.

were married, there were two other weddings. Luban's only Jewish fiddler came to the Rav and proudly told him that he would play only at *his* wedding, and do so free of charge. Reb Moshe shook his head and said that he could not permit the fiddler to play at his wedding unless he played at the other weddings as well.

One Shabbos afternoon, two of Reb Moshe's grandchildren were playing with one of their friends in the lunchroom of Tifereth Jerusalem where Reb Moshe and some others had gathered for *shalosh seudos*. In the midst of their playing, the grandchildren ran to their grandfather, with their little friend tagging along behind them. Reb Moshe gave each of his grandchildren a hug and a kiss and without a moment's hesitation hugged and kissed the other child as well.

Similarly, when an older grandson visited Reb Moshe before leaving for Eretz Yisrael and brought with him a friend who would be accompanying him, Reb Moshe wished them both well and kissed them both goodbye.

❀ ❀ ❀

In Camp Staten Island, there was a young family of four girls and one boy, age seven. One day, the boy came running to Reb Moshe shouting, "My sisters are all fighting with me!" Reb Moshe calmed the boy by saying, "Don't worry, you will yet have a brother." Later, Reb Moshe related this incident to the boy's father and remarked with a smile, "When your son is in trouble, he knows where to run!"

A year later, a baby boy was born, and the little boy had his brother.

One summer day, Reb Moshe was sitting in the lobby of a Catskill Mountains hotel when a 5-year-old child wandered in. Seeing no one but strangers in the room, the child tottered over to the small man with the grey-white beard and friendly look, hopped onto his lap, and announced, "You are my Zeidy!" Reb Moshe put his arms around his little friend and they began an animated conversation. A few minutes later, the boy's father entered the lobby in search of his son, only to find him on Reb Moshe's lap, a very content look on his small face. Before the father could apologize, Reb Moshe said, "Oh, what a shame you weren't here! Your son had so many clever things to tell me!"

Someone remarked to one of Reb Moshe's talmidim: "The Rosh Yeshivah loves his grandchildren so much!" The talmid replied, "You should know that he loves *your* grandchildren as much as you do — that is his level of *ahavas Yisrael.*"

HIS EXTREME SENSITIVITY TOWARD THE FEELINGS AND NEEDS OF OTHERS went far beyond open acts of kindness.

"Could I Hurt His Feelings?" There is a well-known story about someone who had driven Reb Moshe to yeshivah and accidentally slammed the car door shut on the Rosh Yeshivah's fingers. Reb Moshe clenched his injured fingers with his other hand, bit his lip against the excruciating pain, and walked into the yeshivah building without uttering a sound. Several talmidim who had witnessed the incident later asked Reb Moshe why he had restrained himself so. He answered quietly, "The young man was kind enough to drive me to yeshivah. Could I hurt his feelings by letting him know something was wrong?"

> Shortly after World War II, the Shulsinger Brothers Publishing Company published a beautiful *Shas*. It was the first *Shas* of such quality ever published in the United States, and Reb Moshe purchased one as soon as it became available. Once, he left his desk briefly and while he was out, one of his talmidim accidentally tipped over a bottle of ink on the brand-new gemara. The culprit was deeply chagrined. "I wished that the ground would just swallow me up," he recalled. Just then Reb Moshe returned. Seeing what had happened, he broke out in a pleasant smile and said that blue was his favorite color and that the gemara looked even more beautiful than before. With that, he went back to his writing as if nothing had happened.

Driving along a highway one rainy afternoon, Reb Moshe's driver missed an exit sign and was forced to make a lengthy detour. Someone else in the car criticized the driver for not being alert. For about fifteen minutes Reb Moshe did not say a word. Then, he remarked, "My, what a foggy afternoon it is! It is difficult for me to read the road signs … "

On another occasion, a driver got off the highway at the wrong exit, whereupon one of the passengers complained, "Oh, he is lost." The driver tried unsuccessfully to mollify the passenger with humor. A few moments later, Reb Moshe began commenting on the heavy clouds and poor visibility. "It is a miracle that anyone can drive in such bad weather." Only much later did the driver realize that the Rosh Yeshivah's intention was to deflect the criticism of his driving.

A childless woman, a talented artist, came to Reb Moshe for a blessing that she have a child. When the blessing was fulfilled, the woman brought Reb Moshe a painting as a sign of gratitude, which the Rebbetzin hung in the dining room. When the woman's new baby was old enough to travel without difficulty, she brought him to the Feinstein home to show Reb Moshe the fruit of his blessing. As she left the apartment and was waiting at the elevator, Reb Moshe himself came rushing out into the hall. He remembered that her painting was no longer hanging on the dining-room wall and feared that she might feel slighted. Reb Moshe explained to the woman that the dining room had been converted into a shul for a morning *minyan,* so it was not proper for the painting to hang there. The Rebbetzin had hung the picture in the bedroom.

Once, a rosh yeshivah came to discuss something with Reb Moshe. While being ushered in, the visitor was told that Reb Moshe had been lying down, for he was ill. Later, Reb Moshe told his visitor the source of his illness. "I was compelled to say something that caused anguish to another Jew," he said painfully.

As much as he respected Reb Moshe as a man of truth, the visitor found this difficult to believe — until Reb Moshe explained himself: He had been judging a dispute and had stated his opinion. The party he had ruled against could not accept Reb Moshe's decision and continued to adamantly defend his position. Finally, Reb Moshe was forced to remark, "You must realize that it is difficult for a person to see things objectively when he has a personal interest in a matter."

Reb Moshe feared that the man might have felt hurt by this comment. It was this that had caused him to become physically ill.

WHEN REB MOSHE AND HIS FAMILY ARRIVED IN AMERICA IN 1936, THERE WAS only one kosher bakery on the Lower East Side. Reb Moshe knew that the

Heightened Sensitivity

proprietor was a sincere Orthodox Jew, but this did not mean that he was knowledgeable in the halachos that a baker needs to know. Specifically, he did not know whether or not the bakery fulfilled the mitzvah of separating *challah* from each dough. Reb Moshe pondered the matter until he came up with a way of determining this without insulting the owner.

He entered the store, greeted the owner, and said, "Our family has just arrived in America. Since coming here, my wife has yet to fulfill the mitzvah of *hafrashas challah*. Would it be possible for her to come to the bakery every so often to do this mitzvah?" From the owner's response, it was obvious that the bakery fulfilled this mitzvah regularly.

❦ ❦ ❦

When Rabbis Avraham Yeshayah and Menachem Savitz were 17 and 10 respectively, they hit upon a wonderful idea. Their grandmother lived on the Lower East Side not far from the Feinsteins. If they would spend Shabbos at their grandmother's, they would be able to *daven* all the *tefillos* at the *minyan* in Reb Moshe's apartment.

The plan worked perfectly; Avraham Yeshayah even had the opportunity to "speak in learning" with Reb Moshe. At the conclusion of *Minchah* on Shabbos afternoon, Reb Moshe invited the boys to remain for *shalosh seudos*. They were thrilled with the invitation, but said that first they would hurry to their grandmother to inform her of this.

Reb Moshe had not realized that they were staying at their grandmother's. "How often do you come to your grandmother for Shabbos?" he asked.

They replied that she came to them quite often, but this was the first time that they were her guests.

"If so," said Reb Moshe, "I must withdraw my invitation. It would not be right for me to take you away from your grandmother."

❀ ❀ ❀

Reb Moshe and his rebbetzin lived on the third floor of their high-rise apartment building on FDR Drive, directly above the family of Rabbi Tuvia Goldstein. One day, Reb Moshe, probably engrossed in Torah thought, exited the elevator at the second floor by mistake, and rang the Goldsteins' bell. When Reb Tuvia's daughter opened the door, Reb Moshe immediately realized his mistake. When Reb Tuvia appeared at his daughter's side moments later, Reb Moshe explained his error and said, "Now that I am here, would it be all right if I came inside and made a *berachah*?" Apparently, Reb Moshe felt it would be disappointing to the family if he simply said "Goodbye" and left. Reb Tuvia was delighted by the suggestion and soon the two were conversing as Reb Moshe partook of a small snack.

At the wedding of the daughter of Rabbi Tuvia Goldstein (right) to Rabbi Yosef Mermelstein (center). Rabbi Shneur Kotler is at far right.

Moshe, a 21-year-old talmid at Tifereth Jerusalem, purchased his first car — a black Ford Thunderbird with tinted windows. While he was driving in Brooklyn, someone gave him a tongue-lashing for "driving a car unbefitting a *ben Torah*." Shortly thereafter, this *bachur* had the good fortune to drive Reb Moshe home after *Shacharis*.

Reb Moshe's post-*Shacharis* departure was somewhat of a ritual in the yeshivah. Virtually the entire *minyan* would accompany him to the waiting car. People would rush ahead to hold open the beis midrash door, the front door, the car door, and to wish the Rosh Yeshivah a good day. Some tried to ask a quick *she'eilah* (halachic question) before Reb Moshe got in the car and its door had closed.

On the morning when Reb Moshe rode home in the black Thunderbird, he turned to his driver and said, "Moshe, this is the *best* car I've ever been in!"

The *bachur* appreciated the compliment but did not understand. "The best ever?" he asked.

"Yes," replied Reb Moshe, "and I'll tell you why. Every morning a crowd follows me to the car. Some want to say *"Shalom aleichem"* and others have questions to ask. It is impossible to acknowledge everyone. I am sure that when I enter the car and people see me through the window and wish they could speak to me, they feel very bad.

"But your car has tinted windows. Once I'm in the car, people can't see me. I'm sure their hurt is lessened this way."

On the eighth day of Pesach, Reb Moshe's doorbell rang. Rabbi Dovid Birnbaum, a talmid who was a guest at Reb Moshe's table, opened the door to admit a poor, elderly European woman. When Rabbi Birnbaum led the woman into the dining room, Reb Moshe made a point of averting his gaze so that it was obvious he could not see the woman's face.

The woman said that her sister had passed away on Yom Tov and she had a question to ask regarding use of the deceased's possessions. Reb Moshe answered her question and then, in a soft voice, asked, "Today is Yom Tov — why did you ring the bell?"

The woman replied, "I come from Poland and we eat *gebroktz*[16] on the last day of Pesach." She mistakenly thought that the dispensation of this

---

16. I.e. foods in which matzah comes in contact with liquid. Many, especially those of chassidic origin, have a custom not to eat such foods on Pesach, except on the eighth day, which is a holiday only in the Diaspora and is of Rabbinic origin.

custom on the eighth day meant that it had the status of Chol HaMoed or less.

Reb Moshe explained to her that this was incorrect. He then wished her well and she left. Reb Moshe then turned to Rabbi Birnbaum and said, "I kept my eyes averted because I had to point out her error in ringing the doorbell. This way, she will not be embarrassed should we meet again, because she knows I do not know who she is."

To Rabbi Birnbaum, Reb Moshe's interaction with others in all situations was as perfect as possible for a man of flesh and blood. In the way that his brilliant mind could view a complex *sugya* from every possible angle, he was able to immediately size up any situation from every angle and conduct himself in a manner that was exactly appropriate for the other person's needs.

FOR A FEW SUMMERS, REB MOSHE AND HIS REBBETZIN VACATIONED IN HARTFORD,

Special Attention
Connecticut, at the home of the local *shochet*, Rabbi Berman. A relative of the Bermans would visit from time to time. Once, this man decided that he would pay careful attention to Reb Moshe's actions in order to learn from them.

Knowing that Reb Moshe arose very early to study Torah, this man arose early one morning and went to observe Reb Moshe. Reb Moshe was sitting at a table learning; near him was the Berman's youngest child, a little girl of about five, the only child still at home. The man watched in amazement as the girl rolled a ball towards Reb Moshe, who was engrossed in his learning. Reb Moshe seemed to be waiting for the ball, for he looked up from his *sefer,* picked up the ball and rolled it back. This scene repeated itself a number of times. Later, the man asked Reb Moshe, "Why did the Rosh Yeshivah have to interrupt his learning to play with her? If he would not have played ball with her, she would have found something else to do."

Reb Moshe replied: "This little girl is the youngest in her family, a *bas zekunim* (born when her parents were middle-aged). She is the princess of her home, about whom everyone makes a fuss.

"Since I have arrived here, her parents are catering to my needs. They stand ready to provide me with every possible comfort. I have become the center of attention. I have taken away this little girl's kingdom! Isn't is proper, then, that I should appease her in some way by giving her special attention?"

Once, a boy living in Brighton Beach found himself in a quandary. His bicycle tire was flat, his *chavrusa* lived a mile away, and it was

Chol HaMoed. Was he allowed to fix the flat so that he could ride to study Torah with his *chavrusa*? He did not know the answer, so he did what, to his 13-year-old mind, was the obvious thing to do. He opened the phone book and looked up the number of Rabbi Moshe Feinstein.

The boy posed his question. Reb Moshe listened and then asked, "Tell me, have you asked this question to your father?"

The boy replied quietly, "I don't have a father. He passed away when I was three."

After a few moments of silence, Reb Moshe told the boy what to do about his bicycle. He then said, "After you finish learning with your *chavrusa*, I would like very much if you could come visit me — with your mother's permission, of course. Let me explain to you how to get to my house using the subway … "

That afternoon, a shy 13-year-old knocked on Reb Moshe's door. Reb Moshe welcomed the boy warmly and invited him to sit down. He then asked *mechilah* for any hurt he might have caused the boy when asking about his father. Reb Moshe looked at the boy lovingly and said, "From today on, I will be like a father to you. Call me whenever you want, and visit me as well. My door is always open to you."

One Motza'ei Shabbos before *Maariv* was about to begin in his apartment, a young boy entered looking very sad. Someone informed Reb Moshe that this boy had lost a parent six months earlier and was having great difficulty coping with his loss. After *Maariv*, as everyone was leaving, Reb Moshe approached the boy and asked that he remain. He sat down with him and, in his fatherly way, told the boy about the purpose of life, the rewards of the Next World, the great pleasure that a child on this world can bring to his parent in *Gan Eden*, and other words of comfort. Twenty minutes later, the boy left the apartment a changed person. He now could deal with his loss and go on with his life.

❁ ❁ ❁

A young man who was raising his small children alone was having a difficult time. He went to Reb Moshe's apartment hoping for some badly needed *chizuk* and to receive his *berachah*. However, he found Reb Moshe in the middle of a meeting on an important *klal* matter. Reb Moshe interrupted the meeting long enough to hear the man's story and offer his *berachah*.

The following night in the midst of a snowstorm, as the young man was struggling to put his children to bed, the doorbell rang. Reb Moshe had come by car to offer *chizuk* and visit the children. He went upstairs with the children to their bedrooms, tucked each child into bed, and then sat on the bed and spoke words that warmed the child's young heart.

Then he spoke to their father privately and blessed him that his sons should grow to become true *bnei Torah* and his daughters true *bnos Yisrael*, a blessing that has been fulfilled.

❦ ❦ ❦

One summer, Reb Moshe was planning to remain in the city but his family prevailed upon him to spend a couple of weeks in a Catskill Mountains bungalow colony. After one day, Reb Moshe asked that arrangements be made for a driver to take him back to the city with all his luggage. He would not explain what had gone wrong. He simply said, "If a driver cannot be arranged, I will take a bus."

Only later did he explain the problem. His bungalow adjoined that of a widow, whose daughter had a sweet voice. The daughter entertained her mother much of the day with her singing. Halachah did not permit Reb Moshe to hear the singing, and he was not going to deny the widow this pleasure. There was no choice but to return home.[17]

Offering Reassurance

HE ONCE RECEIVED A LETTER OF APOLOGY FROM SOMEONE WHOM HE HAD never met. The writer told of how he and a friend had become involved in a heated halachic discussion. The friend had cited a statement of Reb Moshe's to back up his opinion, to which the writer had responded with a remark to the effect that the proof was of little meaning to him. Later, when the discussion had ended, the man realized that his manner of dismissing the proof was in fact a slight to Reb Moshe's honor. In the letter he wrote how this was troubling him day and night to the point that he had difficulty sleeping. He humbly begged Reb Moshe's forgiveness.

Reb Moshe, who more than once remarked that he had never held a grudge against anyone, forgave the man. However, this was not sufficient — as far as he was concerned. The man was troubled by what he had done and his mind had to be put at ease. It would not be enough to write

---

17. Apparently, he did not want to reveal this reason at first out of concern that someone might speak to the widow about it.

*Dancing at
a wedding*

the man a letter; it could take two or three days for a letter to arrive, and what about the man's feelings until then?

Reb Moshe did what, to him, was the natural thing to do. Using the address on the envelope, he obtained the man's phone number, called him immediately, and put his worries to rest.

> On his way to the elevator after a *chuppah* ceremony, Reb Moshe was surrounded by well-wishers. When the elevator had deposited them on the building's ground floor, Reb Moshe told Rabbi Moshe Rivlin, his companion, that they would have to go back up again. He had been unable to shake a man's hand which was extended as the elevator door closed. They returned to the floor of the wedding, Reb Moshe found the man, shook his hand, and then left.

At the wedding of Rabbi Chaim Twersky's daughter, Reb Moshe arrived unexpectedly. He had been sent an invitation, but Rabbi Twersky had not called to invite him personally in order not to tax his strength. Now that he had arrived, both fathers asked Reb Moshe to be *mesader kiddushin*, but said that they would like him to leave right after the *chuppah*, in view of his need to rest. Reb Moshe thanked them for their concern, but he stayed to dance with the *chasan* before leaving. When his car was nearly at the Manhattan Bridge, he asked the driver to go back to the hall. In the excitement of the wedding, he had forgotten to wish Rabbi Twersky *mazal tov* before leaving.

❧ ❧ ❧

He once visited someone's home on Yom Tov. So enthralled was the family by Reb Moshe's presence that they remained oblivious to a baby crying in a playpen. Reb Moshe interrupted the conversation to say, "For the baby it is also Yom Tov."

Once, a few students of the yeshivah were playing basketball and an errant rebound hit another boy in the face, breaking his glasses. Later the boys came to Reb Moshe to inquire whether they were halachically liable to pay for the glasses. They were in the middle of a series of arguments regarding their responsibility when Reb Moshe cut them off. First, he wanted to know if the victim had been hurt and how he was.

A *yeshivah bachur* traveled to Tifereth Jerusalem to meet Reb Moshe for the first time. He waited his turn after *Shacharis* and requested a *berachah* for success in his endeavors. When the last person on line had left, the *bachur* returned to Reb Moshe. "Can I also have a *berachah* for *gezunt* (good health)?" he asked.

Reb Moshe's face took on the concerned look of a worried father. "You mean you're not well?" he asked.

"No, no, I'm fine, *baruch Hashem*," the young man replied. "I just thought it would be good to ask for a *berachah* that I should stay well."

Reb Moshe smiled broadly and offered his heartfelt *berachah*.

WHEN HE DEVELOPED A PAINFUL LEG INFECTION, THE DOCTOR RECOMMENDED that the leg be kept raised to ease the pain. Reb Moshe would not

In the Midst of Pain

permit a milk crate to be brought into the beis midrash for his leg to be placed on, for fear that this would cause concern among his talmidim.

During that time, he was once driven home from Yeshivah of Staten Island by Rabbi Gershon Weiss, menahel of the yeshivah. One of Rabbi Weiss' children was crying in the car and because of this, Rabbi Weiss could not escort Reb Moshe to his apartment. Instead, another passenger, a talmid in the yeshivah, went along while Rabbi Weiss waited in the car with the child. The high-rise apartment buildings on FDR Drive had separate elevators for even and odd floors. Reb Moshe, who lived on the

second floor, missed his elevator as it began its ascent. Knowing that the talmid would not leave until Reb Moshe was at his apartment door and not wanting to delay the crying child from going home, he took the elevator for odd-numbered floors to the third floor and, limping on his infected leg, walked down a flight of steps to his apartment.

Rabbi Weiss related another anecdote that reveals yet another aspect of Reb Moshe's unusual sensitivity toward others. In the summer camp of Yeshivah of Staten Island, it was the responsibility of a particular student to bring meals from the camp kitchen to Reb Moshe and his rebbetzin in their bungalow. One day, the *bachur* had not arrived in time, and Rabbi Weiss' young son, who happened to be near Reb Moshe's bungalow, was asked to bring the Rebbetzin a container of milk. The boy excitedly raced to the camp kitchen, but when he got there he saw the student bringing lunch, including milk, for the Rosh Yeshivah's family. Not one to easily give up a chance to serve Reb Moshe and his wife, the child clutched the milk container and raced to the bungalow — but he was too late. The student had already arrived with the lunch.

Someone who happened to be in the bungalow at the time told the boy to return the milk to the camp kitchen. Overhearing this, Reb Moshe said to the crestfallen child, "No, don't return it. We need it! We can use it tomorrow!"

Reb Moshe then asked the boy to sit down, while the Rebbetzin went to get him some candy. He asked the boy his age and which *masechta* he was learning at the time. Hearing that he was 11 years old and studying *Bava Metzia*, Reb Moshe smilingly exclaimed, "Oh, when I was 11 years old I also learned *Bava Metzia*! In fact I memorized the entire *masechta* that year. May Hashem help you to do the same."

Instead of being sent away with the container of milk, the child went away with candy from the Rebbetzin and the even sweeter memory of a warm encounter with the giant of the generation.

RABBI DAVID FEINSTEIN REMARKED:

The Torah Personality

My father, *zt"l,* did not attend a "*mussar* yeshivah" like Kelm or Slabodka. I assume that he learned classic *mussar* works such as *Shaarei Teshuvah* and *Mesillas Yesharim,* but he developed his *middos* primarily through his *limud haTorah,* by putting into practice what theTorah teaches us about what a person should be. He drew from the very sources from which *Mesillas Yesharim* was written and learned from there how to perfect himself.

Of the *Shemen HaMishchah* (Oil for Anointment), the Torah states: "With it you shall anoint the *Ohel Mo'ed [i.e. the Mishkan],* and the *Aron*

HaEidus, and the *Shulchan* and all its utensils, and the *Menorah* and its utensils, and the *Mizbei'ach* … "[18]

In eulogizing a chassidic Torah leader who had recently passed away, Reb Moshe said: Oil is a metaphor for Torah. All of this *gadol's* activities, the various aspects of his *avodas Hashem,* were all "anointed" with the sanctity of his Torah and his love of Torah.

The same can be said of Reb Moshe.

After his passing, Reb Moshe's devoted rebbetzin said of him, "He enjoyed life." Reb Moshe suffered persecution in Russia; his early years in America were not easy; he shouldered the responsibilities of a family, a yeshivah, and, in a very real sense, all of *Klal Yisrael.* Yet he was almost always in good spirits, his genuine smile and warmth bringing joy to whomever he encountered. It was a joy born of *simchas haTorah,* of a lifelong attachment to the study and teaching of Torah, and of living an uplifted life devoted to Hashem and to helping others.

---

18. *Shemos* 30:26-27.

CHAPTER ELEVEN

Faith and Zealousness

The lighting of the Chanukah menorah for eight days commemorates the victory of the Chashmonaim over the Syrian-Greeks, after which a flask of oil bearing the Kohen Gadol's seal was found in the Beis HaMikdash. The flask contained a one-day supply of oil for the menorah, but miraculously the oil lasted for eight days.

For centuries, commentators have grappled with an obvious question: Should not Chanukah be celebrated for only seven days, since there was enough oil for one day? Reb Moshe explained that herein lies a fundamental lesson of faith. In decreeing that the festival be celebrated for eight days, Chazal were implying that every occurrence in this world is, in essence, a miracle. Oil burns because it is the will of Hashem that this particular liquid serve mankind as a fuel. If Hashem so willed, vinegar could also burn, as it did for R' Chanina ben Dosa. We light the Chanukah menorah for eight days instead of seven to demonstrate the common denominator between natural and supernatural occurrences — both occur only because Hashem wills them to.

("Kol Rom" [Bastion of Faith], by Rabbi Avraham Fishelis)

REB MOSHE'S FAITH AND TRUST IN HASHEM WERE RARE AND sublime. His firm belief that all is from Hashem and that nothing is beyond His power was apparent to all who were privileged to have a relationship with him.

No Power But Hashem

In an address at the Agudath Israel annual convention following the 1973 Yom Kippur War, Reb Moshe said:

Addressing an Agudath Israel convention

During the Six Day War [when open miracles occurred] we perceived the hand of G-d. Had we all been fully aware of what we witnessed and the impact of all the stories we heard, we would not have needed this recent war to awaken us.

As long as we persist in attributing success to כֹּחִי וְעֹצֶם יָדִי, *the strength and the might of my hand,*[1] we are still in need of the lesson that there is no such thing; "the strength and the might of my hand" are non-existent.

We have an overriding obligation to avoid this pitfall, especially in the era of *Ikvesa d'Meshicha* when we are on the very threshold of Mashiach's arrival. The final mishnah in *Masechta Sotah* describes this era as a time when the honor of Torah will suffer and many economic and material problems will beset us, and there will be no one to rely upon except for our Father in Heaven.

All suffering we endure is geared toward bringing us to this ultimate realization, and the sooner we come to it, the sooner we will be spared. We must imbue all our activities with our belief in אֵין עוֹד מִלְבַדּוֹ, *there is none beside Him.*[2] This must be a guide to our thoughts and our actions.[3]

---

1. *Devarim* 8:17.
2. Ibid. 4:35.
3. From *The Jewish Observer,* November 1973.

THOSE WHO CAME TO REB MOSHE WITH SERIOUS MEDICAL ISSUES SAW FIRST-hand how his rock-firm *emunah* guided him as he guided others.

Medical Issues
Once, he received a phone call from a man whose doctor had told him that he was suffering from an incurable ailment and had but a few weeks to live. The man was calling to discuss an item he planned to include in his will. Reb Moshe refused to discuss the matter. He said that the man should not be so quick to accept the doctor's word as fact, as doctors are only human and can make mistakes. He instructed him to seek the opinion of a second doctor and assured him that Hashem would help him.

The caller followed Reb Moshe's advice. A subsequent series of tests showed that, indeed, the first doctor had erred. The man was ill, but his ailment was not terminal, as the first doctor had said, and the ominous prediction did not come true.

Bnei Brak's Maayanei HaYeshua Hospital is not only a place to heal the sick, but also a place of Torah study. The hospital's founder, Dr. Moshe Rothschild, founded a kollel located in the hospital building, whose members study complex topics of medical Halachah.

Rabbi Yisrael Zicherman, Rav of Brachfeld in Kiryat Sefer, is an alumnus of that kollel. During his kollel years, he became friendly with an American doctor who was a *baal teshuvah*. The doctor told Rabbi Zicherman what had inspired him to live a Torah life:

> During my years in New York, I treated a terminally ill patient whose days were clearly numbered as his body functions grew progressively weaker. After consulting with other specialists, I told the patient and his family that there was only one way to possibly extend the patient's life by a few months. He would have to undergo a complicated, very painful, and very expensive surgery. It was up to them to decide whether to proceed.
>
> "I cannot decide such a question on my own," the patient replied. "I will consult with Rabbi Moshe Feinstein, under whom I studied many years ago."
>
> I offered to accompany him to Rabbi Feinstein and present the intricacies of the case. I had an ulterior motive; I wanted to see how a rabbi would approach such a situation.
>
> It was the first time I had ever consulted with a rabbi of such stature. Respectfully, I explained the details of the case and the hardships and dangers of the surgery, omitting nothing.
>
> What followed will forever remain etched in my memory. Rabbi

Feinstein began to cry. He cried real, bitter tears, for almost twenty minutes. As a physician, I know how we gradually detach ourselves from our patients' feelings, how years of practice numb our sensitivities. Yet, this rabbi who met countless people *every* day was moved so intensely by the plight of my patient — who was neither a relative nor a close disciple, but a student from many years ago.

Rabbi Feinstein finally spoke and said that he needed a day before he could render a decision on this difficult question.

The next day, the two of us returned to Rabbi Feinstein. He greeted us warmly and then, with confidence and equanimity, told the patient, "Go ahead with the surgery. We will pray on your behalf and ask Hashem to grant you many more healthy years. "

The expression on my face must have revealed my skepticism, because Rabbi Feinstein turned to me and said, "In the half-year reprieve that this surgery will grant our friend, he will have the opportunity to answer 'Amen' to many blessings. Each 'Amen' will create a guardian angel on his behalf. These angels will defend him before the Heavenly Court and he will be granted a long life in their merit."

The encounter with this holy *tzaddik* and his response struck a chord in my heart. There is no doubt that Rabbi Feinstein well understood the ordeal facing this terminally ill patient. Nevertheless, he felt that it would all be worthwhile so that the patient would live a little longer and be able to utter the word *"Amen"* many times.

It was then that I first realized that there must be something very profound in Torah and mitzvos.

The surgery was successful and the patient lived for several years.[4]

---

4. Adapted with permission from *Just One Word — Amen* by Esther Stern, published by Feldheim.

REB MOSHE'S DIVREI TORAH ON CHUMASH AND MANY *DERASHOS* THAT HE
delivered in Luban were published posthumously under the title *Darash*

Darash *Moshe.* His deeply rooted *emunah* permeates this work.

Moshe   In a famous piece regarding the Exodus, Ramban writes that
one does not have a share in the Torah of Moshe Rabbeinu
unless he believes that everything that occurs in this world is, in fact,
miraculous and there is truly nothing "natural" at all.[5] In *Darash Moshe,*
Reb Moshe derives this lesson from a particular aspect of one of the Ten
Plagues:

Regarding the plague of *Barad* (hailstones), the Torah relates that when
Moshe Rabbeinu prayed that the plague should end, " ... *the thunder and
hail ceased and rain did not reach the earth.*"[6] As Rashi comments, the
hailstones that were in midair at the time of Moshe's prayer immediately
disappeared and never reached the earth.

We know that Hashem does not perform a miracle unless it is necessary.
That the hailstones disappeared in midair was an additional miracle. Why
was it necessary? Reb Moshe explained:

> We view the halt to the hail's descent as miraculous only because we
> accept as fact the laws of physics, which demand that heavy objects
> such as hail that are suspended in midair must eventually fall. This
> reality is true only because Hashem ordained at the time of Creation
> that heavy objects fall and lighter ones are suspended. Had Hashem
> wanted, He could just as easily have done the opposite.
>
> To Hashem there is absolutely no difference between hailstones
> landing on earth and hailstones stopping in mid-fall. At the time of
> the plagues, when Hashem was acting toward the Egyptians in a way
> that was contrary to the normal order of this world, it was perfectly
> "natural" for the hailstones to disappear as suddenly as they had
> appeared, and not fall to earth. "Miraculous" had become the "natu-
> ral order" of the moment. The lesson is: From Hashem's vantage
> point, nature and miracles are one and the same.[7]

Rabbi Elimelech Bluth was present when a man gave Reb Moshe the
gift of a fountain pen, which he uncharacteristically accepted. The man
explained that his wife had given birth to a healthy child after receiving
Reb Moshe's blessing, and the gift was their token of appreciation. Noting

5. Ramban to *Shemos* 13:16.
6. *Shemos* 9:33.
7. *Darash Moshe,* Vol. II.

Rabbi Bluth's surprise at his acceptance of the gift, Reb Moshe explained, "This is 'my' child."

The mother had given birth to several children with birth defects — and then she developed a disabling condition. As a result, it was considered impossible for her to bear more children. Then the "impossible" happened and she became expectant again. She was worried that in her poor state of health, she would not survive the pregnancy. And she was also concerned about the health of her unborn child.

Reb Moshe was consulted. He told the parents that the pregnancy was a miracle and that they should have faith that Hashem would not let it happen unless mother and child would be healthy. The miracle *did* end happily. The woman had no ill effects and the newborn infant was completely healthy.

THERE ARE FEW INSTANCES WHERE THE TORAH REVEALS THE REASON FOR A specific mitzvah. Yet, on the Seder night, *Chazal* required us to explain the reasons for the Korban Pesach, matzah and maror. This,

Our Outlook on Life

explained Reb Moshe, is because these three mitzvos represent three fundamentals of a Jew's outlook on life:

Korban Pesach represents the exacting Divine Providence with which every Egyptian firstborn was killed while every Jew was spared. This teaches that every moment of our lives is being carefully guided by *hashgachas Hashem*. In Reb Moshe's words: If I drive somewhere and arrive at my destination safely, it is only because Hashem, in His infinite kindness, kept reckless drivers away from the path that I traveled to ensure my safety.

Matzah represents the speed with which the Jews were taken out of Egypt when the moment of redemption arrived. This teaches that a person's fortunes can change in a moment, for nothing can stand in the way of Hashem's will. Therefore, a person who finds himself in a difficult situation should never despair, and someone who is wealthy and successful should never grow complacent. Life can change drastically in an instant.

Maror teaches that a Jew should never become too comfortable in *galus*. As long as Yosef was alive, the Egyptians treated the Jews royally, but when he and his brothers died, the bondage began and life became bitter. As long as Jews are in *galus*, their security is never assured. Only Hashem's kindness keeps them safe and their enemies at bay.

REB MOSHE'S BITACHON (TRUST IN HASHEM) WAS EVIDENT IN MANY WAYS, including the way he took responsibility for his yeshivah's financial viability.

In Everyday Life One Friday as he was about to enter the beis midrash to deliver his *shiur*, an administrator approached him to say that the bank manager had just called. If the yeshivah did not make a $2,000 deposit that day, its checks would not be covered.

Logic dictated that Reb Moshe would immediately place a few phone calls to raise the necessary funds. But Reb Moshe would not do this at the expense of the *shiur.* "Do not worry," he told the administrator, and he proceeded to the beis midrash.

As he was completing the *shiur* some two hours later, a man who did not appear to be wealthy entered the beis midrash. He approached Reb Moshe and handed him a donation of $2,000.

"BLESSED IS THE MAN WHO TRUSTS IN HASHEM,"[8] FOR WITH PROPER TRUST one can live a life free of worry and fear. Additionally, the stronger a per-

With Perfect Faith son's trust, the more he will benefit from Divine compassion, as Dovid HaMelech said, "And he who trusts in Hashem will be surrounded with kindness."[9]

Someone once submitted to Reb Moshe the name of an expectant woman who was experiencing difficulties, asking that he offer his blessings that both mother and child would be well. After Reb Moshe had granted this request, the person said, "The woman is worried about what will happen." One would have thought that Reb Moshe, whose heart overflowed with concern for *every* Jew, would offer words of compassion and comfort for the woman. Instead, he said simply, "Of what help is it to worry?" Reb Moshe's message was that to have faith could do more for the woman than hours of compassionate talk.

> An elderly native of Radin who had been a neighbor of the Chofetz Chaim explained the difference between him and everyone else. He said, "The Chofetz Chaim believed in the World to Come and we believe in the World to Come. But to us, the World to Come is a matter of faith, while to the Chofetz Chaim it was as real as the room next door."
>
> The same can be said of Reb Moshe. The World to Come, reward and punishment, the coming of Mashiach — to him anything men-

---

8. *Yirmiyahu* 17: 7.
9. *Tehillim* 32: 10.

tioned in the Written or Oral Torah was as real as something we can touch, smell, and see.

One summer in Reb Moshe's later years, a virus spread among the residents of Camp Staten Island. Reb Moshe's family, concerned for his health, attempted to limit his contact with others. When he was asked to be *sandak* at a *bris* in the camp, it was suggested that the *bris* take place in his bungalow and that only the immediate family be present. However, Reb Moshe insisted that the *bris* be held in the camp's beis midrash. There were no adverse ramifications. When someone asked Reb Moshe what had prompted his decision, he replied, "The presence of Eliyahu HaNavi [at the *bris*] overrides all concerns [that I might contract the virus]."[10]

A man once came to Reb Moshe with a dilemma. His father was quite advanced in years and his children had delicately suggested that he indicate where he desired to be buried. The father had refused to discuss the matter, and his son now asked Reb Moshe what the family should do next.

Reb Moshe replied, "Let the matter rest! Perhaps your father does not want to discuss it because he believes that he will live until the time of the Redemption. And with such faith he may yet live to see Mashiach!"

In a letter, Reb Moshe stressed the importance of instilling *emunah* in one's children:

> The primary aspect of *chinuch* is to raise one's children with *emunah* in Hashem and His Torah, and in the belief that whatever one possesses is a gift from Hashem. Then the child will acquire a love of Hashem and of his parents, who are Heaven's emissaries to grant him his needs. In this way, he will carry out what he is told with love, with an understanding that he is fulfilling the will of Hashem. He will require discipline only on rare occasions, and when he is disciplined he will understand that it is for his good.[11]

In another letter, Reb Moshe wrote of the *mechanech's* role in instilling *emunah* in his charges:

> The [Torah] teacher must make sweet for them the concept of *emunah* in Hashem, both in regard to His having created all that exists and that He continues to grant life and sustenance to all ... and *emunah* that He gave us Torah and mitzvos. He must also make sweet

---

10. The presence of Eliyahu HaNavi at *every bris milah* is mentioned in *Pirkei D'R' Eliezer* (ch. 29) and *Zohar* to *Parashas Lech Lecha*.
11. *Igros Moshe, Yoreh De'ah III, #76.*

for them the idea that keeping the mitzvos is more precious than all the money and gold that exists, and greater than all the pleasures of this world, for through them one acquires eternal life. As the mishnah states, "Better one hour of spiritual bliss in the World to Come than an entire lifetime on this world."[12] Such instruction in a pleasant manner, which demonstrates the contrast between those who crave the pleasures of this world and those who yearn for Torah and mitzvos, will transform the students into *bnei Torah* so that their outlook will be one of Torah and it [i.e. choosing right from wrong] will not be a test for them at all …[13]

Ready for Mashiach

AS *MAARIV* ENDED AT THE CONCLUSION OF PESACH, REB MOSHE REMARKED wistfully: "I *davened* all Yom Tov that we should be *zocheh* to bring *shalmei simchah*.[14] Let us be *mispallel* that we should be *zocheh* to bring the *Pesach Sheini*."

One year, at the beginning of the month of Iyar, someone heard a sigh escape Reb Moshe's lips. When asked what was the matter, he explained, "*Chazal* have said, 'In Nissan they were redeemed (from Egypt) and in Nissan they will be redeemed.' Now, another Nissan has passed, and we were still not worthy to greet Mashiach."[15]

The birth of a *Parah Adumah* (completely red cow) in Eretz Yisrael some years ago caused great excitement. All Jews today are considered to be in a state of *tumas meis* (ritual defilement brought about through contact with a corpse) and as such are not permitted to enter the Temple area, nor would they be permitted to partake of offerings were the *Beis HaMikdash* to be in existence. The Torah prescribes that only by means of a ritual involving a *Parah Adumah* can people be purified of this defilement. Many saw the rare birth of a red cow as a sign that the redemption was not far off.

Reb Moshe, however, was not moved by the news. "The cow must be at least two years old for its ashes to be fit for this service. What if Mashiach

---

12. *Avos* 4:22.
13. *Igros Moshe, Yoreh De'ah* Vol. III, #71.
14. One of the festival offerings.
15. When Reb Moshe's grandson, Rabbi Avi Feinstein, was a young boy, he told his mother that he wanted to fast on Tishah B'Av. "He is not allowed to," Reb Moshe responded when the question was presented to him. "There is no reason for him to accept upon himself something in which he is not obligated." He went on to explain: "There is no *chinuch* as far as Tishah B'Av is concerned. Every day we are *mispallel* that Mashiach should come and that next year Tishah B'Av will be a Yom Tov."

The following Erev Yom Kippur, Reb Moshe phoned his daughter-in-law to say, "If Avi wants to fast, you may allow him to. Yom Kippur will always be a fast day."

were to arrive tomorrow? Would we have to wait two years in order to become *tahor?* They will have to discover a red cow somewhere that is older than the one just born!" Later some hairs on the cow's hide changed color, rendering it unfit for a *Parah Adumah.*

For a time, Reb Moshe contemplated the idea of writing a code of law on the *Kodashim* section of the Talmud which deals with the Temple service. Such a work, he felt, would help familiarize Kohanim and scholars with laws they would need to know at the time of the Redemption. He decided, however, that in light of the fact that the *Aruch HaShulchan HeAsid* (by Rabbi Yechiel Michel Epstein) and *Likutei Halachos* (by the Chofetz Chaim) already dealt with these subjects, he would devote his time and energy to other areas.

On Yamim Tovim, as he would shake the hand of each Kohen at the conclusion of *Bircas Kohanim,* he would say to him, "May you merit to perform the service in the *Beis HaMikdash.*"

> When he needed a cardiac pacemaker, he asked his son-in-law, Rabbi Moshe David Tendler, to detail the surgical procedure to him. Then he asked Rabbi Tendler to review the procedure, once and then again, something very uncharacteristic of Reb Moshe. Rabbi Tendler asked Reb Moshe what troubled him. Reb Moshe said, "I know that I am not worthy to be a member of the *Sanhedrin,* but in this generation, I may be one of those selected when Mashiach comes. I fear that the surgery will make me a *baal mum,* thus disqualifying me." Only when he had ascertained to his satisfaction that the medical procedure would not have that effect did Reb Moshe consent to the operation.

At the *bris* of a grandson in the last years of his life, Reb Moshe responded with an emphatic *"Amen"* when someone expressed the wish that he would be present at the infant's wedding. Then, his eyes brimmed with tears as he said, *"B'derech hateva* (according to the laws of nature), this does not seem possible, given my age and state of health. But Mashiach can come in an instant. And in any case, nothing is beyond Hashem's power, as we see regarding Sarah Imeinu."[16]

---

16. Sarah was faulted for laughing incredulously when the angel told Avraham that she would bear a child at age 90. Though the angel was disguised as a wayfarer, Sarah should have responded *"Amen,"* for nothing is beyond Hashem's power (see Ramban to *Bereishis* 18:14).

It distressed Reb Moshe when anyone would dare to speak critically of the *Avos* or

In a letter to his nephew, Rabbi Yechiel Michel Feinstein, Reb Moshe discusses the obligation to anticipate Mashiach's arrival and to hope each day that this will be the day on which he suddenly appears. He cites the enactment of Rabban Yochanan ben Zakkai after the *Churban*, prohibiting the eating of the new crop of grain on the 16th of Nissan. This was done because of the possibility that Mashiach would suddenly appear on the late afternoon prior to the 16th or on that very night, which would complicate the timely offering of the *Omer* the next morning.[17] From this enactment, writes Reb Moshe, we see that each day of a person's life he must anticipate the possibility of Mashiach's imminent arrival as something very real.[18]

THE GEMARA STATES: "A PERSON DOES NOT STUB HIS TOE DOWN BELOW UNLESS this is decreed upon him from Above."[19] Suffering on this world is brought

Introspection about through exacting *hashgachas Hashem*. However, the average person is not capable of attributing misfortune to a specific sin. For such a person, affliction should lead to *cheshbon hanefesh* (introspection) and general self-improvement. However, Reb Moshe, who from his early youth devoted his life solely to Torah study and *avodas Hashem*, and who did not divert his mind from this mission for a moment, *was* capable of attributing adversity to a specific incident in his life.

Once, while he was being driven along an icy road, the car skidded and his head bumped against the dashboard. Fortunately, he was not seriously hurt, but upon arriving at his destination, he said that he needed a few minutes to contemplate what possible sin could have caused the mishap to occur. After a few minutes of intense thought, Reb Moshe resumed his studies.

When he underwent surgery for the insertion of a pacemaker, the device malfunctioned almost as soon as it was inserted and another surgery was

---

Imahos, attributing to them failures other than those clearly stated in the Torah or by *Chazal*. He once said that when speaking of Yosef and his brothers, we may speak of their dispute in order to draw lessons of proper behavior for ourselves. At the same time, we must bear in mind that their greatness was far beyond our understanding and we must not view their apparent shortcomings as character weaknesses of ordinary people like ourselves.

17. *Rosh Hashanah* 30a.
18. *Igros Moshe, Orach Chaim* V, #8. On Tishah B'Av, Reb Moshe's pain over the *Churban* was obvious from his mournful countenance — and from the old, worn frock that he wore on that day (preface to *Igros Moshe*, Vol. VIII).
19. *Chullin* 7b.

required. The night before the second procedure, with his family gathered around him, Reb Moshe engaged in some soul-searching, trying to discover the sin that had caused this additional suffering. He reviewed in his mind all the years of his life until he came to his childhood days. There, he found a possible source for his affliction. As a young *cheder* child he and a classmate had both offered an answer to their rebbi's question. Reb Moshe recalled feeling a sense of pride when the rebbi found his reasoning superior to that of his friend. While he had not actually done his friend any harm, it was still wrong for him to feel uplifted by an incident that had embarrassed someone else. Reb Moshe viewed his mistake as an indirect form of מַלְבִּין פְּנֵי חֲבֵירוֹ, *shaming one's friend,* for which the surgery he was to undergo was a fitting punishment.

> He thought of a second possible sin. Once, when someone had come to ask him a halachic question, he had been somewhat abrupt in the manner with which he responded. It was possible that the man's feelings were hurt, and this too might have been the source of his affliction.
>
> Then, Reb Moshe was quiet; he could not think of a third sin.
>
> His rebbetzin spoke up. "It is not your fault that this happened; it is *our* fault. When the decision was made to insert a pacemaker, the top doctor in the department was away. We had the choice of having the surgery done immediately by his competent associate, who is somewhat less renowned and experienced, or to wait for the doctor to return. We decided to wait for the top doctor, for we felt sure that with him in charge, everything would be fine.
>
> "Surely, others heard of our decision and would learn from it that when in a similar situation, they too should wait for the most renowned doctor. We gave the impression that we were putting our faith in the doctor, not in the *Ribono shel Olam*. So the *Ribono shel Olam* caused the doctor to be unsuccessful this time."
>
> Reb Moshe appreciated his rebbetzin's assessment.

IN THE OPENING PARAGRAPH OF *SHULCHAN ARUCH, REMA* WRITES THAT THE verse שִׁוִּיתִי ה׳ לְנֶגְדִּי תָמִיד, *I envision Hashem before me always,*[20] is a great

Tefillah   concept in Torah and in the attributes of *tzaddikim.* Anyone who was privileged to meet Reb Moshe could see this concept etched upon his features, and it found obvious expression in his *tefillah.*

---

20. *Tehillim* 16:8.

He was extremely zealous in all aspects of *tefillah*. Our Sages attach great significance to being among the first ten men who comprise a *minyan*. Throughout the many years that he was healthy enough to walk to the yeshivah alone, Reb Moshe was usually the first person present for *Shacharis*.

He said every word from a *siddur;* during the time when he had trouble seeing, his family had enlarged photocopies of *siddur* pages made for him. At *Modim,* he would bow so deeply — even when suffering from sciatica — that a *yeshivah bachur* who had once observed this as a youth recalled vividly thirteen years later the impression it had made on him. During the repetition of *Shemoneh Esrei* Reb Moshe would stand, following the *chazzan's* every word from a *siddur.*

Reb Moshe would recite pages of *Tehillim* every day. In the years when he would go to a hotel for a brief summer vacation, he would walk along a country road at 6:00 a.m. praying from a *Tehillim* that he held open before him. People would often gather to gaze at the devotion with which he prayed. One man later remarked that it had been worth his trip to the hotel just to watch Reb Moshe recite *Tehillim*.

Reb Moshe always enunciated his prayers clearly and distinctly. His *Pesukei D'Zimrah,* as its name implies, was truly a song of praise. Until his health began to fail, he would stand for *Pesukei D'Zimrah* and recite it in a raised voice. Rabbi Michel Shurkin recalls standing next to Reb Moshe as he recited *Ashrei* and hearing him stress the word כָּל (*all*) in the verse: טוֹב ה' לַכֹּל וְרַחֲמָיו עַל כָּל מַעֲשָׂיו, *Hashem is good to all; and His mercies are on all His works.*[21]

His *Shema* — which he recited with the most careful enunciation, using the melody of the *trop* (cantillation) as if reading from the Torah — was the epitome of *Kabbalas ol Malchus Shamayim,* the acceptance of Hashem's sovereignty.

---

21. *Tehillim* 145:9.

Most of us find it difficult to sense Hashem's Presence as keenly as we should when praying the *Shemoneh Esrei,* but anyone who watched Reb Moshe pray could almost feel it. He would stand motionless during *Shemoneh Esrei,* except when bowing. In explanation, he related that when the Communists took him in for interrogation in Luban, he had been forced to stand at attention as a guard kept watch. Never had he felt so subservient. From then on he decided that he would demonstrate his subservience to the true Ruler by standing this way during *Shemoneh Esrei.*

One day he received very distressing news. Before *Minchah,* he instructed the *chazzan* in Tifereth Jerusalem not to wait for him to finish *Shemoneh Esrei.* That afternoon, it took Reb Moshe almost an hour to recite *Shemoneh Esrei,* as he beseeched his Creator to come to the aid of those in need of His mercy.

❧ ❧ ❧

A grandchild once became quite ill, but the family did not tell Reb Moshe in order not to distress him. However, when the child took a turn for the worse and had to be rushed to the hospital, Reb Moshe was informed, and was asked to pray. "Why was I not told earlier?" he asked, clearly upset. He grabbed a *Tehillim,* and, standing near a window in his dining room, began to pray, as tears streamed down his face.

A few minutes later the phone rang in the Feinstein home. Reb Moshe looked up from his *Tehillim.* "Are they calling from the hospital?" he asked anxiously. Told that the call was not from the hospital, Reb Moshe went back to reciting *Tehillim.* This same scene was repeated several times, as other calls came in. Finally, Rebbetzin Feinstein told her husband, "They're calling from the hospital — *baruch Hashem,* everything is fine. The child was given a new medication and is responding beautifully."

"*Baruch Hashem,*" Reb Moshe exclaimed, as he closed his *Tehillim*, beads of perspiration visible on his forehead. Slowly, he made his way to the bedroom where he collapsed into bed and fell into an exhausted sleep.

One year at Yeshivah of Staten Island minutes before the start of Yom Kippur, a talmid approached Reb Moshe and asked that he pray for his mother's speedy recovery. Reb Moshe withdrew a paper on which were written some one hundred Hebrew names. He added this new name to the list. These names had apparently been submitted to Reb Moshe by petitioners in recent months. Reb Moshe had transcribed the names onto one sheet of paper which he inserted into his *machzor*, so that he could pray for them on Yom Kippur.

A young couple once asked Reb Moshe for some practical advice on child-rearing. Reb Moshe told them to follow the example of Chanah,[22] who prayed both before and after her son Shmuel was born that her aspirations for him be realized.

IN DARASH MOSHE, REB MOSHE SPEAKS OF THE LOVE OF MITZVOS THAT IS SO integral to our service of Hashem:

Love of Mitzvos At the naming of a Jewish child, we offer the parents our wishes that this child "enter to Torah, the *chuppah*, and good deeds." Reb Moshe asked: Does not the blessing of Torah encompass good deeds as well? He answered that there are many situations where a person can take "the easy way out" and avoid doing a good deed.

A classic example of this is the separation of *terumos* and *maasros* from produce grown in Eretz Yisrael. There are ways sanctioned by Halachah through which a farmer can avoid the obligation to separate these tithes, thus leaving more for himself and depriving the Kohen and Levi of their rightful shares. Yet, Hashem knew that the vast majority of Jews would never seek to circumvent these mitzvos. They would give the Kohen and Levi their rightful gifts, and that is why He did not provide Kohanim and Leviim with a portion in Eretz Yisrael. This, says Reb Moshe, illustrates the love of mitzvos of earlier generations.

One who truly loves Hashem's mitzvos, said Reb Moshe, will seek to have some connection to a mitzvah even when he cannot actually fulfill it. For example, someone who for health reasons cannot eat a *k'zayis* of maror should at least taste the maror. One who will be unable to sit in a *succah* should seek to have a share in the building of a *succah*.

---

22. *I Shmuel* ch. 1 and 2.

This is the blessing we express at a child's naming. We hope that the child will grow to have a love of mitzvos so that he will seek to accomplish good deeds even when he is exempt from a mitzvah or when he could find means to be exempt from that mitzvah.[23]

AFTER MOVING TO FDR DRIVE, WHERE HE LIVED UNTIL THE END OF HIS LIFE, REB Moshe remarked to a visitor, *"Baruch Hashem,* I have moved to a new

Zeal for a Mitzvah apartment." The visitor asked, "Is the Rosh Yeshivah's new apartment that much better than his old one?" Replied Reb Moshe, "Oh, no! A dwelling is a dwelling — the advantages of one over the other are insignificant to me. I am happy, though, that I now live farther from the yeshivah than before. I will be able to earn more *s'char halichah* (the reward for traveling or walking to perform a *mitzvah)!"*[24]

His zealousness was apparent in many other ways. He would escort his visitors out the door, usually walking them to the elevator. When an older person would come to see him, he would escort him downstairs to the front door of the building.

> One summer in the Catskill Mountains, Rabbi Zeidel Epstein and his family piled into a van to return to the city after their summer vacation. Reb Moshe was to remain in the bungalow colony another few days. When Reb Moshe saw the van pull out of the colony and pick up speed as it headed down the road, he literally ran behind it to fulfill the mitzvah of *levayah.*[25]

In his last years, he once attempted to escort a former talmid to the elevator. Seeing how weak he was, the talmid insisted that he not accompany him. Reb Moshe would not agree to this without begging the talmid's forgiveness.

Reb Moshe followed the opinion of the Vilna Gaon not to carry anything in his pockets on Shabbos while in a private domain for fear that he might mistakenly carry it to a public domain.

At the Shabbos meal he would sing *zemiros* and invite others to sing as well. Only a few weeks before his passing, he taught a young great-

---

23. *Darash Moshe, Parashas Behaalosecha.*
24. The longer walk did not cause a loss of learning, for surely Reb Moshe was engrossed in Torah thoughts as he walked.
25. *"Levayah"* is the mitzvah of escorting someone a minimum of four *amos* as he embarks on a journey; see *Sotah* 46b.

Performing the mitzvah of kisui hadam (covering the blood of a slaughtered bird) after performing the kaparos ritual in his apartment before Yom Kippur

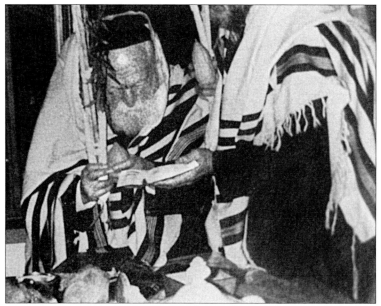

With his arbaah minim on Succos

grandchild a tune for *Mizmor L'David,* customarily sung at the *shalosh seudos* meal. Occasionally, he would discuss the contents of the *zemiros* and would offer possible reasons why certain *zemiros* had become more popular than others.

In his last years, when he was on a strict diet, he refrained from eating white bread. However, in honor of Rosh Chodesh he would have challah.

While fulfilling the mitzvah of taking the *arbaah minim,* Reb Moshe had a unique way of vibrating his hands to make the leaves of the *lulav* rustle.

Someone tried to emulate this practice, but found that his hands hurt too much and gave it up.

AS A RULE, REB MOSHE PERSONALLY SUPERVISED THE BAKING OF HIS PESACH matzos. He would emphasize that he came to perform the mitzvah, and **Matzah-Baking** not because he questioned the *kashrus* of the bakery. There were some who urged him to change to a larger, newer, more efficient bakery, but he always refused, explaining that people might view that as casting aspersions on the *kashrus* of the older bakery.

> Rabbi Avraham Pam related that he was once present when Reb Moshe was supervising the baking of his own matzos. Rav Pam was amazed at Reb Moshe's *zerizus*, his zealousness in performing this mitzvah. With the verve of someone much younger, he rushed from the rolling of the dough to the oven to the cleaning of the sticks and then back. ... Rav Pam commented that a *gaon* possesses not only a superior mind, but also superior physical and spiritual capabilities.[26]

Those who accompanied Reb Moshe to the matzah bakery recall his joy when the finished matzos were removed from the oven. To someone who was overzealous in rejecting matzos, he gave the gentle, humorous rebuke, "Rabbi Akiva would eat our matzos, but we would not eat his." The same person was in the habit of breaking off parts of many matzos because he maintained that they were not well baked.[27] Reb Moshe opposed this practice. He told the gentleman that he should pay for the complete matzos because the breakage was unnecessary.

One year, he asked someone to bring some of the matzos he had baked to a man who had made a number of appeals for funds on behalf of Tifereth Jerusalem. Reb Moshe knew that the man sought nothing in return for his efforts, but was hopeful that the very personal gift he was now sending would be accepted as a token of his appreciation.

---

26. From an article by Rabbi Chaim Aryeh Pam published in the *Yated Ne'eman* in commemoration of Reb Moshe's tenth *yahrzeit*.

27. A matzah with a fold or other irregularity might not have been baked thoroughly and thus might be *chametz*. Often during the pre-Pesach baking, when a small part of a matzah has such irregularities, the *rav hamachshir* (supervising rabbi) will break off the problematic part along with some of the surrounding area, and permit the rest of the matzah to be used on Pesach (see *Mishnah Berurah* 461:32).

RABBI YISRAEL SEKULA, THE SADOVNER RAV, WAS A GAON AND TZADDIK WHO led a *kehillah* and was a great *gabbai tzedakah* for the poor. He also owned

The Halachos of Matzah-Baking
and supervised the "Poilisher Matzah Bakery." The Rav's halachic knowledge and integrity earned him the respect of both chassidic and Lithuanian *talmidei chachamim.* Reb Moshe was one of many roshei yeshivah whose *chaburos* (organized groups) would bake their matzos at the Poilisher Bakery. In each *chaburah,* one member was in charge of accepting and distributing the orders, while a second member, usually the one most knowledgeable in Halachah, would stand at the oven, checking each matzah to ensure its *kashrus* for Pesach.

One year, a particular *chaburah* had someone standing at the oven who seemed to find something wrong with virtually *every* matzah. Often, he would consult a *Sefer Mishnah Berurah* which he had brought along, and would then break off a piece of the matzah, because of what he considered folds or some other defect. After a while, the member in charge of orders complained to the Sadovner Rav that as matters stood, there would not be enough *sheleimim* (whole matzos) for the *chaburah.* The Rav replied that this was the fault of the person at the oven; he was breaking matzos that were perfectly kosher. As the *chaburah's* time was nearing its end, the Rav approached the fellow at the oven and said, "Reb Moshe was here yesterday with one *chaburah,* and he will be here with a second *chaburah* ten minutes after yours is finished. Please stay and hear what he has to say."

As soon as Reb Moshe arrived, the Rav and the other man approached him together. The Sadovner Rav said, "Could the Rosh Yeshivah please tell us how many matzos he had to break yesterday?"

Reb Moshe replied, "The matzos were very good. I did have a *pikpuk* (doubt) concerning one matzah, so I paid for it as a *shaleim* (whole matzah) and at home I broke off the piece in question."

Until that point, Reb Moshe had been facing the Sadovner Rav as he spoke. Now, he turned to face the other man and said, "One cannot bake matzos only with *Shulchan Aruch, Orach Chaim* (in which the laws of Pesach are found). He must also bake with *Shulchan Aruch, Choshen Mishpat* (monetary laws) in mind. *Shleimim* cost more than *shevarim* (broken matzos). If one wants to be *machmir* (stringent) and break matzos that don't really need to be broken, he has caused the bakery owner a loss. The right way is to pay for whole matzos and then, if one wishes, he can break off pieces at home."

SHULCHAN ARUCH CITES THE CUSTOM OF USING MATZOS AT THE SEDER WHICH were baked on the afternoon of Erev Pesach.[28] Today, this custom is fol-

Erev Pesach Matzos

lowed primarily by chassidim. The Lithuanian yeshivah world generally does not use these matzos out of halachic concerns.[29]

Every year, the Sadovner Rav would send a box of Erev Pesach matzos to Reb Moshe. One year, the Rav's grandson, who was a chasan, offered to deliver the matzos, for he wanted to request a berachah from Reb Moshe in advance of his wedding.

When he rang Reb Moshe's doorbell, a talmid came to the door. This was the first time the talmid would be joining the Feinstein family for the Seder. As it was Erev Pesach and Reb Moshe was very busy with pre-Yom Tov preparations, the talmid had been asked to limit access to the Rosh Yeshivah to those with urgent requests. When the Sadovner Rav's grandson stated his purpose in coming, the talmid looked at him in shock and said, "Erev Pesach matzos? I'm sorry, but the Rosh Yeshivah doesn't use those." And he closed the door.

The grandson calmly rang the bell a second time. The talmid opened the door and said, "It is Erev Pesach. The Rosh Yeshivah does not have time for this. He won't eat from such matzos, so you are wasting your time."

The grandson responded, "Obviously, this is your first time here, so you don't know. But my grandfather, the Sadovner Rav, sends the Rosh Yeshivah Erev Pesach matzos every year."

The talmid was not convinced, but he said, "Fine, so I'll give the matzos to the Rosh Yeshivah."

But the grandson had come for a berachah. "Thank you, but I want to deliver them personally into the Rosh Yeshivah's hands."

Reb Moshe had heard bits and pieces of the conversation and when he came to the door, he realized that the young chassid was more than a bit upset. When he told Reb Moshe who he was and why he had come, Reb Moshe's face lit up. "Oh, thank you! Thank you so much!" And he accepted the box of matzos.

The talmid turned to Reb Moshe and asked, "The Rosh Yeshivah eats Erev Pesach matzos?"

Reb Moshe replied, "Our family descends from Koidenov chassidim. They used Erev Pesach matzos, so we are not meshaneh (i.e. we do not act differently)."[30]

---

28. *Orach Chaim* 458:1.
29. See *Mishnah Berurah*.
30. Obviously, Reb Moshe would not have used the matzos had he not had implicit trust

The Sadovner Rav's grandson said, "I am getting married after Shavuos. Could the Rosh Yeshivah *bentch* me?"

Reb Moshe happily obliged, conferring a heartfelt *berachah*.

Reb Moshe then said, "My talmid gave you a hard time and caused you distress. Say that you have no hard feelings towards him and that you are *mochel* him."

"It's fine," the young man replied. "I know he didn't mean it personally."

"Yes," Reb Moshe said. "He simply had no idea that I use such matzos. But he did cause you distress. So please, I ask of you to specifically say that you are *mochel* him."

The Sadovner Rav's grandson complied with this request, wished the Rosh Yeshivah *"Gut Yom Tov,"* and left.

A TALMID ONCE ACCOMPANIED REB MOSHE ON A *SHIVAH* CALL. WHEN THEY entered the house, they saw that the widow was grief-stricken. As Reb

Deeds of Greatness Moshe offered his words of consolation, the talmid watched as the woman's distraught expression changed before his eyes. When they rose to leave, her face reflected hope and appreciation.

As they left the house, Reb Moshe whispered to his talmid, "I hope that I fulfilled the mitzvah of *nichum aveilim* properly." Surprised, the talmid responded, "But of course! Surely the Rosh Yeshivah saw how her mood was transformed by his words."

"Yes," replied Reb Moshe, "I did notice it. But can one be sure of what she was feeling in her heart?"

When they reached the subway station for the return trip home, Reb Moshe insisted on paying the talmid's fare. "You did not know the deceased's family. You came to accompany me. It is only proper that I pay your fare."

The talmid said, "If the Rosh Yeshivah insists on doing this, then it must be in accordance with a halachah in *Shulchan Aruch*."

"No," replied Reb Moshe, "I am simply doing what is proper."

❈ ❈ ❈

When Reb Moshe was in his 80s, a dear friend, Rabbi Chiya Aryeh, passed away. Reb Moshe traveled to Brooklyn for *nichum aveilim*. The *shivah* house was built on a hill and had a steep flight of steps to the front door. Those who accompanied Reb Moshe were afraid that the climb

---

in the supervision and *kashrus* standards of the Sadovner Rav.

Raphael Aryeh, late son of Rabbi Chiya Aryeh, who together with his wife, תבלח"י, were guests of honor at the annual dinner of Mesivtha Tifereth Jerusalem in 1987. The close relationship between the Feinstein and Aryeh families continues to this day.

would prove too strenuous for him. Reb Moshe allowed the Aryeh grandchildren to carry him up the steps so that he could fulfill the mitzvah.

❦ ❦ ❦

One summer when Reb Moshe was in his 70s, he and his rebbetzin vacationed at a bungalow colony in the Catskill Mountains. On weekdays when there was no *minyan* at the colony, Reb Moshe *davened* some two miles away at Camp Yeshivah, the summer home of Yeshivah Chasan Sofer. Each morning, one of the men at the colony was assigned to drive Reb Moshe to and from the camp for *Shacharis*. One day, due to a misunderstanding, all the men at the colony had gone away, leaving Reb Moshe without a driver. It was not until that morning, when there were no men around except for him, that Reb Moshe realized he had no ride to *Shacharis*.

Quickly, he ran upstairs to the third floor of his cottage, where a boy of bar mitzvah age, Shmuel Greenberg,[31] was sleeping. Shmuel often accompanied Reb Moshe to *Shacharis*, but usually had time to awaken later and still be ready for the car ride.

"Shmuel," Reb Moshe said, "we have no ride this morning. You must get up quickly and we will walk to *Shacharis*."

The boy looked at his clock and saw that the hour was late. "But even if we leave quickly we will never make it in time for most of *Shacharis*," he said.

"Yes," Reb Moshe replied, "but it is Monday and we can still make it for *krias haTorah*."

Soon they were walking down the country road on a very hot summer morning. A good part of the walk was uphill, but this did not deter Reb Moshe, despite his age. After some time, he accepted his young companion's suggestion to remove his frock, which Shmuel carried for him.

---

31. Rabbi Shmuel Greenberg is a nephew of Rabbi David Feinstein.

Walking back to his bungalow following Shacharis in Camp Staten Island left to right: Pesach Broyde, Reb Moshe, Dovid Beinish Feinstein

At one point, Reb Moshe looked at Shmuel and saw how he was perspiring. He told the boy, "We are doing what is required of us. One must walk up to 4 *mil* to hear *krias haTorah.*"[32]

Shmuel suggested that they try to "hitch" a ride with one of the passing cars. Reb Moshe rejected this suggestion. He said that toward the end of his life, the Chasam Sofer sought a non-Jew who had once done him a favor. The Chasam Sofer was seeking to return the favor, he said, for before Mashiach's arrival the nations of the world will have to receive their reward for whatever *chesed* they had done for the Jewish people.[33] Said Reb Moshe, "Most of the drivers around here are non-Jews. If one of them gives us a ride, there is no way that I will be able to find him to return the favor."

They arrived at the *minyan* at the beginning of *chazaras hashatz.* Shmuel turned to Reb Moshe and said excitedly, "We're in time for *Kedushah!*" Reb Moshe's face shone with joy.

❧ ❧ ❧

One evening, when still robust but in his 80s, Reb Moshe was about to rush out of his apartment with Rabbi Bluth when the Rebbetzin protested. "Don't run. You are always running! It will affect your health."

---

32. See *Shulchan Aruch, Orach Chaim* 90:16. A *mil* is a distance of 2,000 *amos,* between 3,000-4,000 feet.
33. Reb Moshe cited a passage from *Bava Basra* 10b as proof of this.

Reb Moshe stood straight and still, and answered firmly, "לְכָּךְ נוֹצַרְתִּי (for this I have been created). The Torah says that our days will be increased if we perform Hashem's mitzvos. This will *improve* my health, not harm it!"

WHEN THE JEWISH PEOPLE ENTERED ERETZ YISRAEL THEY TRAVELED TO THE mountains of Gerizim and Eival, where they heard the blessings and

The Goodness in Judgment

curses listed in *Parashas Ki Savo*.[34] Mount Gerizim was designated as the mountain of blessing, while Mount Eival served the opposite purpose. The Jews were also commanded to erect an altar upon Mount Eival upon which they would bring peace-offerings and "rejoice before Hashem."[35]

Reb Moshe asked: Why were the Jews commanded to rejoice upon the mountain reserved for the curses? Would it not have been more appropriate to bring offerings and celebrate upon Mount Gerizim, the place of blessing?

From here, said Reb Moshe, we can learn a basic principle of faith: "All that Hashem does, He does for the good."[36] When Hashem causes tragedy to befall a Jew, G-d forbid, He does so with the person's benefit in mind. *As a man chastises his son, so does Hashem, your G-d, chastise you.*[37] Though it pains a father to inflict punishment upon a child, it is sometimes necessary. Hashem is sometimes forced to deal with His children in the same way.

The peace-offerings and rejoicing on Mount Eival were *Klal Yisrael's* expression that even the curses of the Torah are for our benefit. Whatever Hashem does is ultimately for our good.[38]

This teaching was basic to Reb Moshe's life. He accepted hardship and suffering with perfect faith, never once questioning the Divine will.

Once, he visited a talmid who was observing *shivah* upon the passing of his father. As Reb Moshe walked into the room, the talmid was saying that the doctor had misdiagnosed his father's condition, and that this had very likely caused his father's demise.

Reb Moshe reacted forcefully: "One must not speak this way! His death was decreed by Heaven and it must be accepted as such."

In the summer of 1973, the Feinstein family suffered a tragic loss with

---

34. *Devarim* 27.
35. Ibid. vs. 5-7.
36. *Berachos* 60b.
37. *Devarim* 8:5.
38. From *Sefer Kol Rom* by Rabbi Avraham Fishelis.

the passing of Rabbi Eliyahu Moshe Shisgal, husband of Reb Moshe's eldest child, Faya.

To appreciate the strength of Reb Moshe's faith in accepting the loss of his son-in-law in the way that he did, we must attempt to understand the greatness of Rabbi Eliyahu Moshe Shisgal.

CHAPTER TWELVE

An American-bred Gadol

R ABBI ELIYAHU MOSHE SHISGAL, REB MOSHE'S ELDER SON-IN-law, was a rare *gaon* and *tzaddik,* without a doubt among the most outstanding of his generation, one who seemed certain to emerge as a *gadol* of world stature. To someone who expressed his condolences over Reb Eliyahu Moshe's passing, Reb Moshe said, "You have come to console me? You must console the entire world; you do not know what he was."

A Rare Gaon and Tzaddik

Rabbi Yaakov Kamenetsky once asked a son-in-law of Reb Eliyahu Moshe if he had had the opportunity to become well acquainted with his father-in-law before his passing. After the young man replied that he hadn't, Reb Yaakov remarked wistfully, "No one *really* knew him," meaning that no one had plumbed the depths of his greatness. On another occasion, Reb Yaakov said, "He belonged in an earlier generation."

HE WAS BORN IN THE CITY OF SLUTZK, WHITE RUSSIA, IN THE YEAR 1921. RABBI Isser Zalman Meltzer, who headed the city's yeshivah, was *sandak* at

Growing Up

Eliyahu Moshe's *bris milah.* In later years, Reb Eliyahu Moshe would remark with great feeling how fortunate he was that Reb Isser Zalman had held him and blessed him that he become great in Torah.

His father, Rabbi Avraham Yitzchak Shisgal, had studied in the Slabodka Yeshivah together with Rabbi Yaakov Kamenetsky and other well-known personalities, and then became the Rav of Rostov, White Russia. In 1925, when Eliyahu Moshe was four years old, his family emigrated to the United States. Rabbi Avraham Yitzchak Shisgal entered the American rabbinate in Pawtucket, Rhode Island, where he served until 1933. Young Eliyahu Moshe attended public school in Pawtucket until age 11. Then, his parents sent him to study in Yeshivah Torah Vodaath in the Williamsburg section of Brooklyn, where he boarded with a local family. A year later, his father found a position in Williamsburg. Subsequently, he became a rav on the Lower East Side.

Eliyahu Moshe was a pleasant, friendly, athletic child, but even as a schoolboy he was remarkable. When his friends were given a few cents to spend, they would run to the store for ice cream or candy, but he would save his money until he had enough to buy a *sefer.*

Upon completing elementary yeshivah, Eliyahu Moshe was enrolled at Mesivta Torah Vodaath, then one of the very few secondary yeshivos in America. When he first came to Torah Vodaath, his background had been somewhat weak and he was placed in a class with younger boys. Not for long, though. He made great strides quickly and before long had established himself as a Torah prodigy, complementing a brilliant mind with exceptional diligence.

Rabbi Eliyahu Moshe Shisgal

AT A RELATIVELY YOUNG AGE, ELIYAHU MOSHE WAS PROMOTED TO THE YESHI-vah's highest *shiur,* that of its Rosh Yeshivah, Rabbi Shlomo Heiman. Reb

Rav Shlomo Heiman

Shlomo had gained renown in Europe as a *gaon* and master teacher of Torah, and, at the suggestion of the great Rav of Vilna, Rabbi Chaim Ozer Grodzensky, had been brought to America to serve as head of Torah Vodaath.

Eliyahu Moshe quickly became the apple of his Rosh Yeshivah's eye. "Where is Shisgal?" Reb Shlomo would ask whenever his prize talmid was not present at the start of a *shiur.* Only after Eliyahu Moshe had been seated would Reb Shlomo begin. Often when Eliyahu Moshe asked a question during the *shiur,* Reb Shlomo would say, "Shisgal asks like a *lamdan!*" Rosh Yeshivah and talmid became exceptionally close.

The late Bostoner Rebbe, Rabbi Levi Yitzchak Horowitz, related:

> I learned in Reb Shlomo Heiman's *shiur* in Torah Vodaath. Reb Shlomo would deliver his *shiur* in the morning and would be available in the afternoon to respond to our questions.
>
> One afternoon, however, we could not ask him anything because one particular *bachur* spent the entire afternoon arguing with our rebbi about something he had said that morning in *shiur.* The next day, Reb Shlomo began his *shiur* by saying, "Shisgal *shlugged up* (disproved) yesterday's *shiur* ..."

Reb Shlomo fell ill and passed away at a relatively young age, while still in his prime. At his funeral, Eliyahu Moshe wept so uncontrollably that it interfered with the eulogies. Some of the rabbis were annoyed with him, but one of them said, "Let him be. His is the greatest eulogy."

Each year on Reb Shlomo's *yahrzeit,* Rav Shisgal would repeat a *shiur* his rebbi had delivered on the first *amud* of *Masechta Yevamos.* His awe for Reb Shlomo was such that during the *shiur* he would speak of *"der Rebbe"* but could never bring himself to mention Reb Shlomo by name. One year, a new talmid

Rabbi Shlomo Heiman

attending the *shiur* asked Rav Shisgal, "Who is *'der Rebbe'*?" It was with great difficulty that Rav Shisgal was able to enunciate "Rav Shlomo Heiman."

ELIYAHU MOSHE'S STUDY PARTNER FROM THOSE YEARS AND LIFELONG FRIEND was, יבל״ח, Rabbi Eliyahu Simcha Schustal, presently Rosh Yeshivah of

Unquenchable Thirst

Yeshivah Bais Binyomin in Stamford, Connecticut. Throughout their lives, whenever they met it seemed as though they were returning to an incessant, heated discussion of Torah subjects, as two brilliant minds honed each other in an unending quest for the truth of Hashem's word.

> Throughout his life, at every available moment, Rav Shisgal's mind was engrossed in Torah. He never went anywhere without a *sefer*. On dimly lit subway platforms or under incandescent street lamps, he would strain to read the words of his pocket-size gemara or volume of Rambam. When he arrived at a wedding, he would be discussing Torah even before his coat was off. He would scan the banquet hall in search of a *chavrusa* [study partner] — a yeshivah student, kollel fellow, layman or rosh yeshivah — someone, *anyone,* with whom to discuss Torah. He would pause in his discussion to fulfill the mitzvah of dancing before the bride and groom — only to resume exactly where he left off as soon as the dancing ended.

In his thirst for learning, young Eliyahu Moshe would seek out the greatest Torah minds to discuss his studies. At the age of 21, while spending his summer at Camp Mesivta in Ferndale, New York, he traveled to nearby Woodridge to "speak in learning" with Reb Moshe, who was vacationing there. Reb Moshe was impressed with Eliyahu Moshe's Torah knowledge, as well as his shining personality.[1] Shortly thereafter, Eliyahu Moshe and Reb Moshe's daughter Faya became engaged.

Not long after his marriage, Reb Eliyahu Moshe was appointed to deliver the *shiur* to the first-year beis midrash (i.e. post-high school) class of Torah Vodaath. This seems incredible, considering his young age, but it is understandable when one realizes how exceptional a young man he was. From then on in Torah Vodaath he became known simply as "Rav Shisgal."

---

1. In *Igros Moshe* (*Even HaEzer I,* #179), we find: "The very esteemed *bachur,* Eliyahu Moshe Shisgal, asked me ..."

RABBI AVRAHAM YAAKOV PAM, LATE ROSH YESHIVAH OF MESIVTA TORAH
Vodaath, was a colleague and close friend of Rav Shisgal and compared

Rav Pam

him to the great men of generations past.

In those years, Torah Vodaath was located in the Williamsburg
section of Brooklyn. On Friday afternoons, when classes were dis-
missed early, Rav Shisgal and Rav Pam would walk together to the
Bridge Plaza, discussing Torah. At the plaza they were to part — Rav
Pam to continue on to the subway station and Rav Shisgal to take the
bus over the Williamsburg Bridge to the Lower East Side. However,
rather than see their discussion end, they would walk one another
back and forth, from Bridge Plaza to the subway station, until the
advancing hour left them no choice but to go home.

One summer when the Pam family rented a bungalow in the Catskill
Mountains, Rav Shisgal came to visit his beloved friend. When told that
Rav Pam had just gone to take a nap, Rav Shisgal implored, "Please! Do
not disturb him. I will wait until he gets up — it is *k'dai* (worthwhile) for
me to wait." He had brought along a gemara, and he proceeded to study

At a Moetzes Gedolei HaTorah meeting in the home of Reb Moshe. At table
(right to left): Reb Moshe, Rabbi Yaakov Yitzchak Ruderman, Rabbi Moshe
Horowitz (Bostoner Rebbe), and Rav Pam. Standing in background (left to right):
Rabbi Chaskel Besser, יבל"ח Rabbi Chaim Dovid Zwiebel and Rabbi Shmuel Bloom

from it until Rav Pam awoke. The two greeted one another warmly and proceeded to delve into a Torah discussion.

After Rav Shisgal passed away, Rav Pam paid a *shivah* call to the family. He asked to be shown the room in which his beloved *chaver* had usually studied, a room whose walls were saturated with a never-ending stream of Torah thought. Rav Pam stood silently in the room for a few minutes, as if in the presence of the *Shechinah,* and then left.[2]

In his *hesped* of Rav Shisgal, Rav Pam said that there are two types of *masmidim* (diligent students). The first is the standard *masmid,* one who never leaves his gemara, except when absolutely necessary. Of the second type it can be said that the Gemara never takes leave of him, for wherever he is at any given time, his mind is totally engrossed in the *sugya* (Talmudic topic) which he is presently studying. "This was Rav Shisgal," said Rav Pam. "The Gemara never left him — literally."

THE SPEED OF RAV SHISGAL'S THOUGHT PROCESS WAS ONE OF THE MOST remarkable in his generation, but his talmidim could never have known
A Morsel of Torah this from his *shiurim.* His delivery was slow and deliberate, so that every talmid could grasp each point. He chose each word carefully to convey the intended meaning. Each change of tone was an explanation in itself. He had no desire to compose dazzling *chiddushim,* weaving together concepts from a variety of sources. Instead, he sought to reveal the treasures that lay buried in every word of Gemara, Rashi, and Tosafos. Often, he would point out a difficulty or a proof from a word or sentence that others might have glanced over.

He would often exclaim, "Oh — to understand but a morsel of Torah!" As Rav Pam expressed it, Rav Shisgal amassed many such morsels in becoming one of the *geonim* of his generation.[3]

His search for truth in Torah was such that he would cancel a scheduled *shiur* if he felt that the subject matter was not perfectly clear to him.

His talmid, Rabbi Yitzchak Frankel, recalled:

> He was totally involved in whatever he was learning to the exclusion of all else. And when he began a *sugya,* he approached it as if he had never learned it before.

---

2. Rav Pam related that Rav Shisgal appeared to him in a dream with such clarity that when he awoke, he recalled the entire Torah discussion that had taken place between them.
3. Rav Pam once said that with his clear, logical mind and intense toil in Torah, Rav Shisgal would raise important points related to the Gemara that were not found in the classic commentaries.

Once, when I was already attending *shiurim* of Reb Moshe, I asked
Rav Shisgal to explain a difficult Rashi in *Masechta Shabbos*. I was
shocked when he responded, "But I haven't learned it!" A year later,
he was delivering *shiurim* in that *perek*. He called me over and said,
"Regarding that Rashi that you asked me about last year ..."

Reb Moshe and his illustrious son-in-law were two of the most gentle,
kind, mild-mannered people one could meet. And the love and respect
they had for one another was deep. But when they got involved in
Talmudic debate, "sparks would fly."

For a while, Rav Shisgal, then a *maggid shiur* in Tifereth Jerusalem,
would attend Reb Moshe's Friday-morning *shiur*. At times Rav Shisgal
would challenge a premise put forth by his father-in-law, and as the debate
intensified, these two *gedolim* would become ever more excited, as the
talmidim sat silently, observing the exchange in awe. There could be no
better demonstration of " ...for they [the Torah's words] are our life and
the length of our days."[4]

---

4. From the *Maariv* prayers.

Rav Shigsal discussing Torah with Reb Aharon; in the background is Reb Moshe's mechutan, Rabbi Yitzchak Tendler, a rosh yeshivah in Yeshivah Rabbi Jacob Joseph.

Eventually, Rav Shisgal curtailed his attendance at the Friday *shiur*, out of concern that his arguing in public with Reb Moshe might be perceived as a lack of respect. At that time, he told a talmid to make it known among the talmidim that his arguing in learning with the Rosh Yeshivah in no way detracted from his recognition of the Rosh Yeshivah's greatness in Torah. Rather, this is the way of *"milchamtah shel Torah"* ("Torah warfare") of which our Sages state: Even a father and his son, a teacher and his student, who are studying together, at first become "enemies" of one another (as they challenge and refute), but in the end they are beloved friends.[5]

With Reb Aharon

RAV SHISGAL'S GENIUS WAS PLAINLY APPARENT IN HIS DISCUSSIONS WITH RABBI Aharon Kotler, whose own lightning-quick mind was legendary. Rav Shisgal sought out *every* opportunity to discuss Torah with Reb Aharon. Whenever Reb Aharon attended a wedding in New York, Rav Shisgal would make sure to be there. Reb Aharon delivered a weekly *shiur* in *Seder Zeraim* on the Lower East Side,

---

5. *Kiddushin* 30b.

Reb Moshe and Reb Aharon dancing at a wedding with Rav Shisgal clapping in the background

which Rav Shisgal never missed (though officially the *shiur* was for laymen).[6]

Few who observed the two discuss Torah could follow the pace of their rapid-fire conversation. Reb Aharon spoke almost as quickly as his mind worked, and in discussion with him, Rav Shisgal spoke the same way!

When Rav Shisgal was 32 years old, he traveled to Lakewood, New Jersey, for the annual convention of Agudath Israel. The Shabbos services of the convention were held at Beth Medrash Govoha, Reb Aharon's yeshivah. When Rav Shisgal went to wish Reb Aharon a *Gut Shabbos* at the conclusion of the Friday-night *tefillos,* he was told, "Tonight you will be my guest at the *seudah!*" Of course Rav Shisgal accepted the offer, which in essence was an invitation to discuss Torah with Reb Aharon.

The next morning, prior to the Torah reading, Reb Aharon discussed the distribution of the *aliyos* with the *gabbai.* Although many rabbanim and roshei yeshivah were in attendance, no additional *aliyos* were made.

---

6. Rav Shisgal and Rav Pam would attend the *shiur* together.

Nevertheless, Reb Aharon motioned toward Rav Shisgal and said, "He must be given an *aliyah*. He is young, but a *gadol baTorah*."

At Reb Aharon's funeral in 1962, Rav Shisgal wept uncontrollably, until Rav Yitzchak Hutner, who also knew Rav Shisgal well, succeeded in calming him.

THERE WAS MUCH THAT RAV SHISGAL'S TALMIDIM LEARNED FROM HIM ASIDE from his superlative method of study. His zeal in Torah was obvious in that

Dimensions of Teaching

he was always the first one seated in the classroom at the start of a *shiur*, with his gemara open to the correct page, ready to begin. He would not begin the *shiur* until everyone had found the place, but the talmidim knew that they were expected to find it quickly, for their rebbi could not bear to see precious seconds go to waste.

> During a *shiur*, a talmid disputed Rav Shisgal's interpretation of the Gemara. The contention seemed so ludicrous that the class burst out laughing. Reb Eliyahu Moshe chastised his students, "Why do you laugh? Is this the proper way? Besides, how can one be sure that what he suggested is wrong? Perhaps it is we who are in error. It is possible, you know, for one man to arrive at the truth, while the majority's thinking is wrong."
>
> Having spoken, he excused himself and left the room, returning in a few minutes with a gemara that he had climbed two flights of stairs to get. From it, he read the text of a Rashi aloud and said, "It is apparent from Rashi that our explanation is the correct one."

One day, some students requested of him that he no longer allow questions to be asked during the *shiur*. The class wanted to hear what the rebbi had to say; any difficulties a talmid might have could be clarified after the *shiur*. Reb Eliyahu Moshe responded with typical humility. "What do you mean? There is no rebbi here, nor are there talmidim! We are all studying together and we need one another. This is the way to acquire a true understanding of Torah, through discussion among those who study it."

When a talmid approached him, he would rise in respect. If ever he saw talmidim engage in idle chatter while sitting before an open gemara, he would walk over and gently, respectfully, steer the conversation toward learning.

As mesivta students, Rabbi Paltiel Bender and his classmates would *daven Minchah* on public fast days in the beis midrash of Torah Vodaath.

Left to right: Reb Shaya Wasserman (a rebbi at Tifereth Jerusalem), Rav Shisgal, Reb Michel Barenbaum, Reb Moshe

When the *gabbai* approached Rav Shisgal to ask him his full Hebrew name so that he could call him to the Torah for *Maftir*, Rav Shisgal did not immediately respond. First, he took a moment to adjust his hat and fix his tie. As soon as the *gabbai* announced his name, Rav Shisgal rushed to the *bimah*. It was a demonstration of *kvod haTorah* and *zerizus* for a mitzvah that the young *bachurim* would never forget.

> Once, he was engaged in a Torah discussion with a student of the post-graduate Beth Medrash Elyon in upstate New York. The student excused himself, saying he had to get from Williamsburg to Washington Heights to meet the person who would drive him back to yeshivah. Undeterred, Rav Shisgal accompanied him for the hour-and-a-half trip to Washington Heights to continue their discussion.

A legendary Torah figure on the Lower East Side was Rabbi Yaakov Safsal, known as the Vishker *Iluy*, who was famous as one of the great Torah geniuses of the century. He studied Torah all day by himself in a beis midrash. Rav Shisgal used to visit him regularly to discuss Torah with him. Rav Safsal looked forward to these sessions, and he would say to the much-junior scholar, "Tell me, when can I come to you to speak in learning?"

❀ ❀ ❀

After more than twenty years on the staff of Torah Vodaath, Rav Shisgal accepted a position as rosh yeshivah in Mesivta Be'er Shmuel. He explained to Rav Schustal that in Torah Vodaath he could have a student for only one year, and he felt that he could accomplish more if he could teach the same students year after year. Later, Rav Shisgal became a rosh yeshivah in the Yeshivah of Staten Island, which afforded him the same opportunity.

One of Rav Shisgal's students in Torah Vodaath described the impact Rav Shisgal had on his talmidim: "A student who entered his class still in essence a 'kid' would leave it a full-fledged *yeshivah bachur* and a mature young man."[7]

He would never trouble a talmid to bring him a *sefer.* Yet, when he was at home, he would sometimes ask one of his daughters to come from another room to fetch him a *sefer* that was not far from where he sat. One of the girls asked why he did this, and he replied, "So that you can fulfill the mitzvah of *kibud av.*" His brother-in-law, Reb Reuven, maintains that he also did this to maintain a personal relationship with his daughters.

Mitzvos and Kindness

TO RAV SHISGAL, EVERY MITZVAH WAS A PRICELESS GEM. HE RECITED BLESSINGS with such intense concentration that even scholars many years his senior were inspired by him. Before partaking of food at the *seudas Shabbos,* he would say with feeling, "*L'kavod Shabbos Kodesh*" (in honor of the holy Shabbos). On Purim, he would hear the Megillah-reading in shul and then read it

---

7. From a fictional story by Mr. Wolf Karfiol (*Jewish Observer,* June 1979), in which one of the characters was modeled after Rav Shisgal. In a subsequent issue (October, 1979), the following appeared:

To the Editor:

Reading Wolf Karfiol's article "The Thirty-Year Trip" (June '79) enabled me to make my own personal trip back to the year I spent in Rabbi Shisgal's class, in the first-year beis midrash. A raw young man from the Midwest was inspired and helped along to develop an appreciation for Torah and the yeshivah way of life. Rabbi Shisgal was one of those truly special and unique rebbis who by his very nature was able to serve as a model and to inspire his talmidim. The evenings we spent in his house on the East Side are still very real in my mind, and his *hasmadah* in the beis midrash in the late afternoon hours still serves as an incentive to me to study and learn.

There is so much more one could say about Rabbi Shisgal. Certainly Karfiol's description is true for him, as well as it is for me. Hopefully all of our children will at one time or another experience such a rebbi.

Alan Green
St. Louis, Mo.

aloud at home, for fear of having missed a word due to the banging and other disturbances at the mention of Haman's name. A number of neighborhood women made a point of attending Rav Shisgal's private reading, for they felt inspired by it.

Those who knew Rav Shisgal cannot forget the way he prayed. He pronounced each word slowly, meaningfully. One could easily tell from watching his lips where he was up to in the *tefillah*. Even the slow swaying of his body was full of meaning. He was usually the last person in the beis midrash to complete the *Shemoneh Esrei*, and it usually left him drained of energy. Often, he would mop his brow after finishing.

Rabbi Yitzchak Frankel recalled:

> Whoever did not meet him cannot possible perceive his level of *tzidkus* and *yiras Hashem*. His *Shehakol* over a glass of water was said with more fervor and concentration that we would hope to have at *Ne'ilah* on Yom Kippur.

On an Erev Shabbos toward the end of his life when he was already seriously ill and weakened, Rav Shisgal traveled to Williamsburg for a *dvar mitzvah*. Before returning home, he paid a visit to the Viener Rav, Rabbi Ezriel Yehudah Leibowitz. When Rav Shisgal sat down to have a drink, the Rav went into the kitchen and told his rebbetzin, "Come and listen how a Jew recites a *berachah*."

He distributed *tzedakah* far out of proportion to his modest earnings. He gave until his pockets were literally empty. There were beggars on the Lower East Side who, knowing Rav Shisgal's generosity, would wait for him each morning along the route he took to shul. Often he would give away every cent he had so that he had no money left for carfare. Finally, he began using one pocket exclusively for carfare.

❧ ❧ ❧

Like his father-in-law, Rav Shisgal's insatiable thirst for Torah did not prevent him from performing countless acts of kindness. Each week, he visited a nursing home to brighten the lives of its residents with his warm words and genuine concern. On Erev Shabbos, he would purchase challos for an impoverished widow and hand-deliver them (something which even his own family did not know of until after his death). Often he would give immeasurable encouragement to unfortunate people by asking them for advice. They felt uplifted by the fact that he considered them important and wise.

In his youth, Rabbi Chaim Krinsky accompanied Reb Moshe to a *melaveh malkah* to benefit the yeshivah. By the time it ended the hour was late, and Reb Moshe insisted that his talmid spend the night at his apartment. However, when they arrived there, they discovered that the guest room was already occupied. Reb Moshe phoned Rav Shisgal and asked if he could have a guest for the night. Rav Shisgal was genuinely excited. "*Hachnasas orchim*! When do I have the opportunity for *hachnasas orchim*?"

Rav Shisgal welcomed the *bachur* to his apartment and led him to the guest room. For the next hour or so, Rav Shisgal came to the room every few minutes to see if there was anything more he could do to make his guest comfortable. To Rabbi Krinsky, the way he was served that night was another example of Rav Shisgal's exceptional *tzidkus*.

AFTER HIS FATHER DIED, RAV SHISGAL SUCCEEDED HIM AS RAV OF HIS SMALL Lower East Side shul. It was not a position he sought, especially since he

Devoted Rav continued to serve as a rosh yeshivah, but he took on the responsibility because the shul was his mother's source of income. The shul's members were, for the most part, ordinary people, who would recite *Tehillim* when the Rav was not teaching them *Chumash* or *Mishnayos*. Rav Shisgal served his congregants more like a *shamash* than a Rav, accommodating them in every way possible.

One frigid winter evening, as the hour approached midnight, he walked the few blocks from his home to shul to turn on the heat, so that those who would come early for *Shacharis* the next morning would not be cold.

An elderly man who lived in Staten Island once gave Rav Shisgal a sum of money to purchase a *lulav* and *esrog* for him. Finding an *esrog* for the man was a relatively simple task, in light of the fact that Rav Shisgal paid more than the man had given him. However, when it came to selecting a *lulav,* he had difficulty finding one to his satisfaction. When he finally found one that appeared to be kosher, though not of the best quality, he asked a second person for an opinion. The man, who knew Rav Shisgal well, asked, "Are you buying it for yourself?"

"I am buying it for someone I know," Rav Shisgal replied.

"Well," the man said, "for a man like yourself I would not recommend such a *lulav,* but for an average Jew it is good."

When the man was out of earshot, Rav Shisgal turned to a talmid and said incredulously, "I do not understand what he meant. Why am I different than any other Jew? Either the *lulav* is good or it is not!"

Rav Shisgal decided that the *lulav* was kosher and took it for *himself,* designating the superior *lulav* that he had bought for himself earlier for the man. He explained to his talmid that the middle leaf of the new *lulav* could easily split if shaken too hard, which could render it unfit for use. He would take care to shake it gently so that this should not happen; the elderly man might not be capable of this.

Rav Shisgal then set out for Staten Island where the elderly man lived. Though he had already spent a good part of the day performing a kindness for the man, he did not hurry home after delivering his purchases. Instead, he asked quite innocently if he could see the man's *succah.* While the man thought that this request was made out of curiosity, Rav Shisgal was, in fact, concerned that the *succah* be halachically valid. After inspecting the *succah,* he wished the man *"Gut Yom Tov"* and left.

ON THE LOWER EAST SIDE LIVED AN ODD JEW KNOWN AS "THE PROFESSOR." THE Professor imagined himself to be both a medical genius and a high-ranking

The Professor army official. Attired in a long army coat, he would walk into hospitals and bark orders that were either laughed at or ignored. He was a harmless fellow and most people paid little attention to him.

Rav Shisgal befriended this man as he did other unfortunate souls, and the Professor became a familiar face in the Shisgal home. He would join the family for meals and they would often prepare food for him to take along wherever he might be going.

With Reb Moshe and his son, Reb Reuven, at a wedding

Rabbi Peretz Steinberg, a prime disciple of Rav Shisgal, was privileged to remain close to him until the latter's passing. He once visited Rav Shisgal's home and found that his rebbi had company. "Allow me to introduce you to the Professor," Rav Shisgal said to him. So that his talmid should not think that he was making fun of the poor fellow, Rav Shisgal quickly added, "I call him the Professor because that is what he wants to be called."

The Professor had brought along a transistor radio, which he was proudly showing off. He turned the radio to its highest volume and proceeded to switch from station to station — over and over again. The Professor was enjoying himself immensely, and assumed that the others were as well. Rav Shisgal did not have the heart to dampen the man's spirits by asking him to turn off the radio.

Suddenly, Rav Shisgal had an idea. He put his ear to the radio and said, "Professor, are these military secrets that I hear?"

"Yes!" the Professor shouted excitedly. "This is a military radio and it carries military secrets!"

"Well," said Rav Shisgal, "as you know, I am not a member of the military. I probably should not be hearing these things."

"You are right," the Professor replied, and promptly turned off the radio.

Another "friend" of Rav Shisgal was an emotionally unstable older fellow named Avraham, who found the Shisgal home a place of refuge from his many problems. Rav Shisgal served as Avraham's banker. Whatever money the man earned was given to Rav Shisgal, who kept it in his apartment. Whenever Avraham needed money, he would come to Rav Shisgal and "withdraw" the necessary sum from his "account."

Rav Shisgal was once walking with someone when he noticed a drunkard stagger and fall. Quickly, he rushed over and helped the man to his feet. Noticing his companion's look of surprise, Rav Shisgal said, "He too is a *tzelem Elokim*."

RAV SHISGAL WAS EXCEPTIONALLY WISE AND PERCEPTIVE; HE COULD SEE through to the root of any problem and offer counsel that would set matters straight and uplift one's spirits. As he lay perilously ill only weeks before he passed away, the phone rang frequently in his hospital room. People his family did not know were calling to ask his advice. When one caller was told that Rav Shisgal was too ill to speak with him, the person exclaimed, "Please! You must let me speak with Rabbi Shisgal — just for two minutes! He will save my life!"

Sage Counsel

Following Rav Shisgal's passing, Rebbetzin Shisgal received a letter from a man who was a total stranger to her. He wrote:

Dear Mrs. Shisgal,

With tears coming down my face, I must relate how your husband saved my family from much pain. It was six years ago. Your husband came to my store — I can't even remember for what. Anyway, the way he looked at me I knew that I had to run out from behind the counter and tell him of my problem. My son had announced that he wanted to marry an Italian girl in a few months — her family gave their approval for this match. I could not mix in — after all, he was 24 and had a mind of his own, and how could I, of all people, object if I attended a synagogue only twice a year?

Your husband agreed to see my son in a week. He came by and took him around the block for a walk, returning fifteen minutes later. At first, my son said nothing, but the next morning he said to me, "Father, dear, if we have such a man as part of our people I can't marry her."

At the wedding of Rav Shisgal's daughter, Sarah Rivkah, to Dr. David Krayanek;
seated (right to left): Reb Moshe, the chasan, Reb Yaakov Kamenetsky;
standing directly behind them (right to left): R' Abraham Baker (baal korei in
Tifereth Jerusalem), unidentified, Rav Shisgal, Shmuel Yaakov Feinstein;
behind him is Rabbi Avraham Pam, יבל"ח Aryeh Don Greher

> So you see that your husband saved many people from heartache.
> Of course my son married a nice Jewish girl and just last week he
> told me that he had registered his daughter in an Orthodox day school.
> Let me say that we lost a good public relations man for Judaism.
> Who can replace him …?
> Mr. S.

REB MOSHE AND HIS SON-IN-LAW HAD A DEEP LOVE AND RESPECT FOR ONE
another. Reb Moshe would rise whenever Rav Shisgal entered a room,

Love and Admiration while Rav Shisgal, even in the last pain-racked weeks of his life, would force himself out of bed, adjust his robe, and put on his slippers whenever speaking with Reb
Moshe over the phone.[8]

Whenever the two were together, they engaged in the delight of their
lives — Torah discussion. At gatherings held in the Yeshivah of Staten

---

8. The only other callers for whom he was observed doing this were his mother and Rabbi
Yaakov Kamenetsky.

Island, Reb Moshe and Rav Shisgal could be seen sitting at the head table, involved in lively discussion, taking little note of the food that was placed before them.

In the winter of 1969, New York was hit with a blizzard that blanketed it with more than a foot of snow. A wedding to which Reb Moshe and his family were invited was scheduled for that night at a mid-town Manhattan hotel. That afternoon, Rav Shisgal and his rebbetzin trudged through the snow to Reb Moshe's apartment building, from where a limousine was to take them to the wedding. The limousine never arrived. Someone present suggested to Reb Moshe, "The Rosh Yeshivah cannot go to the wedding in such weather — *no one* will go!" Reb Moshe responded, "No one will go? Then we *must* go!"

They succeeded in borrowing a car but soon after they started out, the car broke down. Reb Moshe, Rav Shisgal, Reb Reuven, and their wives plowed through the snow to a subway station, and went to the wedding by subway. They returned the same way.

The next morning, Rav Shisgal rose early and made his way through the deserted streets to Reb Moshe's building, where *minyanim* were sometimes formed in inclement weather. He met Reb Moshe in the building's lobby; it seemed that there was no *minyan* that morning, so the two set out together on the long walk to Tifereth Jerusalem. Not another soul could be seen on the streets, where huge drifts of snow made their journey a strenuous task.

They had gone only a few blocks when a passing patrol car stopped them. What emergency, the officers wanted to know, had caused the rabbis to venture out in such treacherous conditions? When Rav Shisgal explained the situation, the officers offered to drive them to the yeshivah. Before Reb Moshe and his son-in-law left the car, the officers extracted a promise from them that they would call the precinct for a ride home later that day.

IN THE SPRING OF 1973, RAV SHISGAL BECAME SERIOUSLY ILL. AT THAT TIME, A talmid, unaware of his rebbi's illness, phoned to ask if he could come over

Illness to discuss a pressing problem. Rav Shisgal was in excruciating pain and knew that his talmid would not want to speak with him after seeing him in such a state. But he could not disappoint a talmid who needed his help. So he said, "I think it would be best if we talk about this over the phone right now," and they proceeded to discuss the issue.

When he realized how grave his condition was, he began a study session with a Holocaust survivor, who had been with a number of *tzaddikim* prior to their death. He once chided himself for asking his doctor what the future held for him. The future, he reasoned, was entirely in the hands of Hashem, regardless of the doctor's prognosis.

When his illness became known, a Catholic neighbor approached the Shisgal family to say that he prayed for Rabbi Shisgal's recovery every day.

❈ ❈ ❈

Rav Shisgal's family wanted him to have a private room during his hospital stays. However, he resisted this suggestion, saying that having roommates afforded one the opportunity to perform acts of *chesed*. He assisted his roommates not only physically but also spiritually, teaching those who were not religious to recite blessings over foods. One of his roommates would shout violently at anyone who attempted to speak with him — except for Rav Shisgal, with whom he conversed quite normally.

He always kept cake and fruit in his room to serve his visitors, and would escort them to the elevator on their way out, despite his constant pain. Interestingly, Reb Moshe, who would do the same for his company in his last, infirm years, tried to discourage his son-in-law from escorting him out. However, Rav Shisgal would not relent.

On a Friday in July of 1973, Rav Shisgal was discharged from the hospital for what would be his last time. Rabbi Peretz Steinberg, who took him home that day, recalls that after Rav Shisgal's belongings were packed, he went from room to room saying goodbye to all the patients. Having made his farewells, he began heading toward the elevator. A nurse who spotted him leaving called to the nurses' station, "Come, everyone! The rabbi's leaving!"

The nurses, every last one of them, walked behind him. As he entered the elevator, a nurse exclaimed, "There goes a beautiful man!"

On the way home, he asked that Rabbi Steinberg take him to the home of Rabbi Yosef Eliyahu Henkin. Rav Shisgal requested that Rav Henkin, who was then well past 90, bless him. Rav Henkin, with whom Rav Shisgal was very close, blessed him and then said, "Now, you bless me."

They passed away ten days apart.[9]

---

9. When Rav Shisgal was to marry off a daughter, he extended a personal invitation to Rav Henkin, who said, "I know that many prominent rabbanim and roshei yeshivah will attend your daughter's wedding. I will be happy to attend, but I do not want to be accorded any honor at the *chuppah*."

Rav Shisgal discussed the matter with Reb Moshe, who said that Rav Henkin's request

During the two-month-long illness that took Rav Shisgal's life, Reb Moshe visited his son-in-law every day. Mr. David H. Schwartz, a brother-in-law of Rav Shisgal, recalls spending an entire night with Reb Moshe in a hospital waiting room when Rav Shisgal was rushed there for emergency treatment. Toward morning, Mr. Schwartz dozed for a while and then awoke with a start. Reb Moshe, who was reciting *Tehillim*, smiled at him and nodded reassuringly.

ON THE NIGHT OF 3 MENACHEM AV 5733 (1973), RABBI NISSAN ALPERT LOOKED out the window of his apartment, which overlooked that of Reb Moshe,

The End and saw Reb Moshe returning home from a visit to the hospital where Rav Shisgal lay in a coma. A short while later, the lights in Reb Moshe's apartment went out as he and his rebbetzin retired for the night.

At around midnight that night, Reb Nissan noticed that the lights in the Feinstein apartment were on and Reb Moshe was pacing back and forth. Reb Nissan understood that the worst had happened; Rav Shisgal had passed away.

A member of Reb Moshe's family recalls, "We learned how to handle even tragedy from the Rosh Yeshivah. When we came to the door to inform him of the tragic news, we had to ring the bell because the door was locked with a chain. The Rosh Yeshivah opened the door and understood at once what had happened. 'We will not wake *der mama,*' he said. 'She will have time to grieve. Let her sleep so that she will have strength.'

"He then took the telephone book and instructed each of us whom to call. The Rosh Yeshivah himself called about the gravesite. He asked that the site be 'a worthy one.' After all the details and arrangements had been completed, he allowed his grief to take over. As he wiped the tears streaming down his face he said, 'Now I will go tell *der mama.*'"

> At 6:00 the next morning, Reb Nissan watched as Reb Moshe sat on his terrace, writing his *chiddushei Torah*. Less than an hour later, Rabbi Moshe Zev Feierstein came, as usual, to take Reb Moshe to *Shacharis*. Upon entering the car, Reb Moshe told Rabbi Feierstein the bitter news. On many occasions, Rabbi Feierstein had taken both Reb Moshe and Rav Shisgal to *Shacharis* and would listen in awe as

---

should be ignored. At the *chuppah,* he was called to recite the first two of the *sheva berachos,* a significant honor.

these two *gedolim* who loved each other so argued heatedly over the *pshat* in a Gemara.

On that sad morning, Reb Moshe alighted from the car at Tifereth Jerusalem, went straight to his seat in the beis midrash and resumed writing his *chiddushim* as he did every morning. He would be occupied with the funeral for most of the day and, in spite of his deep sense of grief over the tragedy, he still utilized every available moment for Torah study.

In his eulogy, Reb Moshe wept as he began, but brought himself under control as he quoted the verse הַצּוּר תָּמִים פָּעֳלוֹ כִּי כָל־דְּרָכָיו מִשְׁפָּט קֵל אֱמוּנָה וְאֵין עָוֶל צַדִּיק וְיָשָׁר הוּא, *The Rock (Hashem)! — perfect is His work, for all His paths are just; a G-d of faith without iniquity, righteous and fair is He.*[10] "We do not understand," he said, "but we know that the *Ribono shel Olam* is just. He is righteous and fair and whatever He does is an expression of His mercy."

Reb Moshe's profound grief did not interfere even for a moment with his concern for others. As the funeral entourage stood together at Kennedy Airport, from where Rav Shisgal would be flown to Jerusalem for burial, Reb Moshe had the presence of mind to ask an acquaintance if he had a ride back home. When he saw a second coffin being carried, he walked in back of it as well, fearing that the huge crowd that had come to pay respects to his son-in-law would indirectly cause hurt to the other family and shame to the deceased.

Two weeks after the funeral, someone called Reb Moshe to extend his condolences. When the person started to speak of the enormity of the loss, Reb Moshe interrupted him in mid-sentence. "We must accept Hashem's decrees with love — וַיִּדֹּם אַהֲרֹן, *And Aharon remained silent!*" — a reference to Aharon's silent acceptance of the death of his two sons.[11]

At a *sheloshim* gathering for Rav Shisgal, Reb Moshe cited the *pasuk* in which a farmer, upon bringing his *bikkurim*, declares before Hashem, עָשִׂיתִי כְּכֹל אֲשֶׁר צִוִּיתָנִי, *I have done all that You have commanded me.*[12] "Who," asked Reb Moshe, "can say before the *Ribono shel Olam*, 'I have done all that You have commanded me?'" Reb Moshe began to weep as he cried out, "Rav Shisgal could say it!"

---

10. *Devarim* 32:4.
11. *Vayikra* 10:3.
12. *Devarim* 26:14.

The last family simchah in which Reb Moshe participated was the bar mitzvah of Rav Shisgal's grandson, Dov Nosson Greenfield. Standing at right is Rav Shisgal's son-in-law Rabbi Mendy Greenfield; in the background is the boy's grandfather Rabbi Boruch Greenfield, who was one of Mesivtha Tifereth Jerusalem's first group of musmachim.

The inaugural issue of the *Am HaTorah* journal was dedicated to Rav Shisgal's memory. In a letter of appreciation to the journal's editors, Reb Moshe described his late son-in-law:

> He was a *gadol baTorah;* he toiled strenuously in it all his days, literally. His mouth did not cease uttering its words, nor did his mind ever cease delving into its depth. He was a *tzaddik* and *chassid* (exceptionally pious) and his every word and deed was in accordance with Torah. His *middos* were exceptional and he was pleasing to all; his every action was for the sake of Heaven …
>
> …Let it be recognized and understood that even in this country a man as great as he developed, so that many other students of Torah will follow in his path to become great in Torah and in deed.
>
> One who signs with great pain, but with the hope that many will follow in his path, which will be a merit for his *neshamah* and pleasing to it,
>
> Moshe Feinstein

CHAPTER THIRTEEN

Humblest of Men

"And the man Moshe was exceedingly humble."[1] *It was because of this that Moshe Rabbeinu merited that the Torah was given through him and that the Divine Presence rested upon him. Thus said the prophet Yeshayahu:* רוּחַ ה׳ אֱלֹקִים עָלָי, יַעַן מָשַׁח ה׳ אֹתִי לְבַשֵּׂר עֲנָוִים, *The spirit of Hashem Elokim is upon me, because Hashem has elevated me to bring good tidings to the humble.*[2] *From this we can derive that humility is the most desirable trait of all.*[3]

RABBI SHMUEL GERTZ, ONE OF REB MOSHE'S FIRST TALMIDIM IN America, applied the above Midrash to his revered rebbi. Reb Moshe's humility was true and natural; it was apparent to anyone who was privileged to know him. He honored others at every opportunity, but he sought to escape honor. And when it came to helping his fellow Jew, no deed was beneath his dignity.

Respect for Everyone

In Tifereth Jerusalem, it was not uncommon to see Reb Moshe hurrying from his seat near the *aron kodesh* to greet a bedraggled stranger in the

---

1. *Bamidbar* 12:3.
2. *Yeshayahu* 61: 1.
3. *Midrash Aseres HaDibros.*

back of the beis midrash. "Can I do something for you?" he would ask, his eyes radiating the inner warmth he felt for every Jew.

A poor man once entered the beis midrash while Reb Moshe's *shiur* was in progress and began to ask the students for money. The man was asked to wait until the *shiur* ended, but he refused. He caused such a great commotion that Reb Moshe had no choice but to ask a few talmidim to escort him out. As soon as the lecture ended, Reb Moshe — instead of donning his hat in preparation for *Minchah* — hurried to the back of the beis midrash. He rushed over to the beggar and, holding the poor man's hand, humbly begged forgiveness for what had happened.

> A young man who was a recent *baal teshuvah* had heard so much about the great "Rabbi Feinstein" that he wanted to meet him in person. He traveled to the Lower East Side early one morning so that he could *daven Shacharis* in Tifereth Jerusalem and greet Reb Moshe afterward. Through the course of *Shacharis,* he was trying to determine which elderly gentleman was Rabbi Feinstein, but there were many, and he remained stumped. Finally, as the *davening* drew to a close, he approached someone and asked, "Can you point out Rabbi Feinstein to me?"
>
> The person readily obliged, and the young man gasped. Earlier, Reb Moshe had approached him with his hand extended in greeting, as he did whenever he saw a new face. The young man thought the extended hand was the elderly man's request for a donation, and he had obliged by giving Reb Moshe a quarter. Reb Moshe accepted the quarter, so as not to embarrass the giver, and walked away.

On a hot summer day, someone came with a halachic query. Wishing to discuss the matter in private, Reb Moshe took the visitor to his office — but it was occupied. A student seeking relief from the heat had gone to the office with his gemara and was sitting there with the air conditioner on full blast. Not even remarking on the unauthorized use of his office, Reb Moshe apologized to the student for disturbing him — and went back to the beis midrash.

Rabbi Moshe Rubin studied at Yeshivah of Staten Island in the 1970s. Upon his request, Rabbi Reuven Feinstein arranged for him to spend Shabbos with Reb Moshe and his rebbetzin on the Lower East Side. On Motza'ei Shabbos young Moshe asked for an alarm clock so that he would be up early for his ride back to Staten Island. Reb Moshe replied, "There is no need for a clock. I will be up at that time and I can wake you!"

Reb Moshe did not realize that his guest was uncomfortable with the thought of having the *gadol hador* wake him. Moshe slept fitfully that night and was up before Reb Moshe came into his room at 6:30.

Another time, Moshe had the privilege of driving Reb Moshe from his home to Yeshivah of Staten Island. Upon arriving at the apartment, Moshe found the Rosh Yeshivah home alone. Reb Moshe insisted on serving Moshe a snack before they departed. When a slice of cake was placed before the *bachur*, he saw this as a golden opportunity to learn a halachah about which he often wondered. "Does this piece have the *shiur* (requisite amount) for *Al Hamichyah*?" he asked.

Reb Moshe responded by serving him another slice of cake.

> Reb Moshe's warm, humble nature endeared him to all. Some were shocked when the door of the beis midrash opened one day and in walked Reb Moshe together with a high school student, the *bachur's* arm around Reb Moshe's shoulder as one would walk with a good friend. Of course this was not correct on the *bachur's* part, but to Reb Moshe's talmidim such a sight was no cause for wonder. The *bachur* was too young to perceive Reb Moshe's true stature. What he did know was that the Rosh Yeshivah related to him with the love and kindness of a grandfather, and his true stature was hidden beneath his incredible humility.

RABBI YONOSON STEIF, FORMERLY RAV OF BUDAPEST, HUNGARY, AND LATER OF New York's Khal Adas Yereim, was a *gaon, tzaddik,* and one of the greatest

Humble Contemporaries

poskim of his time.[4] He and Reb Moshe often discussed halachic issues and had enormous regard for one another. Their very different backgrounds did not prevent them from forming a deep bond of friendship and mutual respect.

Every year on Erev Rosh Hashanah, Reb Moshe would call Rav Steif, who was almost twenty years his senior, to wish him "*a gut yahr.*" Rebbetzin Feinstein would call Rebbetzin Steif and do the same. After Rav Steif passed away, Rebbetzin Feinstein would continue to make the pre-Rosh Hashanah call to his rebbetzin, and Reb Moshe would take the phone to also wish her well.

At a wedding following Rav Steif's passing, one of his talmidim mentioned to Reb Moshe that Rebbetzin Steif was in attendance. Reb Moshe

---

4. He passed away in 1958.

With Rabbi Yonoson Steif (seated at right)

requested that she be called to the *mechitzah* so that he could greet her and wish her well.

Reb Moshe's humility was matched by Rav Steif's, as the following anecdotes illustrate:

> Once, the two arrived at a wedding at the same time. Chairs were quickly brought for them, but neither wanted to sit down first while the other stood. Reb Moshe gestured that Rav Steif should sit first, while Rav Steif motioned to Reb Moshe that *he* should sit first. They remained standing the entire time.

On a torrid summer day, Rav Steif's daughter observed him as he spoke on the phone while wearing his hat and frock. After the call ended, she asked him why he was dressed this way at home in such hot weather. Rav Steif replied, "Esther'ke, I was speaking with Rav Moshe Feinstein, and for such a *talmid chacham*, one stands and speaks with *derech eretz*; and must be dressed properly as well."[5]

---

5. Adapted with permission from *Living in the Illuminated Shadow — The Life and Times of Rabbi Yonason Steif*, by his daughter, Mrs. Esther Shulamis Bleier (published by Feldheim).

Once, Rav Shlomo Zalman Auerbach stood the entire time while speaking on the phone, though his son R' Baruch, out of concern for his father's health, asked that he be seated. Upon hanging up the phone, Reb Shlomo Zalman said, "How can one sit when speaking to Reb Moshe?" (From *Chiko Mamtakim*, Vol. II, p. 34).

RABBI MOSHE NEUSCHLOSS, RAV OF NEW SQUARE, WAS ANOTHER GREAT CONtemporary with whom Reb Moshe enjoyed a warm relationship.

Rav Moshe Neuschloss
In their later years, both were patients of the same cardiologist. One afternoon, Rav Neuchloss arrived at the doctor's office shortly past noon for an appointment that was scheduled for one o'clock. He signed in with the receptionist, then sat down in the waiting room. A few minutes later Reb Moshe arrived for his appointment, and the two luminaries greeted one another. The receptionist announced that Rabbi Feinstein should go to the examination room; she explained that his appointment had been scheduled for 12:30.

Reb Moshe was visibly distressed. He walked over to Rav Neuschloss and said, "The Rav should go first. *Kvod haTorah demands* that he go first! And after all, he was waiting here ahead of me!"

Rav Neuschloss could not help but smile. "*Kvod haTorah? Kvod haTorah* demands that the Rosh Yeshivah go first! And as the secretary said, the Rosh Yeshivah has an earlier appointment."

Very reluctantly, Reb Moshe headed towards the examination room. When he emerged, he apologized to Rav Neuschloss, who responded that no apologies were necessary.

Late that night, Rav Neuschloss received a phone call from Reb Moshe. "As I was preparing to retire for the night," he said, "I contemplated what happened today. I feel that I erred in allowing myself to go ahead of the Rav. I ask *mechilah* …"

Rabbi Moshe Neuschloss

It was Rav Neuschloss' practice to visit Reb Moshe on Chol HaMoed Succos. One year, he brought along his seven-year-old son, Yehudah ("Yidde'le"). The sharp-minded child entered Reb Moshe's *succah*, looked up at the *s'chach* and exclaimed, "*Tatte! A passe'le succah!* (Father! An invalid *succah*!)" The *s'chach* was comprised of thin wood slats. In New Square at that time, all *succos* were covered with evergreens or bamboo.

Rav Neuschloss was somewhat embarrassed by his son's outburst, but Reb Moshe seemed amused. "*Mein kind* (My child)," he said to the boy, "what is your name?"

"Yidde'le."

"Come, Yidde'le," said the *gadol hador*, "sit on my lap." Reb Moshe helped Yidde'le climb onto his lap, then made sure that he was comfortable and unafraid.

"Yidde'le," he said, "let us learn a mishnah together."

Reb Moshe opened a *Mishnayos Succah* to a mishnah that discusses the maximum width of a piece of *s'chach*. Reb Moshe taught the boy the mishnah with the patience and clarity of an expert grade-school *melamed*. He demonstrated to him that thin wood slats did, in fact, meet the mishnah's requirements. Then, in his warm, gently way, he quizzed the boy on what he had just learned. Satisfied that Yidde'le understood, Reb Moshe concluded, "So, Yidde'le, look up at the *s'chach* and tell me — is it *kasher* (valid)?"

The boy assured him that it was.

AT *SHALOSH SEUDOS* IN HIS HOME SHORTLY BEFORE PESACH, REB MOSHE dwelled on the beginnings of *Yetzias Mitzrayim*, when Hashem instructed

Levels of Humility Moshe Rabbeinu to return to Egypt from Midian, initiating the process of redemption. The Torah relates that for a week, Moshe argued that he was unworthy of this mission and that his brother, Aharon, should be entrusted with it.

Reb Moshe said: Humility comes in varying forms. Some people enjoy honor and prestige, but they understand that it is wrong to pursue honor and therefore they avoid the limelight. There is a much higher level of humility, when a person truly desires the path of *hatznei'a leches*, to walk modestly with Hashem, and abhors any form of honor or recognition. This was the path of Moshe Rabbeinu, who truly did not want the honor that would naturally come with being the leader and redeemer of *Klal Yisrael*. The Torah relates Moshe's protestations in great detail to teach us this lesson.

Reb Moshe's readiness to perform any *chesed* that needed to be done illustrated how personal dignity meant nothing to him.

> Without the slightest hesitation, he would stand on a bench to shut the lights in the beis midrash after everyone else had left; climb on the desk in his office to lower the setting on a three-in-one light fixture, in order not to waste yeshivah funds; or prepare breakfast for the student who had come to assist him with his morning needs. When, on one occasion, the student protested this, Reb Moshe responded, "What is wrong? Am I not permitted to do a kindness for someone?"

With his son, Reb David, in Camp Staten Island

When the *shamash* of Tifereth Jerusalem was not well, Reb Moshe climbed up on a bench to turn on a *yahrzeit* bulb on the memorial plaque. He explained simply, "People pay for this service. It would be dishonest not to turn on the light."

Reb Moshe would often remain in beis midrash on Fridays long after his one-and-a-half-hour *shiur* had ended. One Friday, a talmid, Rabbi Avraham Yosef Rosenberg, remained to learn as well. When Reb Moshe finally closed his *sefarim*, he made his way around the beis midrash collecting *sefarim* that were lying around and putting them back on their proper shelves. When Rabbi Rosenberg insisted on finishing the job, Reb Moshe showed him the most efficient way of making room on the crowded shelves.

Once, Reb Moshe had to send his son, Reb David, on an important mission. At the time, Reb David was helping a child with his studies. While Reb Moshe felt it necessary for his son to leave at once, he did not want the child to suffer because of it — so he sat down and tutored the boy himself.

Reb David commented:

> I took my father's *anavah* (humility) for granted. This is what I always saw. He had no *gaavah* (pride) whatsoever. If he told someone, "If you have a *she'eilah*, come and ask me," this was because he wanted to help the person, to give him *chizuk*.

Left to right: Reb Dovid Lifshitz, Reb Moshe, Reb Shimon Schwab

He never spoke about himself. If he ever mentioned his years learning under Reb Isser Zalman (Meltzer) or Reb Pesach Pruskin, it was just parenthetically, or when he wanted to show recognition and *hakaras hatov* to Reb Pesach's son, Rav Avraham Pruskin.

Rabbi Shimon Schwab, the legendary Rav of K'hal Adas Yeshurun, recalled an occasion that, to him, epitomized Reb Moshe's humility. The Rosh Yeshivah had spent a Shabbos in Camp Agudah and as he prepared to leave on Sunday morning, he made his way through the large dining room to shake the hands of the many counselors and say "Goodbye" to the hundreds of campers.

A SEATTLE COURT JUDGE WAS HAVING A DIFFICULT TIME DECIDING A CASE involving a Jewish litigant. He agreed to the suggestion that an authority

On Being Crowned "the Greatest" on Jewish law be consulted to see how he would rule in such a matter. Upon inquiry, the judge discovered that the aged dean of a talmudic school on New York's Lower East Side was reputed to be the world's greatest authority on Jewish law. A meeting was arranged between an officer of the court and Rabbi Moshe Feinstein.

At the meeting's outset, the emissary respectfully asked, "Can you tell me how and when you were declared the greatest authority on Jewish law in our day?"

Reb Moshe replied, "I really don't know the answer to your question. All I do know is that people who come to me with halachic questions once often return a second time with something else to ask. So I imagine that they are satisfied with the answers they receive."

A woman who remembered Reb Moshe from Russia asked him what position he occupied in America. "I say a *shiur,*" he replied, "and sometimes I *pasken a she'eilah* (issue a halachic ruling)."[6]

In a letter to an Israeli woman seeking his blessing and prayers, Reb Moshe wrote, " ...there are many G-d-fearing men in Eretz Yisrael whose prayers are certainly desired by Hashem, so what is my role in such matters? However, because your anguish is great, I shall respond ..."[7]

Rabbi Yonah Ganzweig noted that Reb Moshe's humility had much to do with his acceptance as the *posek hador:*

> It is said concerning the Beis Yosef that the reason he became the *posek* of the Jewish people for all generations is that he never said *"Kabel daati! —* you must accept my opinion!"[8] We may say the same of the Rosh Yeshivah: due to his great humility, he never said, *"Kabel da'ati!"* As a result, Heaven decreed that the Jewish people accept him as the preeminent *posek.*

REB MOSHE'S GENUINE HUMILITY SHINES THROUGH IN MANY OF HIS LETters. He was the leader of his generation, his counsel and *psak* were sought

Seeking Forgiveness by petitioners worldwide, and yet he saw the need to apologize for a delay in responding to a correspondent:

However, his honor, my friend, should know that my time is not my own at all — even for a short time. I respond immediately only for practical matters that need to be resolved without delay. This is why I have postponed writing until today. Now, I will fulfill my promise and write, with the help of Hashem, what seems correct in my humble opinion ...[9]

I ask forgiveness for my delay in responding. The demands on my time are indescribable; it is literally impossible for me to respond immediately. There are so many with halachic questions, including

---

6. From *Meged Givos Olam.*
7. *Igros Moshe, Orach Chai,* Vol. IV, #47.
8. See *Chida's Shem HaGedolim, Maareches Sefarim,* "Beis Yosef."
9. *Igros Moshe, Orach Chaim,* Vol. I, #138.

those who write from all over … and I must also deliver shiurim to the talmidim in yeshivah and prepare those shiurim for publication as is the desire of bnei Torah. I hope that his honor will forgive me with a full heart, and I will bless his honor for this specifically.

ONCE, IN AN UNBELIEVABLE DISPLAY OF THOUGHTLESSNESS, SOMEONE called him before 5:00 a.m. to ask him a *she'eilah* that was not urgent. The

Roots of Humility

next morning at the same time, the same person called with a question about a *Tosafos*. The next morning, it happened again. Finally, on the *fourth* morning, Reb Moshe softly told his pre-dawn caller, "The reason I arise so early to learn is so that I can be prepared to answer the questions people ask when they call me later." That was the last time the man called at that hour.

On another occasion, he lamented to the Rebbetzin, "If I can't find time to learn, I will remain an *am ha'aretz*." Coming from someone of such greatness, it sounds as though such words were said in jest, but Reb Moshe meant it, knowing the vastness of the Torah.

It is clear that Reb Moshe realized full well his position as a leader of *Klal Yisrael* and his role as a *posek*. His humility was rooted in

the teaching of Rabbi Yochanan ben Zakkai: "If you have studied much Torah, do not take credit for yourself, for that is what you were created to do."[10] As *Mesillas Yesharim* explains, since intelligence is granted to a person for the purpose of acquiring knowledge, man may not become arrogant for having utilized this gift, any more than a bird may for using its wings to fly.

In this light, Reb Moshe's fear of remaining an *"am ha'aretz"* can be better understood. While we might be quite satisfied were we to amass a fraction of Reb Moshe's Torah knowledge, he was always concerned lest he fall short of the potential inherent in the great mental gifts with which Hashem had blessed him.

The Gemara relates:

> R' Yosef the son of R' Yehoshua ben Levi took ill and (as Rashi explains) his soul actually left his body. Then he awoke, and his father asked him, "What did you see [in the Next World]?" R' Yosef replied, "I saw an upside-down world. The superior ones were on bottom and the inferior ones were on top." "My son," R' Yehoshua ben Levi replied, "you have seen a clear world."[11]

---

10. *Avos* 2:9.
11. *Pesachim* 50a.

Reb Moshe asked: Why did R' Yosef refer to the Next World as "upside-down"? Surely he understood that often a person's true worth is not apparent in this lowly world. In the next world, everyone's true status is revealed for all to see.

The answer, explained Reb Moshe, is that R' Yosef saw that even people who *truly were worthy* were ranked in the Next World below simple people who had accomplished less. The reason for this is that in the Next World our status is determined not by accomplishment but by how much of our potential was realized during our years on earth. A simple shoemaker who was scrupulously honest and strained himself to study Torah whenever he had free time might be ranked higher than a great *talmid chacham* who could have learned much more.

Rabbi Reuven Feinstein sees this insight as a key factor in his father's great humility. Reb Moshe never saw himself as being better than anyone else, for one can never be sure who is truly closer to fulfilling his potential. And, Reb Reuven adds, this attitude made his father's kindness to one and all something natural. If one's attitude toward others is, "They are at least as worthy as me, and possibly much more," then it is only natural to treat everyone with great respect, to lend an ear to their problems, and to offer them *chizuk* when they need it.

And a natural outgrowth of genuine humility is *ahavas Hashem, ahavas Yisrael,* and respect for *every tzelem Elokim.*

Self-Improvement

IN THE SAME WAY THAT HE WAS NEVER SATISFIED WITH HIS ACHIEVEMENTS in Torah, so too did Reb Moshe never cease working to improve his *middos,* which seemed angelic to others even in his youth. The climb up the ladder of righteousness, as with the study of Torah, is endless. It is with this awareness that *tzaddikim* in all generations live with the ever-present thought that their piety is somehow lacking. This, too, was undoubtedly a prime source of Reb Moshe's humility.

> Reb Moshe was extremely mild-mannered; in the most tense and provocative situations he would show not a trace of anger. In reference to this, he once remarked, "Do you think I was always like this? By nature I have a fierce temper, but I have worked to overcome it."

A similar comment was heard from him when a yeshivah student questioned him regarding humility. "It is years that I am working on perfecting this trait," he said.

One Erev Yom Kippur, Reb Moshe was seen studying *HaMeoros HaGedolim,* a collection of anecdotes about the great figures of the *Mussar* movement. As a preparation for the Day of Atonement, he sought to discover avenues of improvement by examining the ways of these *tzaddikim.*

When arriving at a *chuppah* ceremony, Reb Moshe would, for many years, take a seat in the back of the hall, though he would invariably be accorded an honor at the ceremony. Only in his later years — when, as the recognized *gadol hador,* he was the object of everyone's attention and such behavior would have seemed incongruous — did he take a seat toward the front.

IN MESIVTHA TIFERETH JERUSALEM, THE *CHAZZAN* WOULD ALWAYS PAUSE AT the conclusion of *Shema,* in line with the universal custom to wait for the

Thoughtful Humility congregation's leader at that point in the *tefillah.* Reb Moshe recited *Shema* with the proper cantillation *(trop)* and with intense concentration, and usually lagged far behind most of the congregation. Not wishing to keep the others waiting, he would signal to the *chazzan* to go on when he had completed only the first two portions of *Shema.*

Rabbi Reuven Feinstein once accompanied his father to a wedding, where *Maariv* was recited at one point. The *minyan* fell silent as the *chazzan* waited for Reb Moshe to complete *Shema.* Departing from his normal custom, Reb Moshe recited the entire *Shema* without giving any signal. Well aware of his father's custom, Reb Reuven later asked why he had not signaled the *chazzan* to continue. Reb Moshe explained, "In my own yeshivah, it is obvious that the *chazzan* is waiting only for me, and therefore there is nothing wrong in my signaling to him. However, at a wedding, where I am only a guest like everyone else, I have no right to assume that it is for *me* that the *chazzan* is waiting."

❦ ❦ ❦

Someone who assisted Reb Moshe for a number of years once asked him, "Why does the Rosh Yeshivah permit phone calls to disturb his learning at all hours of the day? Would it not be more practical to accept calls at specific hours only?"

Reb Moshe replied, "There is a trace of arrogance in telling someone that I cannot be disturbed and he must call me back at my convenience. That is not for me."

When he spent his summer vacation at Zuckers' Hotel in the Catskills, some talmidim from the nearby Woodridge Yeshivah paid Reb Moshe a nighttime visit. They found him in conversation on a pay phone in the hotel lobby. After finishing the phone call, Reb Moshe turned to his visitors and apologized for keeping them waiting. "I was on the phone with Rav Kruger (a renowned rav) concerning some cases of *agunos*." The *bachurim* were amazed that the *gadol hador* felt it necessary to apologize to them.

A *bachur* was experiencing difficulties in a certain area and his father asked Reb Moshe to speak with him. During the afternoon break in the *bachur's* yeshivah, the pay phone rang. It was Reb Moshe, calling to speak with the *bachur*. Upon being told that he was unavailable at the moment, Reb Moshe said, "Please ask him to call me. Anytime is good, except between 3 and 4 in the afternoon. I get tired then and I need to lie down." Apparently, Reb Moshe felt a need to explain why there was an hour in the day when this yeshivah student would not be able to reach him.

A close acquaintance of Reb Moshe did not inform him of a grandson's upcoming *bris* out of embarrassment that someone other than Reb Moshe was being honored as *sandak*. How surprised this man was when Reb Moshe came uninvited and remained until the conclusion of the *seudas mitzvah*!

Rabbi Yaakov Heftler was a close talmid of Reb Moshe. As Rabbi Heftler was preparing to celebrate the *bris* of a son, he learned that Reb Moshe was not feeling well. Therefore, Reb Moshe was not informed about the *bris*, which would be held in Monsey. Reb Moshe surprised everyone by attending. When Rabbi Heftler expressed his amazement that Reb Moshe had undertaken the trip, he smiled and replied, "If I do it for strangers, shouldn't I do it for those to whom I am close?"

> Rabbi Heftler would call Reb Moshe every Erev Rosh Hashanah to exchange greetings for *"a gut yahr."* One Erev Rosh Hashanah, Rabbi Heftler was extremely busy and unable to make phone calls. An hour before Yom Tov, his phone rang — it was Reb Moshe. Realizing his talmid's shock, he said, "What difference does it make who calls whom — as long as we wish one another *a gut yahr!"*[12]

Reb Moshe was once walking along a street in his neighborhood when he heard a voice calling, "Moshe, Moshe!" Looking up, he saw that the voice was that of an acquaintance, who was behind the wheel of his car. Without blinking an *eye*, Reb Moshe walked over to the car. Upon realizing that Reb Moshe had assumed that he was being called, the man turned crimson with embarrassment.

He said, "I was calling my son, who happened to be on the street as I drove by. I would never have dreamed of addressing the Rosh Yeshivah in such a disrespectful manner. Besides, if I had had something to discuss with the Rosh Yeshivah I would have gotten out of my car and gone over to him — I would not have dared to ask the Rosh Yeshivah to come over to me ..."

Reb Moshe assured the man that there was nothing to be concerned about. "It is already many years that these things mean nothing to me."

REB MOSHE'S HUMILITY DID NOT PREVENT HIM FROM BEING FIRM AND UNYIELD-ing when necessary. As a genuine Torah personality, Reb Moshe would

Firm and Unyielding

respond forcefully when he felt the situation required such a reaction.

Once, when judging a *din Torah,* he caught someone offering testimony that was clearly false. Reb Moshe reprimanded the man and asked him to leave the room.

While judging a dispute, Reb Moshe stated a halachah that was not to the liking of one of the parties involved. The man had the audacity to

---

12. From an article by Rabbi Heftler in the *Kol HaTorah* journal.

accuse Reb Moshe of falsifying the law so that the case would be brought to a speedy conclusion. Reb Moshe rose to his full height and emphatically declared:

"My name is Moshe Feinstein. True, I do not know how to learn. But go in the streets and ask if I am a liar!"

When a manuscript commentary to *Chumash* attributed to Rabbi Yehudah *HeChassid* (12th-century Tosafist) was found to contain questionable statements, Reb Moshe issued a *teshuvah* condemning its publication and sale.[13] To Reb Moshe it was clear that even if Rabbi Yehudah *HeChassid* had written the bulk of the commentary, the statements in question were inserted by heretics. In order to deceive loyal Jews into accepting their views, these enemies of Torah would sometimes insert heresies into the manuscripts of acclaimed scholars who were no longer living.

When the manuscript was published despite his objections, Reb Moshe dispatched emissaries to Hebrew book stores, forbidding the sale of the *sefer*.

❀ ❀ ❀

A widow once accosted Reb Moshe as he was about to leave his yeshivah and, in a sharp and disrespectful manner, she complained about the way her son's rebbi was treating him. Reb Moshe listened in silence to the distraught woman, allowing her to speak her piece. When she was finished, Reb Moshe assured her that he would look into the matter personally. He then asked the student who was waiting to drive him home to take the woman home instead. Reb Moshe went on foot.

Yet his reaction was altogether different when another widow expressed a determination to violate Halachah. She came to him insisting that her husband had been buried in the wrong grave, and she wanted to have his remains exhumed and reburied in the proper place. Reb Moshe dispatched a student to get the cemetery office on the phone so that he could verify the claim. The student could not reach the proper person.

Reb Moshe explained to the widow that, in any case, it was forbidden to move the remains until some time had elapsed after burial. In the meantime, the facts could be established. She left, but came back a few minutes later insisting that it be done immediately. Again, he explained to her patiently that nothing could be done for the time being. She came back a third time. Then he told her sternly, "You will not change the halachah with tears!"

---

13. See *Igros Moshe, Yoreh Deah* III, #114, 115.

After the woman left, Reb Moshe turned to his talmid to explain his behavior. "One should not raise his voice, especially to a person in pain — but sometimes it cannot be avoided, because that may be the only way to make them understand."

THE WHEAT FIELDS OF THE POILISHER MATZAH BAKERY WERE LOCATED A few miles from Camp Staten Island in upstate New York. When the

Feigning Anger

Sadovner Rav and his sons would go out to the fields in the summer to supervise the cutting of the wheat, a taxi would take them to the camp for *Minchah* and *Maariv.*

Once, as they arrived at the camp, Reb Moshe was speaking on a public telephone. As they approached him in order to greet him, they were shocked to hear Reb Moshe shouting into the phone. "*Nein, nein* (No, no)! You are a *meizid* (intentional sinner) and you will not have a *kaparah* (atonement)!"

The Sadovner Rav had never seen Reb Moshe upset, and certainly not as agitated as he appeared to be. He and his sons felt uncomfortable seeing Reb Moshe in this state. However, the moment Reb Moshe hung up the phone, he turned to them with a big smile and extended his hand in greeting. He said, "It [i.e. the phone conversation] was a matter regarding which the halachah says one must show anger, so I showed anger. But now the phone call is over! *Shalom aleichem!*"

Rabbi Aryeh Zev Ginzberg was present when Rabbi Nissan Alpert came to Reb Moshe and was asked, "*Nu*, were you successful?" Reb Nissan responded affirmatively. Reb Moshe then asked, "And how did you accomplish it?" "By learning from a *maaseh rav* (a deed of my rebbi)," Reb Nissan replied. Later, Rabbi Alpert told Rabbi Ginzberg what he meant:

> Once, Reb Moshe told Reb Nissan and another talmid that he wanted them to come to his apartment to serve as witnesses for a *get*. A woman whom he did not know had contacted him and said that she and her husband wanted to divorce.
>
> The woman arrived with a man whom she introduced as her husband, and Reb Moshe began to question them. Suddenly, Reb Moshe's face grew flushed and, to his talmidim's shock, he began to shout at the woman that she was a liar and that he would not write a *get* that was false. After a few minutes, the woman broke down and admitted that it was all a ruse. She wanted to remarry but her husband had not agreed to a divorce. So she arranged for a man to

pose as her husband so that a *get* would be written and she would have "proof" that she was free to remarry.

Reb Moshe's "spiritual antennae" has sensed the falsehood in her words.

Rabbi Alpert concluded, "From that incident I learned that someone who is in a position to render judgment and enforce it must be prepared to divest himself of his real personality and act in a way that is totally out of character — if that is what the situation requires. So I did the same in my recent mission, and in that way I was successful."

REB MOSHE WAS QUICK TO TAKE A FIRM STAND WHEN THE WELFARE OF those who devote their lives to teaching Torah was concerned.

For the Sake of Torah Teachers In his early years at Tifereth Jerusalem, as the yeshivah struggled with a financial crisis, the board of directors conducted a study of how to cut costs.[14] They presented their findings to Reb Moshe, whom they needed to implement their conclusions: if three rebbeim would be fired and classes combined, the yeshivah would save a significant amount of money.

Reb Moshe did not hide his annoyance. "I have a better suggestion," he said. "Fire all the rebbeim and I can teach the entire yeshivah." With those words, he left the meeting and returned to the beis midrash.

A few minutes later, a member of the board who was a *talmid chacham* approached Reb Moshe with tears streaming down his face. "We ask *mechilah* of the Rosh Yeshivah," he said, "and we withdraw our recommendation."

It was not only when his own rebbeim were concerned that Reb Moshe took a firm stand. Decades later in a certain yeshivah, a dispute erupted between rebbeim and the board of directors over salary. Leading members of the board were convinced that their position was correct, and they went to seek Reb Moshe's endorsement of their approach. In advance of the visit, the chairman of the board made it clear that he was seeking not a *"psak"* (definitive ruling) to which the board would be bound, but a non-binding opinion. To this end, he planned to remain standing when speaking to Reb Moshe, to indicate that the meeting was of a casual nature.

However, as soon as the group entered his apartment, Reb Moshe

---

14. This was before Reb Moshe assumed responsibility for the yeshivah's finances. See Chapter Three.

insisted that the chairman be seated. After hearing the issues and positions, Reb Moshe, clearly and decisively, sided with the rebbeim.

REB MOSHE WAS ONCE ASKED HOW ONE BEGINS ON THE PATH TO ACQUIRE true humility. He replied, "By not having *hakpadah*," meaning, to ignore **Starting on** insults and any sort of wrong of which one has been the **the Path** victim. Reb Moshe added, "One must work at this until it becomes his nature. And one should realize: What does one gain from having *hakpadah*? All it accomplishes is to make one ill."

> Once, someone who lost a *din Torah* over which Reb Moshe presided wrote an article in a Yiddish newspaper sharply critical of Reb Moshe. Later, this fellow phoned Reb Moshe and told him that his rationale for writing the piece was a conversation he had with a renowned *talmid chacham* who agreed with him that Reb Moshe had erred in his *psak*. Many years later, this *talmid chacham* came to Reb Moshe with a request that he pen a letter on his behalf. Reb Moshe immediately obliged.
>
> After completing the letter and handing it to the man, he said, "Now I would like to ask you a question." Reb Moshe then told him of the above-mentioned *din Torah* and asked whether or not it was true that he had held that Reb Moshe had erred. The scholar reacted with shock, saying that the matter had never been discussed with him. Reb Moshe asked *mechilah* (forgiveness) for having even entertained the possibility that what he had been told was true.

In relating this incident, which he heard from his father, Rabbi David Feinstein commented, "My father's approach was to make sure that the *Satan* would not interfere. First, he penned the letter for the man, and only then did he bring up the incident that had caused him hurt."

RASHI DEFINES THE WORD עָנָיו WHEN APPLIED TO MOSHE RABBEINU[15] AS A שָׁפָל וְסַבְלָן, *humble and tolerant person*. In his commentary to *Pirkei Avos*,[16] **"Never in** *Rabbeinu Yonah* describes a tolerant person as "one who **My Life ..."** distances himself from anger and responds in a soft tone. Even when he is wronged, he will tolerate it and no bitter word will escape his mouth ..."

---

15. *Bamidbar* 12:3.
16. 2:9.

Reb Moshe's tolerance of the personal wrongs committed against him was the most incredible aspect of his humility.

A student once asked to be forgiven for having once said something improper to him. Reb Moshe said, "You are right to ask forgiveness, but you should know that never in my life have I ever taken offense at something that was said to me."

He once judged a *din Torah* in which the money in question was held by a third party, who was to present it to the person in whose favor Reb Moshe would rule. The case was decided, but the man refused to hand the money over. When Reb Moshe asked why, the man replied, "I will not hand the money over, for your *psak* is invalid! You have overlooked an obvious halachah, namely that monetary disputes cannot be judged at night!" Reb Moshe calmly explained to the man that he had not erred, and the money should therefore be handed over.

Five months later, this man came to Reb Moshe, requesting that he be provided with a certificate attesting that he was a qualified *shochet*. Reb Moshe, who knew the man well, promptly picked up his pen and began to write.

Others present in the room were aware of this man's earlier insolent outburst and were convinced that he was unworthy of Reb Moshe's help. "The Rosh Yeshivah surely recalls the disrespect shown him by this man ...," they began.

Reb Moshe replied adamantly, "Of what relevance is this? Yom Kippur has already passed, at which time I recited *Tefillah Zakah*, declaring my forgiveness of all who have sinned against me. This is not mere child's play! Besides, the man has certainly repented by now." And he continued writing the certificate requested of him.

IN THE FOLLOWING INCIDENT, REB MOSHE TAUGHT THE IMPORTANCE OF VERbalizing one's *mechilah* for the wrong committed against him.

A Time to Forgive Rabbi Meir Zlotowitz once arrived at Reb Moshe's apartment as a *din Torah* was concluding. Reb Moshe rendered his decision in favor of one party and the other party agreed to abide by it. As the litigants prepared to leave, Reb Moshe asked that both men state that they forgave each other for any hurt that might have been caused. One man immediately said that he was *mochel* (forgiving of) his opponent. The other man said, "Rosh Yeshivah, it's fine. Everything is from Hashem; it is *bashert* (Hashem's will). He agreed to pay me my money and there are no hard feelings." However, Reb Moshe was insistent; he would not let the man leave without saying that he was *mochel* the other man. The man complied.

After the two left, Rabbi Zlotowitz asked Reb Moshe why he had been so insistent that the man verbalize his *mechilah* when he had made it clear that he bore his adversary no ill will. Reb Moshe replied:

> The Torah relates that Yosef HaTzaddik sought to comfort his brothers after he revealed himself to them and they felt ashamed and frightened for their having sold him.[17] He told them not to be distressed, for their actions were a manifestation of the Divine will that he be a provider for his father and family during the years of famine. Later, after Yaakov Avinu died, Yosef spoke to his brothers again and, as the Torah states, "He comforted them and spoke to their heart."[18] Yet, the Midrash states that the murders of the *Asarah Harugei Malchus* (ten great sages who were executed by the Romans) were an atonement for Yosef's sale by his ten brothers. This was necessary, says *Rabbeinu Bachya,* because Yosef never explicitly said that he forgave them for what they did. And so they died without having been completely forgiven.[19]

"This is why," concluded Reb Moshe, "I was insistent that he state explicitly that he forgave his adversary. Otherwise, they keep *cheshbon* (an accounting) in Heaven, for even thousands of years, until the wrong is atoned for. I have reviewed this teaching of *Rabbeinu Bachya* many times and made it a part of my *derech hachaim* (path of life)."[20]

MANY YEARS AGO, A RESPECTED *TALMID CHACHAM* PUBLISHED A *SEFER* THAT bore a *haskamah* (approbation) from Reb Moshe. A number of points

Protector of Antagonists

expressed in the *sefer* were sharply decried by some who found them contrary to their own strongly held traditions. Some time later, a pamphlet appeared which viciously attacked the *sefer,* its author, and even derided Reb Moshe for having given his *haskamah* to the work. There was widespread outrage at

---

17. See *Bereishis* 45:5.

18. Ibid. 50:21.

19. In *Rabbeinu Bachya's* words: "Though the Torah states, 'He [Yosef] comforted them and spoke to their heart' (*Bereishis* 50:21), which indicates that Yosef had been placated, nevertheless the Torah does not state that there was *mechilah* on Yosef's part and that he had acquiesced to their request that he 'forgive their spiteful deed' (see 50:17). Thus, they died with their sin not having been forgiven by Yosef, and atonement was impossible without Yosef's forgiveness. Therefore, their punishment was stored away and sealed, to be remembered at a later date by way of the *Asarah Harugei Malchus*" (*Rabbeinu Bachya* to *Bereishis* 50:17).

20. See *"Erev Pesach Matzos"* in Chapter Ten.

this attack on Reb Moshe, not only against the brazen author, but against the group to which he belonged. Most people were convinced that he would not have dared write that way about Reb Moshe unless he had been authorized to do so by his leaders.

A delegation of prominent members of this community visited Reb Moshe to disavow any involvement in the authorship or publication of the pamphlet. They made the point that their Rebbe and Reb Moshe had great mutual respect for one another, and no one who heeded their Rebbe's word would have dared write such slanderous comments.

Reb Moshe informed the delegation that he had not heard the rumors, nor seen the pamphlet; in fact, he was unaware of its contents. There was nothing, he assured them, for which to apologize.

One of the delegates asked Reb Moshe if he would care to see a copy of the pamphlet. Reb Moshe replied, "No. If I read what has been written of me, I may become upset. For this alone (i.e., causing another Jew anguish) the author might incur Heavenly punishment, and I don't want that to happen."

❧ ❧ ❧

One summer, Reb Moshe stayed at a bungalow colony in the Catskills that did not have a *minyan* on weekdays. For *davening*, he would be driven down the road to a colony whose residents were predominantly chassidic.

Many chassidim recite *Tefillas Minchah* after sunset. Reb Moshe was very careful to always *daven* before sunset.[21] That summer, a talmid of Reb Moshe undertook to arrange for a *minyan* in the chassidic colony that would *daven Minchah* before sunset. Most days, there would be a second *minyan* after sunset.

One Sunday, most people were away and it was with great difficulty that a *minyan* for *Minchah* was arranged shortly before sunset. Towards the end of the *davening*, a young chassid, who had a reputation as a rabble-rouser, entered the shul. Seeing that the *tefillah* was nearing its end, he began to shout from the back of the room, "What right does he have to make a *minyan*? He doesn't stay in this colony! He doesn't belong here!"

The brazen fellow then walked to the front of the shul, turned to Reb Moshe, and ridiculed a couple of his famous halachic rulings which were considered controversial in chassidic circles.

---

21. See *Mishnah Berurah* 233:14 and *Igros Moshe, Orach Chaim I*, #24.

At that point, two elderly chassidic gentlemen, both *talmidei chachamim*,[22] began to cry. As tears streamed down their faces, they turned to the young chassidic men who were also part of the *minyan* and said, "*Yungeleit!* We have no strength, but how can you remain silent after hearing such talk! *Gib em a pur petch!* (Give him a couple of smacks!)"

The young men took heed and from different parts of the shul began to converge on the perpetrator.

Suddenly, Reb Moshe, who was then in his 70s, rushed from his seat to block the men from getting any closer. He put up his hands to signal that they should stop their advance and said, "No, no, no! He is right! This is not my place. What right do I have to make *minyanim* here? But I want to appease him by saying to him: In principle, you are right. However, I did not do it without permission; the *gabbai* gave me permission to make the early *minyanim*. But *chas v'shalom* to lay a hand on him. No one should touch him."

And with those words, the crisis was defused.

IN THE 1960S, REB MOSHE ISSUED A *PSAK* THAT AROUSED OPPOSITION IN MANY circles. Of those rabbanim who opposed the ruling, the vast majority did so

Vocal Opposition

with the great reverence due a *gaon* and *tzaddik* of Reb Moshe's stature. Most prominent among those who disagreed with the *psak* was the saintly Satmar Rav, Rabbi Yoel Teitelbaum. The Rav made his feelings known in public *shiurim* and through the organization of chassidic rabbis, the Hisachdus HaRabbanim.

The Satmar Rav

As has often been the case in our people's history, when Torah leaders have a dignified disagreement, men in the street jump into the fray and turn a respectful disagreement into a nasty war. Anonymous individuals who considered themselves Satmar followers hung posters in Orthodox neighborhoods which spoke against Reb Moshe and his *psak* in very disrespectful terms.

When the Satmar Rav was informed of this, he was extremely upset. He

---

22. One was a *sofer*; the other had authored a *sefer*.

At a rally in Manhattan Center to protest the opening of a public mixed swimming pool in Jerusalem. At table (left to right): Reb Yaakov Kamenetsky, Reb Moshe (at podium), Vodioslaver Rav, Rabbi Hertz Frankel (standing), Satmar Rav.

summoned Rabbi Hertz Frankel, an active Agudist who had been chosen to serve as head of secular studies in the Satmar school system. Rabbi Frankel had a relationship with Reb Moshe, Reb Yaakov Kamenetsky, and other roshei yeshivah, and he was the Rav's liaison to these leaders of the Lithuanian yeshivah world. He recalls:

> The Rav was very upset when anonymous individuals took the law into their own hands and engaged in acts that were very disrespectful towards Reb Moshe. The Rav summoned me and asked that I arrange a meeting between Reb Moshe and a delegation that would go to express the Rav's feelings. The delegation, said the Rav, would include the Satmar Rosh Yeshivah, Rabbi Nosson Yosef Meisels, זצ״ל; Rabbi Lipa Friedman, זצ״ל, executive director of the Satmar education system and an esteemed *talmid chacham*; and myself.
>
> I contacted Reb Moshe's secretary on the Rav's behalf and a meeting was arranged. A few days later, we met with Reb Moshe in his office during lunch time at Tifereth Jerusalem. Rabbi Friedman opened the meeting by saying that the posters and letters were the work of individuals who had not sought anyone's authorization for their actions. The Rav had asked that the delegation express his distress over the matter.

With a wave of his hand, Reb Moshe indicated that as far as he was concerned, any reports of the Satmar Rav's involvement were utter nonsense. It was also obvious to him that someone of the Rav's stature would be distressed over such happenings. He said, "For this, there was no need for you to come. *Chas v'shalom* that I should suspect the Rebbe of instigating such things."

For the next fifteen minutes, the delegation and Reb Moshe engaged in friendly conversation; the discussion centered around the Satmar Yeshivah and Tifereth Jerusalem. When we rose to leave, Reb Moshe emphasized again that there was no need for the delegation to have come, though he appreciated the gesture.[23]

A distinguished delegation of chassidic rabbanim volunteered to visit Reb Moshe to convince him to retract the controversial *psak*. Before going, they conferred with the Satmar Rav to seek his advice and blessing. The Rav, who was famous for his scintillating sense of humor, responded, "But what will you do if he speaks with you in learning?"

The group went to Reb Moshe but failed to sway him. Reb Moshe, in turn, dispatched his own emissaries to the Rav, declaring his readiness to rescind the *psak* — if he could be convinced that his halachic logic in the matter was incorrect.

In the end, though Reb Moshe always made it clear that any qualified halachic authority had the right to disagree with him, he refuted all attempts at disproving his *psak* and stood by his ruling.

---

23. Two years later, a private meeting called for by the Satmar Rav and organized and coordinated by Rabbi Frankel was held to address the crisis of forced autopsies in Eretz Yisrael. The participants included the Satmar Rav, Reb Moshe, Reb Yitzchak Hutner, Reb Yaakov Kamenetsky and Reb Yaakov Yitzchak Ruderman. That this meeting took place *after* the disagreement over Reb Moshe's *psak* is sufficient proof that though Torah leaders may disagree strongly, their respect for one another is unaffected.

That meeting was the first time that the Satmar Rav and Rav Ruderman met. Afterward, Rav Ruderman expressed his awe of the Rav's greatness. Some time later, these two *gedolim* sat next to each other at a wedding reception, and took the opportunity to debate their divergent outlooks toward the State of Israel and participation in its government. When the discussion ended, a wealthy chassid who was one of Satmar institutions' main supporters said to Rav Ruderman with pride, "*Ni, zeist vi mein Rebbe ken* ...(Well, so you see that my Rebbe knows [i.e. he won the debate])."

The Satmar Rav's face reddened as he rose from his chair and demanded of his chassid, "Is that how one talks to a rosh yeshivah!"

UNFORTUNATELY, NOT EVERYONE INVOLVED IN A CONTROVERSY HAS THE LEVEL-headedness of Torah giants like Reb Moshe and the Satmar Rav. One fel-

Above the Fray low composed a *sefer*, containing chapter after chapter of refutations to various responsa found in *Igros Moshe*. Not content with the legitimate course of trying to show flaws in Reb Moshe's reasoning, the author filled his work with scornful and derogatory statements. Ridiculous as it may seem, the man somehow thought his efforts would help to undermine Reb Moshe's position as the foremost *posek* of the generation.

For publication, he brought his manuscript to the very same typesetter/printer who produced Reb Moshe's *sefarim*. Seeing the *sefer's* contents, the printer immediately called Reb Moshe, gave him a quick outline of the situation, and asked him how to proceed.

"Well," Reb Moshe replied, "one who writes a *sefer* quite often needs it to supplement his income and achieve renown. One is obligated to do another Jew a favor. You, too, depend on printing to earn your livelihood. Go ahead with the *sefer's* publication."

When the above-mentioned controversy was at its height, one demented individual would call Reb Moshe at all hours of the day and night, shouting any insult that came to mind. Each time the fellow called, Reb Moshe would listen to the tirade in silence and say "Good-bye" when it finally came to an end.

Some understood this behavior as conforming to a teaching cited in *Tiferes Yisrael:* The humble will listen carefully when berated by others, for amid a torrent of insults may lie some truths; by taking heed of such truths, one achieves some degree of self-improvement.

Reb Moshe once told a close talmid, "The best response to personal attacks is no response."

> A well-known rav attacked Reb Moshe's *psak* forcefully. The following summer, Reb Moshe spent some time vacationing not far from where this rav was staying. When Reb Moshe was asked to approve a mikveh in the area, he sent someone to ask the rav to accompany him on the inspection of the mikveh.
>
> "What?" another person asked incredulously. "This is the man who wrote ..."
>
> As was so often the case, Reb Moshe's response was quiet yet firm. "I *must* have him with me on the inspection."
>
> Those close to Reb Moshe were understandably concerned with defending his honor — and why should he dignify someone who had

been publicly disrespectful to him? Reb Moshe had a broader view. His stature would be measured by Hashem, not public opinion. If the status of the mikveh could be enhanced by that rav's endorsement, then he should participate in the inspection.

The rav accompanied Reb Moshe.

Rabbi Michel Barenbaum viewed this incident as an illustration of one of Rabbi Yisrael Salanter's teachings. Reb Yisrael taught that in perfecting the Torah's requirement not to bear a grudge for a wrong committed against oneself, it is necessary to eradicate totally any feeling of ill will toward the wrongdoer. The way to accomplish this is by actively seeking to benefit this very person. By repaying his misdeed with kindness, all bitterness will vanish.

In speaking of Reb Moshe, Reb Michel cited the following Talmudic teaching:

> For three years, the academies of Shammai and Hillel argued. These said that the halachah was as they saw it while the others took the opposite view. A Heavenly voice finally declared: "Both these and those are the words of the living G-d! — but the halachah follows the academy of Hillel."
>
> If both are the words of the living G-d, then why did the academy of Hillel merit that the halachah should follow their views? Because they were soft-spoken and bore disgrace (gracefully) ...[24]

One night, the late *gaon* and *posek* Rabbi Tuvia Goldstein came to the apartment of his neighbor, Reb Moshe, as someone else was walking out the door. Reb Tuvia thought he recognized the man as one of the most vocal and disrespectful opponents of Reb Moshe's above-mentioned *psak*.

Concerned for Reb Moshe's honor, Reb Tuvia asked, "Was that [he named that man]?" Reb Moshe did not respond. "Most probably he came

---

24. *Eruvin* 13b.

to ask for a favor." Again, Reb Moshe did not respond. "And probably," continued Reb Tuvia, "the Rosh Yeshivah agreed to do him that favor." Reb Tuvia assumed correctly that Reb Moshe's silence indicated that his conclusions were correct. "That being the case," said Reb Tuvia, "I must voice my protest for the sake of *kvod haTorah*."

Reb Moshe, however, had a different outlook. He replied, ״יֵשׁ קוֹנֶה עוֹלָמוֹ בְּשָׁעָה אַחַת *(There is one who acquires his portion in the World to Come in a single moment)*.[25] Maybe this is my שָׁעָה (moment)."

In relating this incident, Reb Tuvia said, "Reb Moshe was the *gaon hageonim*, the *posek hador*; he never ceased learning. Yet, he viewed this moment, when he extended kindness to the man who had shown him disrespect, as his שָׁעָה."

With all his efforts at pursuing peace and acting towards his detractors with honor and kindness, Reb Moshe did feel hurt by the shameful attacks against him and his *psakim* at that time. His son Reb David commented, "My father said that he would not have minded if they would have argued against his proofs (through Talmudic debate), but to attack him as they did was inexcusable. He felt that they were not being *ehrlich* (upright)."

To Reb Moshe, being *ehrlich* was paramount. When Rabbi Shmuel Greenberg was a young boy, his father asked Reb Moshe to confer his *berachah* upon him. Reb Moshe's blessing was, *"Du zolst zocheh zein tzu zein an ehrlicher yid (May you merit to be an upright Jew)."*[26]

In his *Emunah U'Vitachon*, the Chazon Ish writes:

> Any deficiency in the nobility of one's soul, specifically with regard to *middos*, will result in a deficiency in his acquiring Torah wisdom, which has its roots in refined character and pleasant disposition …
>
> …One who is bound by the ropes of earthly desire …pursuing the "sweet things" of life, hungry for pleasures, forever angry, full of arrogance — even if his soul is endowed with superior intellectual abilities, even if he has been granted a double portion of insight and understanding, he will never find true success in Torah study. Contemptible *middos* dull a person's mind and desensitize the heart.

---

25. *Avodah Zarah* 10b.

26. Reb Moshe and his son Reb Reuven were once discussing a story that had happened in Luban in which a Jew had made a tragic mistake. Reb Reuven asked his father, "What sort of Jew was he?" Reb Moshe replied, ״אַן אֶמֶתֶע עֶרְלִיכֶע אִיד״ *("A truly 'ehrliche' Jew")*. In relating this, Reb Reuven commented, "To my father, that's what was most important." Mr. Beinish Kaplan commented, "In Tifereth Jerusalem, your self-worth was measured by your dedication to Torah study and *ehrlichkeit*."

They close before him the doors to wisdom and the gates to under-standing.

Conversely, outstanding *middos* make it possible for the student to attain his potential in Torah scholarship.

Small wonder that Reb Moshe achieved a level of Torah greatness that was akin to that of earlier generations.

CHAPTER FOURTEEN

Transcending Nature

Moshe replied …, "The people come to me to seek Hashem"
(Shemos 18:15).

"…the people come to me to seek Hashem," that I should pray
for their sick (Ramban).

OR DECADES, THEY WOULD COME AT ALL HOURS OF THE DAY; IN his final years, when he was plagued by illness and his strength had to be conserved, an appointment had to be made in advance.

An Open Door   Reb Moshe's "agenda" was unlimited. The halachic questions covered the full gamut of *Shulchan Aruch* from awesomely complex questions of life and death, to matters of modern technology for which only someone of his caliber could find applicable precedents and principles in the classic sources, to questions that were so simple that one wondered why they had to be asked at all.

There were other types of petitioners, too. They were of all ages, from all walks of life; men and women, young and old, Ashkenazim and Sefardim, chassidim and *misnagdim.* They sought blessings and prayers regarding anything that was important to a Jew: a *shidduch* for an older child, a baby for a childless couple, a cure for the sick, a livelihood for a breadwinner …

It was a matter of principle to Reb Moshe that he had to be available to anyone who needed him. For many years, he even had a telephone next to his seat in the beis midrash. As he grew older, one of his confidants put a note on Reb Moshe's apartment door giving hours when he could be reached. When Reb Moshe saw it, he removed it, commenting, "If someone comes to me now, he needs me *now*. I have no right to make him wait." Eventually he had to admit that he would have to limit his availability. This time, however, *he* composed the note giving the hours when he could see people. Its text and tone were apologetic, reflecting his sincere regret that troubled and tormented people would be forced to wait for *his* convenience.

He greeted each visitor with that warm smile that made people feel that he was their friend as much as their guiding light. He would listen patiently to each request, sometimes interjecting a question or two. He wanted to understand the situation well, because he cared. When the entire picture had been presented, Reb Moshe would offer his advice or blessing. Often he would include the people in his prayers, especially the sick, either having them in mind during *Shemoneh Esrei* or by reciting *Tehillim* on their behalf. Fortified by the blessing and prayers, the petitioner would take leave of Reb Moshe, his burden eased and his spirits raised.

A WELL-KNOWN *TALMID CHACHAM* ONCE SAT WATCHING AS A LINE OF PETITioners approached Reb Moshe, one by one, seeking his blessing. When the last person had gone, the scholar turned to Reb Moshe and related the following tale:

On Seeking a *Chacham's* Blessing

A woman once requested a blessing from Reb Yisrael, the Maggid of Kozhnitz, for a matter of major importance to her. The Maggid said, "I will grant your request, but only if you give me 100 gold coins to distribute to the poor." The woman pleaded that it was impossible for her to meet such a demand. Yet the Maggid insisted that his condition be met.

Some time later the woman returned to the Maggid and placed a sack containing 80 gold coins before him. "I have gone through much sacrifice to raise this sum," she said. "Please consider it sufficient for my request to be granted."

"I will not," came the firm reply. "I made it clear that you were to return only if you had raised the specific sum. You should not have returned with less than the full amount. You have wasted your time in coming here."

That was enough for the distraught woman. She never dreamt that someone with a reputation for righteousness and benevolence could be so unbending toward someone in need. In her distress, the woman cried out, "I will manage without your blessing! I will rely on the *Ribono shel Olam* alone, and He will help me."

Upon hearing these words, the Maggid's demeanor suddenly changed. Gently he said, "*That* was what I have been waiting to hear. The first time you came to me, I sensed that you were placing your entire trust in me alone. But a Jew must never forget Who is the *real* source of all blessing. A Jew must show his faith in Hashem through prayer and good deeds. That will be a source of merit for him.

"I never wanted your money. I purposely demanded the impossible, in order to force you to change your way of thinking. Now that you realize toward Whom your prime trust should be directed, I offer you my blessings."

Reb Moshe did not dispute the story's message, but he defended those who came to him with their requests. "They are fulfilling a teaching of our Sages that when misfortune strikes, one should ask a *chacham* to seek mercy on his behalf.[1] I am not the *chacham* of whom our Sages speak, but if people think that I am and come to me for this reason, then I must honor their request."

Others, however, could speak of Reb Moshe's powers in more open terms. The Steipler Gaon, Rabbi Yaakov Yisrael Kanievsky, whose blessings effected countless miracles, is reported to have remarked shortly before his own passing, "Reb Moshe has been given the keys to granting blessings in this generation."

He took the matter of conferring *berachos* very seriously. Once, a young man studying in kollel asked Reb Moshe for a *berachah* for success in his learning and *nachas* from his children. Reb Moshe replied, "And what

---

1. *Bava Basra* 116a.

The Steipler Gaon

about *parnasah?*" meaning, why was he not requesting a blessing that he should always be able to provide for his family? The young man replied, "*Baruch Hashem*, I have *parnasah.*"

Reb Moshe was upset with this reply. "Do you think that *parnasah* is guaranteed?" he asked. "A person can have today, and not have tomorrow. One must constantly pray for *parnasah.*"

On another occasion, a young *talmid chacham* asked for a *berachah* that he grow in *yiras Shamayim*. Reb Moshe responded with a blessing for success, good health and other good things, but he made no mention of *yiras Shamayim*. When the man repeated his request a second and then a third time, Reb Moshe responded, "One cannot gain *yiras Shamayim* through a *berachah*. For that, one needs to invest effort."[2]

ONCE, AN EIGHT-YEAR-OLD BOY DEVELOPED A MALIGNANT GROWTH ON HIS leg. Doctors said that the leg had to be amputated — but even then, there

Concern for His Petitioners

was no guarantee that the child's life could be saved. A friend of the family brought the distraught father with his son to the beis midrash of Tifereth Jerusalem, where the man told his story to Reb Moshe. The Rosh Yeshivah broke down in tears. The father, too, wept uncontrollably. After a few minutes, Reb Moshe took the man's hand in both of his and said, "I cried and you cried. The One Above will note our tears and your son will have a *yeshuah* (salvation)." The amputation was performed, and there was no recurrence of the malignancy.

Reb Moshe's concern over a petitioner's troubles did not end when the person left him. Once, a rosh yeshivah called him requesting that he pray for a sick child. A few days went by without Reb Moshe having heard anything new about the child's condition. Then, he and the

---

2. Prayer is a personal effort, and thus on *Shabbos Mevorchim* we ask for a life of *yiras Shamayim*.

At Yeshivah of Staten Island on Motza'ei Yom Kippur with the yeshivah's Mashgiach Ruchani, Rabbi Chaim Mintz

rosh yeshivah happened to meet. Reb Moshe anxiously asked, "How is the child? I have gone around for days without a head!"

Prior to a serious medical test, a talmid asked Reb Moshe for a *berachah*. A week later, Reb Moshe approached the talmid and asked, "How was the test?" "Fine, *baruch Hashem*," the talmid replied, "everything's fine."

Reb Moshe responded, "People come to me with their problems but they forget to come back to tell me the good news that the problems have been resolved." Like this talmid, many did not realize to what extent Reb Moshe was *nosei b'ol* (sharing the burden) as he made their problem his very own and kept it in mind until he heard good news.

Rabbi Shmuel Greenberg related:

> Once, a friend of mine was experiencing a minor health problem. I brought my friend to the Rosh Yeshivah for a *berachah*. The Rosh Yeshivah asked for my friend's Hebrew name. A few months later, I was astounded when the Rosh Yeshivah asked me, "How is Moshe ben Shoshanah feeling?"

During the Yamim Noraim season, hundreds — perhaps thousands — would seek Reb Moshe's *berachah*. Joining the scores of others requesting a *berachah* on Erev Yom Kippur was a talmid who had experienced a particularly difficult year. When his turn came he said to Reb Moshe, "Please give me a *berachah* that the coming year should be one of *menuchas hanefesh* (peace of mind)." The following year on Erev Yom Kippur, Reb Moshe asked this talmid, "So, was the past year one of *menuchas hanefesh*?"

Left to right: Reb Yaakov Kamenetsky, Reb Yaakov Yitzchak Ruderman, Reb Moshe, Reb Chaskel Besser

It happened that the phone in Reb Moshe's bedroom rang at 3 a.m. The caller was a former talmid whose newborn was experiencing life-threatening complications. Doctors had all but given up hope for the infant. The father asked Reb Moshe to pray for his son's recovery.

Two days later the young man held in his hands a special-delivery letter from Reb Moshe, written only hours after the phone call of that fateful morning. In it, Reb Moshe assured the worried parents that their baby would get well. Sure enough, the baby recovered.

In relating this incident, the late Rabbi Chaskel Besser commented, "Reb Moshe always viewed a problem from *every* possible angle. All the parents sought was salvation for their baby, but Reb Moshe also sought salvation for the parents by giving them peace of mind."

REBBETZIN FEINSTEIN RECALLED HER HUSBAND'S ELATION UPON HEARING that someone for whom his blessing had been sought had seen the wish **Overjoyed** fulfilled. She quickly added that never did Reb Moshe take credit for whatever had occurred. He was ecstatic only that another Jew's life had become happier.

One summer toward the end of his life, the phone rang in the bunga-low of his son, Reb Reuven. The caller's wife was soon to give birth; her previous pregnancies had not ended well. He was asking for the Rosh Yeshivah's *berachah* that this time all should go well. Rebbetzin Shelia Feinstein brought the phone next door and Reb Moshe con-ferred his *berachah*.

The next morning, Reb Moshe remarked, "I wonder what's doing with the couple who called last night." Moments later the phone rang. The woman had given birth to a healthy baby girl. Reb Moshe was overjoyed.

One morning, Rabbi Elimelech Bluth heard Reb Moshe muttering; "Six months … a miracle … ?" Rabbi Bluth asked if the Rosh Yeshivah would explain the significance of these words, and he did:

Six months *earlier*, a childless couple had come to him for a blessing. As always, he had complied with their request, but in a somewhat strange fashion. "May you inform me in six months' time of happy tidings," he said. Now, six months later, the couple had called Reb Moshe with the news that they were going to have a baby, and expressed their apprecia-tion for the "miracle he had brought about."

Reb Moshe summed up his feeling on the matter: "A miracle or not a miracle — what is the difference? As long as there are *simchos* among Jews!"

ON A VISIT TO ERETZ YISRAEL, RABBI SIMCHA BUNIM COHEN WENT TO SEE Rabbi Shlomo Zalman Auerbach. Rebbetzin Auerbach came to the door

A Humble Explanation and said that her husband was resting and was unavail-able. However, when she heard that her visitor had brought regards from Rav Moshe Feinstein, she told him to wait. She returned moments later and invited Rabbi Cohen to come inside. She said, "The Rav is in bed writing and he did not want to be disturbed. But when he heard Rav Feinstein's name, he said that you should come in."

Rabbi Cohen entered Reb Shlomo Zalman's bedroom and relayed Reb Moshe's message. Reb Shlomo Zalman asked, "So what is new by Reb Moshe?" Rabbi Cohen told him that Reb Moshe had recently written a *teshuvah* explaining why he is obligated to confer *berachos* upon those who request them of him.[3]

---

3. *Igros Moshe, Yoreh De'ah* IV, #51.

There, Reb Moshe writes that a simple Jew who is asked to pray for his fellow is obligated to do so, for "it is possible that for whatever reason, Hashem will hearken to this man's *tefillah* or *berachah*. For Hashem knows and remembers one's every deed and thought, and perhaps this person has some *zechus* because of which his *tefillah* will be accepted." Regarding himself, Reb Moshe cites the teaching that when someone is ill, his family should ask a *chacham* (Torah scholar) to seek Hashem's mercy on his behalf. Reb Moshe concludes that though he himself is not the *"chacham"* of whom the Gemara speaks, nevertheless, since his petitioners view him as that *chacham* and therefore come to him, Hashem will accept his prayers on their behalf in the merit of their faith in the words of *Chazal*.

Hearing these words, Reb Shlomo Zalman responded, "My rebbi, Reb Isser Zalman [Meltzer], had the same humble explanation as to why he conferred *berachos* on those who requested it."

MANY STORIES ABOUT REB MOSHE INDICATE CLEARLY THAT HE HAD WHAT CAN only be described as *ruach hakodesh*, the ability to see beyond what was visible.

Divine Insight

In the summer of 1970, Arab terrorists hijacked three TWA jets, forcing the pilots to land in the Jordanian desert, where the passengers were held hostage for some time. Among the hostages were Rabbi Yitzchak Hutner, Rosh Yeshivah of Mesivta Rabbi Chaim Berlin and one of *Klal Yisrael's* leading Torah figures, and his family. While Jewry prayed for the safe release of *all* the prisoners, there was special concern for the fate of Rav Hutner, to whom so many turned for teaching and inspiration, and whose advanced age made prolonged captivity especially dangerous.

During the many days that the hostages were held, there was a heat wave in New York. Reb Moshe remarked to his talmid, Rabbi Yosef Brick, that Hashem had brought the intense heat upon them so that they should feel the suffering of the hostages.

One afternoon, Reb Moshe entered the beis midrash of Mesivtha Tifereth Jerusalem in a jovial mood. "So, Rav Hutner has been released!" he smilingly told someone. The person, looking somewhat confused, informed Reb Moshe that the news reports had made no mention of the hostages' release.

That night it was learned that the crisis had indeed ended with the safe release of all hostages.

Dancing with Rabbi Yitzchak Hutner at a wedding

The sequel to this episode demonstrates the *middah* of *nosei b'ol* (sharing another's burden) which certainly was a factor in Reb Moshe's meriting Divine insight. Roshei Yeshivah instructed their yeshivos to charter buses so that senior talmidim could join them at Kennedy Airport to greet Rav Hutner upon his arrival from Jordan. The scene was a joyous one, and to add to everyone's rejoicing, a group of Orthodox musicians had come on their own to play lively music in honor of Rav Hutner's deliverance from captivity.

Reb Moshe approached the band leader and told him not to play any music. "Six captives have still not been released," he said. "We cannot rejoice until everyone is freed."[4]

---

4. The very next morning, Rav Hutner phoned Rabbi Moshe Sherer to say that he was "tormented" by the fact that six hostages were still being held captive. Even after the six were freed, neither he nor Reb Moshe rested until they were home with their families. The renowned Sefardic *chachamim* Rabbi Yosef and Rabbi Avraham Harari-Raful were among them, and were scheduled to land at Kennedy Airport late in the afternoon of Erev Rosh Hashanah. Rabbi Sherer contacted Reb Moshe to ask exactly until what time they could be driven home. Police drove the brothers through traffic and they arrived home well before candle-lighting time. Only then did Reb Moshe, Rav Hutner and Rabbi Sherer breathe a sigh of relief. (See the biography of Rabbi Sherer, published by ArtScroll/Mesorah, pp. 393-397.)

Dancing with Rabbi Shneur Kotler and Rabbi Gedaliah Schorr (his back to the camera) at a wedding

When Rabbi Shneur Kotler, revered Rosh Yeshivah of Beth Medrash Govoha, lay stricken with the illness that would eventually take his life, Reb Moshe prayed for him constantly, never forgetting to have his private *minyan* recite the *Mi shebeirach* prayer on his behalf. Reb Moshe, who was then confined to his home because of his own poor physical state, would frequently ask his family to inquire as to Reb Shneur's current condition.

When Reb Shneur passed away on Thursday, 3 Tammuz, 5742 (1982), it was decided not to inform Reb Moshe, lest his own health be affected adversely. At the Torah reading on the following Shabbos, Reb Moshe made no request that a *Mi shebeirach* be said. In fact, he never again asked about Reb Shneur's condition. When he happened to glance at a Yiddish newspaper which had been left lying in his apartment, Reb Moshe's face registered no shock or even faint surprise at the headlines telling of Reb Shneur's huge funeral.

A BUSINESSMAN CLOSE TO REB MOSHE WOULD OFTEN SEEK HIS GUIDANCE ON business-related matters. Once, he informed Reb Moshe that he was

Sensing a Lack of Jewishness
being pressured to terminate his dealings with a certain individual who had harmed other dealers in their industry. He had not encountered any problem doing business with this man, and on the surface did not see a reason to bow to pressure.

Reb Moshe asked him, "Is the man Jewish?" "I believe so," the man replied. "He presents himself as a Jew and I have no reason to think he is lying." During the course of their conversation, Reb Moshe asked a number of times whether he was certain that the man was Jewish.

A short while later, the man discovered that this individual was, in fact, a German gentile who had been masquerading as a Jew.

In another incident, Reb Moshe insisted that his determination of someone's lack of Jewishness had nothing to do with *ruach hakodesh*.

One day, a man rushed into the beis midrash of Tifereth Jerusalem and told Reb Moshe that a Jewish *bachur* had just been hit by a car in front of the yeshivah. Reb Moshe replied, "Don't refer to him as a 'Jewish *bachur*' — he's not Jewish."

The bearer of the tidings was dumbfounded. "But Rosh Yeshivah, I just saw his yarmulka lying next to him in the street." Reb Moshe repeated that the boy was not Jewish.

Soon the facts emerged. The teenager was a non-Jew who had been harassing a Jewish boy. The Jewish boy ran away and the teenager gave chase. The victim's yarmulka fell off as he ran and he was afraid to stop to pick it up. The teenager was hit by the car just where the yarmulka had fallen off.

When Reb Moshe was asked how he knew that the teenager was not Jewish, he is reported to have said, "I was studying Torah in the yeshivah at the time. It is inconceivable that this could have happened to a Jewish child right outside."

Reb Moshe was exceedingly humble, but he could not deny the protective power of Torah.[5]

Lest one think that the above story indicates a lack of concern for the accident victim because he was not Jewish, the following story refutes this:

As a talmid of Reb Moshe, Dr. Melvin Zelefsky would visit him to discuss the halachic ramifications of new advances in the field of medicine. Once, when Dr. Zelefsky came to the yeshivah to discuss a new breakthrough in cardiac surgery, Reb Moshe told him, "I have at home a *teshuvah* on this topic that I have recently completed. Come home with me; I will give you the *teshuvah* so that you can make a copy for yourself."

They arrived at the high-rise apartment complex where Reb Moshe resided and approached the elevators in the main lobby. Dr. Zelefsky

---

5. See *Makkos* 10a regarding the protective powers of Torah. The Gemara (ibid 11a) also relates that a man was devoured by a lion 3 *parsah* (roughly 8 miles) from R' Yehoshua ben Levi, and as a result Eliyahu HaNavi did not reveal himself to R' Yehoshua for 3 days. R' Yehoshua was held accountable for the occurrence of such a tragedy in his vicinity.

On a fund-raising trip, Reb Moshe made time to study Torah with his host's son

pressed the "up" button. The elevator arrived and its doors opened, but Reb Moshe made no move to enter. The doors closed and the elevator began its ascent without them. Bewildered, Dr. Zelefsky pressed the button again. However, when the elevator arrived, Reb Moshe again did not enter. Instead, he gestured toward a little girl at the other end of the lobby who did not appear to be Jewish. The girl, who was alone, was playing with a toy. Reb Moshe said, "She is too young to be left alone without supervision. I don't want to leave until the person responsible for her appears."

A few minutes later, the door of the building's rental office opened. A woman who obviously was the little girl's mother appeared and took hold of her hand. Then Reb Moshe entered the elevator, remarking to Dr. Zelefsky, "*A klein kind darf hoben shemirah* (a young child requires supervision)."

RABBI YISROEL BELSKY RELATED TWO INCIDENTS INVOLVING REB MOSHE THAT to his mind indicate special *siyata diShmaya* (Divine assistance) for some-

Siyata DiShmaya

one whose every word, deed, and thought were for the sake of Heaven.

Rabbi Belsky attended a function for the benefit of Tifereth Jerusalem. When Reb Moshe entered the room, he noticed Rabbi

Belsky, took him by the hand, led him to a table reserved for rabbanim, and indicated which seat he should take. During the course of the evening, Rabbi Belsky made the acquaintance of the rav sitting next to him, whom he had never met before.

A few days later, Rabbi Belsky received a phone call from a talmid. The young man's mother, a divorcee, was seeking to remarry, and someone had suggested a rav who also was seeking to remarry. Would Rabbi Belsky by any chance know this rav well enough to provide information about him? This rav was none other than the one who had sat next to him on that evening! Rabbi Belsky provided very positive information, and the two married.

On another occasion, Rabbi Belsky inquired of Reb Moshe concerning an obscure halachah related to the laws of marriage. Reb Moshe stated his opinion and then repeated a couple of times for emphasis, "And this is how I rule in all such situations."

A few months later, Rabbi Belsky attended a wedding in the Midwest, and this question arose before the *chuppah*. None of the rabbanim present were sure how to proceed — until Rabbi Belsky repeated the *psak* that Reb Moshe had stated with such conviction.

Shidduchim and Marriage

ONCE, THE DAUGHTER OF SOMEONE CLOSE TO REB MOSHE BECAME engaged to a boy from a distinguished family. The *kallah's* family was troubled when the *chasan's* parents informed them that they had very little money to contribute toward the wedding expenses. The *kallah's* family were people of modest means and even paying their share of the expenses was not easy.

When they consulted Reb Moshe he said, "This time you will pay, later they will pay. Hashem will help you."

Through wondrous ways, the *kallah's* parents found the means to pay for the wedding without having to borrow money. A few years later, the *chasan's* parents surprised their *mechutanim* by purchasing a home for the young couple.

When Rabbi Yisrael H. Eidelman was first asked by Reb Moshe to serve as the *baal tefillah* for Yomim Nora'im at Yeshivah of Staten Island, he politely declined on the grounds that he was a *bachur* (and *Shulchan Aruch* states that preferably the *baal tefillah* for Yomim Nora'im should be married). Reb Moshe accepted this response, and someone else served as *baal tefillah*. The following year, Reb Moshe made the same request of Rabbi Eidelman and received the same response. This time, however,

With Rabbi Lipa Eidelman, father of Rabbi Yisrael H. Eidelman and a rosh yeshivah at Mesivtha Tifereth Jerusalem. With them are (left to right): Rabbi Mordechai Tendler, Rabbi Shloime Frankel, Rabbi Elimelech Bluth

Reb Moshe responded, "In the coming year, you will be married." Rav Eidelman served as *baal tefillah* and was married a few months later.

Rabbi Michel Shurkin recalled:

> At *sheva berachos* celebrations, we sometimes saw open Divine insight. On one occasion, Reb Moshe did not know the *chasan* personally. Much of his *derashah* was devoted to the destructiveness and shamefulness of anger. The *chasan's* friends knew that he possessed this negative trait, and Reb Moshe's words were perfectly suited to him.
>
> Another time, the *chasan* was a very unsuccessful fellow. Those who knew him doubted whether he would be able to support a family. Reb Moshe offered an abundance of blessings for his material success in life, and he became wealthy.[6]

On one occasion, a childless couple asked for Reb Moshe's blessing. To their surprise, he asked if they had ever given a gift to their *shadchan* (matchmaker). They had not. He told them that they were halachically

---

6. From *Meged Givos Olam*.

required to do so and they should attend to it without delay. Within a year they had their first child.

❦ ❦ ❦

It was common for yeshivah students to seek his blessing that they find their proper mate. One very diligent student was concerned that the mental and physical stress of *shidduchim* would hamper his learning; however, he made no mention of this when seeking Reb Moshe's blessing. He was therefore quite amazed when Reb Moshe concluded his blessing with, " ...and may your quest cause only minimal loss to your Torah study."

When this same young man was married and his wife was expecting their first child, he again requested Reb Moshe's blessing. After conferring his usual good wishes for mother and child, Reb Moshe added cryptically, "At times, complications arise at childbirth; one need not be alarmed by this." Sure enough, as the pangs of childbirth set in, doctors detected a problem that posed a danger to the child — but concern soon gave way to joy as a healthy baby was born.

Another student was debating whether or not he was ready for marriage. While he mulled the matter over in his mind, he was certain of one thing: It was not too early to receive Reb Moshe's blessing that all go well whenever he would seek a *shidduch*. Again, the petitioner made no mention to Reb Moshe of his personal considerations; all he asked for was a blessing. Reb Moshe said, "May Hashem help you find ... and you should begin the search now!"

IN NEFESH HACHAIM, RABBI CHAIM OF VOLOZHIN WRITES:

Nature Will Be His
A person who accepts upon himself the yoke of Torah for its own sake (Torah lishmah) will be raised above everything in this world. Hashem will watch over him with a Providence that will transcend the laws of nature ... for he is attached to the Torah and to Hashem, as it were ... The laws of nature will be placed in his power, according to what he will decree upon them ...[7]

---

7. *Nefesh HaChaim* 4:18.

Rabbi Heshy Jacob was very close to Reb Moshe and often had *shalosh seudos* with him in his apartment. Once Rabbi Jacob's six-year-old son was hit in the *eye* by a thrown rock and suffered a cut cornea. The eye was quite bloodshot, and the ophthalmologist said the wound would take about a month to heal. The next Shabbos, Rabbi Jacob took his son to Reb Moshe's apartment for *Minchah* and *shalosh seudos*. Reb Moshe noticed the *eye* and asked what had happened. Seeing Reb Moshe's anguish, Rabbi Jacob regretted having brought the child, but it was too late. He told Reb Moshe the story. Reb Moshe held the boy's face between his hands and stared into his eyes without saying a word. By the following Shabbos the eye was completely healed. The ophthalmologist said that in his 30 years of practice he had never seen such a recovery.

A woman was experiencing serious complications in the early stages of pregnancy. There was uncertainty whether or not the baby was alive. When her husband asked Reb Moshe for a *berachah*, he said that he would offer a *tefillah al tenai* (conditional prayer), on the assumption that the baby was alive.[8] Reb Moshe expressed the hope that "she should carry well and with ease, the child should be well, and her delivery should go well ..." Reb Moshe repeated this prayer *four times*.

Almost immediately the complications disappeared and it became apparent that the pregnancy was viable. The remaining months went smoothly, but at the time of birth, there were major complications. The birth ended joyfully, with a healthy mother and child. The doctor said that in all his years of practice, he had never seen a labor with such severe complications end successfully.

Rabbi Peretz Steinberg was visiting Reb Moshe on Purim when the phone rang. The caller was scheduled to undergo chest surgery and was requesting a *berachah* that all should go well. Reb Moshe responded, "Do

---

8. The Gemara states that a prayer to change an established fact is a prayer in vain and should not be said (see *Bava Metzia* 41a).

not have the surgery without first consulting *'der frummer doctor'* (the religious doctor)."

The caller was baffled. "Who is *'der frummer doctor'*? I have one doctor, he is not *frum*, and he said that I *must* have this surgery!"

"First *see der frummer doctor*," Reb Moshe repeated.

Rabbi Dovid Twersky, the late Skverer Rebbe of Boro Park, was well versed in medical matters and well connected to top doctors in their respective fields. When this patient called to relate his conversation with Reb Moshe, Rabbi Twersky said, "That hospital does have a *frum* doctor in this department and he recently received an award for outstanding performance. I will arrange an appointment for you."

The doctor studied the man's test results and determined that he was not in need of surgery.

❧ ❧ ❧

When a mother of four in the Midwest went into labor, her husband called Reb Moshe for a blessing. The woman's family was from the East Side, and had a close personal relationship with Reb Moshe. Whenever there was a family celebration or crisis, they would share the news with him. In response to the present call, Reb Moshe said, "Your wife will have a complete recovery and the four children will be well." The father responded that he wanted a blessing for the fifth child — the newborn. Reb Moshe repeated himself, "Your wife will have a complete recovery and the four children will be well." But he added, "Whatever Hashem does is for the best, and you and your wife should accept it."

When the father came to the hospital and saw his new baby, he noticed that the infant was breathing heavily. The doctor said it was normal, but the condition worsened. Reb Moshe was called again and once more he would not give a blessing for the new baby, but urged the father to strengthen his wife and encourage her to have faith that whatever Hashem wills is for the best. The baby died soon after.

Only a few months later, the same woman began having severe headaches. She underwent tests to find the cause of the malady, and her family doctor told her there was nothing to worry about; the condition would correct itself within a week or two.

A few days later, shortly after *Havdalah,* the phone rang. The husband answered; it was the doctor. "Is your wife listening?" he asked. After being assured that she was not on the line, the doctor said that she had a brain tumor, but that he had not wanted to tell them until he had made arrangements for a hospital bed and the best surgeon in the area. She was to enter the hospital on Monday and the operation was scheduled for Tuesday.

But she *had* been listening to the conversation and, not surprisingly, was frozen with fear. Again they called Reb Moshe. The Rebbetzin said that he was at a fund-raising *melaveh malkah* for Tifereth Jerusalem, but would call back as soon as he got home. The call came after midnight, and Reb Moshe assured husband and wife that the operation would be a complete success and she would be perfectly healthy again.

Their spirits were as high as could be expected, until Monday. The surgeon told the husband, "The tumor is accessible and operable. I can remove it completely, but I have to cut through tissue and your wife will be paralyzed permanently on her left side." Again they went to the telephone to consult Reb Moshe. He laughed and told the caller to ignore the doctor; his wife would have a complete recovery.

The operation was performed and, when the surgeon came to the waiting room to report to the husband, he said, "The operation was a success and there is no paralysis. It is a phenomenon."

A local rabbi who also served as the hospital chaplain was with the husband. He exclaimed, "Why do you call it a phenomenon? Why can't you admit it was a miracle?"

Sullenly, the doctor said, "That's what I meant. There is no medical explanation for it."

> Rabbi Elimelech Bluth was present when a woman came to Reb Moshe with a request. She was childless after many years of marriage and had suffered through a long succession of traumatic occurrences related to her problem. Her husband had come to Reb Moshe each year for the blessing that he hoped would finally bring the longed-for child; so far, this hope had not been fulfilled. Now, she desired something more than a blessing.
>
> "I want the Rosh Yeshivah to decree that Heaven grant me a child," she said amid sobs.
>
> Reb Moshe was taken aback by the woman's request. "I should decree ...? What power have I to do such things ?"
>
> "Yes, the Rosh Yeshivah can decree ... he can ..."
>
> Her incessant weeping became so intense that at one point Rabbi Bluth took the initiative in trying to comfort her. Reb Moshe, however, stopped him. "No, no ... it is good, it is good," was all he said. His intention may have been, simply, that crying can unburden a person of the anguish building up inside, or, as Rabbi Bluth suggests, that

*Eli Stern,
Rabbi
Elimelech
Bluth,
Reb Moshe,
Pesach
Broyde*

the bitter tears of a righteous Jewish woman can help bring about her own salvation by arousing Divine mercy on her behalf.

Finally, as the woman continued crying, Reb Moshe said, "I cannot decree, but I will say this. In the merit of your faith in the power of Torah scholars — for this, you *deserve* a child."

Reb Moshe's words calmed his broken-hearted petitioner; her pure faith, which Reb Moshe had found so praiseworthy, told her that with the Rosh Yeshivah's utterance, her wish had been granted. However, she was not yet finished.

"Rebbi — when?" she persisted.

Reb Moshe was not disturbed by the question. He thought and began counting off the Hebrew months on his fingers. The ninth month was Kislev, the month of Chanukah. "It can't be before Chanukah," he said. "Right after Chanukah."

On the last day of Chanukah, her child was born.

A young woman, stricken with a debilitating disease, had received frightening news from her doctor. She was expectant and, according to her doctor, because of her illness neither she nor her child would survive a full-term pregnancy. The doctor insisted that drastic measures be taken to save her life.

The woman's husband consulted a prominent chassidic rav, seeking his guidance. "This is not a question for me," the rav replied honestly. "This is a question for Reb Moshe."

The couple soon found themselves in the dining room of Reb Moshe's small apartment. The aged sage gently asked the woman to repeat exactly what the doctor had said. He questioned her on a number of points to make certain that he understood the facts clearly. Then he stated his opinion.

"Do not be frightened by what the doctor said. You are going to give birth to a healthy child, and in fact, your own condition will improve. There is nothing to fear."

A few months later, Reb Moshe's prediction came true.

The story, however, did not end there. One Erev Shabbos a year after the baby's birth, the phone rang in the kitchen of the woman's home.

"Hello, this is Moshe Feinstein calling. How are you feeling? Good, very good ... and how is your baby? ... *Baruch Hashem*. Today is your baby's birthday — may Hashem bless your entire family with good health and success!"

IN TRUTH, MANY OF REB MOSHE'S "MIRACLES" WERE INTERTWINED WITH strands of his compassion, loving-kindness, and other outstanding traits.

Source of Miracles This is not merely coincidental, as someone remarked after hearing the following two incidents:

A young man had taken a vocational course after spending several years in a kollel, but for many months had been unable to find a job. His concerned mother was granted an appointment with Reb Moshe so that she could request a blessing for her son. Reb Moshe assured the worried mother that her son would find a means of livelihood. A few days later, the young man was called for an interview by someone who had rejected his application some months earlier; this time, he was hired. The story, though, did not end there.

Some time later, the above story was repeated to a prominent senior rosh yeshivah, who exclaimed in amazement, "Now I understand!" He explained that the young man's employer was his former talmid; the mother of the young man had once implored him to call the employer on behalf of her son. He tried a few times but had been unable to get through for one reason or another, and eventually forgot about it. Then, one night, he dreamt that Reb Moshe was asking him to speak to this same person on behalf of the unemployed young man. He made the call the next day and the former talmid promised to cooperate.

The dates were checked. The dream had come on the night of Reb Moshe's blessing.

The second story is not a miraculous one — or perhaps it is, if we have a true appreciation of Reb Moshe's greatness.

Years ago, Reb Moshe would have *shalosh seudos* and recite *Tehillim* in his yeshivah every Shabbos afternoon. One Shabbos, as he was reciting *Tehillim,* a special-needs child stood watching him. The boy went over and turned Reb Moshe's *Tehillim* on an angle to the right, and Reb Moshe continued reciting. Then the boy turned the *Tehillim* to the left and Reb Moshe continued reciting. The boy took the *Tehillim* and turned it completely around and Reb Moshe continued reciting. Not satisfied, the boy turned the page, but Reb Moshe was still not disturbed.

A man sitting nearby had watched all this and, although people went out of their way to be patient with the boy, the man had seen what he felt was too much. He snapped, "Stop it already. Let the Rosh Yeshivah *daven!*"

Reb Moshe turned to the man and said, "He is only playing with me. I *enjoy* it when he plays with me. I love him like my own child!" With that, Reb Moshe embraced the boy and kissed him.

Said one person after hearing the above two stories, "Stories like the first one could happen because stories like the second one happened."

Reb Moshe himself once said as much, though in an opposite sense, when someone came to him with a bizarre story. A stranger claiming kabbalistic powers had frightened someone terribly by accosting him suddenly and announcing that it had been revealed to him that one of the man's close relatives was deathly ill. The stranger told the man that his relative's illness would soon become apparent unless the family followed an order of prayer and repentance that he would prescribe.

The man had accepted all the stranger had said as fact.

However, he asked someone close to Reb Moshe to relate the story to the Rosh Yeshivah, and ask if any additional repentance was necessary. After hearing the story, Reb Moshe was visibly upset. He said, "The man has nothing to worry about. The stranger's telling of his 'revelation' in a manner that frightened the poor man so shows a total lack of sensitivity on his part. He is lacking in *middos*, and Hashem does not communicate with someone lacking in *middos*. He did not have a revelation."

If *middos* and Divine inspiration are so intertwined, then it is no wonder that Reb Moshe was among the very few in his generation to whom the hidden was revealed.

CHAPTER FIFTEEN

The Final Years

I N THE FINAL YEARS OF HIS LONG LIFE, REB MOSHE SUFFERED from a number of physical ailments. Until his very last day, he strained to carry on his holy mission in this world with every ounce of his waning strength.

Spiritual Nobles A number of years before his passing, at *shalosh seudos* in Tifereth Jerusalem, Reb Moshe posed a question: In *Tehillim*, Dovid HaMelech cautions us, "Do not rely on nobles, on a human being, for he holds no salvation."[1] Is this not obvious? Was it necessary for Dovid HaMelech to caution a believing Jew not to place his trust in men of power, who can lose that power as quickly as they attain it?

Reb Moshe answered that the term נְדִיבִים, *nobles,* in this verse does not refer to men of material wealth or political clout. It refers to "spiritual nobles," the Torah leaders of each generation. When issues arise, whether halachic or otherwise, requiring extensive Torah knowledge, it is natural to rely on Torah leaders to resolve the matter. Reb Moshe declared that each person has a responsibility to become very knowledgeable in Torah so that he need not always depend on others.

---

1. *Tehillim* 146:3.

Reb Moshe's response to the young man who wanted to donate a year of his life to him

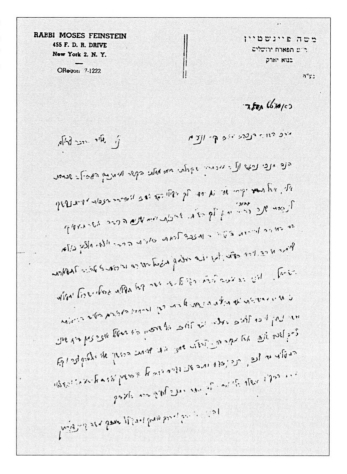

Rabbi Shlomo Avigdor Altusky was among the participants at that *shalosh seudos*. He recalls the feeling everyone had that Reb Moshe was speaking of the generation's dependency on himself. At that time, Reb Moshe was in his early 80s and showing no signs of slowing down. He was as accessible as ever.

However, not long after, he began to experience heart problems and other health issues. He became less accessible, though he still was the *gadol hador*. One could always be sure that an important question could be brought to Reb Moshe for immediate resolution.

AFTER REB MOSHE TOOK ILL IN 5738 (1978), HE RECEIVED A LETTER FROM A *BEN Torah* who wrote that he was donating one year of his life in the hope that

Precious Letters

in this merit Reb Moshe's life would be extended. Reb Moshe responded:

I was tremendously moved by your letter, which I received during the days of my difficult illness, regarding the sacrifice of which

*you wrote. However, know, my precious one, you will not lose even
a moment of life; to the contrary, in the merit of your mesiras nefesh
to donate a year for my sake, Hashem Yisborach will grant you many
years of good health in which to toil in Torah …*

A few days after Succos 5740 (1979), Reb Moshe penned a letter to an
old friend from Russia, Rabbi Nochum Trebnik, a rav in Kfar Chabad.[2] In
it he writes:

*Because of my weak state of health, ר״ל, I did not write [letters] on
the eve of this new year, as I usually do … Because of this, I also did
not send the check to his honor's home … I am greatly distressed
over this, but I am certain that his honor, my friend, will forgive me.*

A HEART AILMENT, WHICH NECESSITATED THE IMPLANTING OF A PACEMAKER,
forced him to curtail the heavy schedule of public appearances that had

Fighting Infirmity

been part of his life for decades. However, this condition did
not prevent him from rising at dawn to study Torah as he
always had, nor did it prevent him from continuing to rule
on matters of Halachah, and publish *sefarim* on both Talmud and
Halachah.

---

2. He was the brother of the *gaon* Rabbi Shimon Trebnik, *Hy"d,* a childhood friend of Reb
Moshe. More than a dozen *teshuvos* to Reb Shimon are found in *Igros Moshe,* as well as
one to Reb Nochum.

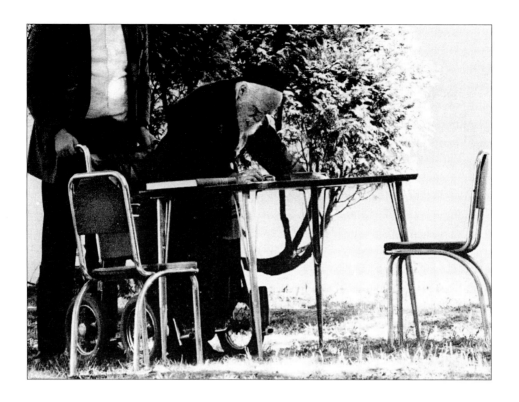

In 1981, in his preface to the sixth volume of *Igros Moshe,* Reb Moshe writes:

> I have already reached, through the kindness of Hashem and His infinite mercy, into my 80s ... He continues to grant me the strength to clarify the Halachah properly, with knowledge and understanding, as in my earlier years ...

Around that time, Reb Moshe suffered sciatica attacks. A neighborhood boy who often attended him once initiated a discussion in learning, only to realize that Reb Moshe was in agony. "Please forgive me!" the boy said. "I will ask the Rosh Yeshivah another time ... " "No!" Reb Moshe insisted. "We can continue talking now. *'For they* (i.e. the words of Torah) *are our life and the length of our days'* — this is what I live for ... "

When Eretz Yisrael's Torah community was again facing the threat of *giyus banos* (forced conscription of girls), the renowned *posek* Rabbi Moshe Sternbuch arrived in America to convene a meeting of rabbanim and *askanim* (activists). He was granted a private appointment with Reb Moshe but was told that for the past year, poor health had prevented the Rosh Yeshivah from attending meetings. Rav Sternbuch requested only that Reb Moshe write a letter for the cause. However, Reb Moshe responded, "I consider myself ill when my own needs are concerned, not when the community's needs are concerned." He attended the meeting and succeeded in galvanizing others to action.

One day his talmid Rabbi Michel Shurkin came to visit.

"How is the Rosh Yeshivah?" Rabbi Shurkin asked.

"Not good, not good," replied Reb Moshe. "The doctors have ordered me to sleep one more hour each night. What will become of me? I will remain a complete *am ha'aretz* (ignoramus)!"[3]

> Those who were privileged to take part in the *minyan* in his apartment during periods of illness could see clearly how he ignored pain and infirmity during *tefillah*. In the midst of excruciatingly painful sciatica attacks, when standing was agonizing for him and he needed assistance to rise from his chair, he insisted on standing for *Baruch She'amar* and then, a few minutes later, getting up again for *Mizmor L'Sodah* and of course for *Shemoneh Esrei*. He would stand again for *Modim D'Rabbanan*. Despite the pain in his back, he maintained his usual practice of bowing very deeply during *Shemoneh Esrei*. During that time, someone once observed how Reb Moshe's knees buckled from pain as he was reciting *Shemoneh Esrei*. As he began to fall forward, his hands pressed against a wall, helping him regain his balance, and he continued *davening*.

As Purim approached that year, Reb Moshe was still in great pain. Those close to him assumed that a *minyan* would be convened in his home for the *Megillah* reading. However, Reb Moshe insisted on *davening* in Tifereth Jerusalem in order to proclaim the miracle [פָּרְסוּמֵי נִיסָא] in the presence of a large multitude. The Rebbetzin pleaded with him not to exert himself. He compromised by having a *minyan* in his apartment in the evening, but going to the yeshivah in the morning.

When he spent Yom Kippur at the Yeshivah of Staten Island, he was implored, for the sake of his health, not to fall to the floor and bow, as is customary during the *Mussaf* prayer. Reb Moshe, however, could not be dissuaded. He explained that to be in shul and not kneel with the rest of the congregation was a *chillul Hashem*.

The last two years of his life, his failing health forced him to spend Yom Kippur at home, where a *minyan* was convened. His close ones appealed to him not to bow, and he agreed to step out of the room at that part of

---

3. From *Meged Givos Olam*.

Learning in his final years with the aid of two lamps and a magnifying glass

the service. When the time came to bow, however, someone peeked into the hallway — and there was Reb Moshe, bowing along with the *minyan*.

His failing vision caused him to fall behind in his study of *Daf Yomi*. Yet, he continued to press on as he strove to complete *Shas* for yet another time. He was observed engrossed in *Masechta Bechoros* (using a magnifying glass), studying not only the basic text, but all the emendations of *Bach* and *Shitah Mekubetzes* in very small print on the side of the *gemara*! It was a source of satisfaction to him that he eventually did complete the cycle of *Daf Yomi*, though he did not complete it in time for the world-wide *siyum* celebration in the fall of 1983.

HE SOUGHT TO HELP OTHERS AS MUCH AS HIS STRENGTH ALLOWED. HE WOULD obtain the phone numbers of some of the many sick people for whom he

Helping Others was asked to pray, speak with them for a while, and wish them well. On Friday nights, he would knock on the door of a widow living on his floor to wish her "*Gut Shabbos.*" And, of course, he continued to advise both individuals and organizations on matters affecting them.

One hot, humid summer day, a neighbor was asked to try to repair a broken air conditioner in Reb Moshe's apartment. When the neighbor arrived, he found Reb Moshe sweltering in the heat as he recited *Tehillim* for a sick woman.

During this period, Rabbi Yisrael Eidelman went to Reb Moshe's apartment to ask that he write a letter to a wealthy individual, requesting a donation for the yeshivah. It took quite some time for Reb Moshe to complete the letter. When he finished, he said, "I must rewrite the letter. I did not inquire as to his wife's well-being. She is a great *baalas chesed* [and it would be wrong not to inquire about her] ... " And he rewrote the entire letter.

During this very difficult period of his life, his grandson, Rabbi Mordechai Tendler, assumed even greater responsibility for assisting and protecting Reb Moshe. There was regular tension between Reb Moshe's sense of responsibility to be available and the opposing need to conserve his strength, protect his health, and differentiate between those who genuinely *needed* him and those who wanted simply to be near him. Most of the time, the buffer, protector, and screener was Reb Mordechai.

IN RECALLING THOSE FINAL, DIFFICULT YEARS, RABBI EPHRAIM GREENBLATT wrote:

Talmidim Remember During that period, the Rosh Yeshivah suffered from difficult, painful afflictions, yet whenever I inquired as to his state of health, he would respond: "Not bad; one should never refer to the workings of Hashem as 'bad,' *chas v'shalom*. I just have pain every now and then."

Despite his extreme weakness, he prevailed over his situation and demonstrated his spiritual greatness. He strove to continue with his fixed learning sessions, though he had to refrain from delivering *shiurim* ... He told me that he would not take pain-killers because they would weaken his power of concentration and his ability to learn. It was through such perseverance that he attained *shleimus* (spiritual perfection).[4]

Rabbi Eliyahu Dovid Kaufman, a great-nephew of Reb Moshe and a talmid, was among those who attended Reb Moshe in his final years. He recalled:

After the Rosh Yeshivah's heart problems began, he returned to yeshivah to deliver his *shiur*. He did not look well, and when he began to speak he was noticeably weak. But as the *shiur* progressed, the color returned to his face and he was his former vibrant self. It

---

4. *She'eilos U'Teshuvos Rivevos Ephraim*, Vol. V, preface III.

was something amazing. And once the *shiur* ended, his complexion changed and he appeared weak once again.

In his final, pain-filled years, I had the *zechus* to assist him both in his home and at the hospital. The Rosh Yeshivah allowed me to help him dress, but would never allow me to tie his shoes. He explained that he would permit a grandchild to do this, but not a talmid. "For a talmid," he said, "it is a *bizayon* (degrading)."

When reciting the bedtime *Shema*, he would say the prayer *Ribono shel Olam*, in which one declares his forgiveness of anyone who may have offended him, slowly and with great concentration.

On Shabbos morning, he would complete the mitzvah of being *maavir sidrah* before the daytime *seudah*. He would recite each word of the *sidrah* as carefully as one recites *Shema*. At the *seudah*, he would often ask me to lead the *zemiros* — and always asked that I pause when the Rebbetzin brought in the next course.

As the Rosh Yeshivah's condition worsened and he was hospitalized, he continued to serve Hashem to whatever degree was possible. He would force himself out of bed to stand for *Shemoneh Esrei* and, as always, would stand absolutely still, while I stood behind him holding on to him to make sure that he would not fall. On one occasion, doctors entered the room as he was *davening*, looked at his chart, and expressed amazement that it was possible for him to get out of bed and stand.

AS TIME PROGRESSED, REB MOSHE WEAKENED STEADILY. IN THE WINTER OF 5745 (1985), he was hospitalized with a condition that, for a time, caused him

In the Presence of Holiness

to drift in and out of a semi-coma. Jews the world over poured out their hearts in prayer for him. Their entreaties were accepted; though still extremely weak, Reb Moshe was eventually discharged from the hospital. Approximately a year later, in the winter of 5746, he was again hospitalized and subsequently released.

> It was obvious to the hospital staff that, in treating Rabbi Moshe Feinstein, they were in the presence of holiness. He strained to get dressed for *davening*; at the very least, he would don his hat. All were amazed how he would often stand for *Shemoneh Esrei* despite excruciating pain. When too weak to stand but strong enough to sit, he would be careful not to lean back or even to make use of the arm-rests. Amazingly, he would force himself up from his wheelchair to bow at *Modim*. However, it was more than his performance of deeds between man and G-d that impressed the doctors and nurses. They saw before their eyes an angel whose concern for other human beings was of a quality they had never seen.

When someone would come to administer an injection or some other treatment, he would force himself closer to the person to make the task easier. He never forgot a "thank you" for anything that was done for him. Before leaving the hospital he again thanked and blessed all who had come to his aid. He strained not to cry out when painful treatments were performed, so as not to cause anguish to the one administering them.

His solicitude for the feelings and welfare of others was undiminished by his own suffering. Several times a day he would inquire about the Rebbetzin and wanted to be sure that concern for him did not cause her to be neglected.

Someone who administered a treatment known to cause excruciating pain asked Reb Moshe how he was able to bear the suffering without crying out. He replied, "You are doing what must be done for my benefit. It is worthwhile for me to have a little more pain, rather than to cause you distress."

During one hospital stay, the women of the family brought cakes to the hospital and distributed slices to doctors, nurses, orderlies, attendants — anyone who had rendered Reb Moshe a service in any way. Instead of eating their portions, they showed them off and treasured them, and most took them home to their families. To them, these were not ordinary pastries, but mementos from an extraordinary man. The hospital staff was so devoted to Reb Moshe that many of them wept when they heard about his death.

IT HAD BEEN REB MOSHE'S PRACTICE FOR MANY YEARS TO SPEND SHAVUOS AT the Yeshivah of Staten Island. For his last Shavuos, in 5745 (1985), he

Strength for a "Thank You"

remained at home. Mr. and Mrs. Jaeger, the yeshivah's devoted cooks, had always prepared a special cake and blintzes in Reb Moshe's honor. This time, they sent these foods, prepared in accordance with Reb Moshe's strict diet, to his Lower East Side apartment. After Yom Tov was over, Reb Moshe wanted to call the Jaegers and thank them. Someone attempted to dissuade him, saying that he was too weak even to hold the telephone receiver. Reb Moshe said, "To give the Jaegers some pleasure by thanking them, the *Ribono shel Olam* will give me the strength to hold the phone."

> One day, a great-granddaughter came to insert drops into Reb Moshe's eyes. As she was preparing them in another room, the Rebbetzin said to Reb Moshe, "But you were already given those drops a little while ago!" "Yes," replied Reb Moshe, "but she doesn't know that. And I know that she takes pleasure in giving them to me. Better that I be given them again than for her to have come for nothing."

For a time, a gentile male nurse cared for Reb Moshe at his home. A yeshivah student would also sleep in the apartment, in case of emergency. Once, a substitute nurse was there, who was unfamiliar with the accommodations in the apartment. Realizing that the nurse might not know how to set up the makeshift bed for himself, Reb Moshe sent the student to make sure the nurse was resting comfortably.

ABOUT A YEAR BEFORE REB MOSHE'S PASSING, SOMEONE CAME TO RABBI David Feinstein with the delicate question of whether or not a member of

Siyata DiShmaya

his family should undergo major surgery. Reb David presented the question to Reb Moshe, who was then so weak that he could barely speak. Reb Moshe advised that the surgery be performed. When Reb David relayed his father's decision, the

The last picture taken with the Rebbetzin

sick person's family expressed reservations. Reb Moshe was extremely ill; perhaps he had not fully grasped the problem. Was it possible that in healthier times he would have advised differently?

Reb David told the family members that they need not be concerned. "If the Rosh Yeshivah understood the question properly, then you certainly must listen to him. And even if he did not understand it, he still had the *siyata diShmaya* to say what is correct." The surgery was performed with successful results.

A FEW MONTHS BEFORE REB MOSHE'S PASSING, A MAN RESIDING IN Jerusalem developed a serious medical problem. Doctors recommended a surgery that was complicated from a halachic standpoint. The patient presented the problem to his rav, Rabbi Yechiel Michel Stern, a renowned *talmid chacham* and author of *sefarim*. Rav Stern did not feel comfortable ruling on such a complicated issue with such serious ramifications, so he brought the matter to the *gaon* Rabbi Shlomo Zalman Auerbach.[5]

"Ask the Gadol Hador"

---

5. Rav Stern is married to the daughter of Rabbi Avrohom Dov Auerbach, a brother of Reb Shlomo Zalman.

Reb Shlomo Zalman pondered the matter and said, "Such a question must be decided by the *gadol hador* — call Reb Moshe." He recited Reb Moshe's phone number from memory; Rav Stern made the call but the line was busy. Rav Stern said, "I will call my cousin, Rav Nissan Alpert, who is among Reb Moshe's closest talmidim, and ask him to present the *she'eilah*."

Reb Nissan himself was seriously ill at the time; he passed away just a few months after Reb Moshe. Yet, he immediately agreed to speak to Reb Moshe. However, he cautioned, "The Rosh Yeshivah is very weak these days and it may not be possible to ask him to rule on such a serious matter."

Reb Nissan found Reb Moshe feeling quite ill. Few halachic questions had been brought to him in recent weeks because it was too difficult for him to focus on the matter at hand. When Reb Nissan presented the question, Reb Moshe listened and responded, "It is difficult to be *matir* (to permit the surgery). However, the *she'eilah* is not *nogei'a* (relevant)."

Reb Nissan was stunned. *The she'eilah was not nogei'a? But there was a man in Jerusalem waiting to hear whether or not he should undergo the surgery!*

Reb Nissan posed the question a second time and received a similar response. *"Der she'eilah is nit ken she'eilah"* ("The question is not a [relevant] question.") Reb Nissan phoned Rav Stern and related what Reb Moshe had said. Rav Stern, too, was mystified.

He went to Reb Shlomo Zalman and related Reb Moshe's strange response. The *gaon* replied matter-of-factly, "Well, the *she'eilah* is not *nogei'a*," but he did not elaborate.

Rav Stern was expecting the patient to return to find out the *psak*, but he did not return. Two days later, Rav Stern met the man. "Where have you been?" he asked him. "Don't you want to know the *psak* regarding your surgery?"

"It's not *nogei'a*," the man replied. "The doctors discovered other medical issues that make the surgery irrelevant."

Rav Stern immediately took a taxi to the Shaarei Chesed neighborhood where he told Reb Shlomo Zalman what had just happened.

Reb Shlomo Zalman replied, "Why are you *nispa'el* (amazed)? If the *gadol hador* is weak and infirm, he still has *siyata diShmaya*."[6]

See Chapter Five about the relationship between Reb Moshe and Reb Shlomo Zalman.
6. Related by Rabbi Dovid Weinberger, who heard it from Rav Yechiel Michel Stern. Rav David Feinstein told Rav Weinberger that this was probably the last halachic query brought

Announcement by rabbanim and roshei yeshivah calling for prayers, Torah study and the giving of tzedakah as a source of merit for Reb Moshe's recovery

AT ONE POINT, REB MOSHE SUFFERED FROM A CALCIUM DEFICIENCY THAT LEFT him disoriented. On Yom Tov, his son Reb Reuven recited *kiddush* for the

A Pure Neshamah

family and some of the wine was passed to Reb Moshe. His non-Jewish nurse took the cup of wine and put it to Reb Moshe's lips, but he closed his lips and shook his head, indicating that he would not drink it. As the nurse placed the cup down, she commented, "I can't understand it. He is such a cooperative patient — why does he refuse to drink?"

A grandson who was present then picked up the cup and put it to Reb Moshe's lips. He drank it without difficulty.

Though the wine was *mevushal* (and halachically permissible after being handled by a non-Jew), Reb Moshe did not know this. And though he was

---

to his father.

disoriented, his pure *neshamah* would not permit him to partake of wine that seemingly was forbidden.[7]

In the summer of 1985, someone saw Reb Moshe straining his eyes to study *Parashas Vayikra* more than two months after it had been read as the weekly Torah portion. The person was apprehensive that perhaps Reb Moshe's memory was failing and he was confused as to which was the *parashah* of that week. Delicately, the person mentioned that *Vayikra* had been read some time ago. Reb Moshe said, "The halachah states that one who is G-d-fearing should review the weekly *sidra* with both *Targum* and *Rashi*. I fell behind while I was in the hospital so now I am simply paying up my debts!"

On Chanukah of his final year, Reb Moshe stood ready to kindle his menorah, as his Rebbetzin and a yeshivah student who often attended him looked on. Reb Moshe recited the blessing and then directed the lit candle which he held toward the wick in the menorah. He lit the first wick, but with his weak eyesight he could not find the next one. He tried moving the candle about, but still could not locate the wick.

The student came over and gently took Reb Moshe's hand and started to guide it, but Reb Moshe would not let him. He wanted to fulfill the mitzvah without assistance. He tried once more, but again was not successful. Reb Moshe seemed on the verge of tears. He loved every mitzvah so much and wanted so badly to fulfill it …

Suddenly the flame found the wick and it caught. Immediately, Reb Moshe's mood changed. He lit the remaining wicks and, joyfully, began to chant *Haneiros Halalu*.

---

7. In relating this incident, Reb Reuven Feinstein commented that genuine *ameilus baTorah* (toil in Torah) uplifts the student and brings his fulfillment of mitzvos to a higher level. If it does not, then something is lacking in the *ameilus* (see *Rashi* to *Vayikra* 26:3). Torah was so much a part of Reb Moshe's essence that even without clarity of thought, his *neshamah* simply could not partake of that which seemed forbidden.

Reb Moshe's lack of strength during those last months made it difficult for him to concentrate. Still, he tried his utmost to persevere. When a young man told him a *chiddush* with which he disagreed, Reb Moshe immediately contended with him. Not wanting to cause Reb Moshe undue strain, the young man said, "We can discuss it another time." But Reb Moshe could not rest knowing that someone believed something to be true when, in fact, it was false. To remain silent would have been a greater strain for Reb Moshe than to speak. He patiently showed the young man where he had erred.

WHEN IT BECAME TOO STRENUOUS FOR HIM TO PRAY THE LONG SHABBOS morning *davening* with a *minyan*, Reb Moshe would recite the *Shacharis*

The Final Shabbos

prayers alone, and later a *minyan* would come to his apartment for the Torah reading and *Mussaf*. On the Shabbos of *Parashas Zachar*, the last Shabbos of his life, an *aufruf* was held at Tifereth Jerusalem. Since those who regularly formed Reb Moshe's *minyan* would be attending the *aufruf* and would not be at his home until much later than usual, it was thought best for Reb Moshe that he *daven Mussaf* privately, and hear the Torah reading with a *minyan* later in the day.

Rabbi Reuven Feinstein hurried to his father's home that day well before the *minyan* was to gather. He suggested to Reb Moshe that he recite *Mussaf* and eat something before the *minyan* arrived for the Torah reading.

"Why won't there be a *minyan* for *Mussaf*?" Reb Moshe wanted to know. Reb Reuven explained that the *aufruf* had made this impractical. Reb Moshe, however, was adamant. He wanted to *daven Mussaf* with a *minyan*, as he had always done. It was past noon by then and most people had already *davened*, but, seeing how distressed his father was, Reb Reuven made the effort to gather a *minyan*. His quest was successful; soon a *minyan* convened in Reb Moshe's dining room for *Krias HaTorah* and *Mussaf*.

Later, as they sat eating the *seudas Shabbos,* Reb Moshe turned to Reb Reuven and said, *"Gedenk! Men darf arein-chappen vifil men ken!"* (Remember! One must grab as many [*mitzvos*] as he can.)

ON THE FOLLOWING SUNDAY NIGHT, THE EVE OF TAANIS ESTHER, 5746 (1986), a call was sounded to the Hatzolah emergency rescue squad: Rabbi Moshe

The Light Is Extinguished Feinstein had to be rushed to the hospital immediately.

As the ambulance was speeding to the hospital he felt his strength waning. He said, *"Ich hob mehr nisht ken ko'ach* (I have no more strength)." Those were his last words.

How much strength had he had for the last several years? Very little, but whatever strength was left in him was devoted to Hashem, to Torah, and to *Klal Yisrael.* As long as he had strength — *any* strength — his service continued. He would not stop working at his full capacity, as he had for 91 years. And then he had no more strength.

> In the beis midrash of the Yeshivah of Staten Island, boys and young men were fervently reciting *Tehillim,* imploring Hashem to spare him. At 9:50 p.m., the light fixture over his seat near the *Aron HaKodesh* flickered and went out. Then it glowed for a moment and went out again.
>
> Reb Moshe was gone, and then it was dark.

It has been pointed out that the 5,746th verse in the Torah reads, *And it came to pass after Moshe had finished writing down the words of this Torah in a book to the very end.*[8] Appropriate words for the *gadol hador* who was named after Moshe Rabbeinu and who passed away in the year 5746.

NEWS OF HIS PASSING SPREAD QUICKLY, CASTING A PALL ON THE JOYOUS preparations for Purim. Everywhere there was a sense of having been

Farewell orphaned. It had been a world *with* Reb Moshe, and now it was a world *without* Reb Moshe. True, he had been very ill and virtually inaccessible, but he had still been among us. He was like a sun obscured by clouds. We could not *see* it but we were warmed and comforted by the knowledge that it was there. But now, the sun had set and was gone — and we knew the sky was empty. People heard the news and gasped. Then wept.

The *chevrah kadisha* members who performed the *taharah* and pre-pared Reb Moshe for burial were some of the most respected and expe-

---

8. *Devarim* 31:24.

נצחו אראלים את המצוקים
ונשבה ארון הקודש

מתוך צער רב ויגון מודיעים אנו על פטירת

מורנו ורבנו רבן של כל בני הגולה

מרן ראש הישיבה

הגאון **הרב משה פיינשטיין** זצוקללה״ה

הלוי׳ תצא ממתיבתא תפארת ירושלים

145 איסט בראדוויי

145 EAST BROADWAY

בשעה 1:00

והקבורה תהי׳ בארץ ישראל

וכל בית ישראל יבכו את השריפה אשר שרף ה׳

הנהלת מתיבתא תפארת ירושלים

rienced practitioners of this ultimate kindness. They shook their heads in reverent amazement. The body radiated such holiness, such purity!

All night, devoted disciples met with the family and police to plan the funeral. The Police Department prepared for the largest funeral American Orthodoxy had ever known.[9] As the *niftar* lay in the beis midrash of Mesivtha Tifereth Jerusalem surrounded by reverent Jews from four generations reciting *Tehillim*, the subways and highways were somber arteries of grief, as mourners converged on the Lower East Side.

The cross-section of people was breathtaking: Chassidic rebbes, rabbanim, roshei yeshivah, yeshivah students, Bais Yaakov girls, teachers, merchants, professionals, civil servants, some clad in black hats and long coats, some in *kipot serugot* and sport jackets, community leaders, elected officials. Businesses chartered buses so that groups of employees could take turns going to the funeral. Schools and offices closed for the day.

---

9. The official who coordinated the police presence at the funeral came during *shivah* to express his condolences and his admiration for the massive crowd's orderliness and cooperation.

Orthodoxy had lost its father, and 100,000 of his children crowded the Lower East Side to mourn their loss and share their grief.

AS THE WORDS OF TEHILLIM BOOMED OVER THE HUGE OUTDOOR LOUDSPEAK-ers, it seemed as if all of creation was in mourning. Rabbi Michel

The Funeral in New York Barenbaum tearfully eulogized his mentor and friend, and poignantly said that if Reb Moshe could speak he would express his compassion for the tens of thousands

of people who were standing in the street and would ask the speakers to be brief.

Rabbi Yaakov Yitzchak Ruderman — painfully thrust into the position of America's senior rosh yeshivah by the successive deaths of Rabbi Yaakov Kamenetsky and Reb Moshe — wept as he eulogized, "The teacher of us all … a great *tzaddik* and *baal middos* … his loss is so painful that one cannot find the words to express what he feels." Indeed, he couldn't. It was impossible for him to contain his sense of loss, and his unfettered emotions spilled out into the hearts of the multitude.

Other roshei yeshivah and rabbanim who eulogized him were (in order of their appearance) Rabbi David Lipschutz of Yeshivas Rabbi Yitzchak

The funeral in New York

The funeral procession down East Broadway

Elchonon; Rabbi Chaim Stein of the Telshe Yeshivah; Rabbi Shraga Moshe Kalmanowitz of the Mirrer Yeshivah; Rabbi Yaakov Joffen of Yeshivas Beis Yosef; Rabbi Levi Krupenia of the Kamenitzer Yeshivah; Rabbi Nissan Alpert; Rabbi Moshe David Tendler; the Satmar Rav; Rabbi Reuven Feinstein, and Rabbi Mordechai Tendler. Speaker after speaker mourned the catastrophe. Only the facts that it was Taanis Esther and that the *niftar* had to be taken to the airport limited the eulogies.

By the time the eulogies were over, it was late afternoon. The crowd walked in mournful silence as the Hatzolah ambulance bearing Reb Moshe's coffin slowly made its way down East Broadway. From there the procession continued on to Kennedy Airport.

The crowd dispersed ... it was difficult to imagine that Purim was just a few hours away.

IN ERETZ YISRAEL, THERE WAS DISAGREEMENT AS TO WHEN THE FUNERAL should take place. The plane was scheduled to land in the afternoon of 14

The Funeral in Jerusalem Adar, so it would have been feasible to hold the funeral on the evening of Shushan Purim, when Jerusalem performs all the mitzvos of Purim. Some felt that the funeral should be held at night, as is commonly done in Jerusalem. Rav Elazar Menachem Shach and other *gedolim* were concerned that the mas-

*Posters announcing the funeral in Jerusalem. With the exception of the poster
on far right, posters state that the funeral will take place on the night of Shushan
Purim. The poster on far right corrects this, stating that because of "mechanical
problems on the plane" the funeral was postponed for Shushan Purim day.*

sive crowd in the dark could create a situation of *sakanah* (danger), and
therefore the funeral should be held on Shushan Purim day.[10] As Rav
Reuven Feinstein put it, "It was upsetting to think that the funeral of someone who had pursued *shalom* all his life should be the cause of
machlokes."

In the end, Heaven resolved the matter. After a couple of hours in flight,
the pilot announced that the plane was experiencing radar trouble and
was returning to New York. It remained at Kennedy Airport for hours until
the problem was fixed. By the time the plane arrived in Tel Aviv,[11] it was
midnight of Shushan Purim in Eretz Yisrael, and there was no choice but
to hold the funeral during daylight hours.

On Shushan Purim in Jerusalem, 250,000 people paid their respects, in
the largest funeral since the time of Rabban Yochanan ben Zakkai, some
2,000 years earlier.

---

10. There were those who sought to minimize the concerns of *sakanah* by saying that the
crowd would not be more than 50-60,000. They reasoned that the fact that people were
busy with Purim, combined with the fact that Reb Moshe had not been to Eretz Yisrael
since 1964, would minimize the size of the crowd.

11. Many *gedolim* were at the airport when Reb Moshe's coffin arrived.

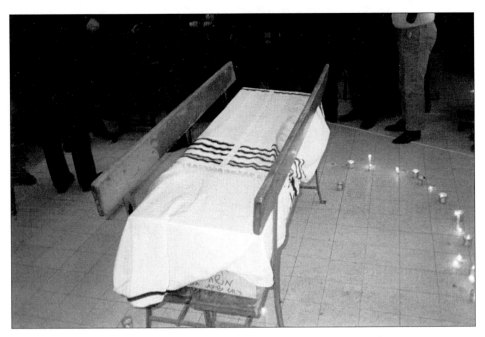

Rav Moshe's aron, during the funeral at Yeshivah Eitz Chaim in Jerusalem

Reb Moshe had been in Eretz Yisrael only once in his lifetime, but he belonged to Eretz Yisrael as much as to America and as much as to Uzda, Starobin, and Luban. He was the *sar haTorah,* the prince of Torah, and every citizen of the world of Torah was his subject and child.

Rav Shach, his voice choked with tears, cried, "Torah, Torah, gird yourself in sackcloth! Prepare yourself to mourn for your only, unique son … Reb Moshe was the *gadol hador,* without embellishment, without exaggeration … He was an only son to our generation."

He was followed by his colleague and Reb Moshe's boyhood friend, Rabbi Dovid Povarsky; the Chief Rabbi of the Eidah HaChareidis, Rabbi Yaakov Yitzchak Weiss; Reb Moshe's illustrious nephew, Rabbi Yechiel Michel Feinstein; the Sefardic rosh yeshivah Rabbi Yehudah Tzadkah, and Rabbi Reuven Feinstein.

At the conclusion of the eulogies, Reb Moshe's coffin, escorted by hundreds of thousands, was carried on foot from Yeshivah Eitz Chaim on Rechov Yaffo all the way to Har HaMenuchos. There, he was laid to rest near his rebbi, Reb Isser Zalman; his close colleague, Reb Aharon; his son-in-law, Reb Eliyahu Moshe Shisgal; and in close proximity of the holy Belzer Rebbe.

As his grandson through marriage, Rabbi Aryeh Don Greher, stood on Har HaMenuchos and looked down at the seemingly endless masses who

The funeral in Jerusalem

had come to accord Reb Moshe his final honor, a verse from *Megillas Esther* came to mind: כָּכָה יֵעָשֶׂה לָאִישׁ אֲשֶׁר הַמֶּלֶךְ חָפֵץ בִּיקָרוֹ, *This is what shall be done for the man whom the King desires to honor.*[12]

❧ ❧ ❧

A thought that Reb Moshe once said encapsulates the void his passing created.[13]

On the words "And Yaakov departed from Be'er Sheva,"[14] Rashi comments that the departure of a *tzaddik* from a place leaves a profound void.

12. *Esther* 6:9.
13. The following is from *Darash Moshe* (part I) to *Parashas Vayeitzei*.
14. *Bereishis* 28: 10.

For a *tzaddik* is the glory, splendor, and beauty of the place in which he resides. When he departs, these qualities leave with him.

Reb Moshe explained:

Glory [הוֹד] refers to the influence that the presence of a *tzaddik* has upon others without any active effort on his part. The mere fact that others observe his ways and greatness in Torah has a powerful influence upon them. This trait is called הוֹד, *glory*, in that people appreciate how glorious the *gaon* and *tzaddik* is.

Splendor [זִיו] denotes the active influence that a *tzaddik* exerts on others. Onkelos uses this word[15] to describe the ray of light that shone from Moshe's face upon his return to the camp after the forty days he spent on Mount Sinai receiving the Torah from Hashem. Like the sun, it sheds its light over great distances. Similarly, the influence of a *tzaddik* can reach people who live far away from him.

Beauty [הִדּוּר] denotes the intrinsic beauty of the *tzaddik*, which is far greater than the benefit others derive from him. Thus we find this word used in reference to an *esrog* to indicate that its beauty is inherent in itself. This is the greatest trait of all, for it represents all the great qualities that the *tzaddik* possesses.

With the passing of Reb Moshe, the glory, splendor, and beauty that he embodied had departed.

---

15. *Shemos* 34:35.

Of Honor and Disrespect

WHEN REB MOSHE'S FUNERAL PROCESSION REACHED THE burial spot on Har HaMenuchos, they found that the open grave needed to be widened somewhat. Someone picked up a hoe and

Miracle at the Burial

began to chop at the ground. The crowd was so dense that there was little room to move and people were inadvertently being pushed. At one point, the hoe came down hard on the foot of Rabbi Aryeh Don Greher and he fainted from the pain. He was revived, and the burial proceeded.

Though his foot was throbbing with pain, Rabbi Greher asked to participate in the custom of placing earth on the grave. He was handed a shovel, placed one shovelful of earth on the grave — and immediately, the pain in his foot disappeared. Later, he found that not only had the hoe torn his shoe, it had also ripped his sock. Yet, on his foot there was nothing more than a red mark, and the pain never returned.

Reb Moshe's tombstone on Har HaMenuchos

פ"נ

מרן הגאון הגדול
שר התורה והיראה
ה' חסיד וה' עניו
רבן של כל ישראל
רבי **משה פיינשטיין**
זצוקללה"ה
שהיה אבד"ק אוזדא וליובאן שברוסיא
ואח"כ ראש מתיבתא תפארת ירושלים
בנוא יארק כיובל שנים

בן הגאון הצדיק החסיד והעניו
רבי **דוד** זצוקללה"ה
אבד"ק ......
והרבנית מרת **פייא ביטל** ע"ה
ממשפחת הגר"א, בעל סדר הדורות,
הרד"ט, השל"ה ולמעלה בקודש
נולד בכ' אדר תרנ"ה
נ..... אראלים ויצאה נשמתו הטהורה
או.... ליום שני י"ג אדר שני
תענית אסתר שנת שמו"ת
ומ.... באדמת הקודש בשושן פורים
ת נ צ ב כ"ה

A SHORT WHILE AFTER REB MOSHE'S PASSING, SOMEONE IN ERETZ YISRAEL began experiencing excruciating headaches that no doctor was able to

Unwarranted Complaint

treat. Frightened, the man rushed to a leading rav in Eretz Yisrael, in search of his blessing and guidance.

Upon hearing that the man's troubles had begun around the time of the funeral, the rav asked if he had ever said anything disrespectful of Reb Moshe. The man replied that he had not. Then the rav offered counsel that was somewhat unusual. Rather than instruct him as to which doctor to use or the most preferred medical procedure to undergo, he told the man that the *Goral HaGra* should be cast. Perhaps through this, the man would find the real source of his suffering.

The *goral* was cast. The verse it pointed to stared back at the man: " … *and why did you not fear to speak against My servant Moshe?"*[1]

At first glance, these words meant nothing to the man. Then suddenly, it hit him like a bolt of lightning … Of course! He had been there, among the multitudes that had thronged the streets of Jerusalem on the day of Reb Moshe's funeral. Reb Moshe was a *gaon*, a *tzaddik* … how could one not come and pay his respects? He was upset, though, by the number of eulogies and the length of the funeral in general. It was Shushan Purim and Jerusalem was supposed to be engaged in the mitzvos of the festive holiday. It did not seem right, the man had felt, for a funeral — anyone's funeral — to ruin the Purim of hundreds of thousands of people.

The man had expressed his opinion to others.

"Why did you not fear to speak against My servant Moshe?"

The rav then told him that the *Shulchan Aruch* prescribes what he must do — indeed, the only solution to his suffering. He must gather ten people and, in their presence, ask forgiveness of Reb Moshe at his gravesite.

The man assembled a *minyan* of men and, accompanied by them, made his way up Har HaMenuchos to the site of Reb Moshe's grave. There, he begged forgiveness for his words.

The man's headaches soon disappeared.

RABBI SHOLOM EISEN WAS ONE OF JERUSALEM'S GREATEST *POSKIM* A GENERA-tion ago. During his final illness, Reb Sholom's doctors advised that he be

Reb Sholom's Dilemma brought to America for treatments. The treatments were not successful and he returned home in grave condition.

Taanis Esther arrived and with it came the tragic news that Reb Moshe had passed away. Reb Sholom wanted very badly to participate in the funeral on Shushan Purim, but his family insisted that he was physically not up to it. Bedridden and pitifully weak, he accepted their position and remained at home.

Later, he called his son to his bedside and said, "I would like you to gather a *minyan*, go the grave of Reb Moshe, and ask forgiveness for my not having participated in the *levayah*."

"But why, *Tatte?*" asked his son. "Weren't you exempt because of weakness?"

Reb Sholom replied, "As far as the obligation to attend the funeral of a *gadol hador*, I believe that I was exempt. But when I was hospitalized in

---

1. *Devarim* 12:8.

New York, Reb Moshe, זכר צדיק לברכה, visited me. Out of *hakaras hatov* (gratitude), I should have attended his funeral — and I do not think that my illness freed me from that obligation."

Only after his son carried out his wish and, in the presence of a *minyan*, asked forgiveness at Reb Moshe's grave, was Reb Sholom Eisen at peace.

Greater in Death Than in Life — Four Stories

גְּדוֹלִים צַדִּיקִים בְּמִיתָתָן יוֹתֵר מִבְּחַיֵּיהֶן.

Tzaddikim are even greater in death than in life.[1]

REG ROSEN[2] WAS RAISED IN A COMPLETELY SECULAR ENVIRONMENT; his grandfather was president of a Reform temple. Greg visited his grandparents often.

A Book in the Mail On one such visit, Greg entered his grandfather's study and perused its library of books. One book caught his eye — *Reb Moshe*. His grandfather had received it in a mailing from Yeshivah of Staten Island. Greg was struck by the photo of the sage on the cover, wrapped in his *tallis* and *tefillin* and immersed in his prayers. He opened the book and began to read.

A few minutes later, his grandfather entered the room. "Put away the book, Greg. When I move out of this house, you can have it." It was a strange thing to say, because Greg's grandparents had lived on Long Island for many years and had never expressed any intention of moving.

---

1. *Chullin* 7b.
2. Name has been changed.

The following year, Greg's grandmother passed away. Not long after, Greg visited Israel as part of a youth tour. He returned greatly inspired but unsure how to channel his inspiration.

A short while later, his grandfather stunned the family by announcing that he needed a change of scenery and would be moving to Florida. During the weeks of packing, he asked his daughter to give Greg the book *Reb Moshe*, in fulfillment of his promise.

That night, Greg stayed up late reading about this great Jew, Rabbi Moshe Feinstein. The book was an *eye-opener* for him; he had thought that such pure, good-hearted, wise people did not exist — and certainly he had no idea that Torah could produce such an individual.[3]

When Greg graduated high school, he enrolled in a college in Washington, D.C., which offered a kosher meal plan. He began to keep kosher and at the same time traveled often to nearby Silver Spring, Maryland, to attend Torah classes. During summer recess, he made a decision that changed his life: he left college and enrolled in a yeshivah.

Eventually, Greg emigrated to Eretz Yisrael, where he continued his full-time Torah studies and developed into a fully committed Jew whose life revolves around Torah and mitzvos.[4]

RICH[5] WAS A BAAL TESHUVAH STUDYING AT A UNIVERSITY IN LONDON. NOT long after embracing a life of Torah, he joined a Project SEED program.

A Dose of Emunah One of the lecturers spoke about the greatness of Reb Moshe, who had recently passed away. Rich visited a Judaica store and purchased *Reb Moshe*. He read the book and felt greatly inspired by it.

After graduating, Rich was hired by a huge management firm that recognized the young man's extraordinary talents. When a major project in Brussels required the expertise of a team of five, Rich was one of those selected. He was sent to Chicago for special training before heading out to Belgium.

The project was exciting, the work stimulating, but Rich found that his heart was not in it. In London, he had gotten his first real taste of Torah learning, and he yearned to travel to Eretz Yisrael and become part of a yeshivah.

---

3. Greg also studied the glossary dozens of times, as a start towards building a Hebrew vocabulary.
4. Adapted from *Visions of Greatness*, Vol. V, by Rabbi Yosef Weiss (CIS Publications).
5. Name has been changed.

But he felt that he could not quit at this point. His company had invested so much in his training for this project, and he was the only member of the project team with a *kippah*. To quit now, he felt, would be a *chillul Hashem*.

Rich recalls that period in his life:

> It was a tough time. I tend to tense up in difficult situations, and I was worried about my future. Also, my apartment in Brussels was not working out and this contributed to my anxiety. But I found a way to calm down. I had the book about Reb Moshe with me.
>
> I reread the chapter on "Faith and Zealousness." I reminded myself of Reb Moshe's unshakable *emunah* in all situations. I told myself, "There is nothing to worry about. Relax. It's all in Hashem's hands." This had a calming affect on me.

And salvation soon came in a very unexpected way. In the huge office building where Rich worked, there was a warehouse managed by Arabs. To get to his office, Rich had to walk past this warehouse. His *kippah* did not go unnoticed by the warehouse management.

One day, Rich was summoned to a meeting by the head of his department.

"Rich, I'm sorry to have to tell you this, but we have a problem. Those guys who manage that warehouse aren't happy with your head-covering. They demand that either you remove it or be transferred out of this building. We feel very bad about this, but we have no choice. We understand that you're a man of religious conviction. If you want to keep the skullcap on, we can transfer you back to London."

Rich appeared upset, but inwardly he was quite pleased. This was the opportunity for which he had been waiting. Now, no one would blame him for resigning.

A short while later, his dream was fulfilled as he enrolled in a yeshivah in Jerusalem. Today, more than 20 years later, he looks back at that episode and recalls the *chizuk* he received from Reb Moshe as a crucial component of his salvation. Rich reflects, "I once read in a *sefer* that when you read about a *tzaddik* with the intention of learning from him, you become connected to him in a very real sense. Perhaps at that crucial time, Reb Moshe was interceding on my behalf."[6]

---

6. Based on an interview with "Rich." For more about Rich's story, see "The Kippah Club" in *"It Could Have Been You"* by Nachman Seltzer (published by Artscroll/Mesorah).

IN THE FALL OF 1990, THIS AUTHOR RECEIVED THE FOLLOWING LETTER FROM A young man living in Northern Israel:

A Soldier's Companion For some time now, I have had the urge to write to you to offer you my *berachos* on your wonderful *sefer, Reb Moshe.*

I am a 33-year-old religious Jew who had, of course, heard of Reb Moshe but knew nothing about his life and had not even read one of his *teshuvos* (although I was familiar with several).

I am writing to tell you what this *sefer* means to me. You quote the *Gemara* in *Chullin* that *tzaddikim* are greater in death than in life; in my own personal life, I have seen the truth of this teaching personified in Reb Moshe.

It is obvious that you tried very hard to keep the superlatives in this *sefer* to a minimum, but Reb Moshe's character, which was the embodiment of every superlative, shines forth from every page.

Though I am light-years away from such *middos*, this did not prevent me from taking his example in daily matters. For example, on those weary early mornings when I feel particularly lazy during *Shacharis*, I think of Reb Moshe in agonizing pain struggling to stand up during *Mizmor L'Sodah* … and I jump to my feet.

It has become my custom to take the *sefer* to shul during the month of Elul and to keep it at my place there until after Yom Kippur. I do not know if it is halachically correct to glance through it during the long *chazaras hashatz* on Rosh Hashanah and Yom Kippur, but it certainly keeps me in the right frame of mind.

In addition, I take the *sefer* — now suitably plastic-covered — with me to *miluim* (army reserve duty). There it serves two purposes. Firstly, when encountering improper language and behavior, which unfortunately is prevalent in the army, I think of Reb Moshe's example and distance myself from these people *without* alienating myself.

Secondly, and far more significantly, when the going gets tough, I think of Reb Moshe's implicit trust in Hashem; this elevates and strengthens me. Last year when we were in Tulqarem for most of Tishrei and the Intafada was hot and furious, Reb Moshe helped to guide me to a level of *bitachon* which I had never before attained. Simply put — I overcame my fear.

This year, we are on the banks of the Jordan River — and your *sefer* is beside me!

No words can describe my gratitude for this *sefer*, which has informed the world who Reb Moshe was.

RABBI DAVID FEINSTEIN RELATED:

"This Is a Human Being!" One afternoon in the early 1990s shortly before Shavuos, I completed my afternoon *shiur* and found someone waiting to see me. He was dressed like a common laborer. I invited him into my office where I have a photograph of my father, *zt"l*, hanging on the wall. The man looked up and said, "I also have that picture." Then he reached into his bag and took out the book *Reb Moshe* and said, "You see this book? This book is what made me become religious."

He then told me that a few years earlier, he had been fabulously wealthy, to the point that he could have covered our yeshivah's entire budget. "And I would have done it," he added. Now, however, he had suffered major losses and was no longer in that position. He left me a check for the yeshivah for $500, and said that he would return before Rosh Hashanah.

He returned before Rosh Hashanah and was pleased when I recognized him and greeted him by name. He left another check for $500. After that he returned often, each time bringing with him a donation. He was in the wholesale electronics business and he would bring equipment and appliances for the yeshivah to make use of at its discretion.

On one visit, he related how the book about my father had inspired him to become a *baal teshuvah*. "I read about his personality, his *middos,* and I said to myself, '*This* is a human being. If you're not like this, you're not a human being. I'm not a human being.' And so I became a *baal teshuvah.* "

Around a year later, he passed away. He left the yeshivah a significant sum of money — and he died a *baal teshuvah*.

Reb David concluded: "If this man would have viewed my father as a *malach* [i.e., an angel of seemingly supernatural qualities], he would not have related to him. 'If he's a *malach*, what do you want from me?' He saw my father as a human being, and that is what made him want to emulate him."

Reb Moshe once remarked that sometimes the *Ribono shel Olam* takes a *tzaddik* away from this world because it is only then that people take proper stock of his lofty ways and mighty deeds in an effort to emulate him.

To follow in Reb Moshe's ways — how much there is to follow! As Rabbi Nissan Alpert expressed it, "Reb Moshe was so outstanding in every way, yet so simple in the way he went about things, that one tended to lose sight of his greatness."

Rabbi Elimelech Bluth said, "I don't think there was a mind in the world superior to that of the Rosh Yeshivah — and I'm really not sure which was greater, his mind or his heart."

In Rabbi Ephraim Greenblatt's words:

> The Rosh Yeshivah was like the miraculous oil of Chanukah; he illuminated the world until the end of his life … From his youth, he drew strength only from the Torah, and until the end he never diverted his mind from the Torah.
>
> In his last days he remarked, "I want to live a bit more and accomplish for the sake of Torah."
>
> The Rosh Yeshivah was one of a kind; a *gaon* in Torah and in *tzidkus*, a *gaon* in *pashtus* (simplicity) and *temimus* (sincerity), a great *gaon* in *middos tovos*. In *middos* he was the *gaon hageonim* (genius of geniuses) — there was no one like him.
>
> It is common to find a line of demarcation between intellectual genius and *middos*, but with the Rosh Yeshivah there was no such thing. His Torah and *middos* were firmly intertwined. He carefully avoided even *avak lashon hara*[7] and would not listen to *lashon hara*. He was the man of peace who stayed far away from all *machlokes*. His merit protected all of *Klal Yisrael*.

Reb Moshe was loved and respected because he offered love and respect to all who knew him. He was admired by everyone for his greatness, but he devoted his life to teaching that what he had accomplished could be attained by anyone who is willing to dedicate his life to serving Hashem with all his might. This is difficult, but not impossible. Reb Moshe was not a "miracle man," but, like the Moshe whose name he bore, was indeed a "man of G-d." Even more, he was an *eved Hashem*, servant of Hashem. Rabbi Elchonon Wasserman explained that, by Torah law, an *eved* has no personal rights or possessions; he exists only to serve his master. Moshe Rabbeinu's utter devotion to Hashem was such that he dedicated *every* deed, thought, and moment to His service.[8]

---

7. Lit. the dust of *lashon hara*, words that are not intrinsically *lashon hara* but are forbidden nonetheless.

8. See Reb Elchonon's *Kovetz Maamarim*.

Rabbi Simcha Wasserman[9] once presented his rebbetzin with a gift of two biographies; one about a *tzaddik* who was known to be a "miracle-worker," the other the book on Reb Moshe. Reb Simcha explained the difference between the two: The thrust of the first book shows the greatness of a person who merited that the *Ribono shel Olam* fulfilled his *every* decree. The biography of Reb Moshe shows the greatness of a person who was able to do everything that the *Ribono shel Olam* wanted *him* to do.[10]

Rambam teaches, "Every person can be as great as Moshe our teacher."[11] Can we really be as great as Moshe Rabbeinu? Can we be as great as Reb

9. Son of Reb Elchonon and Rosh Yeshivah of Yeshivah Ohr Elchonon in Jerusalem.
10. From *Greatness in Our Midst — The Life of Rabbi Simcha Wasserman* by Dovid Fox (Feldheim Publishers).
11. *Hilchos Teshuvah* 5:2.

Moshe? No. But we can aspire to equal their zeal to serve Hashem. That is what we should learn from Reb Moshe's life — every moment of it.

Reb Moshe lived for the day when there would be love and fear of Hashem, and when this would bring love and unity to all of *Klal Yisrael*. He longed to see peace among us, to know that each and every one of us truly cared for our fellow — and he was convinced that such peace and love would bring Mashiach.

We thought that he would lead us to greet Mashiach — Hashem decreed otherwise. But if the lessons of Reb Moshe's life penetrate our minds and hearts, surely Mashiach's footsteps will not be far away.

May the image of Reb Moshe, the *gaon* of Torah and *middos tovos,* remain with us forever.

GLOSSARY

All entries are Hebrew unless otherwise noted:
(Yid.) Yiddish, (Ar.) Aramaic.

Acharonim: Talmudic commentators and *poskim* from 16th century to the present

Aggadah: the philosophical, ethical, poetic and historical exposition of Scripture

agunah (pl. *agunos*): woman who cannot remarry, either because there is no proof that her missing husband is dead, or because her husband has willfully left her without giving her a divorce

ahavas haTorah: love of Torah

ahavas Yisrael: love for one's fellow Jew

Al Hamichyah: blessing recited after eating cake, cookies and the like

aliyah (pl. *aliyos*): call to the Torah for the public reading

anav: humble person

arbaah minim: four species (*lulav, esrog,* myrtle, willow) used during Succos services

Aron HaKodesh: Ark for the Torah scrolls

Ashkenazi: Jew of European ancestry

aufruf (Yid.): special *aliyah* for a *chasan* on the Shabbos before his wedding

avodah: service

Avos: *Pirkei Avos,* Chapters of the Fathers

baal gaavah: conceited person

baal middos: one with outstanding character traits

baal mum: one with a physical defect

bachur (pl. *bachurim*): unmarried man

bas Yisrael: Jewish girl

Baruch Hashem: "Thank G-d"

Baruch She'amar: opening blessing of *Pesukei D'Zimrah* in the morning service

Bavli: Babylonian Talmud

beis din: rabbinic court

Beis HaMikdash: Holy Temple in Jerusalem

beis midrash: study hall

ben (pl. *bnei*) *Torah*: Torah student(s)

berachah: blessing

bimah: podium for the Torah reading in *shul*

Bircas Kohanim: Priestly blessing recited on holidays

blatt (Yid.): one full leaf (two pages) of the Talmud

bris milah: circumcision

chas v'shalom: "G-d forbid"

Chasam Sofer: Rabbi Moshe Sofer (1762-1839), Rav of Pressburg and great halachic authority

Chashmonaim: Maccabees

chasan: bridegroom

chassid: pious person; or, follower of Chassidic movement founded by Rabbi Yisrael Baal Shem Tov

chavrusa: study partner

Chazal (acronym for *Chachameinu, zichronam livrachah*): our Sages, of blessed memory

chazzan: cantor; one leading the prayers

cheder: Torah school, elementary level

chesed: kindness

Chevrah Mishnayos: society for studying chapters of Mishnah

chiddush (pl. *chiddushim*), *chiddushei Torah*: original analyses and interpretations of difficult points of Torah

chillul Hashem: desecration of Hashem's Name

chinuch: education

Chumash: the Five Books of Moses

chuppah: marriage canopy or ceremony

daf: a *blatt*

Daf Yomi: systematic study of the entire Talmud in 7 1/2 years, one *blatt* per day

daven, davening (Yid.): to pray, prayers

derashah (pl. *derashos*): Torah discourse(s)

Dibros Moshe ("The Sayings of Moshe"): Reb Moshe's *chiddushim* on the Talmud

din Torah: case before a *beis din*

dinar: a coin common in Talmudic times

drashah (pl. *drashos*): sermon or discourse

drush: non-literal Scriptural interpretation

dvar Torah: discourse on Torah subject

erev: the eve of (a Sabbath or Festival)

Eretz Yisrael: the Land of Israel

esrog: citron, one of the *arbaah minim*

gabbai: synagogue official

gadol hador: the greatest Torah leader of the generation

gaon: brilliant Torah scholar

gedolei Yisrael, gedolim: The Torah leaders of the generation

Gemara: the part of Talmud that elaborates on the *Mishnah*

gemara: a volume of Talmud

geonus: Torah brilliance

goral haGra: Vilna Gaon's method of casting lots to indicate a particular Scriptural verse as a solution to a problem

Gut Shabbos (Yid.): Sabbath greeting

Gut Yom Tov (Yid.): Festival greeting

hadran: prayer recited at a *siyum*, generally accompanied by a discourse

Haggadah: book of textual readings and rituals used at the Passover *Seder*

Hakadosh Baruch Hu: the Holy One, Blessed is He; i.e. G-d

hakaras hatov: gratitude

Halachah: the body of Torah law

halachah: a Torah law

Hallel: Psalms 113-118, recited on certain festive days

HaNeiros Hallalu: prayer following kindling of Chanukah *menorah*

Hashem ("the Name"): G-d

hasmadah: diligence

hatzalah: rescue

Hatzolah: volunteer first-aid corps operating in many Jewish communities

Havdalah: blessing recited over wine, candle and spices to mark the end of Shabbos

hosafos: additional *aliyos*

Hy"d (acronym for *Hashem yinkom damo*): may Hashem avenge his blood

iluy: genius

Igros Moshe ("Correspondence of Moshe"): collection of Reb Moshe's *teshuvos*

kallah: bride

kashrus: the laws defining kosher food

kavod: honor

kehillah: congregation or community

kesubah: marriage contract

kibud av (va'eim): mitzvah of honoring one's father (and mother)

kiddush: ritual prayer recited over wine on the night and day of Shabbos and yom tov; alt. a festive gathering with food and drink preceded by the recitation of *kiddush* on the morning of Shabbos or yom tov following prayer services

Klal Yisrael: the Jewish people

Knessiah Gedolah: World Conference of Agudath Israel World Organization attended by many Torah leaders

Kohen (pl. *Kohanim*): male descendant of the priestly family of Aaron

Kohen Gadol: chief *Kohen* who served in the *Beis HaMikdash*

kollel: post-graduate yeshivah

Krias HaTorah: public Torah reading

kushya: Talmudic question

Lag BaOmer: thirty-third day of *Sefirah*

lamdan: Torah scholar

lulav: palm branch, one of the *arbaah minim*

Maariv: the evening prayer

machlokes: dispute

maggid: preacher

Maharam: Rabbi Meir of Lublin (1558-1616), Talmudic commentator

Maharsha: Rabbi Shmuel Eidelis (1555-1631); Talmudic commentator

malach (pl. *malachim*): angel(s)

masechta, maseches: Talmudic tractate

mashgiach: spiritual mentor of students in a yeshivah

Mashiach ("Anointed One"): the Messiah

matzah (pl. *matzos*): unleavened bread

mechilah: forgiveness

Megillah, Megillas Esther: Scroll of Esther, read on Purim

melamed: Torah teacher of young children

melaveh malkah: meal eaten after *Havdalah* in honor of the departing Sabbath

menahel: school principal

menorah: eight-branched candelabrum kindled on Chanukah

mesader kiddushin: officiating rabbi at a wedding ceremony

Mesillas Yesharim: *mussar* classic written by Rabbi Moshe Chaim Luzzato (1707-1747)

Mi shebeirach: prayer recited on behalf of a sick person, usually at public Torah reading

middos: character traits

Midrash: classic anthology of the Sages' Aggadic teachings of the Torah

mikveh (pl. *mikvaos*) : ritualarium

Minchah: the afternoon prayer

minhag: custom

minyan: quorum of ten men for conducting a prayer service

misnaged (lit. opponent): one opposed to Chassidism; loosely, any non-*chassid*

Mishnah: Tannaitic dicta compiled by Rabbi Yehudah HaNasi; together with Gemara comprises the Talmud

Mishneh LaMelech: classic commentary on *Rambam's Mishneh Torah*

mitzvah (pl. *mitzvos*): Torah commandment

Mizmor L'David: Psalm 23, customarily sung at *shalosh seudos*

Mizmor L'Sodah: Psalm 100, recited during *Pesukei D'Zimrah*

Modim: a blessing of *Shemoneh Esrei*

Modim d'Rabbanan: congregational response when *chazzan* reaches *Modim*

Moshe Rabbeinu: Moses, our Teacher

Motza'ei Shabbos: The night following Shabbos

Mussaf: the additional prayer of Shabbos, Festivals and Rosh Chodesh

mussar: ethical and moral teachings

Mussar movement: a movement founded by Rabbi Yisrael of Salant which encouraged the study of *mussar* and self-improvement

na'anuim: the shaking of the *arbaah minim* at certain points in the prayers on Succos

nachas: pleasure

Neilah: concluding service of Yom Kippur

nichum aveilim: comforting mourners

niftar: deceased

oleh: one called to the Torah at the public reading

oneg Shabbos: a gathering in honor of Shabbos, usually with light refreshments

Parashas Zachor: portion of the Torah beginning *"Zachor . . ."* (lit. Remember), read on the Shabbos before Purim

pasken (Yid.): decide a question of Torah law

pasuk: verse of Scripture

Pesach: Passover

Pesukei D'Zimrah: Psalms recited at the beginning of *Shacharis*

P'nei Yehoshua: Rabbi Yaakov Yehoshua Falk (1680-1756), Talmudic commentator

posek (pl. *poskim*): halachic authority

posek hador: the leading halachic authority of the generation

psak: decision of Torah law

Rambam: acronym for Rabbi Moshe ben Maimon (Maimonides); codifier, halachist, commentator on Mishnah, and seminal figure of Jewish philosophy (1135-1204)

Ramban: acronym for Rabbi Moshe ben Nachman (Nachmanides); Talmudist, Kabbalist and teacher, author of classic commentaries to Scripture and Talmud (1194-1270)

Rashi: Rabbi Shlomo ben Yitzchak; most basic and widely studied commentator on Scripture and Talmud (1040-1105)

rav (pl. rabbanim): rabbi

Rav Akiva Eiger: One of the 19th century's greatest Talmudists

rebbe: leader of a Chassidic sect

Rebbetzin (Yid.): rabbi's wife

rebbi (pl. *rebbeim*): Torah teacher

refuah sheleimah: a complete healing

Ribono shel Olam: Master of the Universe, G-d

Rishonim: early Talmudic commentators and *poskim*, 10th to 15th centuries

Rosh Chodesh: first day of a Jewish month

rosh yeshivah (pl. *roshei yeshivah*): dean of a Torah institution

ruach hakodesh: Divine inspiration

sandak: one who holds the baby during circumcision

Sanhedrin: Supreme Rabbinic Court in the time of the Holy Temple

s'chach: *succah*-covering, such as branches

Seder Zeraim: first of the six orders of the Mishnah

Sefardi (pl. *Sefardim*): Jew of Spanish or Oriental ancestry

sefer (pl. *sefarim*): book

sefer Torah (pl. *sifrei Torah*): Torah scroll

Sefirah: Forty-nine-day period between Passover and Shavuos, during which certain laws of mourning are observed

segulah: spiritual remedy

semichah: rabbinic ordination

seudas mitzvah: meal in honor of a mitzvah

Shabbos (pl. *Shabbosos*): Sabbath

Shabbos HaGadol: the Sabbath before Passover

Shabbos Shuvah: the Sabbath between Rosh Hashanah and Yom Kippur

Shach: commentary on *Shulchan Aruch*,

by Rabbi Shabsai HaKohein (1621-1662)

Shacharis: morning prayer service

shalach manos: gifts of food sent on Purim

shalosh seudos: third Sabbath meal, eaten in the afternoon

shamash: synagogue caretaker

Shas: the Talmud

Shechinah: Divine Presence

shechitah: ritual slaughtering

she'eilah (pl. *she'elilos*): question of Torah law

Shema: Jew's declaration of faith recited at morning and evening services

Shemoneh Esrei: the Amidah prayer

sheva berachos: seven blessings recited during wedding ceremony, and at meals during the week following a wedding

shidduch (pl. *shidduchim*): marriage match

shiur (pl. *shiurim*): Torah lecture

shivah (lit. seven): seven days of mourning following death of a close relative

shliach tzibbur: Lit., emissary of the community, commonly used as a reference to the one who leads the prayers

shlita (acronym for *sheyizkeh l'yamim tovim aruchim*): may he merit a good and long life

shmad: religious persecution; alt. apostasy

shmuess: ethical discourse

shochet: ritual slaughterer

shtetl: town or village

shul (Yid.): synagogue

Shulchan Aruch: Code of Jewish Law, written by Rabbi Yosef Caro (1488-1575)

Shushan Purim: the fifteenth of Adar, part of the Purim holiday. In Jerusalem, it is the main day of celebration.

siddur: prayer book

Sidra: weekly Torah portion, also referred to as *Parashah*

simchah: joy or joyous celebration

siyata diShmaya: the help of Heaven

siyum: conclusion of the study of a book of Scriptures or Talmud

sofer: scribe who writes or repairs *sifrei Torah, tefillin* and *mezuzos*

succah: booth in which the Jew is commanded to dwell during Succos

sugya: Talmudic topic

Taanis Esther: the Fast of Esther, observed the day before Purim

tahor: ritually pure

tallis kattan: small *tallis* worn beneath a man's outer garments during the day

talmid (pl. *talmidim*): Torah student

talmid chacham: Torah scholar

Tanach: Scriptures

Targum: Aramaic translation of *Chumash*

techias hameisim: resurrection of the dead

tefillah (pl. *tefillos*): prayer

Tefillah Zakah: prayer recited before *Kol Nidrei* in which, among other things, supplicant declares his forgiveness of all who have wronged him

Tehillim: Psalms

teshuvah (pl. *teshuvos*): responsum

Tosafos: 12th-century commentary printed in all editions of the Talmud

Tur: classic halachic text by Rabbi Yaakov ben Asher (c.1275-1340)

tzaddik (pl. *tzaddikim*): a saintly person

tzedakah: charity

tzelem Elokim: the image of G-d in which every person was created

tzidkus: righteousness

Tzom Gedaliah: fast day observed the day after Rosh Hashanah

Vilna Gaon: Rabbi Eliyahu of Vilna (1720-1797), one of the greatest spiritual leaders of Jewry in post-medieval times

yahrtzeit: anniversary of a Jew's death

Yam shel Shlomo: Talmudic commentary by Rabbi Shlomo Luria (1510-1573)

Yerushalmi: Jerusalem Talmud

yetzer hara: evil inclination

yetzer tov: good inclination

Yom Tov (pl. *yamim tovim*): Jewish holiday (holidays)

yungeleit: young men, often a reference to young Torah scholars

zemiros: songs of praise, especially those sung at the Sabbath and Festival meals

INDEX

זֶה סֵפֶר תּוֹלְדֹת אָדָם
This is the book of the generations of man
(Genesis 5:1)

This volume is dedicated to the memory of
שלימה בת מרדכי ע״ה
Sylvia Zerring
ט״ו אב תשמ״ו / August 20, 1986

Her life was a book of kindness and devotion, of nachas
and joy, of generations binding the future with the past.
— As the mother of Elliot, Jacqueline, and Marvin
— as wife of Sol
— as grandmother of Erin and Julie
— as sister of Goldie

she remains etched in our memories as a rare person
whose sensitivity and commitment were lavished
not only on her immediate loved ones, but on
her extended family — the entire Jewish people.

May we always be inspired by her kindness and concern,
and may we follow in her path of tzedakah and chessed.

קָמוּ בָנֶיהָ וַיְאַשְּׁרוּהָ בַּעְלָה וַיְהַלְלָהּ
Her children arise and praise her;
her husband, and he lauds her
(Proverbs 31:21)

Sol, Elliot, Marvin, Jacqueline, Erin,
Julie, Goldie and family

בתודה לבורא עולם שזיכני לראות את הקולות של תורה
בראותי את המנהגות של מורי ורבי רבן של כל ישראל זצ"ל
וחס ושלום שתשתכח תורה זו מישראל
לכן מלאני לבי לזכות בהדפסת הספר הזה
שהיא כטפה מן הים ממדותיו וגמילות חסדיו.

לזכרון נצח

אבי מורי

ר׳ אלטער יוסף בן ר׳ שלום ז״ל

Joseph Jacobs

נפ׳ ג׳ מרחשון תשמ"ו

ואמי מורתי

מרת עטיא בת ר׳ אברהם מאיר ע"ה

Ethel Jacobs

נפ׳ ב׳ מנחם אב תשמ"ט

יהי זכרם ברוך

יצחק דזשייקאבס

This volume is dedicated to the memory of our parents

Louis and Fanny Miller

ר׳ אליעזר בן ר׳ מרדכי ע"ה
מרת פייגא בת ר׳ אריה לייב ע"ה

who nurtured seeds of Jewish growth
during their exemplary lifetimes;

and to our brother and his wife and son

Emanuel, Lillian, and Philip Miller

ר׳ עמנואל בן אליעזר ע"ה
וזוגתו מרת לאה אסתר בת ר׳ פייוועל ע"ה
ובנם פייוועל ע"ה

whose lives ended in a tragic accident
with their futures still ahead of them.

Mr. and Mrs. Milton Miller

We are privileged to dedicate
this biography of a giant of our century
in honor of our parents

Mr. and Mrs. Meyer Ratner

Mr. and Mrs. Joseph Saperstein

and their grandchildren

Richard and Tracy Ratner

*Reb Moshe added steel to the thread
that binds us to our glorious Torah heritage;
future generations will be linked to Sinai
because he was here to teach and inspire us.*

*What was his strength? The Torah!
It was his essence and he was its embodiment.*

*May his memory continue to inspire and guide us;
may we build upon the foundations he laid for us;
and may we be worthy of the sacrifices
he made for us.*

Joan and Sheldon Ratner

This volume is dedicated to the memory of
our beloved father

SAM KLAGSBRUN

ר׳ יהושע שלום בן ר׳ שמעון הכ״מ

ט׳ באב תשמ״ו

and to our beloved mother

ESTHER KLAGSBRUN

מרת אסתר סעריל בת ר׳ אברהם ע״ה

ט״ו בשבט, תשמ״ג

Our paternal grandmother

Sima Klagsbrun

מרת סימא בת ר׳ משה יוסף הי״ד

who was martyred with nine of her children
and many grandchildren by the Nazis, in Melitz, Poland.

Shimon Klagsbrun, Rose Srebro, Shirley Wininger

In honor of

David H. and Raizel Schwartz